'Over the last decade, China rapidly became a major player in global investment. In recent years, China's Outward Direct Investment (ODI) already surpassed its inward Foreign Direct Investment (FDI). Against this background, the editors of this volume, both from China Investment Corporation, China's sovereign wealth fund established a decade ago, assembled an impressive and diversified group of more than 30 academics, policy makers, business consultants and investment professionals from inside and outside China to contribute to a wide range of analysis on China's ODI. The result is a timely and valuable book, which in my view will benefit those who want to understand the economic, business and investment logic of the rise of China's ODI, to interpret related government policies, and to think about its global implications'.

Yingyi Qian, Professor and Dean, School of Economics and Management, Tsinghua University

'This book provides a valuable examination of China's emergence as a global economic powerhouse – from a global manufacturing hub to a global investor. It details, from a variety of perspectives, the shifting focus of Chinese overseas investment, including the role of state and private entities, the consequences for rebalancing of China's domestic patterns of growth, and the experiences of a variety of Chinese firms and entrepreneurs. These are understudied areas that warrant much more attention. *From World Factory to Global Investor* is an important contribution. It provides a window into China today and an important dimension of its likely future economic priorities'.

Merit E. Janow, Dean, School of International and Public Affairs, Professor of Practice, International Economic Law & International Affairs, Columbia University

'In the past few decades, China has successfully transformed itself from a capital-shortage economy to one of the largest global investors. Today, as the world's second largest economy and the largest trading nation, China's economic influence has reached every corner of the globe. China has made and continues to make great contributions to the world economy, yet the country is often misperceived and misinterpreted as new colonialism and imperialism. How has China risen to a world economic power, and how is China changing the world economy? *From World Factory to Global Investor* provides a most authoritative account of China's miracle by focusing on China's outward direct investment. Written by most prestigious scholars in their field, all the chapters are equally strong and solid. All who are interested in the current and future role of China in the world economy should read this excellent book.'

Zheng Yongnian, Professor and Director of East Asian Institute, National University of Singapore

FROM WORLD FACTORY TO GLOBAL INVESTOR

Chinese outward direct investment (ODI) has been growing rapidly in recent years. As an important phenomenon in the global economy, China's ODI deserves more thorough analysis. This book looks at China's ODI activities from multiple perspectives. With the rebalancing of China's own structural growth and China's shift towards a net capital exporter, her initiatives such as 'One Belt One Road' (OBOR) have had profound implications on the traditional super-sovereign or multilateral financial and investment cooperation mechanism. As China's investment destinations and investment methods become more diversified and sophisticated, this book offers unique and refreshing insight into China's ODI activities.

The book covers the whole range of history and policy development of China's ODI and analyses China's ODI trends and characteristics in recent years. It reviews China's major policy changes after the Third Plenary Session of the 18th Central Committee of the Communist Party and how they may impact China's ODI strategy and activities. The book addresses potential challenges and risks of rising ODI activities from practitioners' perspective, and it discusses how recipient countries may react and respond to the surge of Chinese capital. The book also offers policy implications and a future research agenda in relation to the Chinese investments.

Xuedong Ding is Chairman and CEO of China Investment Corporation (CIC). Prior to this, he was Deputy Secretary General of the State Council and has held several positions in the Ministry of Finance, including Vice Minister and Assistant Minister. He recently published *Incentives for Innovation in China: Building an Innovative Economy* with Routledge in 2015.

Chen Meng is Director at China Investment Corporation (CIC) and Visiting Scholar at Leeds University Business School (LUBS), UK, and University of International Business and Economics, Beijing. He previously held senior positions in venture capital businesses in China and the UK. He started his career as Lecturer in Chinese Business and Economy at LUBS. He published *Multinational Banking in China: Theory and Practice* with Edward Elgar in 2009.

FROM WORLD FACTORY TO GLOBAL INVESTOR

A Multi-Perspective Analysis of China's Outward Direct Investment

Edited by Xuedong Ding and Chen Meng

Routledge
Taylor & Francis Group
LONDON AND NEW YORK

First published 2018
by Routledge
2 Park Square, Milton Park, Abingdon, Oxon OX14 4RN

and by Routledge
711 Third Avenue, New York, NY 10017

Routledge is an imprint of the Taylor and Francis Group, an informa business

British Library Cataloguing-in-Publication Data
A catalogue record for this book is available from the British Library

Library of Congress Cataloging-in-Publication Data
Names: Ding, Xuedong, 1960– editor. |
Meng, Chen, 1978 November 14– editor.
Title: From world factory to global investor : a multi-perspective analysis of China's outward direct investment / edited by Xuedong Ding and Chen Meng.
Description: First Edition. | New York : Routledge, 2018. | Includes bibliographical references and index.
Identifiers: LCCN 2017036610| ISBN 9781138210233 (hardback) | ISBN 9781138210240 (pbk.) | ISBN 9781315455815 (ebook)
Subjects: LCSH: Investments, Chinese. | Corporations, Chinese—Law and legislation—Foreign countries. | International business enterprises. | International finance.
Classification: LCC HG4538 .F76 2018 | DDC 332.67/351—dc23
LC record available at https://lccn.loc.gov/2017036610

ISBN: 978-1-138-21023-3 (hbk)
ISBN: 978-1-138-21024-0 (pbk)
ISBN: 978-1-315-45581-5 (ebk)

Typeset in Bembo
by Apex CoVantage, LLC

CONTENTS

List of figures *x*
List of tables *xii*
Foreword by Michael Spence *xiii*
Foreword by Justin Yifu Lin *xvi*
Acknowledgements *xviii*
List of contributors *xix*
Abbreviations *xxii*

Introduction and overview 1

PART I
Review of Chinese outward direct investment **5**

1 Outward direct investment by Chinese enterprises: a survey (2005–2016) 7
Chen Meng, Zhihua Lyu and Chunyang Jiang

2 From 'World Factory' to international capacity cooperation: China's evolving role in the global value chain 23
Xuedong Ding

3 China's economic transition and outward direct investments 33
Lawrence J. Lau

4 Challenges in GVC and ODI development: what can China do? 46
Jiong Gong, Xinding Yu and Zhongxiu Zhao

5 Chinese outward foreign direct investment – an opportunity to revisit international business theory 60
Peter J. Buckley

PART II
Policy development and implications 69

6 Recent changes in China's outbound investment policies and their implications 71
Zucai Hu

7 China builds up free trade areas to facilitate OFDI 79
Xiangchen Zhang

8 Asian Infrastructure Investment Bank (AIIB): a new mechanism for global financial cooperation 87
Yaobin Shi

9 RMB internationalization: history and outlook 94
Jun Ma and Huaizhu Xie

10 Japan's experience of foreign investment and China's policy options 109
Wenling Chen and Guanqun Mei

PART III
The dynamics of Chinese ODI 121

11 From active buyers to active owners 123
Gordon Orr and David Cogman

12 Execution is the strategy: The key to Lenovo's success in IBM PC division acquisition 137
Chuanzhi Liu and Neng Liang

13 Why go global? The logic behind investing overseas 156
John Zhao

14 The dynamics of Chinese outbound investment – challenges and case studies 163
Andrew Wood and Yu Cao

15 Capitalizing on opportunities and tackling major legal challenges and risks: a practitioner's perspective 177
Joseph C. Shenker, Chun Wei and Jordan H. Oreck

PART IV
Chinese ODI in a global context 189

16 Policy implications of FDI on financial sector development 191
Andrew Sheng

17 The history and evolution of Chinese companies going global: what to expect in the years ahead 205
Yibing Wu

18 Chinese investment in the UK: great expectations? 216
Lord Sassoon and Giles Blackburne

19 The 'New Normal' and its implications for Chinese investment in Africa 232
Jacko J. H. Maree and Jeremy J. Stevens

20 The return of bilateralism: China, post-Brexit Britain and Trump 243
Erik Berglof and Vince Cable

PART V
Conclusion 255

21 Summary and conclusions 257
Xuedong Ding and Chen Meng

Index 267

FIGURES

1.1 Growth of Chinese ODI, 2005–2016 11
1.2 Cross-border M&A flows 11
1.3 Cross-border M&A stock breakdown between SOEs and non-SOEs (by number of transactions) 12
1.4 Cross-border M&A stock breakdown between SOEs and non-SOEs (by value) 12
1.5 Investment flow distributions (billion USD) 13
1.6 Top ten destinations by amount of ODI (billion USD) 14
1.7 ODI distribution by industry 15
1.8 ODI distribution by industry, 2005–2016 (by number of transactions) 15
1.9 Dynamics of ODI motives 16
1.10 ODI breakdown between listed and private enterprises (by number of transactions) 16
2.1 Breakdown of a country's foreign trade 24
2.2 Domestic value added rate of main countries 25
2.3 Comparison of RCA index between China and other emerging markets 26
2.4 International comparison of unit labour costs 28
3.1 Chinese exports and imports of goods and services as a percentage of GDP, 1970–2015 34
3.2 Chinese national savings and gross domestic investment as a percentage of GDP since 1952 35
3.3 Chinese inbound and outbound direct investments, US$ billions 36
4.1 Share of intermediate inputs in exports 47
4.2 Changing trends in different types of production activity as a share of global GDP (1995–2014) 47
4.3 China's ODI and IDI share in developing economies 49

4.4 BRICS countries' IDI and ODI level (in billions of US dollars), 1990–2015 50
4.5 Share of BRICS countries in global ODI and IDI, 1990–2015 50
4.6 Average wage of employed persons in urban units of China (in RMB) deflated by CPI (year 2000=100), 2000–2015 51
4.7 Pure domestic consumption portion of GDP 52
4.8 Average selling price of residential and office buildings, 2005–2015 52
4.9 China's net ODI stock by sector at the end of 2015 55
4.10 Forward/backward linkage GVC participation ratio, 2000–2014 56
7.1 OFDI flows from selected economies, 1970 to 2015 (USD 100 million) 80
7.2 OFDI stock of major countries in 2015 80
7.3 Breakdown of China's OFDI stock by industry as of the end of 2015 81
9.1 RMB's share as an international payments currency 95
9.2 Monthly RMB settlement under the current account 99
10.1 Comparison of investment overseas between China and Japan 110
10.2 Comparison of Chinese FDI and ODI 111
10.3 Structure of Japan's ODA 112
10.4 Structure of spending of JBIC 114
10.5 Change of Japan's industrial structure 116
11.1 Investment mix for resource deals 124
11.2 Sector mix of diversification/relationship-building deals 125
11.3 Non-control investments generally did worse than control investments 126
11.4 Success rates by deal size 126
12.1 PC industry market share, 2004–2015 138
12.2 Lenovo sales by region 138
12.3 PC industry structure by concentration ratio 152
16.1 South–South trade already equal to North–North trade 195
17.1 Total resources deals have declined as a percentage of China's outward direct investment 208
21.1 China's emerging driving forces 262

TABLES

1.1 Chinese ODI, 2006–2016 8
1.2 Variables Description 10
1.3 Top ten provinces in ODI transactions 17
1.4 Top ten Chinese enterprises in cross-border M&A (by number of transactions) 18
1.5 Most active ODI enterprises by industry (by amount of investment) 18
1.6 Ten largest M&A transactions since 2008 19
1.7 Difference between SOEs and non-SOEs 19
1.8 Correlation between industry, share acquired and destination 20
4.1 FDI inflows (millions of dollars) and top-three FDI inflow economies 48
5.1 Organisational form and ownership of EMNEs 62
5.2 Home country characteristics that determine internalisation decisions 65
6.1 History of simplifying administrative procedures for overseas investment projects 74
9.1 Currency distribution of OTC foreign exchange turnover 96
9.2 RMB assets held onshore by non-residents 97
9.3 RMB settlement under the current account 100
9.4 Geographical distribution of cross-border RMB receipts and payments (2016) 100
9.5 RMB settlement of cross-border direct investment 101
9.6 Overseas RMB clearing banks 106
12.1 Matches made in hell 140
16.1 China, Malaysia and US – NIIP, 2004 vs 2016 (US$ billion) 197
16.2 China, Malaysia and US – crude leverage ratio, 2004 vs 2016 198
18.1 Chinese investment into the UK by sector, 2005–2016 217
18.2 Chinese investment into the UK and Europe, 2005–2016 218

FOREWORD

Michael Spence[1]

China has been a crucial part of the world's convergence story in narrowing income differentials between emerging and developed countries. The China story is dramatic, moving in a relatively short span of time from an agrarian closed economy to an open, market-led economy. By now it is reasonably well known. As the core of the global supply chain – 'The World's Factory' – China today produces nearly 80% of all air conditioners, 60% of cement, 50% of steel and 27% of automobiles, becoming at the same time the largest trading nation with the most trading partners.

But convergence with advanced countries also means that China has shifted from a major recipient of global capital, technology and management know-how, to a global investor and owner along the evolving supply chains. Its major companies are becoming global brands and significant multinational enterprises. This is a remarkable and profound shift in status, mindset and culture, requiring a deep shift in thinking and understanding on part of investors and recipients.

Since 2006, China has become the world's largest net savings provider, but its outward direct investment (ODI) only surpassed its inward foreign direct investment (FDI) in 2015, and its ODI reached 9% of GDP in 2015, still small compared with 33% for the US and 30% for Japan, but significant as it is now a very large economy. While Chinese ODI is rapidly growing from a relatively small base, its scale and speed of growth has attracted attention among academics, policymakers and investment professionals, for good reason.

China's ODI deserves more thorough analysis, especially because Chinese ODI is related to the rebalancing of China's own structural growth patterns as its private and state-owned enterprises seek to diversify their markets and gain access to technology, skills and working relationships within different cultures and processes. According to the IMF and World Bank forecasts, China is expected to contribute over 25% of world GDP growth between now and 2030, so Chinese ODI in areas such as the One Belt One Road region – covering all countries within the ancient Silk Road and Maritime routes – will make huge differences to the global need for and supply of infrastructure and public goods.

What are the policy drivers, and how will China become a leading player in global ODI? What are the implications of China's rapid ODI to the global economy, businesses and policies? These deserve to be studied objectively and analytically from multiple perspectives.

This book makes a major contribution to this goal. Mr Xuedong Ding (former chairman) and his colleague Dr Chen Meng at the China Investment Corporation (CIC), the leading Chinese sovereign wealth fund, have endeavoured to commission and publish a pioneering collection of essays and studies by world-leading academics, policymakers and investment professionals from both inside and outside of China.

They have edited a book titled *From World Factory to Global Investor: A Multi-perspective Analysis of China's Outward Direct Investment*, with contributions from 34 economists, investment professionals and policymakers.

The book covers the whole range of history and policy debates within and outside China on this important part of China's globalization. Part I of the book surveys the evolutionary development path of Chinese ODI and identifies the major trends and emerging characteristics. Part II introduces major policy changes after the important Third Plenary Session of the 18th Central Committee of the Communist Party in late 2013, to help readers better understand the rationale behind these policy changes and how they may affect Chinese ODI strategies. Part III provides interesting studies to illustrate the dynamics of Chinese enterprises' internationalization processes from business practitioners' perspective. Part IV examines, from a recipient's (host country) perspective, how it reacts and responds to the surge of Chinese capital. Part V offers useful concluding implications and proposes an agenda for future research.

The book is unique in that both editors bring a wealth of experience in policymaking, investment and research within China and abroad. Mr Ding served as Chairman and CEO of CIC for over three years, and was involved intimately at the cutting edge of China's outbound investment as a key investment decision maker and policymaker. He served previously as Deputy Finance Minister, bringing rare and highly valuable experiences and policy perspectives. Dr Meng has held senior positions in private equity and venture capital businesses in China and the UK, having also taught at a British university.

The contributing authors include leading academics such as Professors Erik Berglof, Peter Buckley, Lawrence Lau, Neng Liang and others; minister-level policymakers from China and the UK such as Sir Vince Cable, Zucai Hu, Lord Sassoon, Andrew Sheng, Yaobin Shi and Xiangchen Zhang; in addition to top financial professionals such as Chuanzhi Liu, Jacko Maree, Gordon Orr, John Zhao and others.

This is a timely book that I would highly recommend to all stakeholders who need to assess and interpret China's outward investment and engagement with the rest of the world. Those who wish to understand why and how China will become a leading player in global ODI, along with its vital implications to the global economy, for businesses and for investment options, will profit from this valuable contribution.

Milan
July 2017

Note

1 Michael Spence is 2001 Noble Laureate in Economic Sciences; Senior Fellow at the Hoover Institution; and Philip H. Knight Professor and Dean, Emeritus, at the Graduate School of Business, Stanford University.

FOREWORD

Justin Yifu Lin[1]

China's rapid rise since its opening up in 1978 is among the most important economic development events for the world over the last three decades. Many economists, policymakers as well as business leaders – myself included – have provided useful analyses on how China went from an agrarian, closed economy to an open economy that has been at the core of the global supply chain, often called 'The World's Factory'.

Over the course of China's rapid growth and development in the last three decades, its contribution to world growth has also been lifted from insignificant in the 1980s to around 30% in recent years, and China's savings has also been lifted from insignificant to the world to the largest of the world in 2006.

As is well known, China's development and growth strategy relies on 'reform and opening up'. On the 'opening up' strategy, China, as a result of its rapid growth, has shifted from relying heavily on attracting foreign investment, especially inward foreign direct investment (FDI), in the 1980s, to both attracting FDI and providing outward direct investment (ODI) in recent years. In 2015 China's ODI surpassed its inward FDI. It is not surprising that China has made new policy initiatives that address the new challenges for globalization and connect to China's ODI strategy, including the 'Belt and Road' initiative.

In light of China's economy size (the second largest in the world), its expected high growth rates in the coming decades (China is expected to contribute over 25% of annual world GDP growth to 2030 according to the World Bank and IMF forecasts) as well as its high savings, this important turning point is important not only for China but also for the world and needs to be thoroughly analysed.

A range of important questions needs to be answered from different perspectives objectively and comprehensively. For example, will China become a leading player in global ODI? What are the policy drivers for ODI, from rebalancing domestic economy as well as from addressing new challenges in globalization after the 2008 global financial crisis? What are the implications and opportunities of China's rapid ODI to the world economic growth, international business and global investment?

The new book – titled *From World Factory to Global Investor: A Multi-perspective Analysis of China's Outward Direct Investment* and edited by Mr Xuedong Ding (former chairman) and his colleague Dr Chen Meng at the China Investment Corporation (CIC) – provides excellent answers to the above and other related questions. They have invited contributions from leading economists, top investment professionals and senior policymakers from China and abroad, and each of them brings unique and insightful, as well as objective and comprehensive, perspectives.

As I have explained on many occasions (as the World Bank's Chief Economist and before and after that role), the world needs massive new investment, and there are adequate savings to finance the needed investment, but much of the savings are not utilised and earn excessively low rates of return; hence, addressing low world growth through monetary policies would be inadequate. China's increasing ODI will help world growth, benefit the international business communities and create new opportunities for international finance.

I thus thoroughly enjoyed reading the new book and would strongly recommend it to all interested readers and stakeholders. The book has great vision and deep insights. The issues it addresses are highly relevant for China and the world in decades to come, especially when globalization faces many acute new challenges. I hope you will, like me, very much enjoy reading it.

Beijing
July 2017

Note

1 Justin Yifu Lin is Founding Director of the New Structural Economics Research Centre; Founding and Former Director of China Centre of Economic Research (CCER); Honorable Dean of the National School of Development, Peking University; and Former Senior Vice President and Chief Economist of the World Bank.

ACKNOWLEDGEMENTS

The authors and publisher gratefully acknowledge permission for use of the following material:

Chapter 1: A large part of this chapter first appeared in the *Journal of WTO and China*, Vol. 5, No. 2, February 2015, pp. 105–127.

Chapter 2: An earlier version of this chapter was published in *Globalization*, Vol. 48, No. 7, July 2015, pp. 12–20.

Every effort has been made to trace all the copyright holders, but if any have been inadvertently overlooked, the publisher will be pleased to make the necessary arrangements at the first opportunity.

The authors are also grateful for all contributors and thankful for feedback from three anonymous referees during the early stage of this book project.

CONTRIBUTORS

Erik Berglof is Professor and Director of the Institute of Global Affairs (IGA), London School of Economics and Political Science (LSE).

Giles Blackburne is Director Fellow at China-Britain Business Council.

Peter J. Buckley is Professor of International Business at Leeds University Business School, and Cheung Kong Scholar Chair Professor at University of International Business and Economics (UIBE).

Vince Cable is Professor in Practice at London School of Economics and Political Science.

Yu Cao is Partner at Haiwen & Partners.

Wenling Chen is Chief Economist and Deputy Executive Officer of China Center for International Economic Exchanges (CCIEE).

David Cogman is Partner at McKinsey & Company, and Senior Member of McKinsey's Corporate Finance Practice.

Xuedong Ding is Chairman and CEO of China Investment Corporation (CIC).

Jiong Gong is Professor at the Department of Economics, University of International Business and Economics.

Zucai Hu is Vice Minister of the National Development and Reform Commission (NDRC) of the People's Republic of China.

Chunyang Jiang is Analyst at China Investment Corporation.

Lawrence J. Lau is Ralph and Claire Landau Professor of Economics at Chinese University of Hong Kong, and Kwoh-Ting Li Professor in Economic Development, Emeritus, Stanford University.

Neng Liang is Professor at China Europe International Business School.

Chuanzhi Liu is Chairman of the Board of Legend Holdings Corporation, and Founder of Lenovo Group Limited.

Zhihua Lyu is Analyst at China Investment Corporation.

Jun Ma is Chief Economist at the Research Bureau of the People's Bank of China (PBOC).

Jacko J.H. Maree is Deputy Chairman and former Chief Executive of Standard Bank Group.

Guanqun Mei is Senior Economist of China Center for International Economic Exchanges.

Chen Meng is Director at China Investment Corporation.

Jordan H. Oreck is Senior Associate at Sullivan & Cromwell (Hong Kong) LLP.

Gordon Orr is Senior Advisor and Senior Partner Emeritus at McKinsey & Company.

Lord Sassoon is Chairman of China-Britain Business Council.

Andrew Sheng is Distinguished Fellow at Asia Global Institute, University of Hong Kong.

Joseph C. Shenker is Chairman of Sullivan & Cromwell LLP.

Jeremy J. Stevens is Economist at Standard Bank Group.

Yaobin Shi is Vice Minister of Ministry of Finance of the People's Republic of China.

Chun Wei is Partner at Sullivan & Cromwell (Hong Kong) LLP.

Andrew Wood is Counsel at Haiwen & Partners.

Yibing Wu is Joint Head of Portfolio Strategy & Risk Group of Temasek Holdings, and Joint Head of Temasek Holdings China.

Huaizhu Xie is Research Fellow at the Research Bureau of the People's Bank of China.

Xinding Yu is Assistant Professor at School of International Trade and Economics, University of International Business and Economics.

Xiangchen Zhang is Vice Representative for International Trade at the Ministry of Commerce of the People's Republic of China (MOFCOM).

John Zhao is Chairman and CEO of Hony Capital.

Zhongxiu Zhao is Vice President and Professor at Research Institute for Global Value Chains, University of International Business and Economics.

ABBREVIATIONS

ADB	Asian Development Bank
AI	artificial intelligence
AIIB	Asian Infrastructure Investment Bank
ASEAN	Association of Southeast Asian Nations
BCEG	Beijing Construction Engineering Group
BIT	bilateral investment treaties
Brexit	Britain exiting from the EU
BRICS	Brazil, Russia, India, China and South Africa
BVI	British Virgin Islands
CAS	Chinese Academy of Sciences
CAUK	Changan UK R&D Centre Ltd
CBRC	China Banking Regulatory Commission
CDH	Investments China DINGHUI Investments
CEPA	closer economic partnership arrangement
CFETS	China Foreign Exchange Trade System
CFIUS	Committee on Foreign Investment in the United States
CGC	Credit Guarantee Commissions
CGN	China General Nuclear Power Group
ChemChina	China National Chemical Corporation
CIBM	China Interbank Bond Market
CICC	China International Capital Corporation
CIPS	China international payment system
CIRC	China Insurance Regulatory Commission
CITIC	CITIC Group Corporation of China
CNAPS	China National Automated Payment System
CNOOC	China National Offshore Oil Corp
CNPC	China National Petroleum Corporation

COFCO	COFCO Corporation
COSCO	China Ocean Shipping (Group) Company
CSAs	country specific advantages
CSR	China South Railway Corporation
CSRC	China Securities Regulatory Commission
DMNC	multinationals from developed economies
ECFA	Cross Strait Economic Cooperation Framework Agreement
EME	emerging market economy
EMNE	emerging-market MNE
EMNC	emerging economy-based multinational companies
EPC	engineering, procurement and construction
FDI	foreign direct investment
FinTech	financial technology
FPI	foreign portfolio investment
FSAs	firm-specific advantages
FTA	Free Trade Agreement
GA	General Atlantic
GAC	general administration of customs
GCC	Gulf Cooperation Council
GDP	gross domestic product
GVA	gross value added
GVC	global value chain
HNA	Hainan Airlines Group of China
ICBC	Industrial and Commercial Bank of China
ICT	information and communications technology
IDI	inward direct investment
IoT	Internet of things
JASME	Japan Finance Corporation for Small and Medium Enterprise
JBIC	Japan Bank for International Cooperation
JEXIM	Export-Import Bank of Japan
M&A	merger and acquisition
MIDAS	Manchester's Inward Investment Agency
MinMetals	China National Metals and Minerals Import and Export Corporation
MNE	multinational enterprise
MOFCOM	Ministry of Commerce of China
MYR	Malaysian ringgit
NAFTA	North American Free Trade Agreement
NDRC	National Development and Reform Commission of China
NIIP	net international investment position
OBOR	One Belt One Road Initiative
ODI	outward direct investment
OECF	overseas economic cooperation fund
OFDI	outward foreign direct investment

PBC/PBoC	The People's Bank of China
PCD	PC division
PE	private equity
PENT	pre-establishment national treatment
PMO	project management office
PPP	public-private partnership
PTAs	preferential trade agreements
R&D	research and development
RCA	revealed comparative advantage index
RCEP	Regional Comprehensive Economic Partnership
RMB	renminbi
RQDII	RMB Qualified Domestic Institutional Investors
WTO	World Trade Organization
SAFE	State Administration of Foreign Exchange
SAIC	Shanghai Automotive Industry Corporation
SASAC	State-Owned Assets Supervision and Administration Commission of the State Council of China
SDI	Scottish Development International
SDIC	China's State Development & Investment Corporation
SDR	special drawing right
SME	small and medium enterprises
SOE	state-owned enterprise
SSA	sub-Saharan Africa
STEM	science, technology, engineering and mathematics
TMT	technology, media and telecoms
TPP	Trans-Pacific Partnership Agreement
TSL	two-step loans
TTIP	Transatlantic Trade and Investment Partnership
UNCTAD	United Nations Conference on Trade and Development
VAiT	value added in trade
WTO	World Trade Order
ZTE	Zhongxing Telecommunication Equipment Corporation

INTRODUCTION AND OVERVIEW

China has become well known as the 'World Factory', which is one of its biggest economic achievements since the 'open-door' policy was introduced in 1978. According to incomplete statistics, China now produces nearly 80% of the world's air conditioners, 60% of cements, 50% of pork and steel, 39% of mobile phones and shoes, 30% of solar batteries and 27% of cars. China ranks world number one in over 500 world industrial products in terms of production capacity.

Undoubtedly, China will remain the World Factory for quite some time and will not only consolidate its status as a manufacturing power but also upgrade from a manufacturing power into a powerhouse. However, things have been changing in recent years. For instance, some global brands are moving their local factories from eastern to mid-western China, and some from the Chinese mainland to Vietnam, the Philippines and Bangladesh, or they are establishing new assembly lines in neighbouring countries. In coastal regions of China, factory managers encounter great difficulty in finding and securing peasant workers due to the rapid rise of base salaries. Weak global demand, the slowdown of China's economy, and the rise in currency volatility and protectionism have all pushed competition in world export markets to an even fiercer edge. As a result, the overall competitiveness of Chinese exports has been declining over the past few years, and the traditional labour-intensive and export-orientated development mode is under huge pressure.

So how should the current challenges be tackled? Drawn from international business literature and the experiences of other nations, the natural response would be either (1) Chinese enterprises producing in even lower-cost destinations, similar to what the US and Japanese multinational enterprises (MNEs) did in the mid-twentieth century or (2) Chinese companies moving towards a higher-value chain, either through intensive R&D spending or via cross-border acquisitions, i.e. internalizing foreign technology or know-how to improve productivity.

Both strategies view foreign direct investment as the preferred means of exploiting competitive advantage, rather than exporting. This is clearly reflected in the Chinese government's recent efforts to promote domestic innovation and international capacity cooperation.

The 'Going Out' strategy of Chinese enterprises is essentially a process of corporate internationalization. The underlying motive is to enhance competitive strength via market-seeking, resource-seeking or asset-seeking direct investments (such as in technology, management know-how, sales networks, and brands). Outward direct investments can also serve the purpose of risk diversification. In recent years, the international community has paid increasing attention to the outward investments of Chinese enterprises. The possible reasons for this are as follows: first, Chinese outward direct investment (ODI) has been growing rapidly, at an annual average rate of 23% over the last decade according to official statistics. The types of ownership of Chinese enterprises, investment destinations and investment methods have become ever more diversified and sophisticated. In particular, large scale cross-border mergers and acquisitions (M&A) have appeared in an endless stream, drawing great attention – and sometimes concern – from the recipient country's government, regulatory authorities and media.

Second, according to statistics from the Ministry of Commerce (MOFCOM) and State Administration of Foreign Exchanges (SAFE), Chinese ODI flows in 2014 reached 116 billion USD, representing a 15.5% growth rate over 2013; inward foreign direct investment flows amounted to 119.6 billion USD – a difference of 3.6 billion USD. However, if Chinese enterprises' offshore financing and direct investments are taken into account, in real terms outward direct investment would increase to as much as 140 billion USD, exceeding inward foreign direct investment by around 20 billion USD. Technically speaking, China had already become a net capital exporter,[1] which was a major shift.

Third, the Chinese central government recently introduced several new concepts, including the 'One Belt One Road' (OBOR) Initiative, BRICs Development Bank, and Asian Infrastructure Investment Bank (AIIB), all of which were either initiated or led by China. This undoubtedly brought a refreshing breeze to the mechanisms of traditional super-sovereign or multilateral financial and investment cooperation. Given its foreign exchange reserve amounting to some several trillion USD, what kind of role China will play is surely an intriguing question for the rest of the world.

Of course, China's shift from World Factory to truly global investor is undoubtedly a long and uneasy path. China will most likely traverse a dual development path, remaining the World Factory while also being a net capital exporter for quite some time. Some may argue that being a net capital exporter is currently more of a statistical inflection point. This is partially true. However, it has to be admitted that Chinese enterprises have made visible progress in their internationalization process. In particular, given the increasing prominence of the domestic cost-push effect and adjustments in the global value chain, the allocation and behaviour of Chinese enterprises' overseas investments have evolved over time, and this is also imbued with profound policy implications. Therefore, at such a transition stage, an examination of China's ODI activities is of great value and importance.

Outward direct investment involves a complex and dynamic decision-making process. The strategies adopted by Chinese enterprises are dictated by multiple variables including country-, firm-, policy-, culture- and transaction-specific factors. Any one of these dimensions in isolation would not offer a complete understanding of Chinese ODI activities and behaviours. Therefore, in this book our aim is to provide a full-frame analysis of China's ODI activities. This is clearly a challenging and ambitious task. Fortunately, our expert contributors, with their different backgrounds, agreed to give it a try. They range from academics and policymakers to entrepreneurs and business practitioners – both Chinese and non-Chinese. If readers find that this book lacks a coherent structure, this is probably because we asked our contributors open-ended and general questions, so that they had great flexibility in determining their own (ODI-related) theme or angle, without a predetermined hypothesis. The benefit of this is the complete independence of views expressed by each of the contributors. To some extent, this book is designed more like a symposium.

The book is structured as follows. Part I provides an overview of China's ODI activities from both theoretical and statistical perspectives. The purpose is to reveal the evolutionary development path of Chinese ODI and identify major trends and emerging characteristics. Additionally, by revisiting traditional international business theory, we try to clarify whether the internationalization of Chinese firms is a special case. Part II introduces major policy changes after the Third Plenary Session of the 18th Central Committee of the Communist Party. This helps us to better understand the rationale behind these policy changes and how they may affect Chinese ODI strategies. Part III aims to demonstrate the dynamics of Chinese enterprises' internationalization process, from a business practitioner's perspective: the reasons for investing overseas, Chinese firms' decision-making mind-set, as well as the challenges facing their decisions are fully addressed. Part IV examines, in a global context, how to react and respond to the surge of Chinese capital. It is essential for host-country policymakers and business partners to learn how to seek synergies with Chinese enterprises and reach a win-win outcome. Part V concludes the book, offering useful implications and also proposing an agenda for future research.

Note

1 Foreign portfolio investment is not included here.

PART I

Review of Chinese outward direct investment

1

OUTWARD DIRECT INVESTMENT BY CHINESE ENTERPRISES

A survey (2005–2016)

Chen Meng, Zhihua Lyu and Chunyang Jiang[1]

Introduction

This article surveys Chinese outward direct investment (ODI) using a database of over 3,400 investment transaction records between January 2005 and December 2016. The objective is to investigate and examine the evolutionary development path of Chinese ODI in the last decade. Our analysis reveals several key findings. First, Chinese private enterprises have become an important force of overseas investment, and there are significant differences between the investment styles and preferences of state-owned enterprises (SOEs) and private enterprises. Second, there is a clear shift of target sectors. Investments in energy and natural resources have decreased over recent years, while investments in the real estate, high technology and services sectors picked up substantially. This also reflects a change in investment motives. Third, developed markets, especially the US and Europe, are the preferred investment destinations. Fourth, financing methods become increasingly diversified and sophisticated. In particular, many domestic Chinese private equity funds have been actively involved in cross-border mergers and acquisitions (M&A), indicating further integration between traditional Chinese enterprises and their financial counterparties.

A new era of Chinese outward direct investment

Chinese ODI growth picked up very quickly from 2006, with an average annual growth rate of 23.2% (Table 1.1). In 2014, Chinese ODI reached USD 123.1 billion according to official statistics (Ministry of Commerce and National Bureau of Statistics of the People's Republic of China, 2015). This was the first time that Chinese ODI and inward foreign direct investment (FDI) balanced up, indicating that China might be stepping into a new era of being a net capital exporter. In the

TABLE 1.1 Chinese ODI, 2006–2016

Year	*Flow*		*Stock (bn $)*
	Amount (bn $)	*YoY Growth (%)*	
2006	21.1	43.8	90.6
2007	26.5	25.3	117.9
2008	55.9	110.9	184.0
2009	56.5	1.1	245.8
2010	68.8	21.7	317.2
2011	74.7	8.5	424.8
2012	87.8	17.6	531.9
2013	107.8	22.8	660.5
2014	123.1	15.5	882.6
2015	145.7	18.3	1,097.9
2016(E)	170.1	44.1	1,268

Source: Ministry of Commerce.

same year, China's ODI stock reached USD 882.6 billion, ranking eighth in the world – the first time that China entered the global top ten (UNCTAD, 2016). One year later, in 2015, Chinese ODI flow surpassed FDI.

Stepping into 2016, Chinese enterprises performed remarkably well, with several eye-catching transactions drawing the world's attention. For example, ChemChina made an official bid to acquire Syngenta AG for USD 43 billion, a new record in Chinese ODI history. Hainan Airline Group continued to impress the world by acquiring the CIT Group, a leading global aircraft leasing company based in the US, for USD 10 billion. According to official statistics, in the first half of 2016, Chinese ODI stood at USD 89 billion, representing year-on-year (YoY) growth of 58.7%. Capital mainly flowed into business services (24.6%), manufacturing (19.8%) and wholesale and retailing (16.4%); of these, the manufacturing sector recorded the highest YoY growth rate of 245.6%. The Ministry of Commerce estimated that the overall ODI flow would reach nearly USD 1,268 billion by the end of 2016.

The surge of Chinese ODI activity in recent years may be driven by several factors. First, the world economy was hit by the global financial crisis and Euro zone debt crisis. Many countries were in desperate need of capital, creating a good opportunity for Chinese companies to invest abroad. Second, the Chinese economic slowdown and deepening economic reforms may push many Chinese companies to seek market expansion or technological upgrade opportunities abroad via direct investments. Third, the Chinese government introduced several policy initiatives that helped boost overseas ODI activities. For instance, on 8 October 2014, the State Council relaxed the rules for government approvals on ODI. Except for those projects involving sensitive countries, regions, or industries, outward direct investments need only to fulfil filing requirements instead of obtaining government approvals and inspections. Deregulation on outward investment is also reflected by the establishment of the China (Shanghai) Pilot Free Trade Zone and easing of foreign exchange controls. The Chinese government recently introduced a series of bilateral or multilateral free trade and investment schemes, such as the Sino-Korea and Sino-Australia Free Trade and Investment Agreements, as well as the introduction of the One Belt One Road (OBOR) Initiative and the establishment of the Asian Infrastructure Investment Bank. All of these will be catalytic factors.

Among the aforementioned policy initiatives, the OBOR Initiative received the most attention. In 2016, Chinese enterprises signed 8,158 engineering and construction contracts with 61 countries along the OBOR region, with a contractual value of USD 126 billion. This represented YoY growth of 36% and accounted for 51.6% of newly signed contract value in total. Although China's non-financial ODI in these 61 countries along the OBOR region was USD 14.5 billion, down 2% as compared to 2015 and accounting for just 8.5% of China's total ODI during that period, it is estimated that capital flows into the OBOR region will continue to increase in the coming years.

Data and analysis

Given such a background, it is anticipated that Chinese companies will continue to be internationalized and become an increasingly powerful force of cross-border direct investments. Therefore, it would be very meaningful and important, at this time in particular, to establish a better understanding of Chinese companies' investment motives and behaviours as well as the major trends and characteristics of Chinese ODI activities. In order to do so, we constructed an ODI transaction database by consolidating various information sources, including the Heritage Foundation, Dealogic, China Venture and news releases. A total of 3,421 transactions between January 2005 and December 2016 were retrieved. Each data entry was cross-compared and verified, and was standardized to conform to the following variable categories (Table 1.2). After excluding 62 failed transactions, construction contracts and investments carried out by entities from Hong Kong, Macau and Taiwan, a total of 1,944 valid transaction records were finally used for statistical analysis.

Main trends and characteristics of Chinese ODI

Our survey shows that Chinese ODI transactions grew rapidly during the last decade, reaching USD 179 billion in 2016, which is nearly 15 times larger than in 2005 (Figure 1.1). The average annual growth rate of Chinese ODI in 2005–2016, measured by value, was 25%. Cross-border M&A has become a major form of ODI. Over the last 12 years, Chinese enterprises carried out 1,137 M&As overseas, accounting for about 58.5% of all ODI transactions.

TABLE 1.2 Variables Description

Variables	*Dimensions*	*Description*
Investment Motives	Market	expand market overseas
	Resources/Assets	acquire natural resources or real assets
	Technology	acquire advanced technologies and industry know-how
	Brand	acquire or take advantage of renowned brands; establish own brands in international markets
	Cost Reduction and Diversification	reduce cost by utilizing the market and resources overseas; relocate excessive domestic production capacity; diversify business risk
Ownership	SOEs	state holdings ≥ 50%
	Non-SOEs	private enterprises and state holdings <50%
Industry	Real Estate	land acquisition and real estate development
	Transportation and Infrastructure	construction, transportation and public utilities infrastructure
	Finance	banking, insurance, etc.
	High Technology and TMT	advanced industrial technology, TMT and Internet
	Mining and Energy	mineral exploitation and energy utilization
	Agriculture	farming, breeding, timber, forestry, fishery and agriculture logistics
	Manufacturing	general industrial manufacturing, chemicals and machinery
	Consumption Goods	food and beverages, apparel and other consumable goods
	Services	administration, technology service and others
Acquisition Methods	Absolute Control	equity holdings ≥ 50%
	Minor Active	10% ≤ equity holdings < 50%
	Minor Passive	equity holdings < 10%

Notes: The categorization of industry follows international practice. Some adjustments were made to suit the size of the database.

As Chinese ODI is growing at a rapid pace, several trends and characteristics have emerged. First, private enterprises have entered into a fast-track in terms of cross-border M&A since 2010. Measured by number of transactions, private companies overtook SOEs after 2011. Measured by the value of transactions, private companies started to lead SOEs from 2015 (Figure 1.2).

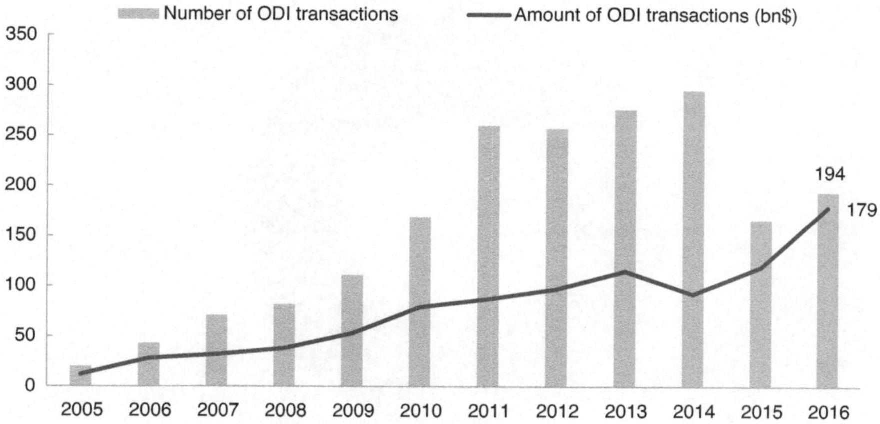

FIGURE 1.1 Growth of Chinese ODI, 2005–2016

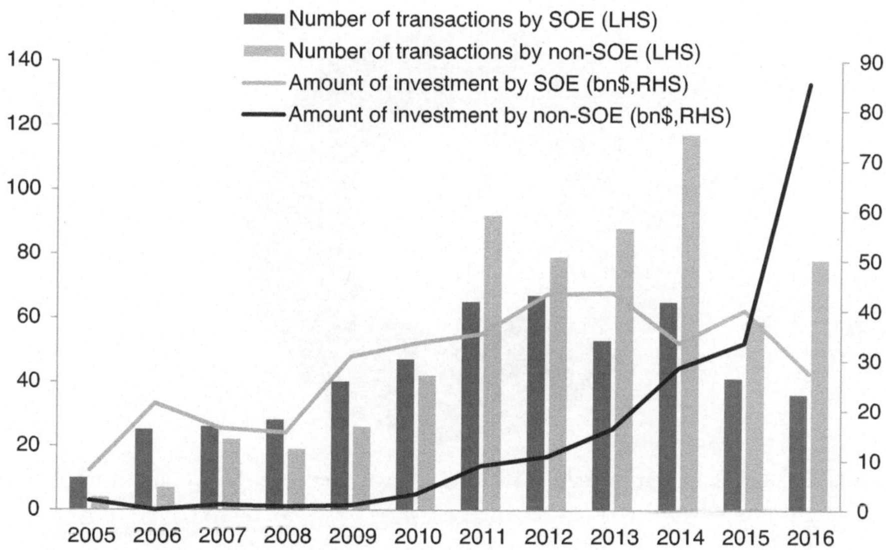

FIGURE 1.2 Cross-border M&A flows

Of the 117 transactions announced in 2016, 78 were conducted by private enterprises, with a total value of USD 85.6 billion, representing an increase of 255% over the previous year. If we look at the M&A stock statistics over the last decade, transactions by private enterprises accounted for about 56% by number of transactions and 35% by value invested (Figures 1.3 and 1.4). The average value of a single transaction by private companies increased from USD 70.62 million before the 2008 financial crisis to the present level of USD 602.3 million.

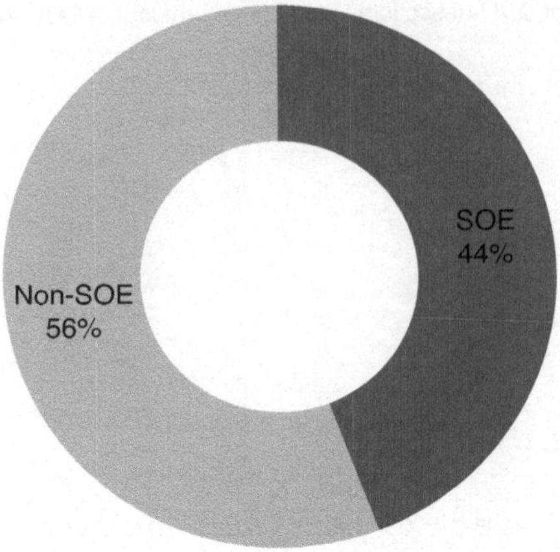

FIGURE 1.3 Cross-border M&A stock breakdown between SOEs and non-SOEs (by number of transactions)

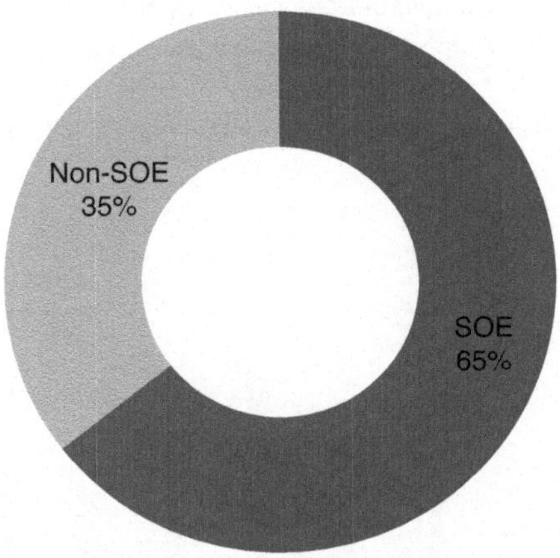

FIGURE 1.4 Cross-border M&A stock breakdown between SOEs and non-SOEs (by value)

Second, developed markets, mainly North America and Europe, are the preferred investment destinations. This has become increasingly visible since 2010. Asia attracted nearly one third of ODI 12 years ago, almost equivalent to the total investments flowing into the US and Europe. In 2014, however, Chinese enterprises conducted 34 M&A transactions in Asia, accounting for just 19% of all overseas investments. In contrast, investments in the US and Europe have grown dramatically in the last ten years (Figure 1.5). The average annual growth rate of Chinese ODI in Europe was 57%, as compared to 17% in Asia, 8% in Oceania and 16% in Latin America. Investments into the US peaked in 2012 and 2016. At a country level, the US (USD 153 billion), Australia (USD 82 billion) and Canada (USD 55 billion) are

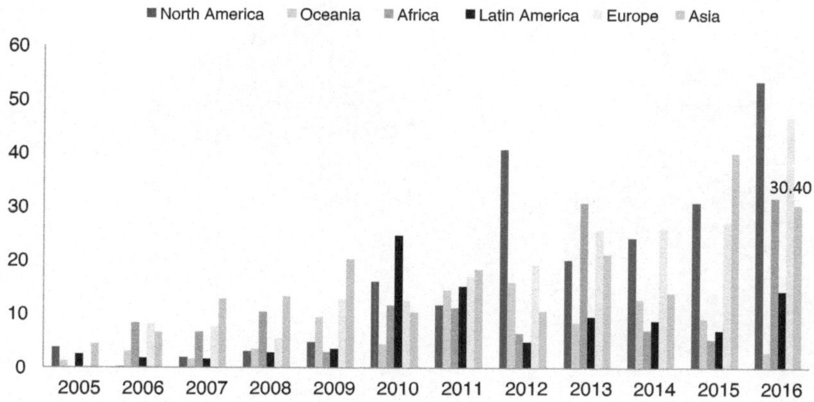

FIGURE 1.5 Investment flow distributions (billion USD)

the top three destinations in terms of the aggregate amount of ODI (Figure 1.6), followed by Brazil (USD 54 billion), the UK (USD 38 billion), Singapore (USD 24 billion), Russia (USD 22 billion), Italy (USD 19 billion), France (USD 18 billion) and Switzerland (USD 18 billion). Preliminary statistics show that total amount of Chinese ODI to the ten largest destinations between 2005 and 2016 was USD 485 billion, accounting for about 52% of overall ODI in the same period.

Third, the target industries have become diversified. By the end of 2016, minerals, energy and manufacturing still accounted for 60% of the aggregate amount of Chinese ODI (Figure 1.7). However, diversification is now a clear trend. Investment flows to high technology, telecommunications, finance, agriculture, real estate and services have increased dramatically. The percentage (by number of transactions) of mineral investments decreased from 50% in 2005 to 23% in 2016 (Figure 1.8). Meanwhile, the number of investments in agriculture, real estate, finance and high technology increased by 49%, 89%, 19% and 5% between 2011 and 2014.

Fourth, Chinese ODI is driven by multiple objectives such as seeking market expansion, resources and assets, brands, technology and know-how. Acquiring resources and energies used to be the priority, but the situation has changed in recent years (Figure 1.9). Acquiring high-value-added companies or assets has become the predominant motive. For example, investments in developed markets mainly aim to seek high-quality assets, and access to global marketing channels, advanced technologies, products and brands which may be beneficial to or consumed in the Chinese market. In addition, brand recognition plays an important role during investment decision-making. Chinese enterprises are hungry to acquire globally established brands or build up their own brands in order to foster their domestic market position and strengthen access to the global market.

Fifth, financing to support M&A activities has become increasingly diversified over the past decade. Around 64% of M&A transactions in 2016 were conducted

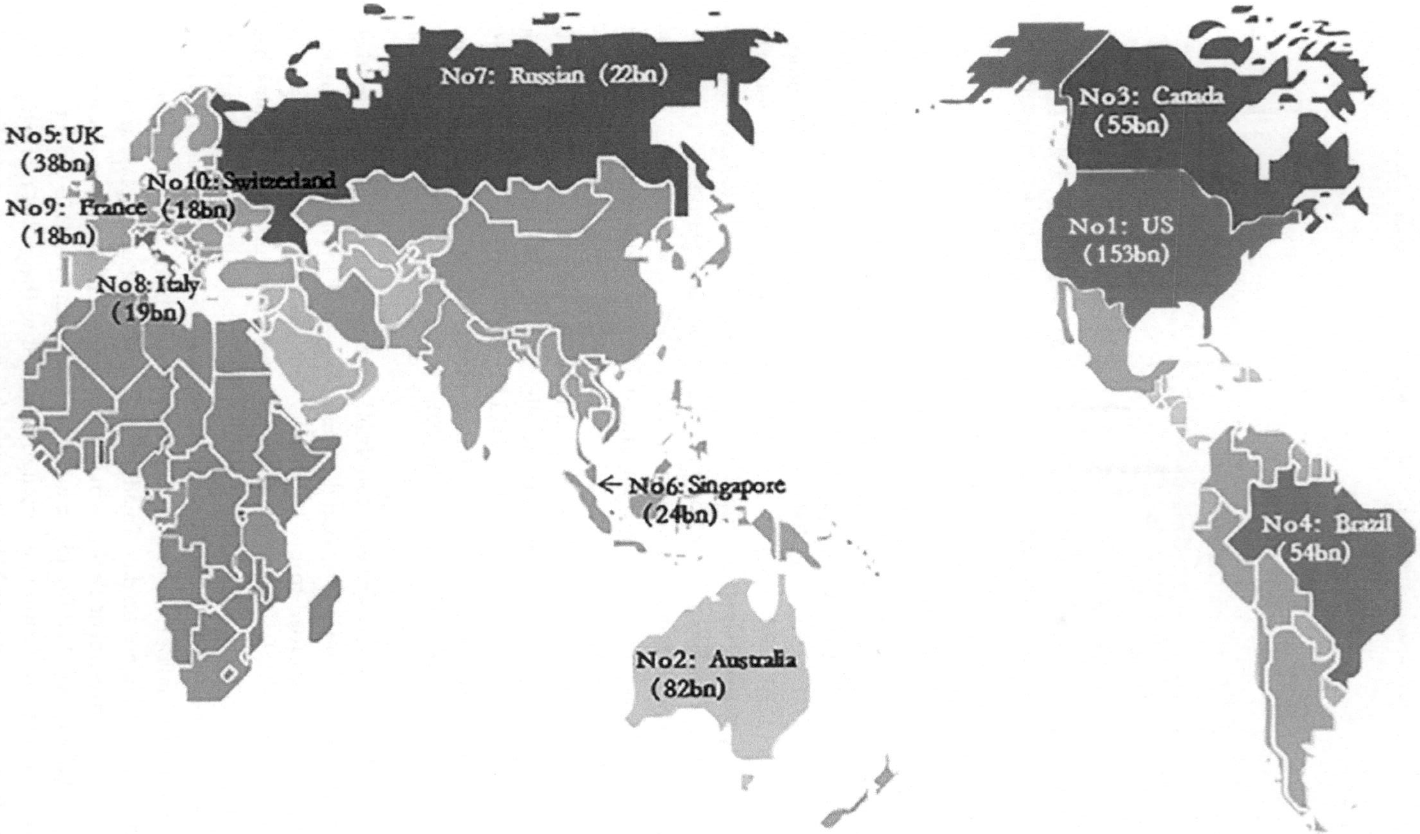

FIGURE 1.6 Top ten destinations by amount of ODI (billion USD)

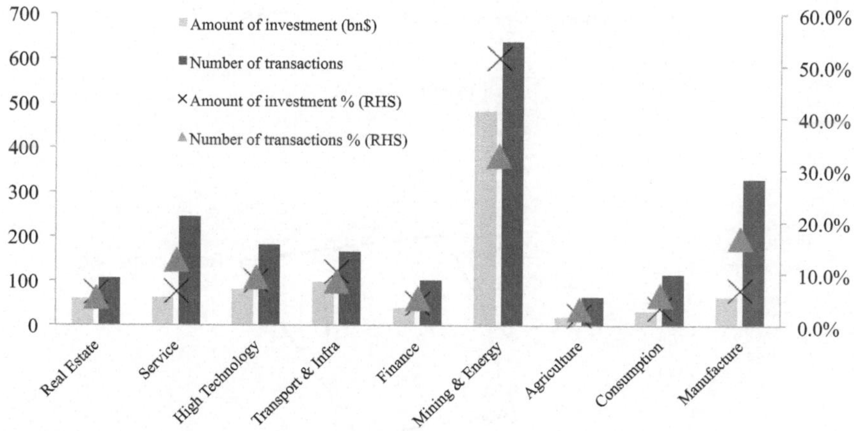

FIGURE 1.7 ODI distribution by industry

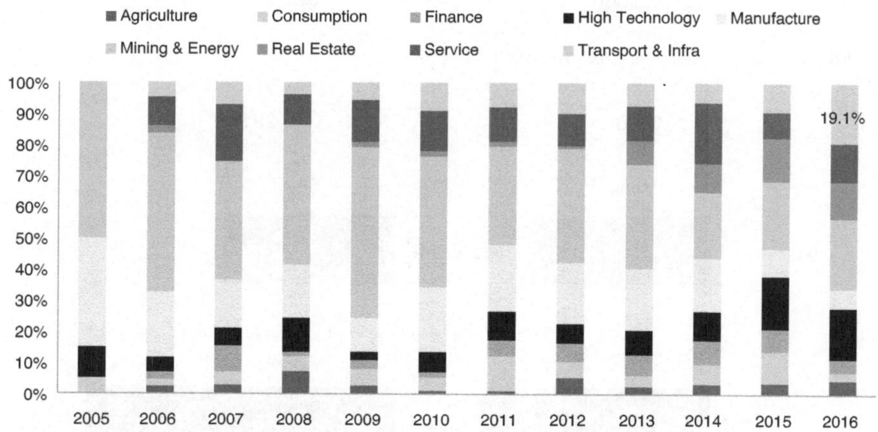

FIGURE 1.8 ODI distribution by industry, 2005–2016 (by number of transactions)

by companies listed in Hong Kong or the Chinese mainland stock exchange (Figure 1.10). Public listed companies have more diversified access to financing, including issuing new shares, issuing bonds, and bank loans. Hong Kong to a large extent has become an important financing platform for Chinese enterprises. Meanwhile, with the development of the Chinese private equity (PE) industry, the number and size of domestic PE funds have increased several times since 2010. It can be observed that domestic PE funds are increasingly active in providing capital and know-how to support cross-border acquisitions, and sometimes they themselves are independent leading acquirers. Meanwhile, large financial institutional investors – such as sovereign wealth funds, asset management companies backed by local governments and insurance companies – are active participants in cross-border M&A and often act as important partners for strategic investors. The development of the domestic financial market also encourages Chinese enterprises

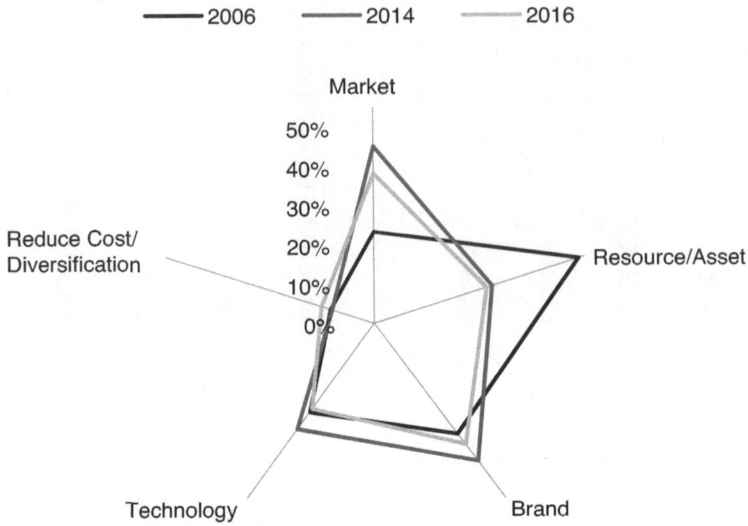

FIGURE 1.9 Dynamics of ODI motives

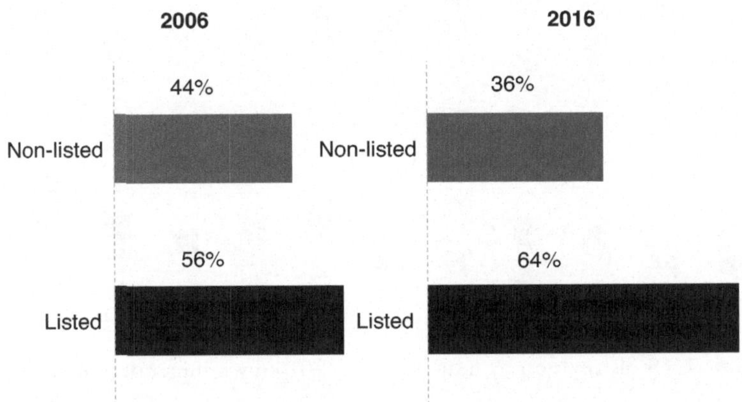

FIGURE 1.10 ODI breakdown between listed and private enterprises (by number of transactions)

to seek innovative financial instruments or vehicles. For instance, over 50 private enterprises jointly established China Minsheng Investment, an investment consortium with a size of 50 billion renminbi (RMB) focusing on overseas manufacturing investments. Another example is Fosun, a well-known Chinese private enterprise, which established joint PE funds with international asset managers.

Sixth, Beijing and coastal provinces are the most active in overseas investments. A large number of SOEs and listed enterprises are clustered in Beijing, making it the most active region in overseas investment, both by number of transactions and by size of investment, followed by Guangdong, Shanghai, Shandong and Zhejiang provinces (Table 1.3).

TABLE 1.3 Top ten provinces in ODI transactions

By aggregated number of transactions		*By aggregated amount of investment flow*	
Province	*Number of transactions*	*Province*	*Amount (USD bn)*
Beijing	706	Beijing	548.53
Guangdong	205	Guangdong	64.91
Shanghai	204	Shanghai	62.29
Zhejiang	129	Shandong	44.74
Shandong	104	Hubei	28.78
Jiangsu	100	Liaoning	21.03
Liaoning	50	Zhejiang	20.28
Hubei	49	Henan	18.61
Fujian	36	Sichuan	17.52
Hunan	33	Jiangsu	17.26

Dynamics of ODI enterprises and transactions

At the firm level, Sinopec, CNPC and Sinochem are the most active, continuously acquiring oil-related assets to expand upper stream resource allocations. They are followed by CNOOC, CITIC, ICBC and ChemChina as the most active SOEs seeking overseas investment opportunities. Among private enterprises, HNA, Fosun, Tencent, Haier and Lenovo have been very proactive in cross-border M&A (Table 1.4). Table 1.5 shows the most active Chinese enterprises in overseas investments by industry domain.

At the transaction level, Table 1.6 shows the ten largest overseas M&A transactions since the 2008 global financial crisis. CNOOC's buyout of Nexen is the single largest acquisition, with a total investment of over USD 18 billion. It can be seen that major oil companies such as Sinopec, CNPC and CNOOC dominate the top transactions. If we exclude oil companies, the top M&A transactions have become more diversified, ranging over the mining, telecommunications, infrastructure and energy industries. Our survey also shows that the average amount of cross-border M&A transactions taken by SOEs is about USD 887 million.

Analysis of investment preferences

Four dimensions were considered in our analysis: type of ownership, preference in industry, geographic destination and acquisition method. We compared the results between the periods 2005–2009 and 2010–2016 in order to illustrate the dynamics and evolution of Chinese ODI behaviours.

Table 1.7 shows the correlation between type of ownership, target industry, destination and acquisition method. SOEs and non-SOEs differ significantly in their investment preferences. For instance, SOEs invest more in energy, mining,

TABLE 1.4 Top ten Chinese enterprises in cross-border M&A (by number of transactions)

Rank	*SOE*	*Non-SOE*
1	Sinopec	HNA
2	CNPC	Fosun Group
3	Sinochem Group	Tencent
4	CNOOC	Anbang Insurance Group
5	CITIC	Haier
6	ICBC	Lenovo
7	ChemChina	Wanda Group
8	Zijin Mining Group	Guangming Diary
9	State Grid	HiSoft
10	Chinalco	Alibaba

TABLE 1.5 Most active ODI enterprises by industry (by amount of investment)

Industry	*1st*	*2nd*	*3rd*
Transport & Infra	COSCO	China Three Gorges Corporation	China Three Gorges Corporation
Finance	ICBC	China Development Bank	China Minsheng Investment Group
Real Estate	Greenland Holding Group	Greenland Holding Group	Shangdi Guanqun Investment Corporation
Consumption	Shuanghui Group	Guangming Diaries	Guangming Diaries
High Technology	CDH Investments	Tsinghua Holdings	Lenovo
Agriculture	COFCO	Beidahuang Group	State Power Investment Corporation
Services	Lenovo	Anbang Insurance Group	JinJiang International
Mining & Energy	CNOOC	Sinopec	Sinopec
Manufacturing	ChemChina	Sinopec	Sinochem

transportation and infrastructure, while non-SOEs concentrate on services, consumption and manufacturing. Africa is a preferred destination of SOEs, whereas Europe attracts non-SOE investments. After the 2008 global financial crisis, SOEs' investments to Africa and to Latin America and non-SOEs' investments to the high technology sector and to North America have all increased. In terms of acquisition methods, SOEs tend to seek absolute control of the target firm with acquired equity holdings exceeding 50%. In contrast, non-SOEs adopt a more flexible investment strategy. Very often, they act as an active minority shareholder.

TABLE 1.6 Ten largest M&A transactions since 2008

Rank	*Company*	*Time*	*Industry*	*Target*	*Country*	*Amount (USD bn)*
1	CNOOC	2012	Minerals and Energy	Nexen	Canada	18.2
2	Sinopec	2009	Minerals and Energy	Addax Petroleum	Switzerland	9.0
3	ChemChina	2015	Manufacture	Pirelli	Italy	9.0
4	Tencent	2016	Service	Supercell	Finland	8.6
5	Sinopec	2010	Minerals and Energy	Repsol Brasil	Brazil	7.1
6	Shuanghui	2013	Consumption	Smithfield Foods	US	7.1
7	MinMetals	2014	Minerals and Energy	Xstrata Las Bambas SA	Peru	7.0
8	State Grid	2013	Minerals and Energy	Singapore Power	Australia	6.7
9	HNA	2016	Service	Hilton Worldwide Holdings Inc.	US	6.5
10	HNA	2016	High tech	Ingram Micro	US	6.0

Note: While this chapter was being written, ChemChina's acquisition of Syngenta AG was not yet closed.

TABLE 1.7 Difference between SOEs and non-SOEs

		SOE	*Non-SOE*
Industry	Real Estate	N/A	N/A
	Services	–	+
	High Technology	N/A (–)	N/A (+)
	Transportation & Infrastructure	+	–
	Finance	N/A	N/A
	Energy & Mining	+	–
	Agriculture	N/A	N/A
	Consumption	–	+
	Manufacturing	– (N/A)	+(N/A)
Destination	North America	N/A (–)	N/A (+)
	Oceania	N/A	N/A
	Africa	+	–
	Latin America	N/A (+)	N/A (–)
	Europe	– (N/A)	+ (N/A)
	Asia	N/A	N/A
Acquisition Methods	Minor Passive	–	+
	Minor Active	–	+
	Absolute Control	+	–

Notes: (1) Tables 1.7 and 1.8 show the correlations between the variables: + indicates a positive correlation, – indicates a negative correlation, and N/A indicates that there is no significant correlation. (2) Parentheses in Tables 1.7 and 1.8 indicate the change of correlation since 2009.

TABLE 1.8 Correlation between industry, share acquired and destination

	Real Estate	*Services*	*High-Tech*	*Transport & Infra.*	*Finance*	*Mining & Energy*	*Agriculture*	*Consumption*	*Manufacture*
North America	N/A (+)	+	+	N/A (-)	N/A	–	N/A (–)	N/A	N/A
Oceania	N/A	–	N/A (–)	N/A	N/A	+	N/A (+)	N/A	N/A (–)
Africa	N/A	–	N/A (–)	N/A	N/A	+	N/A (+)	N/A (-)	N/A (–)
Latin America	N/A	N/A	N/A	N/A (+)	N/A	+	N/A	N/A	N/A (–)
Europe	N/A	N/A	N/A	N/A	N/A	–	N/A	N/A	+
Asia	N/A	+ (N/A)	N/A	N/A	N/A	N/A	N/A	N/A	– (N/A)
Minor Passive	N/A	+	N/A	N/A	N/A	–	N/A	N/A	N/A
Minor Active	N/A	+ (N/A)	N/A	N/A	N/A	–	N/A	N/A	N/A
Absolute Control	+ (N/A)	–	N/A	N/A	N/A	+	N/A	N/A	N/A

Our analysis also demonstrates that industrial concentration correlates with investment destination. For instance, high-tech and service sector investments concentrate in North America; natural resources investments concentrate in Africa, Oceania and Latin America; and manufacturing investments focus in Europe. In addition, companies investing in the energy, mining and real estate sectors mostly seek absolute control of the target firm or assets. However, investments in the services sector mainly consist of active minority acquisitions. While examining the changes of correlations before and after 2009, we found that M&A in the real estate sector in North America, in transportation and infrastructure in Latin America, and in agricultural investments in Africa and Oceania increased after the global financial crisis. In contrast, high-tech investments in Oceania; agriculture, transportation and infrastructure investments in North America; and manufacturing investments in Africa, Latin America and Oceania decreased. In addition, different acquisition methods seemed to be more widely adopted across industries with only two exceptions: companies preferred absolute control in the mining and energy sectors and preferred minority investment in the services sector.

Challenges facing Chinese ODI

We conducted a more in-depth analysis on the 62 failed M&A transactions and found that in its rapid growth, Chinese ODI also encountered great risks and challenges.

First, SOEs, given their governmental background, face more obstacles in their overseas investments as compared to private companies. For instance, CNOOC planned to acquire Unico for USD 18.5 billion in 2005, and the transaction was accepted by Unico. However, the deal eventually failed due to obstruction by the US Congress. SOEs' attempts to control assets in 'sensitive' industries such as energy and resources are likely to raise the suspicions of the recipient country government, regulatory authorities and media. Given the lessons learnt from the acquisition of Unico, CNOOC chose to invest in Canada, which was more investment 'friendly' to Chinese capital, and adopted a more proactive public relations strategy by properly communicating with the Canadian government, regulators and local media before and during the transaction, eventually securing its acquisition of Nexen in Canada.

Second, without careful due diligence and an in-depth understanding of the host country investment environment (investment rules, political sentiment, labour laws and so on), there are added difficulties in securing, executing and managing overseas projects. For instance, Minsheng Bank concluded the acquisition of 9.9% of United Commercial Bank in 2009 within only few weeks, without proper due diligence. After the acquisition, Minsheng Bank found that the corporate governance of United Commercial Bank was flawed, and their financial statements were also questionable. More importantly, Minsheng Bank misjudged the possibility of the Federal Reserve's bailout of United Commercial Bank. As a result, Minsheng Bank suffered a loss of USD 800 million. Many cases have proved that in-depth knowledge of the target entity and industry, as well as sustained communication with the executives and regulatory authorities (including the establishment and maintenance of public and private relations), are vital for the success of a cross-border buyout. Adequate preparation and prudent decision-making can reduce asymmetric information and thus lessen the possibility of an investment failure.

Third, lack of managerial capabilities often leads to investment failure. SAIC Motor's buyout of SsangYong Motor Company in South Korea serves as a good illustration. SsangYong's employees were against the buyout since the beginning of the deal negotiation and went on a 43-day strike, triggered by SAIC Motor's plan to lay off 986 employees. Management of SAIC Motor underestimated the difficulty of business integration and paid insufficient attention to the obvious difference in corporate culture. Internal managerial conflicts became fierce, and strategic integration became unlikely. In the end, SsangYong went bankrupt three years after SAIC Motor's acquisition. Several other similar cases have also shown that differences in culture and values, as well as labour disputes, are major problems in post-investment management. Lack of qualified managerial capability and understanding of the host country culture is often a major hindrance. This may to some extent satisfy their need for capital.

Fourth, private enterprises face greater capital constraints. SOEs are supported by central or local governments, which enable them to access to low-cost capital. On the other hand, sources of capital for private enterprises are rather limited, and the funding cost could be very high as compared to SOEs. In practice, most private enterprises rely on bank lending, sometimes via the 'shadow banking' system. Listed private enterprises may raise capital via public markets; however, the scale is relatively small. Recently, it can be observed that some private enterprises are seeking closer alliances with financial institutions in their cross-border acquisitions. For instance, Sany Heavy Industry teamed up with CITIC Private Equity in acquiring Putzmeister. Lenovo allied with TPG, New Bridge Capital and General Atlantic while taking over IBM's PC unit.

Conclusion and implications

Our survey shows that Chinese ODI has grown rapidly in the last decade. In terms of investment distribution, motives and strategies, Chinese ODI is increasingly diversified and moving towards the upper industry value chain. SOEs' dominant role in overseas investments has weakened, and instead private enterprises have very quickly grown in importance. With the Chinese economy and financial market becoming more liberalized and increasing policy support from the Chinese government, Chinese enterprises demonstrate greater ambitions and confidence in their overseas expansion. We estimate that Chinese ODI will maintain its fast growth trajectory and that Chinese enterprises will continue to accelerate their process of internationalization.

Our survey also suggests several implications. First, more reforms of China's financial system are urgently needed in order to accommodate and facilitate the rapid growth of Chinese ODI. Deregulation and more market-orientated supervision is the key. Second, direct financing such as IPO markets and the private equity business needs stronger support in order to satisfy the financing needs of private enterprises, improve market efficiency and lower the cost of capital. Third, Chinese enterprises need to improve their multinational management capabilities and invest heavily in high-quality international professional managers, which is crucial in successful internationalization. Fourth, facing more competitive Chinese enterprises and a surge of Chinese capital, host-country governments and regulators need to establish and maintain a more transparent and fair investment environment and policy framework so that they can continue to optimize their mutual benefits.

Note

1 All opinions expressed herein are the authors' own and do not necessarily reflect the views of any of the organizations with which the authors are affiliated.

References

Ministry of Commerce of the People's Republic of China, National Bureau of Statistics of the People's Republic of China 2015, *2015 Statistical Bulletin of China's Outward Foreign Direct Investment.*

UNCTAD 2016, *World Investment Report 2016 – Investor Nationality: Policy Challenges.*

Yuanyuan Pan & Ruiyun Huang 2015, *The Quarterly Report of China's Outward Investment (Second Quarter 2015).*

2

FROM 'WORLD FACTORY' TO INTERNATIONAL CAPACITY COOPERATION

China's evolving role in the global value chain

Xuedong Ding[1]

Background

The world economy has undergone profound change since the 2008 financial crisis, as reflected by the transforming landscape of the global value chain (GVC). For instance, it can be witnessed that multinational enterprises (MNEs) are re-allocating their production and supply chains globally so as to reduce production costs. This is clearly the case in Asia. Some developed economies such as the US are calling on their manufacturing companies to return to the home market by providing attractive tax treatment. On the international policy front, bilateral and multilateral trade and investment talks start to receive increasing attention. The most well-known examples are the Trans-Pacific Partnership Agreement (TPP) and the Transatlantic Trade and Investment Partnership (TTIP), which will undoubtedly transform the international policy system.

China has experienced rapid economic growth since reform and opening up in 1978 and then becoming the 'World's Factory' by producing goods for other countries. However, both of its external and internal environments have dramatically changed in recent years. Some MNEs are moving their factories from the China Mainland to Bangladesh, the Philippines and Vietnam in response to rising production costs and intensified competition. The scale of inward foreign direct investment (FDI) in China has been shrinking. Meanwhile, China itself suffers from a sluggish economy. Its excessive capacity needs to be transferred, and the industrial structure needs to be upgraded. Facing such challenges, the Chinese government has announced the 'Made in China 2025' initiative and policies focusing on international capacity cooperation. Generally speaking, it is time for China to adjust its role in the global value chain.

Expanding outward direct investment (ODI) by setting up overseas factories, forming joint ventures and conducting cross-border mergers and acquisitions

(M&A) is widely practiced by many countries, with the aim of reaching out to the global market, moving up in the value chain and transferring domestic advantaged capacity. In turn, this increased ODI also benefits the economy by stimulating growth and structural adjustments in bilateral and multilateral trade.

In 2014, China's FDI and ODI[2] almost balanced up. Based on this fact, some argue that China has entered an era of 'capital exporting' and therefore needs to transform from being the 'World's Factory' to a major capital exporter. This chapter thus aims to address the following questions: what role China plays in the global value chain; which stage China is going through; and what roadmap and policy are needed to support China in moving up the global value chain.

China's current position in the global value chain

A lot of work has been done in theoretical and empirical studies of the global value chain (Buckley and Casson, 1976; Thomas, 1985; Hummels et al., 2001; Helpman, 1984). However, due to data availability and transfer pricing within multinational enterprises, an accurate analysis of GVC appears to be not very straightforward. So far, value added in trade (VAiT) and comparative advantage are two concepts that are mostly employed by international institutions such as UNCTAD, WTO and OECD, to evaluate specialization in the global value chain (OECD, WTO, UNCTAD, 2014). Value added in trade takes only the domestic value added in a country's exports[3] into consideration, which is the real value added (Figure 2.1). According to the OECD, China's domestic value added accounted for 67.4% of its gross exports in 2009, totalling USD 865 billion (Figure 2.2). This is a significant step forward compared with the level in the 1990s. However, processing trade is still a large part of China's exports. As a result, although China has become the largest nation in trading goods, the role it plays on the global stage is still limited to a 'processing factory' or 'assembly workshop'.[4] With the world's largest trade volume, China is still in the middle stream of the global value chain based on an evaluation of value-added trade.

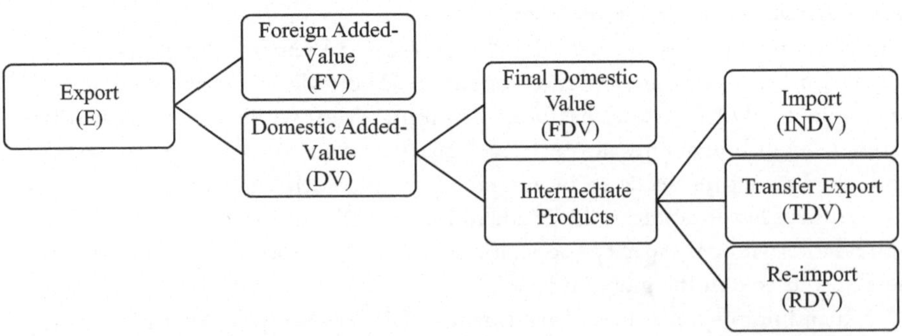

FIGURE 2.1 Breakdown of a country's foreign trade

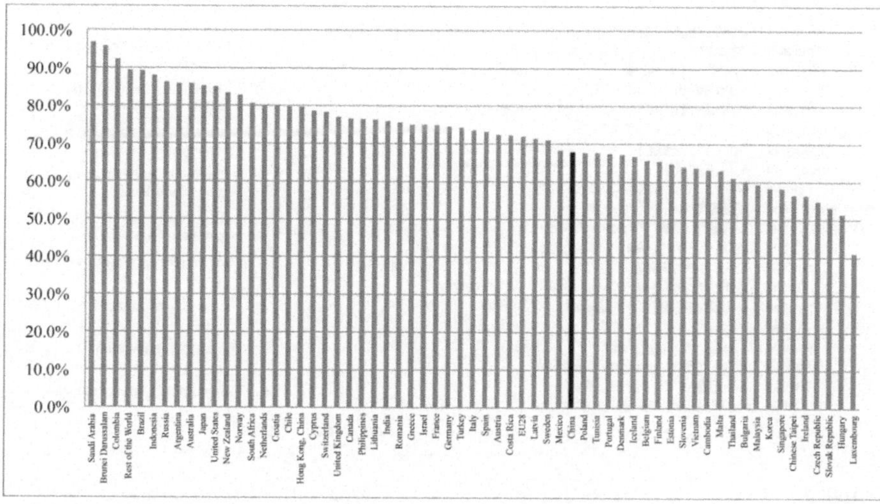

FIGURE 2.2 Domestic value added rate of main countries

Source: author's calculation based on OECD database.

To better understand the statistics shown above, the size of one country's economy and the composition of its exports need to be considered. Countries whose exports mainly consist of raw materials could demonstrate value-added rates higher than 90%, such as Saudi Arabia, Russia and Brazil. However, such a high level does not necessarily mean that these countries are competitive in manufacturing. On the contrary, Germany's value-added rate is only about 75%, but it is in the upstream of the global value chain due to its advanced industrial intelligence. Therefore, a comparative analysis of the industrial landscape is often complementary to an analysis of VAiT.

For example, according to the theory of comparative advantage, one country could make profits by producing and exporting goods with comparative advantages, while importing goods with comparative disadvantages. The Revealed Comparative Advantage (RCA) index is used by the OECD to evaluate the distribution of comparative advantages or disadvantages among industries in a certain country. The index is the ratio of the proportion of a certain kind of goods in the country's exports to the proportion of the same kind in the global total. A comparative advantage is 'revealed' if the index is greater than 1, while RCA of less than 1 indicates that the country is at a comparative disadvantage in this kind of goods or service (OECD, 2009).

A cross-country RCA study conducted by the OECD[5] pointed out China's strengths and weaknesses in international trade. First, several of China's industries have noticeable comparative advantages, including textile and clothing, as well as electronic and optical equipment manufacturing. Second, some of China's capital- and technology-intensive industries (such as electronic and optical equipment, transportation facilities) have become stronger in terms of comparative advantages,

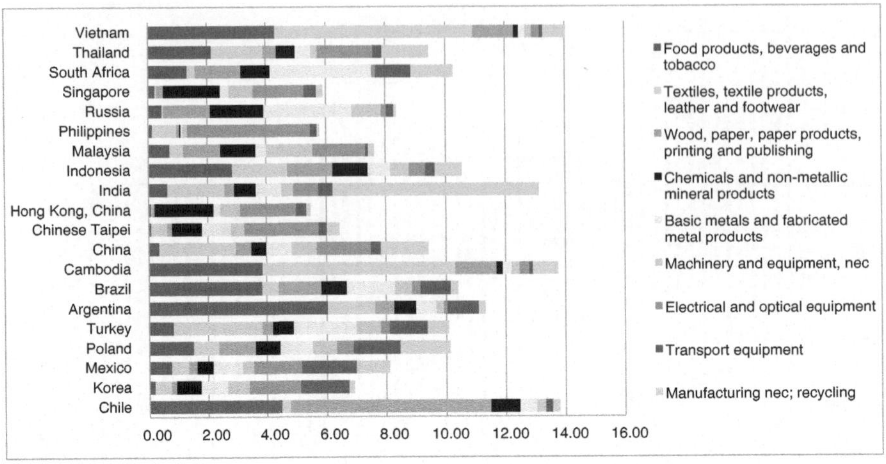

FIGURE 2.3 Comparison of RCA index between China and other emerging markets
Source: author's calculation based on OECD database.

while other industries find themselves in a downward trend. Third, developed countries such as the United States have comparative advantages in almost all manufacturing industries, particularly in technology- and capital-intensive industries. China is behind these developed countries in terms of overall competitiveness, but it stands out in a number of industries (such as textiles, machinery equipment manufacturing, metal products, and electronic and optical devices) compared with other emerging markets (Figure 2.3). Furthermore, China's comparative advantages are complementary to those of some emerging markets. For example, Latin American countries like Brazil, Argentina and Chile are more competitive in timber manufacturing and the food and beverage industry.

A study on China's role in the global value chain, conducted by the Ministry of Commerce of China, confirmed China's value-added rate estimated by the OECD. In 2013, the domestic value added per USD 1,000 exported was USD 640, indicating a value added rate of 64% (MOFCOM, 2014). In overall terms, China is now at the middle level of the global value chain and still has a long way to go to catch up with developed countries. Nevertheless, it has advantages compared to developing countries and emerging economies, and it is ready to export industrial capacities in some fields.

Direction and roadmap of future development

Current stage and future direction

Based on previous analysis, we can draw the conclusion that since reform and opening up, China's domestic value added has increased significantly and has been moving up the global value chain. However, China is still positioned at the middle level of the global value chain, and its industrial composition of export falls behind developed countries. In order to climb further up the global value chain, China needs to strengthen its international competitiveness in high-end manufacturing industries. To achieve this goal, it is important to accumulate knowledge and experience in the fields of core technology, goods, services, human resources and international management know-how. All of this takes time, and progress has to be made step by step.

Undoubtedly, China's overseas investment has grown rapidly in recent years. Official statistics show that China's ODI almost equalled inward FDI in 2014 (MOFCOM, 2015). If we consider that Chinese enterprises use overseas retained profits to reinvest or invest through a third country, China's ODI figure may have exceeded its FDI by roughly USD 20 billion. Technically speaking, this made China a capital exporter for the first time. However, whether or not China has stepped into an era of capital exporting needs further discussion.

Experience of other countries indicates that an advanced capital exporter country needs to be strong not only in the capital volume but also in the 'quality' of its capital outflow. For instance, Japan's capital outflow in the mid-1970s was considered to be a practice of international trade in the wide sense, as most of its capital was deployed to facilitate its export of goods and services. In the late 1970s, after the Japanese government started financial liberalization reforms and loosened restrictions on capital accounts, capital outflow gradually became one of the driving forces for economic growth along with trade and technology, casting a greater stimulus on its economy. Eventually, financial portfolio investment and outward direct investment started to dominate Japan's capital exports, during which time public capital was overtaken by private capital and an increasing amount of capital flowed into developed countries. In the 1980s, Japan surpassed the United States and became the world's largest capital exporter (The Library of Congress Country Studies, 1994), making it a major power in international capital circulation.

China's capital exporting, by contrast, is at its preliminary stage. Although its volume has been growing rapidly, the overall quality is still low compared to developed countries. Its ODI stock is concentrated in developing countries, with the goal of obtaining natural resources and supporting exports of goods and services. This will likely continue for the foreseeable future. Given that 55.2% of non-financial ODI stock is contributed by state-owned enterprises, it will take time for Chinese private capital to catch up. Apart from this, the domestic regulations on capital account outflows are still restrictive to some extent, hindering large-scale and diversified capital exports.

Based on the above analysis, it will be a long and incremental journey for China to become a strong capital exporter. In a reality context, China will continue to expand its scale of outward direct investment. At the same time and equally importantly, it needs to maintain its status as the 'World's Factory' by optimizing and upgrading its industrial structure and promoting the internationalization of its technology, industrial standards and advanced industrial capacity. Failure to retain comparative advantages in traditional manufacturing industries

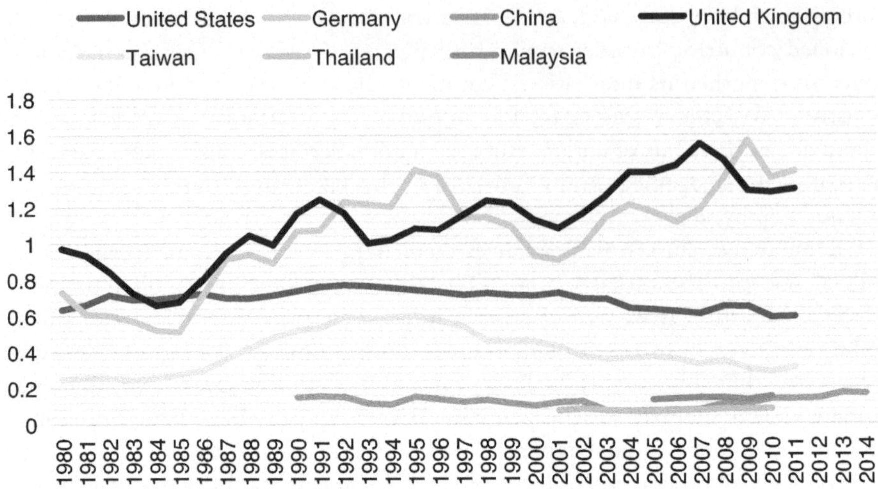

FIGURE 2.4 International comparison of unit labour costs

Source: Wind.

would be a serious mistake, and this would put further pressure on its economic growth and employment. In fact, China still has room to manoeuvre. For instance, China's unit labour cost in the manufacturing industry remains relatively low due to significant improvements in labour productivity. Measured by unit labour cost, China's manufacturing cost is at about the average level compared to its competitors in Asia, and it is still competitive compared to developed countries (Figure 2.4). The solution lies in rebalancing the domestic industrial layout and innovation in a global policy setting. Some traditional manufacturing industries in the eastern coastal region could be relocated to the middle and western regions. This is already an ongoing process. In addition, the One Belt One Road Initiative has provided unprecedented opportunities for Chinese enterprises to participate in international cooperation.

The roadmap

To strengthen and upgrade domestic manufacturing industry, China needs to make use of its capacities fully and effectively. Domestically, the industrial layout should be optimized by relocating traditional manufacturing industries to inner regions. Internationally, China needs to export its advantageous capacity, technology and standards, so that China's manufacturing standards will have a stronger influence. In order to do so, we need a well-thought plan and appropriate execution. For instance, policymakers should put labour-intensive manufacturing sectors on the priority list of the relocation; energy efficiency and environmental protection should be taken into full account along with sustainable local economic growth when selecting a specific location; certain goods and services that can be produced and consumed locally should be prioritized; and export-oriented industries should be given policy support, such as customs clearance and export tax rebates, so as to reduce total cost.

Apart from rebalancing the domestic industrial layout, ODI is also essential. Cross-border M&A and joint ventures, especially in technology-intensive and capital-intensive industries, are key to acquiring core technology, brands, international sales channels, innovative business models and advanced management experience from high-end manufacturing enterprises. This knowledge and experience will drive China's industrial upgrade and then invigorate its manufacturing competitiveness.

Furthermore, China also needs to strengthen cooperation with foreign countries in production capacity, including working with foreign partners in the other countries, and to relocate advantageous industrial capacity to other countries. High-speed railway and nuclear power represent China's top manufacturing level. They play a significant and leading role in promoting international capacity cooperation. China can also seek cooperation opportunities in infrastructure project design, construction and management, as well as other sectors such as steel, cement, chemical industry, building materials, non-ferrous metal, glass and shipbuilding. Based on its solid foundation and comparative advantages in the industries mentioned above, China can perform production tailored to local demand. However, collaboration in these fields often proves to be challenging as well, due to geopolitical factors, protectionism and international competition. In addition, investment risks are high due to the large investment scale, long payback period and uncertainties embedded with green field investments.

Suggestions

The internationalization of Chinese enterprises not only depends on their competitiveness but also depends on policy support. Recently, the Chinese government has proposed several initiatives to facilitate the 'going-out' of domestic manufacturing companies and to boost international cooperation on industrial capacity. Among these initiatives, OBOR as an open and inclusive policy set-up will further facilitate Chinese ODI and international cooperation. In addition, these initiatives have also provided guidance to overseas investment. But more support and efforts are needed to enhance the competitiveness of Chinese enterprises and to level up China's overall position in the global value chain.

First, China needs to bring innovation to the international cooperation of production capacity, and to enhance its ability to improve the global location layout of its industries. Innovative equity structures will certainly benefit international capacity cooperation. Specifically, it is encouraged to expand outward direct investment in equity – obtaining ownerships or long-term management rights of international assets and thus hedging some periodic risks (including exchange rate fluctuations and local government changes) via long-term stable cash inflows. A proper equity structure should be built to allow strong liquidity in order to meet investors' needs for equity transfer and divestment. In large-scale overseas infrastructure projects, public-private partnership (PPP) helps to relieve the pressure of providing a sovereign guarantee as faced by host country governments, and it encourages Chinese enterprises to participate in equity investment and post-investment management. Moreover, financial leasing – in other words renting domestically manufactured equipment to foreign nations – is also worth considering. In this way, China-made equipment can not only generate profits but also gain access to foreign markets. Apart from these measures, China needs a balanced industrial layout and to integrate resources to better arrange its industrial landscape. By setting up financing platforms that link industrial practitioners and financial institutions, building bilateral and multilateral industrial zones and free trade zones, and acquiring project ownerships while enhancing the role as the project contractor, China will fuel its upstream and downstream businesses to go abroad and promote domestic design, technical standards, operations, management as well as talent.

Second, China needs to enhance financial support for the internationalization of its enterprises, especially by making the support system more diversified. By integrating domestic financial policies and consolidating financial resources, the issue of financial institutions lacking cooperation can be solved. An integrated financial support plan involving foreign aid, government subsidies, policy-based finance and commercial capital will decrease the overall financing cost and reduce arbitrage activities by enterprises. In addition, multilateral financial cooperation is helpful in solving issues of bad credit and poor solvency of some countries, thus boosting international cooperation. Multilateral financial institutions initiated by China, such as the Asian Infrastructure Investment Bank and BRICS Development Bank, are essential for regional cooperation and will also enhance collaboration with other multilateral institutions such as the World Bank, the IMF and ADB. Further, domestic financial institutions are encouraged to set up overseas branches to improve their support for Chinese enterprises in overseas businesses. Meanwhile, the financing pressure for some large-scale overseas projects can be relieved by diversifying the capital structure. For example, a multi-layer or multi-trench capital structure can be designed to attract multiple investors.

Third, China needs to improve administrative efficiency and labour productivity. Administrative cost can be further reduced by streamlining administration processes and decentralizing power to improve efficiency. Private enterprises will benefit more from further opening-up, such as expanding the free trade zone and 'negative list' management to a wider area, removing unnecessary monopoly and market access barriers, and promoting PPP cooperation in competitive public sectors. In addition to improving administrative efficiency, it is also vitally important to improve labour productivity. Expanding investment in R&D and education is a practical way to nurture Chinese talent and establish an innovation-oriented environment in the long run. Moreover, by pushing ahead with the 'Made in China 2025' policy, China will increase its chances for making breakthroughs in high-end equipment technology in a number of fields (e.g. information technology, new materials, biological medicine, digital control machines, robots, aeronautics and astronautics, marine engineering, high-speed rail transportation and renewable energy). In addition, foreign direct investment into China should be guided and utilized more wisely with a focus on importing advanced technology and management skills to serve the development of domestic industries.

Fourth, China needs to cultivate and employ talent with global vision and professional skills. Human resources often become an obstacle to the internationalization of Chinese enterprises and their participation in international industrial capacity cooperation. To address this issue, Chinese enterprises need to attract and recruit top talent from across the world and learn to manage global business using global talent. Training of domestic talent is also essential. To become global, Chinese enterprises need qualified managers who not only understand the Chinese culture but also can compete globally.

Finally, Chinese enterprises need to improve their international image. They should not only be self-confident but also enhance mutual trust with host countries. In order to achieve this goal, enterprises are encouraged to seek positive publicity, to properly interact with the culture of host countries and to obey market rules and local regulations. Furthermore, enterprises need to undertake corporate social responsibilities – protecting the local environment, showing respect for local religions and participating in charity events. Importantly, enterprises need to thoroughly understand the local economic and social needs, provide more job opportunities, and pursue mutual benefits in an open and inclusive manner. By doing so, China can enhance mutual trust and understanding with neighbouring countries, eliminate unnecessary doubt and therefore create a favourable international investment environment.

Notes

1 All opinions expressed herein are the author's own and do not necessarily reflect the views of any of the organizations with which the author is affiliated.

2 China's foreign direct investment in 2014 was USD 119.56 billion, and outward direct investment was USD 123.12 billion, according to the National Bureau of Statistics of China.

3 For example, country A exports a $100 intermediate product to country B. After processing and assembly, country B creates $50 added value and exports a $150 product to country C. Following the value added in trade method, the real export of country B is $50, not $150. The conventional method virtually adds $100 of additional value into country B's export. Thus, country B has a trade surplus of $50, not $150.

In international trade, about 28% goods are imported merely as the intermediate product to produce goods and services for export. For example, of USD 19,000 billion global exports in 2010, nearly USD 5,000 billion of goods are imported as intermediate products, and thus are double-counted in accounting (UNCTAD, 2013).

4 China surpassed the US to become the largest trading country in 2012, but the domestic value-added rate of exports was around 67%, far below those of most developed countries.

5 OECD Statistics Database: http://stats.oecd.org/.

References

Buckley, PJ & Casson, MC 1976, *The Future of the Multinational Enterprises*, Macmillan, London.

Helpman, E 1984, 'A simple theory of international trade with multinational corporations', *Journal of Political Economy*, vol. 92, no. 3, pp. 451–471.

Hummels, D, Ishii, J & Yi, KM 2001, 'The nature and growth of vertical specialization in world trade', *Journal of International Economics*, vol. 54, no. 1, pp. 75–96.

The Library of Congress Country Studies 1994, *Japan Capital Flows*, CIA World Factbook, US.

Ministry of Commerce People's Republic of China 2014, *The Research of Global Value Chain and Chinese Trade Added-Value Calculation.*

Ministry of Commerce People's Republic of China 2015, *Brief Statistics on China's Import & Export in December 2014.*

Ministry of Commerce People's Republic of China 2016, *Brief Statistics on China's Non-Financial Direct Investment Overseas.*

National Bureau of Statistics of China 2014, *Annual International Trade Database.* Available from: http://data.stats.gov.cn/easyquery.htm?cn=C01.

OECD 2009, *OECD Communications Outlook*, OECD Publishing, Paris.

OECD 2011, *OECD Statistics Database.* Available from: http://stats.oecd.org/.

OECD, WTO, UNCTAD 2014, *Implications of Global Value Chains for Trade, Investment, Development and Jobs*, G-20 Leaders Summit Saint Petersburg.

Thomas, P 1985, 'Internalization as a general theory of foreign direct investment: A critique', *Weltwirtschaftliches Archiv*, vol. 121, no. 3, pp. 570–575.

UNCTAD 2013, *Trade and Development Report, 2013: Adjusting to the Changing Dynamics of the World Economy.* Available at: http://unctad.org/en/pages/newsdetails.aspx?OriginalVersionID=600&Sitemap_x0020_Taxonomy=Globalization%20and%20Development.

3

CHINA'S ECONOMIC TRANSITION AND OUTWARD DIRECT INVESTMENTS

Lawrence J. Lau[1]

Introduction

China is the world's fastest growing economy, averaging growth of 9.6% per annum since 1978. No other economy has ever grown as fast for as long a period as the Chinese economy. However, Chinese economic growth has begun to slow, to an average annual rate of around 6.5%, in a process of transition to a 'New Normal'. In 2016, the Chinese economy grew 6.7% in real terms. Chinese total international trade in goods and services also grew rapidly, from US$20.3 billion in 1978 to US$4.67 trillion in 2015, making China the second-largest trading nation in the world, just after the US with its total international trade of US$4.99 trillion. However, Chinese international trade has also begun to slow down recently. Both Chinese exports and imports reached a peak as a percentage of GDP in 2006 and have been falling since (see Figure 3.1). Nevertheless, China continues to have a trade surplus on the order of 3% of GDP.

What does the 'New Normal' imply? On the demand side, the 'New Normal' is characterized by, first, a reduced reliance on exports. Chinese exports of goods and services declined absolutely and as a percentage of Chinese GDP, and they are not expected to grow at the same rapid rates as seen in the first decade of this century. Second, it is also characterized by reduced investment in fixed assets in the manufacturing sector and in residential real estate, as there are huge excess production capacities in almost every traditional industry – coal, steel, cement, plate glass, solar panels, ship-building, aluminium smelting and even electric power – and excess supplies of residential housing in all except the first-tier cities of Beijing, Shanghai, Guangzhou and Shenzhen. And even in the latter cities, there are risks of housing price bubbles. Third, it is also characterized by a greater emphasis on household consumption and a better environment – for example, clean air, clean water and clean soil.

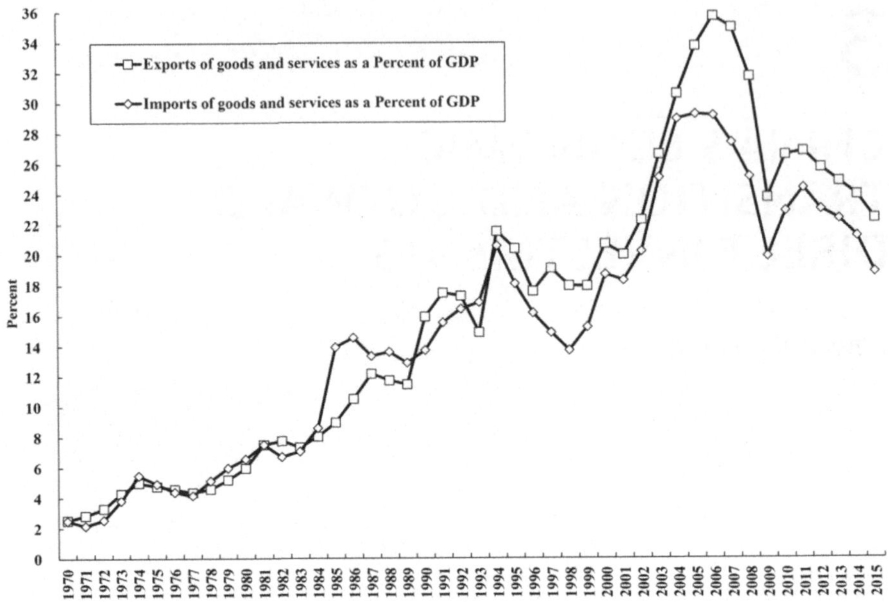

FIGURE 3.1 Chinese exports and imports of goods and services as a percentage of GDP, 1970–2015

On the supply side, the Chinese economy will continue to have strong economic fundamentals going forward – a high domestic saving rate, abundant surplus labour and a huge domestic market. However, the 'New Normal' implies that Chinese economic growth will be increasingly driven by innovation and technical progress, in addition to the growth in tangible inputs. Supply-side structural reform, which is intended to increase the efficiency in the use of capital through reducing wasteful and duplicative investment, is a continuing long-term effort. However, increases in tangible inputs will continue to play a role in Chinese economic growth as the tangible capital per unit of labour in China still lags far behind those of the United States and other developed economies.

One important unique feature of the Chinese economy is its very high national saving rate. Except for the early 1950s, China has always had a high saving rate. During the past decade, the average national saving rate was almost 50%, the highest in the world. In contrast, the average national saving rate around the world is probably around 25%. This high national saving rate has enabled a rapid accumulation of tangible capital in China – structures, equipment and basic infrastructure – without relying on foreign capital, including foreign direct investment, foreign portfolio investment, foreign loans and foreign aid. The growth of the tangible capital stock in China has been the source of the bulk of Chinese economic growth since China began its economic reform and opened to the world in 1978.

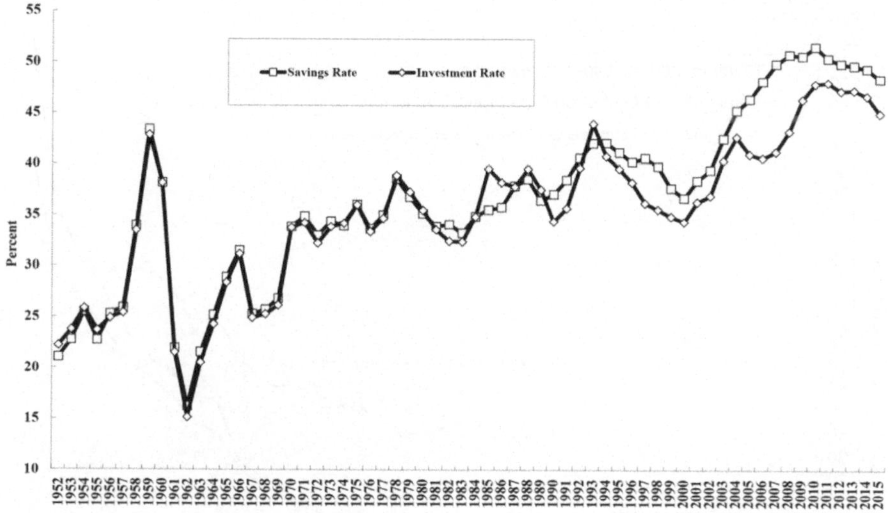

FIGURE 3.2 Chinese national savings and gross domestic investment as a percentage of GDP since 1952

However, this high national saving rate has also caused a serious savings-investment imbalance. Since 1994, the Chinese national saving rate has always been higher than the Chinese investment rate (see Figure 3.2), which means that as much as China has been investing in structure, equipment and basic infrastructure, it is unable to fully utilize all of its national savings. At its peak (2007), the excess of Chinese savings over investment was almost 9% of GDP. It has since declined to around 3% of GDP, but China must seek better and more productive uses for its savings. As investment opportunities in China have become quite limited because of the existing excess capacities in many manufacturing industries and in residential real estate, Chinese enterprises (and households) must look for investment opportunities outside of China. This is where outward direct investment comes in. Of course, it is also possible for China to invest more in research and development (R&D), which supports innovation. However, R&D expenditures are projected to reach 2.5% of GDP only by 2020 (compared with 2.1% in 2015) and cannot productively absorb more resources. Another possibility is to increase investment in the provision of domestic public goods such as clean air, clean water, clean soil, education, health care and elderly care. To do so will require government commitment and leadership.

In Figure 3.3, we present inbound and outbound direct investment of China (including total outbound and non-financial outbound). Inbound foreign direct investment began to take off in 1992, soon after the famous 'Southern Tour' of the late Chinese paramount leader DENG Xiaoping, and reached US$126 billion in 2016. Outbound direct investment (including both financial and non-financial direct investment) started much later, in 2003, with less than US$3 billion. However, it grew rapidly and surpassed inbound foreign direct investment in 2014,

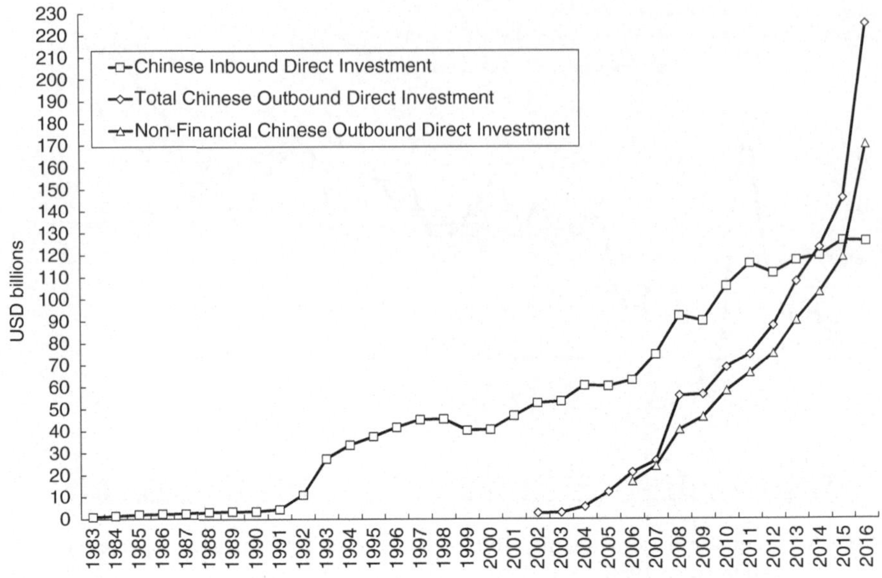

FIGURE 3.3 Chinese inbound and outbound direct investments, US$ billions

Sources: Ministry of Commerce, National Bureau of Statistics and State Administration of Foreign Exchange, *2014 Niandu Zhongguo Duiwai Zhijie Touzi Tongji Gongbao* (Statistical Bulletin on Chinese Outbound Direct Investment [2014]), as adjusted by the author; National Development and Reform Commission, *Work Report for 2016*, p. 56, Chart 13. Data on total outbound direct investment for 2016 according to Dealogic.

reaching US$225 billion in 2016. Even excluding financial investments, outbound direct investment amounted to US$170 billion in 2016, substantially exceeding the inbound direct investment. In the last couple of years, financial outbound investment has grown much faster than non-financial outbound direct investment. Net total direct investment currently runs at a rate of approximately minus US$100 billion per year. This is still a relatively small number relative to the trade surplus in goods and services, which is of the order of US$400 billion a year.[2]

While the excess domestic savings in China provide a strong motivation for outbound direct investment, the aging demographics also support outbound direct investment at this time, with the expectation of capital repatriation years later. The rate of return to capital has been falling in China, in part because of rising wages, in part because of the decline in the working-age population, and in part because of over-investment in many industries, all of which shift the terms of trade between capital and labour against capital. In addition, since capital is already relatively abundant in China but relatively scarce in the rest of the world, it can earn a higher rate of return elsewhere. China Investment Corporation, the sovereign wealth fund of China, was specifically set up to make investments overseas. Similarly, the Silk Road Fund was set up to invest in countries and regions along the new Silk Roads linking East Asia and Western Europe through Russia, Central Asia, South Asia, Southeast Asia and the Middle East.

The outlook for inbound foreign direct investment is not as promising as it used to be. China remains a huge market for both consumer goods and producer goods. Its middle class has been expanding rapidly and has been projected to be as high as 700 million. Even 300 million is already an extremely attractive potential market. However, today, China no longer lacks money. If all that a foreign direct investor can bring to China is money, it should not come. There is no shortage of money for investment in China. In addition, China has also become technologically more sophisticated and can produce many goods that it was unable to produce before. Only a foreign direct investor with innovative technologies, superior designs, new business models (protected by patents, trademarks and copyrights) or unique access to markets can have a good chance to prosper in China.

Reasons for outbound direct investment

Why do Chinese enterprises invest overseas? As explained above, Chinese national savings far exceed Chinese national investment, which means there are excess savings to be productively deployed elsewhere. Chinese domestic household consumption currently constitutes less than 50% of GDP, compared to the more typical 65–70% for a developed economy. Even though it has been increasing at approximately one and a half times the rate of growth of GDP, because of its low base, it will be a long time before Chinese household consumption as a percentage of GDP approaches the level of developed economies. So the Chinese national saving rate will remain high for a long time. Moreover, the lack of good opportunities for investment in fixed assets (and for portfolio investment) in China also means that excess savings will continue to exist and that enterprises (and households) must look to invest overseas.

Seeking lower costs

One important reason for investing overseas is to seek lower production costs. During the last decade, Chinese wage rates have gone up substantially, and the renminbi has appreciated by approximately 25%. In addition, land costs and energy costs are no longer low in China. Setting up manufacturing facilities in overseas markets, despite higher labour costs, can make sense as land and energy costs are much lower, transportation costs can be greatly reduced, and labour costs can be saved through automation and robotics. More recently, since the election of Donald Trump as President of the United States, there is also the possible implementation of a border adjustment tax to be considered, which makes it even more favourable to the establishment of manufacturing facilities in the United States.

Increasing market share and market power

Another important reason for investing overseas is to protect as well as increase market share and market power. Proximity to market makes it much easier to respond to the preferences and needs of customers in a timely manner and to achieve deeper and more durable market penetration. Acquiring a local enterprise in the same line of business can increase both market share and market power instantly. The acquirer can also leverage the existing customer base and distribution system of the acquisition target. Examples of such overseas investment include the US$5.4 billion acquisition of General Electric's appliance unit by the Haier Group and the US$3.4 billion unsuccessful offer for the US crane maker Terex Corp. by Chinese manufacturer Zoomlion Heavy Industry Science & Technology Co.

Acquisition of natural resources and raw materials

Yet another important reason for investing overseas is to ensure the security of supply of indispensable imported natural resources such as oil and iron ore, and potentially the supply of agricultural commodities through the acquisition of agricultural land. Past examples include the US$15.1 billion acquisition of Canada's Nexen Inc. in 2013 by China's CNOOC Ltd. as well as the failed bid by state-owned Aluminum Corp. of China for a significant stake in the Anglo-Australian miner Rio Tinto in 2009. Not all such overseas investment deals were consummated, and not all of the completed transactions turned out to be profitable for the acquirers.

Acquisition of technology

The Chinese government actively promotes innovation and entrepreneurship. In order to support domestic innovation, many Chinese enterprises scour the world to find technologies and high technology companies that can contribute to innovation in China. For example, China National Chemical Corp., also known as ChemChina, made an offer to acquire Swiss pesticides and seeds group maker Syngenta AG, for US$43 billion in 2015.[3] Another example is the acquisition of Kuka, a German robotics company, by the Midea Group for US$5 billion more recently.

Upgrading the quality of domestically produced consumer goods

The rapidly expanding Chinese middle class has become a major source of consumer demand in China. As the disposable incomes of the middle-class households have risen, their tastes have shifted towards consumer goods of higher quality and greater variety. Foreign brands and labels are often preferred because they serve as a form of quality assurance. As Chinese manufacturers of consumer goods gradually abandon the low ends of their markets and move up to produce higher-quality goods, the acquisition of foreign brands, labels and designs becomes important to them as a way of facilitating their own transformation. An example is the acquisition of Swedish automobile manufacturer Volvo Cars by Geely in 2010, even though in this case technology transfer was also an important consideration.

Trade follows investment

It has been well established that trade follows investment. For example, the German automobile makers that set up manufacturing operations in the US import critical components and parts from Germany. Similarly, Japanese automobile makers in China also import critical components and parts from Japan. Thus, Chinese overseas investments can help to expand exports from the outbound direct investors to their investee countries and regions. However, it is not clear how this would work if the border adjustment tax of US President Donald Trump becomes a reality.

Diversification

Of course, diversification must also have been an important motivation of outbound direct investment. Even though the Chinese economy continues to grow faster than almost all other economies in the world, with the possible exception of India, it is only prudent for any successful enterprise to diversify its sources of revenue and profit. It is simply too risky to rely on a single market or a single location of production given all the uncertainty in the world. That is why most successful enterprises try to diversify by investing overseas.

Moreover, one important fact that should be borne in mind is that most owners and managers of enterprises prefer to stay in the same business but operate in a different location rather than to go into another business and operate in the same location. This is because the industry-specific expertise that they have accumulated over the years is much more valuable than a general knowledge of the local situation. Thus, as labour cost rises and the renminbi appreciates, enterprises making garments and toys in China would rather move to Bangladesh, Cambodia and Vietnam to continue in the same line of business rather than enter another business in China.

Diversification is also relevant to portfolio investment. Almost all Chinese wealth is currently invested in Chinese assets of various kinds. It is also prudent for households to diversify their investment portfolios. There is, of course, still capital control in China at the present time. If and when capital control is lifted in China, there is likely to be a one-off outflow of portfolio investment as a result of the stock adjustment of the existing wealth portfolio, which may take several years. This is likely to be followed by a stable annual outflow of portfolio investment, perhaps amounting to 10% of the annual increase in the wealth of Chinese households. However, for the rest of the world, there is also a one-off stock adjustment in its wealth portfolio, resulting in a one-off inflow of capital into China, also followed by a steady annual inflow of foreign portfolio investment into China. Thus, the Chinese capital accounts may still remain in reasonable balance even after capital control is lifted.

Irrational investments

Of course, there are Chinese outbound investment projects that do not appear to make much economic sense. Some Chinese government officials, such as Governor

ZHOU Xiaochuan of the People's Bank of China and Minister ZHONG Shan of the Ministry of Commerce, have even made references to the so-called irrational investments. These are investment projects with low expected returns. They can be motivated by a desire to move money out of China, regardless of the rate of return. They can also be the result of deliberate over-payments for the projects, benefitting the agents and brokers and perhaps ultimately the principals themselves. They can also simply be trophy properties such as football clubs, for which returns do not matter. But capital control still exists in China (even though in principle, outbound investment of less than US$1 billion does not require prior approval from the State Administration of Foreign Exchange). Recently, enforcement of the capital control regulations has been tightened up considerably. It is hoped that such 'irrational investments' will be appropriately discouraged.

Is it necessary to wholly own?

A subject of considerable controversy is whether Chinese enterprises investing overseas should always insist on 100% ownership or a controlling stake. The same controversy also applies to foreign enterprises investing in China. Currently there are restrictions in many industries that have upper limits of permissible foreign ownership in China. There are also explicit or implicit restrictions on foreign and/or Chinese ownership in certain industries in other countries. For example, foreign ownership in US airlines is limited to 25%. Some foreign, including Chinese, direct investments into the US are also subject to the approval of the Committee on Foreign Investment in the United States (CFIUS).

However, there are times when 100% ownership or controlling ownership may not be the best arrangement for a foreign direct investor. Sometimes a local partner may be needed to help with the distribution, as a guide to local preferences and tastes, or to help navigate local politics. Greenfield investments overseas will typically benefit from having a local joint-venture partner. However, partial ownership for the local partner may be needed to provide the right incentive for the local partner, so that the interests of the local partner can be more aligned with those of the foreign direct investor.

It may also be useful to consider alternative business models that may operate well without 100% or even partial ownership. The important consideration is to make sure that any arrangement is win-win and incentive-compatible. Suppose a Chinese enterprise (it does not matter whether it is state-owned or non-state-owned) is interested in investing in an oilfield in a Central Asian country with rich oil reserves, with the objective of ensuring the supply of this critical commodity in the future. However, the oil is in the ground, and the oilfield has to be developed. Moreover, once lifted, the oil has to be transported to China by pipeline. Both the development of the oilfield and the construction of the pipeline require a very substantial investment. Of course, the Chinese enterprise can simply make a large direct investment to develop the oilfield and to build the pipeline. However, ownership of both the oilfield and the pipeline does not in itself assure security of the supply of oil, as the government of the Central Asian country may decide to do something else once oil starts to flow and a better customer than China can be found, or it may decide to levy an export tax on the oil or an additional transit fee for the use of the pipeline. If any of this happens, the Chinese enterprise will need to write off or write down its investments in both the oilfield and the pipeline.

Instead of investing directly in the oilfield and the pipeline, a more prudent alternative for the Chinese enterprise is to sign a long-term (say 30 years) supply contract with the state oil company of the Central Asian country, committing to purchase a fixed quantity of crude oil from it every year, to be delivered to the Chinese border, at a pre-agreed price formula (for example, it can be cost-plus, subject to auditing, or it can be pegged to the price of Brent crude), backed by an irrevocable letter of credit issued by a Chinese state-owned bank. With such a contract, backed by the letter of credit, the Central Asian state oil company as well as the Central Asian government should be able to obtain financing for the development of the oilfield and the construction of the pipeline from both public and private investors, lenders and even multilateral financial institutions. In fact, the pipeline may well be partially financeable by the Asian Development Bank or the Asian Infrastructure Investment Bank. The Central Asian state oil company will then have every incentive to develop the oilfield, construct the pipeline to the Chinese border and start the oil flow to China, because it will need the revenue to service the debts related to the project. And as long as the oil is delivered to the Chinese border, the Chinese enterprise is required to take the oil at the pre-agreed price. So this arrangement is completely incentive-compatible. The Central Asian state oil company needs the revenue, and the Chinese enterprise needs the oil. If no oil is delivered, the Chinese enterprise does not need to make any payment. The Central Asian country may still have concerns that the Chinese enterprise may renege even with the letter of credit. But it is the responsibility of the Chinese enterprise to arrange to have the pipeline on the Chinese side built. As long as it has been built, the Chinese enterprise also has every incentive to accept and pay for the oil; otherwise, the Chinese portion of the pipeline would become worthless. A further consideration is that the Chinese enterprise may encounter much greater difficulties than the Central Asian state oil company in trying to build the pipeline in the Central Asian country.

Similarly, in order to assure the supply of grains such as maize or wheat from overseas, it is not necessary to own the underlying agricultural land or to organize and manage the production directly in the foreign country. In fact, the massive purchase of land by a foreign investor often arouses significant local opposition, but it is totally unnecessary. Moreover, it is generally more difficult for a foreign investor to manage farms and farm labour. Again, a long-term supply contract with a local producer or consortium of producers, providing for the delivery at Chinese ports at an agreed price formula and backed up by an irrevocable letter of credit from a well-established bank, can do just as well. A long-term contract is essential in order to provide the incentive for the producer in the overseas country to develop new supply. New agricultural land will have to be put into production, and this can occur only if there is sufficient assurance that the export demand is continuing and long-term. A long-term supply contract backed by a bank letter of credit can also enable the financing of new agricultural production in the overseas country.[4]

Another feasible approach to foreign direct investment is some form of joint ownership. For example, instead of a Chinese enterprise acquiring a company in Europe, the Chinese enterprise can arrange to inject new capital into the European company in return for a significant percentage of the company and, in so doing, enable the European company to launch an operation in China and elsewhere. The European company receives much needed capital for expansion, and it acquires a Chinese partner that can help it expand in China. The Chinese enterprise can share in the worldwide profits of the European company and can also learn about what is going on in the company, in the industry and in Europe generally through its representatives on the board of directors. So the net result is win-win for both the Chinese investor and the European investee, which is not necessarily achievable with 100% Chinese ownership.

Another possible approach is the model of Royal Dutch Shell and Unilever. These two companies are joint Anglo-Dutch companies and are always identified as such. There is no reason why there cannot be similar Chinese-German enterprises, registered in both China and Germany and owned predominantly by the nationals of the two countries.[5] It can be listed on both the Frankfurt and the Shanghai Stock Exchanges.[6] For example, Volkswagen AG could become such a company overnight, through the conversion of its Shanghai-based joint-venture subsidiary with Chinese partners into a wholly owned subsidiary and issuing to its Chinese partners new shares in the parent company in exchange. After completing such a transaction, Volkswagen AG can then obtain a secondary listing of its shares on the Shanghai Stock Exchange so that Chinese as well as other shareholders can trade their shares in Shanghai as well.[7]

Thus, it may be advantageous for Chinese direct investors to consider alternative ways to achieve the same objectives as they venture forth overseas.

Bilateral investment treaties (BIT)

China and the US, as well as China and the European Union, have been engaged in negotiations on their respective bilateral investment treaties for quite a few years. Apparently the negotiations of the China-US Bilateral Investment Treaty are about 90% complete. It is based on the principles of national treatment and reciprocity, subject to respective negative lists (which forbid investments in certain industries as well as provide for maximum foreign ownership percentages in certain other industries). The negative lists in principle do not have to be the same in both countries. Nevertheless, the negative lists are still regarded as too long. There is also no consensus on the appropriate treatment of state-owned enterprises.

First, it is mutually beneficial for China and the US (and for China and the European Union) to have negative lists, as then direct investors from all of these countries know for sure what can or cannot be acquired, which saves them a great deal of time and money. The negative lists do not have to be the same for both parties to a bilateral investment treaty. Instead of waiting until the negative lists can be pared sufficiently by both parties, one way to proceed is to accept the current negative lists for now but for both parties to commit to a gradual but steady reduction of each side's negative list, say, by 10% a year for the next ten years. For example, if China has 50 industries on its negative list and the US has 30 industries on its negative list, China will have to delete five industries from its negative list in each of the first two years, and then four industries for the next two years, followed by three industries each for the next three years, and two industries each for the final three years. At the end of ten years, the Chinese negative list will be down to 21 industries. Similarly, for the US, in ten years, its negative list will be down to 11 industries. At the end of ten years, both countries can agree on further reductions over time, subject to the provision that each side can maintain up to ten (or some other number of) industries on the negative list. In this way, over time, the number of industries on the two negative lists will become broadly equal. I believe some variation of such a proposed scheme may allow the bilateral investment treaty to go forward, with firm commitments from both countries to reduce gradually the sizes of their respective negative lists. This should greatly reduce the uncertainty facing both Chinese and US direct investors and make it faster as well as more likely for deals to be completed. It also helps to reduce friction between the two countries.

Second, it may also be useful to make a distinction between state-owned enterprises and sovereign government-entities in the bilateral investment treaty. Essentially, direct investors which are state-owned enterprises should be treated like any other direct investor from that country from the point of view of complying with the laws of the investee country. State-owned enterprises should not be allowed to claim sovereign immunity and other sovereign privileges unless they are truly sovereign entities such as a sovereign wealth fund or a central bank or monetary authority.

Local currency financing as a natural hedge

In fact, for outbound direct investment, especially an investment that involves an acquisition and merger of an existing ongoing business, it is actually better for the outbound investor to make the investment in the currency of the investee country or region as much as possible. This minimizes the amount of foreign exchange that the outbound investor needs to purchase from the State Administration of Foreign Exchange. Moreover, it also provides a 'natural hedge' for the outbound investor against future exchange rate risks for the life of the outbound direct investment.

How does this work? Let us consider a concrete example. Suppose a Chinese enterprise wishes to make a direct investment in Malaysia: it is possible for it to purchase US dollars from the State Administration of Foreign Exchange with renminbi first, and then acquire the assets in Malaysia with the US dollars. The Malaysian seller will then exchange the US dollars into Malaysian ringgits. Alternatively, the Chinese direct investor can try to borrow, say, 80% of the purchase price, in the form of a Malaysian-ringgit-denominated loan, secured by the assets that it plans to purchase. This can be readily done because the target of acquisition is a going concern, with revenue and profit and a track record. This would reduce the foreign exchange required by the Chinese investor to, say, only 20% of the purchase price. (Moreover, it can also try to pay the Malaysian seller the remaining 20% in its own currency, the renminbi, if it is agreeable to the seller.) Furthermore, by borrowing in Malaysian ringgit to purchase the assets, the Chinese direct investor has also acquired a 'natural hedge' against the exchange rate risk for the lifetime of its investment. When the renminbi appreciates with respect to the ringgit, the value of the Malaysian assets of the direct investor will decline in terms of renminbi; however, this is largely offset by the decline in the value of the liabilities of the investor (recall that a ringgit-denominated loan has been taken out to finance the direct investment). When the renminbi devalues with respect to the ringgit, the value of the Malaysian assets of the direct investor will appreciate in value in terms of the renminbi, offset by the rise in value of its liabilities in terms of renminbi. Moreover, the revenue from the Malaysian investment, which is likely to be in Malaysian ringgit, can be used to service the ringgit-denominated loan. Thus, the Chinese direct investor will be largely immune to the effects of exchange rate fluctuations between the renminbi and the ringgit for the life of the investment.

Such an arrangement can reduce both the transaction costs and exchange rate risks for the direct investor. The amount of foreign exchange that is needed to support the transaction is also significantly reduced. The direct investor also benefits from the 'natural hedge' because after all, it is not an expert on exchange rates, and no one can successfully predict exchange rate movements more than a couple of years out. In any case, it is almost impossible to buy currency hedges of more than two years into the future, and, even if they are available, they will be very expensive and are still subject to significant counterparty risk. The seller of the currency hedge may not be able to honour its commitment to exchange the Malaysian ringgit for either the US dollar or the renminbi when it is needed.

One question that arises is whether commercial banks are willing to lend to Chinese enterprises on their outward direct investment. Past experience suggests that both Chinese and foreign banks have proved to be eager lenders. For example, J.P. Morgan Chase & Co. provided a US$7.4 billion bridge loan for the Pirelli purchase by ChemChina for US$7.7 billion. Local banks are probably even more eager to provide local-currency loans to Chinese enterprises, especially if they are secured against local assets.

One possible application of this method of financing outbound direct investment is to the infrastructural projects in the China-Pakistan Economic Corridor. Most of the capital expenditures of these projects will be in Pakistani rupees (for example, all labour costs). Any future revenues upon completion of these projects will also be in Pakistani rupees. Thus, it is possible to finance these projects in Pakistani rupees.

Concluding remarks

Chinese outbound direct investment is likely to increase rapidly during the next five to ten years for many of the reasons discussed above. If and when capital control is lifted, there will be significant one-time stock adjustments in order to rebalance the wealth portfolios. There will also be continuing outflows of portfolio investment driven by the annual increases in the total national wealth. At the same time, one can also expect a portfolio investment inflow into China from the rest of the world that also includes a one-time stock adjustment of the world's wealth portfolio and a continuing annual flow, motivated by diversification considerations. It is too early to tell for sure, in steady state, whether the outflows or the inflows will be higher. However, if the rate of growth of the Chinese economy continues to be higher than those of the other developed economies, the probability is that the inflows are likely to exceed the outflows as investments seek higher returns.

Notes

1 All opinions expressed herein are the author's own and do not necessarily reflect the views of any of the organizations with which the author is affiliated.
2 There is, however, an unofficial forecast of an outbound direct investment of US$750 billion five years from now.
3 This acquisition is still in progress. It will be largely financed by loans from a consortium of banks including the HSBC Group. It still awaits final clearance by the various governments concerned.
4 There is of course the risk that the foreign government may decide to impose export control. In order to ensure security of supply, the long-term supply contract can specify that one year's worth of supply has to be put into storage facilities in China as a 'bond'. If export control is imposed, the Chinese importer can take the grains stored in China, and the long-term supply contract will be terminated. This provision removes the incentive for the foreign government to impose export control.
5 Of course, Anglo-Chinese, Chinese-French and other combinations of companies are also possible.
6 One of the listings can be a secondary listing.
7 There are feasible arrangements that can be made to provide for arbitraging between the two stock markets so that the prices of the same shares on the two separate stock exchanges can be equalized. The lack of space does not permit a detailed discussion here.

4

CHALLENGES IN GVC AND ODI DEVELOPMENT

What can China do?

Jiong Gong, Xinding Yu and Zhongxiu Zhao

Background: rising importance of global production sharing

In a world of resource and endowment heterogeneity, specialization is fundamental to the market economy through the division of labour and capital. In the modern world, specialization has certainly crossed national borders. One of the defining characteristics of the world economy today is the globalization of production and trade.

There is no dispute among most economists and policymakers that the structure of today's international trade has completely changed (Feenstra, 1998; Gereffi and Fernandez-Stark, 2016; Koopman et al., 2014; Timmer et al., 2014; Werner et al., 2014). The change is characterized by a new phenomenon known as the global value chain (GVC), which consists of fragmenting production stages across different countries/sectors, triggering meanwhile a significant growth of trade in intermediate inputs.[1]

As shown in Figure 4.1, during the past 15 years, intermediate inputs have accounted for around 75% of global exports, and the share is even higher in developed countries such as the United States and Japan. The share of intermediate goods in China's gross exports is relatively lower than in other countries, but it is growing at a much higher level than the world average.

Indeed, the input components that go into making a final product may come from multiple cross-border sites but be assembled in another place and later exported to yet another destination for final consumption. The GDP decomposition results from Wang et al. (2017) show that the domestic value added exported via cross-country production sharing activities ('Simple GV' with only one border crossing, and 'Complex GVC' with more than two border crossings) is increasing dramatically, while the relative importance of value added for 'Pure Domestic' production activities is diminishing over time.

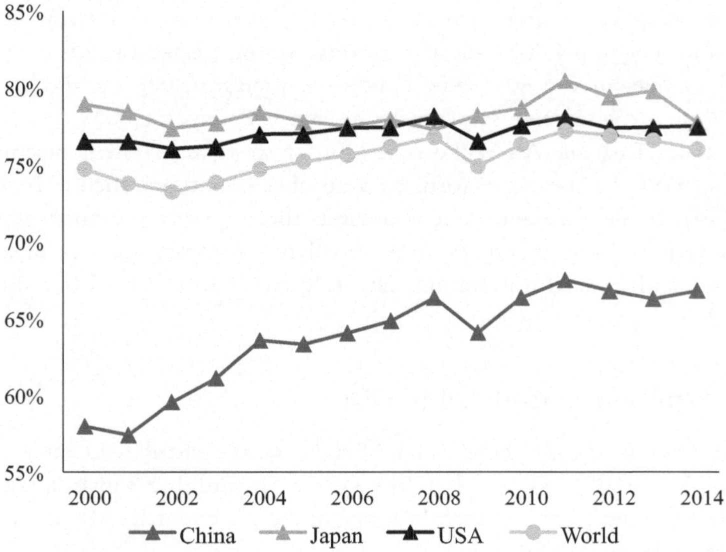

FIGURE 4.1 Share of intermediate inputs in exports

Data source: author's calculation based on the World Input Output Database (WIOD), Version 2016. Gross fixed capital formation and changes in inventories are classified as intermediate inputs.

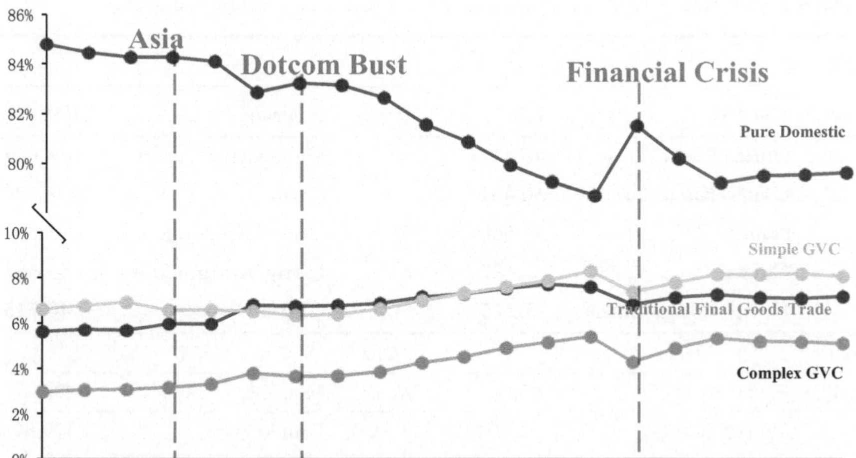

FIGURE 4.2 Changing trends in different types of production activity as a share of global GDP (1995–2014)

Source: Wang et al. (2017).

Various other names and terminologies have been used to describe more or less the same phenomenon, such as fractionalization, dispersion, disintegration, unbundling, outsourcing etc. Some famous examples include the iPod and the Nokia N95 smartphone, whose value chains have been investigated extensively by Dedrick et al. (2010) and Ali-Yrkkö et al. (2011) respectively. Systematic empirical evidence of GVC has been put forth by a number of authors, such as Hummels et al. (2001). In such a context, it is obvious that the way intermediate goods and services are produced and consumed involves a complex network of sectoral interactions with crucial implications not only on a national level but also on a global scale.

China's experience: from IDI to ODI

China has been a primary beneficiary of such seismic changes in international trade over the last 20 years, mostly in the form of inward direct investment (IDI), as the country has ranked consistently as one of the top countries, if not the top in most years, in terms of attracting IDI.

Several theories have been proposed to explain why China has been able to maintain such an enviable market position among emerging market economies. For example, early IDI was driven to a large extent by Chinese diaspora investors from Taiwan and Hong Kong, especially in labour-intensive sectors such as toys and textiles. China is indeed fortunate in that the country with the largest population also has the world's largest diaspora population. China is fortunate in another way, as the timing of China's economic take-off stage, driven by the government's

TABLE 4.1 FDI inflows (millions of dollars) and top-three FDI inflow economies

1990			*2000*		
Rank	*Economy*	*IDI*	*Rank*	*Economy*	*IDI*
1	United States	48,422	1	United States	314,007
2	United Kingdom	30,461	2	Germany	198,277
3	France	16,506	3	United Kingdom	115,304
11	**China**	**3,487**	**6**	**Hong Kong, China**	**54,582**
12	**Hong Kong, China**	**3,275**	7	**China**	**40,715**
2010			*2015*		
Rank	*Economy*	*IDI*	*Rank*	*Economy*	*IDI*
1	United States	198,049	1	United States	379,894
2	**China**	**114,734**	**2**	**Hong Kong, China**	**174,892**
3	Brazil	83,749	**3**	**China**	**135,610**
4	**Hong Kong, China**	**72,319**			

Data source: UNCTAD, World Investment Report 2016.

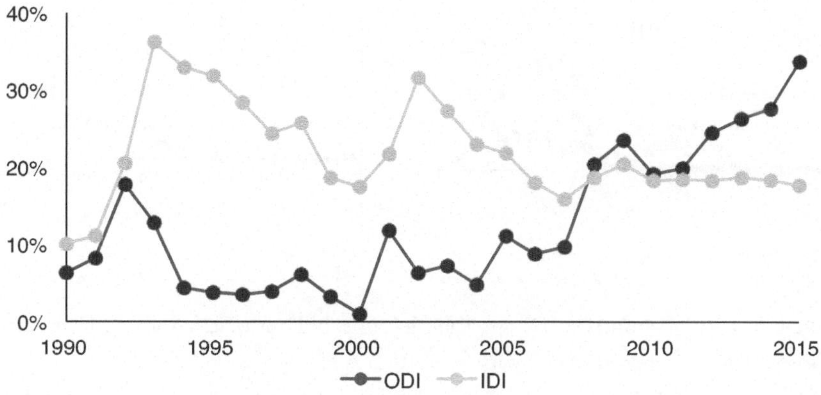

FIGURE 4.3 China's ODI and IDI share in developing economies
Data source: UNCTAD, World Investment Report 2016.

reform and open-door policy, corresponded exceptionally well with Corporate America's massive off-shoring movement starting in the mid-1990s.

By and large, China was – and remains – a good destination for foreign investment capital due to its large market size; its cheap, disciplined and abundant blue-collar labour supply; and a reasonably effective education system that is able to provide a well-trained white collar workforce, especially in STEM (science, technology, engineering and mathematics) areas.

However, FDI is certainly not a one-way street. In more recent years, history has also witnessed another direction of foreign direct investment, which we call outward direct investment (ODI) away from China. Later in the paper, we will analyse who the participants of this movement are and what is driving it. But for the moment, it is safe to state that right now China's cross-border capital movement is characterized as being in a mixed mode, with impressive amounts of both IDI and ODI compared with other developing countries.

As shown in Figure 4.3, China's ODI share in developing countries reached a peak of 36.4% in 1993 and then gradually decreased, but it has still accounted for about 18% in recent years. Meanwhile, China's IDI share showed a high rate of growth after the year 2000, surpassing ODI in 2008.

It might be a good exercise to first describe the overall picture of China's current IDI and ODI in comparison with emerging economies. And for this, we resort to the block of BRICS countries for the convenience of available statistics. In both IDI and ODI accounts, China ranks top among the BRICS countries (Figure 4.4). It is worth mentioning that China was a late starter in outward direct investment but has come from behind within only ten years.

Judging from the inward and outward foreign direct investment stock of the BRICS countries, their positions in the world and in developing countries continued to rise. The share of BRICS countries in global inflows increased from 10.4% before the 2008 financial crisis to a peak of 20.8% in 2014, doubling their pre-crisis

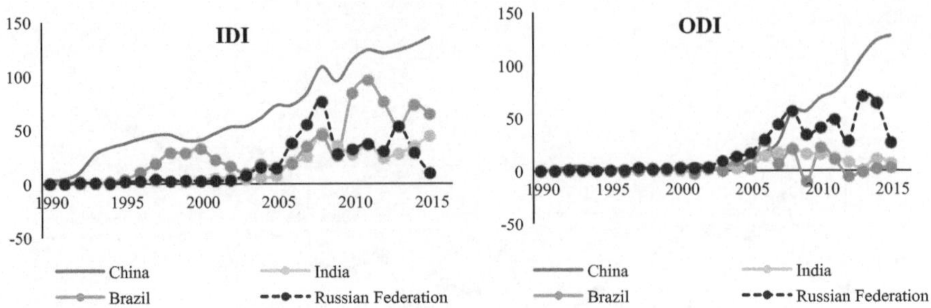

FIGURE 4.4 BRICS countries' IDI and ODI level (in billions of US dollars), 1990–2015
Data source: UNCTAD, World Investment Report 2016.

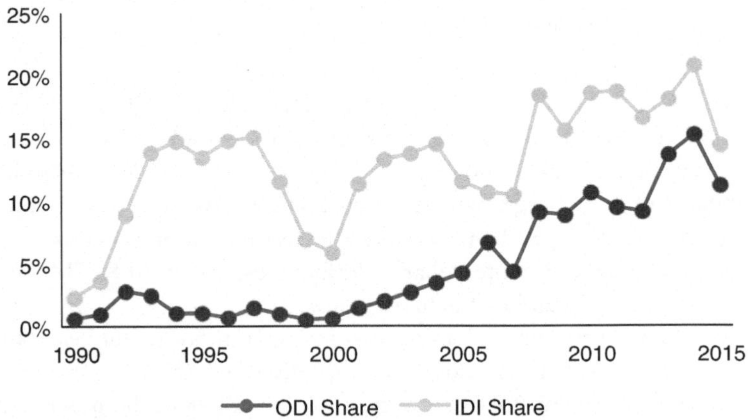

FIGURE 4.5 Share of BRICS countries in global ODI and IDI, 1990–2015
Data source: UNCTAD, World Investment Report 2016.

level. The share of BRICS countries in global outflows reached its peak of 15.3% in 2014. China ranked first among the BRICS countries, in terms of utilization of both IDI and ODI. Mutual investment between the BRICS countries and outside of the BRICS countries will become a new focal point of global economic growth. Exchanges and cooperation in high-tech sectors will become the focus in BRICS countries' future ODI investment.

Driving forces of China's ODI development

Rising costs

It is clear that China will continue to maintain policies to attract IDI, but it is also inevitable that we will see an increasing amount of ODI in the next few years.

This of course will have a profound impact on China's prospect for jobs, tax revenues and GDP growth.

Why do we claim this trend is inevitable? There are several reasons and players at work. First is the reshoring movement among Corporate America back to the US. This is more than simply driven by the recent political climate in Washington, as heralded by the new US President Donald Trump's obsession with built-in-America and creating American jobs. The more fundamental force at work in reshoring is factor price equalization, which has been proven true time after time with respect to strong trading nations such as Japan, South Korea and many others. China is of course no exception.

This is most evident if one looks at the wage curve over the last 15 years (Figure 4.6). Historically, China's low wage has been driven by a seemingly inexhaustible supply of migrant labour – but not any more in recent years, as economists have postulated that China's Lewis turning point has already been passed, and the country is on route to an era of rapid wage rises. Also, in China's rush to wean itself from being an export-driven economy and into a consumer-based economy, it is the government's policy to place more disposable income in the hands of wage earners. This means that China has a specific agenda of raising workers' salary levels on a continuous basis.

The downturn in the global economy today and the political pressure from the US with respect to its ongoing trade deficit with China also led China to realize the vulnerability of its economic model as being overly dependent on the demands of overseas markets. To transform and rebalance its economy, China has been actively promoting the development of its service sector, high-tech industries and domestic consumption so as to ensure sustainable growth.

According to the GDP decomposition results from Wang et al. (2017), the share of the domestically consumed portion in China's GDP can be depicted as a

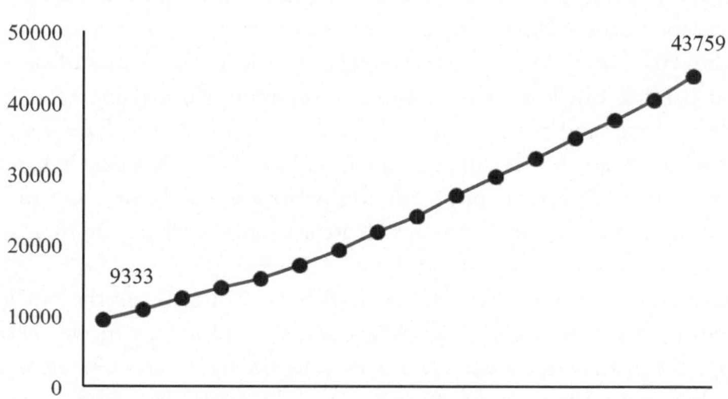

FIGURE 4.6 Average wage of employed persons in urban units of China (in RMB) deflated by CPI (year 2000=100), 2000–2015

Data source: National Bureau of Statistics of the People's Republic of China.

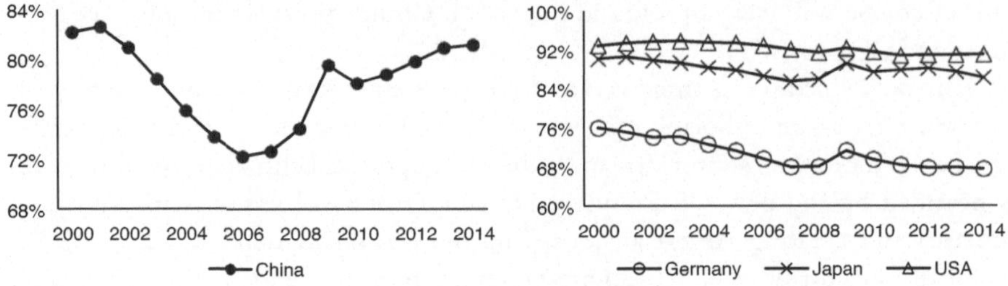

FIGURE 4.7 Pure domestic consumption portion of GDP

Data source: Wang et al. (2017).

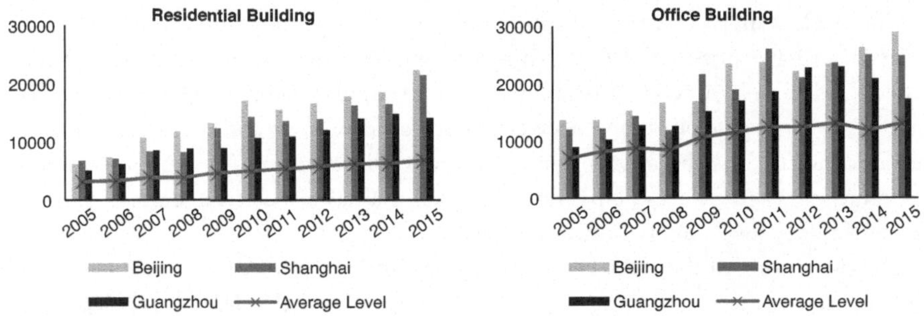

FIGURE 4.8 Average selling price of residential and office buildings, 2005–2015

Data source: National Bureau of Statistics of the People's Republic of China.

'V-Shape', which reflects rising demand from the domestic market after the year 2006 – while in other countries such as Germany, Japan and the United States, the relative importance of their domestic demand is diminishing over time.

In this respect, the Chinese government has driven up minimum wages and allowed the yuan to appreciate, thus increasing the costs of manufacturing in China and driving out low-end, low-tech businesses. Annual increases in Chinese worker salaries and the increasing mandatory associated welfare benefits are even making some local governments in China have to strike a fine balancing act between making companies happy with no further raises to labour cost and workers demanding higher salaries – which will attract more workers and increase local consumption.

The famous or infamous real estate market in China is another major reason that doing business in China is getting so much more expensive these days. Property prices in first-tier cities such as Beijing, Shanghai and Guangzhou have quadrupled over the last ten years (Figure 4.8). This basically drives up employee housing costs and costs for everything else that needs a brick-and-mortar store presence, including rental prices, costs of retail, restaurants and many more. The high property prices are also providing skewed incentives to the local governments to expel manufacturing to leave room for property developments.

China is also catching up with paying for the costs of public goods that have been previously neglected and shuffled aside during the growth boom days. And this translates into higher costs for doing business as well, for things like regulatory and antitrust compliance and like respect for intellectual property rights, just to name a few.

For example, the recent decades of China's export-driven economic growth has come arguably at the cost of severe pollution to the environment, which has in turn posed a threat to the health of its inhabitants. The Beijing smog has bloomed into such international notoriety that it has now become a national embarrassment for China. Thus more money has to be poured into remedying these previous deficiencies in public wellbeing, which ultimately have to be paid for by companies and consumers, albeit China is indeed moving into the league of modern civilized societies as it addresses these issues.

In summary, rising cost is a major reason why Corporate America in China is packing up and heading home. But it is certainly not just Corporate America. Companies from Japan, Korea and Europe are also taking action.

Samsung might be a good case in point. Samsung's electronics business has a very long value chain, with many of its upstream suppliers of electronic parts and components located in Tianjin and Suzhou. They are also surrounded geographically by many Chinese indigenous companies through Samsung's value chain. Such locational clustering is a common phenomenon for consumer electronics companies. And for an essentially corporate legion like that, offshoring to some other country is no less than like ants moving home. For many years Samsung has been studying and delaying the big move out of the concern that its whole value chain will have to be relocated en masse. It now looks as if the long debate over Samsung China or China Samsung is at the beginning of the end, as it unveils its grand plan in Vietnam. There are many cases like this that will inevitably have a profound impact on local economies in terms of jobs, tax revenues and growth prospects.

And it is not just the class of foreign multinationals that is initiating ODI as part of their grand GVC design. Many China economists and commentators have voiced concerns over the increasing costs in China and over the ramifications for indigenous companies who are also struggling in the face of rising costs from all angles – labour, raw materials and high taxes among other things.

One recent event that stirred a national debate is a case in point. Fuyao Glass Industry Group is the largest automobile glass supplier in China with two-thirds of the domestic market share and is the number-four supplier worldwide. Its client list includes all the big-name auto giants in the world, including Volkswagen and General Motors. Its recent US$600 million investment hits the industrial heartland in America – Ohio – a place that enjoys a cost advantage for serving the North America market compared to domestic locations in China, according to Fuyao Glass's boss, Cao Dewang. The phrase 'Cao Dewang has escaped' became a hot topic, generating nearly 10 million views on the Twitter-like Weibo microblog and many comments urging China to 'not let Cao Dewang run away'.

Other driving factors

Costs may not be the only reason that Chinese indigenous companies are offshoring or expanding overseas. At least five additional reasons come to mind. For example, traditionally, China's central role in the global value chain has revolved around manufacturing, which typically occupies the slimmest part of the value chain in the middle, and also the bottom part of what is called the smiley-faced value curve. Naturally, as Chinese companies accumulate more capital stock through years of profitable operations, there is a need to expand into the more value-added part of the value chain. That means acquiring branding assets as well as marketing and sales channels in the downstream, and acquiring foreign technology assets and R&D capabilities in the upstream.

Regarding Chinese companies gaining access to globally recognized brands, international brands benefit Chinese companies by helping to bridge the 'trust gap'. Building a brand from scratch can take decades, millions of dollars, and savvy public relations that Chinese companies usually lack. Given their relative short history, many Chinese firms lack the decades of international experience necessary to build globally recognized brands on their own. Then there comes the alternative to follow the path of Pearl River Piano and Wanda and buy another firm's long-term established brand in the same industry.

Instead of competing on ever-shrinking profit margins in a highly competitive domestic market, Chinese firms are also seeking to access world-class technology overseas in the US and Europe. Chinese firms are able to offer a better product or service than their domestic competitors at a higher profit per unit. Goldwind's acquisition of German wind energy firm Vensys is a good example of this type of ODI strategy.

Chinese companies' relocation overseas may be also driven by domestic industrial upgrade and changing consumer preferences. As Chinese consumers get wealthier and living standards are constantly raised, some low-end industries are finding that domestic demand is increasingly shrinking. For example, the once high-flying instant-noodle industry has seen years of revenue decline. Instant noodle is gradually phasing out of the normal Chinese diet. Companies in this industry have to move to lower income countries in Southeast Asia or Africa in order to survive.

The bicycle, electric bicycle and motorcycle industries are another good example. China is dominant in all these industries, with a total volume of about 100 million units in total sales in 2015. Over 90% of the world's manufacturing capacity in these industries is located in China. However, they are all sunset industries in China, experiencing close to a double-digit decline last year, as people are moving into cars en masse. China now represents the world's largest automobile market with close to 30 million vehicles sold last year. However, companies in these traditional industries are quite successful in moving manufacturing to Southeast Asia and Africa. As companies become more reliant on foreign markets, it is highly likely that they will move their entire value chain overseas, bringing with them their component suppliers and vendors.

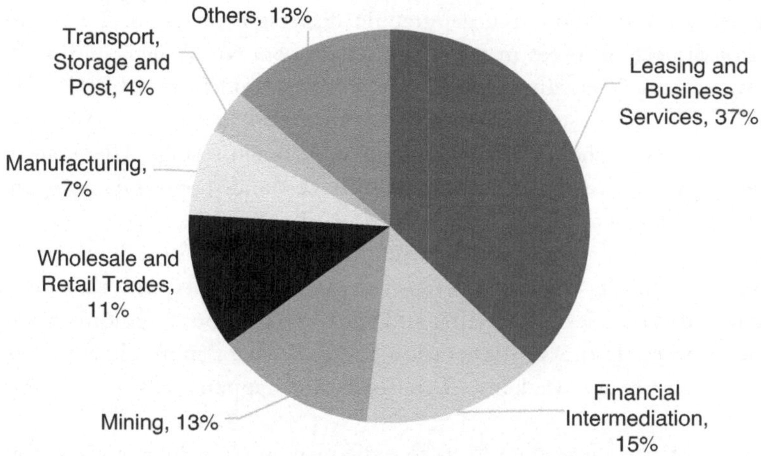

FIGURE 4.9 China's net ODI stock by sector at the end of 2015
Data source: National Bureau of Statistics of the People's Republic of China.

And yet there is another reason that ODI is happening on a large scale, this time led by state-owned behemoths. Chinese firms' going global aligns with Chinese government policy. The 'going out' policy remains the primary policy framework through which the government supports Chinese overseas investment, both economically and politically. Some investments by large SOEs in mineral assets may be motivated by the objective of securing strategic raw material supply. Figure 4.9 shows the industrial structure of China's ODI. The mining sector ranks in the top-three industries in terms of ODI stock share.

It may also be driven by the aspiration to become 'national champions' in world markets. National champions indirectly boost China's economic influence as well as its soft power on the international stage. This is particularly true in light of the latest 'One Belt One Road' Initiative. Chinese companies expand overseas in strategic locations, especially to build infrastructure capabilities in developing countries, such as ports and railroads, to facilitate China's worldwide trading routes.

Challenges in China's GVC and ODI development

From the above analysis, we are drawn to the conclusion that ODI from China is going to be a long-term phenomenon in the next few years. Globalization of the Chinese economy and Corporate China appears to be an inevitable trend.

Viewed from a more theoretical perspective and put into a broader historic context, the ODI phenomenon in China merely echoes the New Economic Geography literature pioneered by Paul Krugman in the 1990s. The New Economic Geography perspective views the corporate locational outcome as balancing dispersion forces and agglomeration forces.

Dispersion forces favour the geographic dispersion of stages. There are two prominent dispersion forces in the supply-chain context. Skilled- and unskilled-labour wage gaps determine vertical specialization, and firm-level specialization determines horizontal specialization. Agglomeration forces are the opposite of dispersion forces – they encourage geographical clustering. There are many agglomeration forces, such as knowledge spillovers and supply-side and demand-side linkages for global supply chains.

While the interplay of agglomeration and dispersion forces determines the equilibrium location of industries, lowering trade costs and transportation costs makes distance less of an issue and thus weakens both agglomeration and dispersion forces. If the agglomeration forces weaken more than the dispersion forces, clustering weakens; if the opposite happens, clustering get more pronounced.

This line of reasoning then leads to explain why clustering tends to follow a 'hump shaped' pattern as trade costs fall. Historically the 'hump shaped' pattern has been observed several times, with a concentration of economic activity in Europe, in North America and later in China, followed each time by dispersion away from these areas in the North. Does that suggest the next round of dispersion of economic activity is going to inevitably happen to China? Are the ODI forces as we described above merely part of the dispersion? And maybe the next round of agglomeration will happen in the South? These are legitimate issues that appear to ordain China's historic destiny in a new world.

ODI away from China notwithstanding, most economists argue that the global value chain is potentially beneficial for all participants in terms of economic growth, technology transfer, skill upgrading, productivity enhancement, and diversification of exports, sophistication, and other spillover effects. In particular, developing economies consider this participation as a stepping-stone for their economic development. As shown in the data presented in Figure 4.10, compared with developed countries like Japan and the United States, both the forward and the backward linkage based GVC participation ratio[2] are much higher for China and India in all sample years.

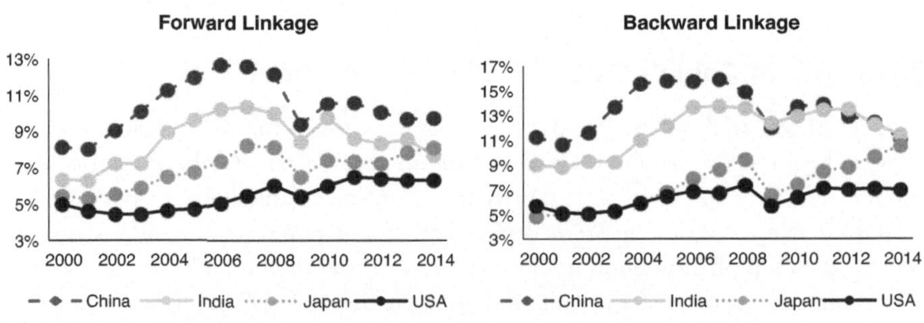

FIGURE 4.10 Forward/backward linkage GVC participation ratio, 2000–2014

Data source: Wang et al. (2017).

The combination of China's globalized economy and ODI provides immense benefits to the developing world. Yet, China itself can also benefit from its potential network of global value chains and investment interests around the world. Trade and FDI are fundamentally a means of seeking gain from specialization. But China also needs to face the prospect of capital and investments moving outside of China, which inevitably leads to an adverse impact on the domestic local economies. That means loss of jobs, tax revenues and other domestic growth opportunities.

Policy suggestions: what can China do?

To address these concerns, we provide the following suggestions that may help China to better transition towards a more open and globalized economy.

First, it is unwise for local governments to adopt policies that deliberately kick manufacturing out of the country in lieu of so-called service industries or real estate development to drive economic growth. Winston Churchill's famous warning ('I would rather see finance less proud and industry more content') comes to mind. Indeed, manufacturing as a means of economic multiplier functions differently from service industries in that it creates a stronger spillover effect in other related sectors, which translates into more jobs and economic activities.

Second, China still needs to maintain an active environment that welcomes foreign IDI. Although the country is not in dire need of capital as it was some 20 years ago, IDI still brings in its fair share of new jobs and new technologies. Measures like financial incentives, tax reductions, free trade zones and other preferential treatment for new investments allowable within the boundary of the WTO and other free trade agreements should still be seriously considered.

The vast heartland of China's western, southwestern and northwestern areas are still quite competitive in terms of wage levels and other costs of doing business. As the coastal area of China sees more manufacturing dispersion, the central government should provide various incentives for businesses to be relocated to the inner heartland. After all, how can countries like Vietnam and the Philippines be more competitive than China's inner provinces? The central government should also continue to invest in infrastructures to make communications and transportations between the inner heartland and the coastal areas as convenient and seamless as possible. These include high-speed railroads, highways, airports, container barge transportations and other logistics facilities that make transport cost competitive. China's highway toll system is one of the most expensive in the world, greatly hindering inter-provincial commerce and the co-integration of a unified national market. A centralized solution such as a national fuel tax needs to be at least investigated as a means to eliminate the expensive and totally inefficient toll system.

Structural upgrade and innovation have been discussed a lot in China as a strategy to keep the country competitive. But in fact this is an area where the government can do very little and should do very little, while leaving most of it to the market. While the government pushes forward supply-side structural reform to provide it with more impetus for growth, more should be done on the government side to trim the governance structure and make it smaller, more efficient and cost effective. In terms of taxation burdens for companies, China ranks quite high among nations. It is about time to slash the government's size and reduce tax so as to make the investment environment in China yet more attractive to domestic and foreign capital alike.

At the municipal city level, lessons can be learned from Shenzhen's experience of trying to retain businesses or at least keep them connected with the city. Shenzhen's future economic growth still looks brisk even against the background of the recent overall challenging macroeconomic environment in China. The city has successfully gone through several rounds of transformations in the past from an initially labour-intensive industrial base to a capital-intensive industrial base and, in more recent years, to a technology-intensive industrial base.

Like many large cities in China, Shenzhen also faces tremendous challenges: for example, shortage of further development space, soaring land and housing prices, soaring labour costs and a fleeing workforce due to high living costs, and other bottleneck public utility and service issues typically associated with crowded metropolises in the world.

The city has implemented several policy instruments to address these challenges. It has been trying to introduce affordable housing to attract more young people to stay. It has made arrangements with the Canton provincial government to set up Shenzhen's 'enclaves' in other parts of Guangdong to relocate some of the city's manufacturing activities to those lower-cost areas in the province. It has also initiated an intensive campaign to attract world-class universities and research institutions to set up Shenzhen campuses so as to turn the city into a knowledge hub and attract high-tech talent. The city has introduced measures to encourage innovation and start-up entrepreneurship and to turn the city into a cluster of venture capital start-ups.

Conclusion

ODI is an inevitable trend driven by global value chain locational realignment. This is driven by the changing macroeconomic conditions as a result of trade and economic growth. Cycles of global dispersion and agglomeration mediated by trade and transportation cost dynamics can be observed in economic history, so it is not surprising to see a torrent of IDI to China in the past but trickles of ODI away from China now. And these trickles are likely to become torrents in the near future.

This will have a seismic impact on China's economy. Is the country ready for it? What are the central government policies and strategies to address these challenges? These are very legitimate questions if China is to sustain its growth as it did in the past. This chapter offers some suggestions and policy instruments that may be considered in the short run. In our opinion, it is impossible to stop the movement of ODI, but the government can at least slow it down via various policy options, making its impact less abrupt and the resulting transition less painful.

Notes

1 'The multiplication of input trade has been facilitated by cuts in tariff and non-tariff barriers within the framework of bilateral and multilateral trade agreements' (Daudin et al., 2011).

2 The forward linkage based participation index proposed in Wang et al. (2017) can be understood as 'What is the percentage of value added that flows into the cross-country production sharing network?' – while the backward linkage based participation index can be understood as 'What is the percentage of value added embodied in final products that comes from the cross-country production sharing network?'

References

Ali-Yrkkö, J, Rouvinen, P, Seppälä, T & Ylä-Anttila, P 2011, 'Who captures value in global supply chains? Case Nokia N95 Smartphone', *Journal of Industry, Competition and Trade*, vol. 11, pp. 263–278.

Daudin, G, Rifflart, C & Schweisguth, D 2011, 'Who produces for whom in the world economy', *Canadian Journal of Economics*, vol. 44, no. 4, pp. 1403–1437.

Dedrick, J, Kraemer, KL & Linden, G 2010, 'Who profits from innovation in global value chains', *Industrial and Corporate Change*, vol. 19, no. 1, pp. 81–116.

Feenstra, RC 1998, 'Integration of trade and disintegration of production in the global economy', *Journal of Economic Perspectives*, vol. 12, no. 4, pp. 31–50.

Gereffi, G & Fernandez-Stark, K 2016, 'Global value chain analysis: a primer', 2nd Edition, Center on Globalization, Governance & Competitiveness, Duke University.

Hummels, D, Ishii, J & Yi, K-M 2001, 'The nature and growth of vertical specialization in world trade', *Journal of International Economics*, vol. 54, pp. 75–96.

Koopman, R, Wang, Z & Wei, S-J 2014, 'Tracing value-added and double counting in gross exports', *American Economic Review*, vol. 104, no. 2, pp. 1–37.

Timmer, MP, Erumban, AA, Los, B, Stehrer, R & de Vries, GJ 2014, 'Slicing up global value chains', *Journal of Economic Perspectives*, vol. 28, no. 2, pp. 99–118.

Wang, Z, Wei, SJ, Yu, X & Zhu, K 2017, 'Measures of Participation in Global Value Chains and Global Business Cycles', NBER Working Paper 23222.

Werner, M, Bair, J & Fernández, R 2014, 'Linking up to development? Global value chains and the making of a post-washington consensus', *Development and Change*, vol. 45, no. 6, pp. 1219–1247.

5

CHINESE OUTWARD FOREIGN DIRECT INVESTMENT – AN OPPORTUNITY TO REVISIT INTERNATIONAL BUSINESS THEORY

Peter J. Buckley

Background

China's outward foreign direct investment (OFDI) is growing rapidly. Figures from the Ministry of Commerce (MOC) show that it grew 16.5% year-on-year to $87.3bn for the first three quarters of 2015. Foreign contracted projects reached $137.6bn between January and September 2015, year-on-year growth of 26.5%

China's search for resources and technology (and brand names) is relentless – backed by state-owned enterprises (SOEs) and sovereign wealth funds channelling finance to internationalisation projects. Mergers and acquisitions (M&A) are an increasing component of Chinese outward foreign direct investment. Chinese companies have become more experienced in international dealings, and this gives them the confidence to carry out takeovers. State encouragement is a factor in this growth; the 'One Belt One Road' Initiative has resulted in countries along 'The New Silk Road' (49 nations) accounting for $13.17bn of the total (an annual growth of 36.7%). Building connectivity is good for Chinese MNEs – particularly SOEs in construction, transport and communications.

This collection of recent evidence confirms that Chinese OFDI represents a challenge to international business theory. This chapter examines the means by which international business theory can meet the challenge.

The challenge to theory of Chinese OFDI

The challenge that Chinese OFDI poses to established international business theory arises from its specific characteristics. Classic explanations of outward FDI (Hymer, 1960, 1976; Vernon, 1966; Buckley and Casson, 1976; Dunning, 1979; Rugman, 1981) were in response to FDI from private, largely manufacturing, 'Western' (including Japan) MNEs. Explanations of where these MNEs invested were put forward in the 'stages' or Uppsala theory of FDI (Johanson and Wiedersheim-Paul, 1975; Johanson and Vahlne, 1977) which predicted that FDI would go in sequence to progressively more 'psychically distant' countries. Therefore, MNEs would invest in culturally close countries to minimise 'the liability of foreignness' (Zaheer, 1995) and thus risk before gradually seeking investments in more psychically distant locations.

Later versions of Dunning's eclectic theory and its variants emphasised the 'firm-specific advantages' (FSAs) possessed by MNEs that enabled them to overcome the disadvantages of foreign operation (Rugman, 1981; Rugman and Verbeke, 2003, 2004; following Kindleberger, 1970). However, Chinese MNEs and emerging-market MNEs (EMNEs) in general were perceived to lack FSAs. This led to a view that (either) EMNEs relied upon country-specific advantages (CSAs) (Nguyen and Rugman, 2015) or EMNEs had evolved new kinds of FSAs, such as the ability to operate in highly regulated or bureaucratic environments – skills that were internationally transferable (Ramamurti, 2009a, 2009b, 2012).

There are further challenges for theory arising from Chinese OFDI. First is the issue of global value chains – MNEs cannot be considered to be free-standing entities; they are embedded in – and often central to – globally dispersed value chains. MNEs are not vertically and horizontally integrated but operate within extensive networks of collaborating, and free-standing, companies. Geographically, MNEs are not freely distributed across economic space but clustered in certain preferred locations, giving rise to centre-periphery effects. In the Chinese case, their OFDI clusters and the coincidence of timing of the outward ventures of groups of Chinese MNEs give rise to a 'phalanx effect' (Buckley, 2017, forthcoming).

In addition, the role of the state looms large in Chinese OFDI. Many of the foreign investors are state owned, and SOEs are intimately connected to 'favoured' private companies. China's external policy centres on the 'go global' strategy, with positive state encouragement for (some) OFDI. The push factor is significant in the desire of some Chinese companies to avoid their restrictive domestic environment. Capital flight is also a motive for Chinese OFDI – foreign environments are often judged as 'safe' havens for capital by the ultimate owners. This links strongly to the significant amounts of Chinese OFDI that goes to tax havens (Buckley et al., 2014).

China's international strategy can be described as 'state driven' rather than 'state controlled'. It combines a number of elements – 'top down' investment from the state via state-owned companies and sovereign wealth funds, and 'bottom up' investment by companies, both public and private, often utilising external acquisition of key foreign assets including technology, brands, skills and market access, network influence, and umbrella macro strategies such as 'One Belt One Road'. This complexity – and the variety of actors involved – is a challenge for theory.

Finally, it can be argued that the strategy of Chinese MNEs differs radically from conventional Western company motives to invest abroad. Chinese firms are alleged to 'go abroad in order to compete at home' – this involves seeking resources (technology, brand names, critical inputs) in order to bring them back to China and enhance their competitive position in the home market. This may lead to a rather different outcome than the traditional 'globalisation' motive. Chinese firms, despite conducting OFDI, may be primarily focused on the domestic Chinese market, not the global market.

To the extent that these factors hold true, they represent a major challenge to extant theory. The following section takes up that challenge.

Chinese OFDI as an opportunity for theory development

The first issue to recognise is that a variety of actors are involved in Chinese OFDI as Table 5.1 shows.

These include state-owned companies, private companies and individual entrepreneurs. When individual Chinese entrepreneurs migrate permanently – as many have done to Africa – they do not count as foreign direct investors, but if their permanent residence remains in China, then they are included.

A second issue is the sectoral make-up of COFDI. This is largely non-manufacturing. Services figure prominently, as does real estate.

Third, the phenomenon is often not the outcome of a single company decision. Chinese companies may be pulled abroad by their membership of global value chains or pushed abroad by governmental direction or by involvement in a cluster of investors – the phalanx effect (Buckley, 2017, forthcoming). Other push factors may be the desire to avoid a restrictive home environment (Witt and Lewin, 2007) or a simple case of 'capital flight' – companies and individuals seeking a safe haven for protection of capital.

Further, Chinese firms may not be seeking to become global competitors but be investing abroad in order to compete at home. This strategy is focused on the acquisition of foreign assets (brands, technology, skills and proprietary information) in order to import this back to China to gain Chinese (home) market share. Foreign market share is less important in this scenario. Technology is brought back to China rather than being globalised.

TABLE 5.1 Organisational form and ownership of EMNEs

		Ownership	
		State owned	*Private*
Organizational form	Corporate investor	**State-owned corporations** • National champions	**Non-state-owned corporations** • World-stage aspirants • Global niche players • Private equity funds
	Entrepreneurial investor		**Entrepreneurial and family businesses** • Entrepreneurial cluster participants • International entrepreneurs

The question remains as to how to meet this complexity and its theoretical challenge.

One response has been to refine the theoretical approach to FDI based on firm-specific advantages (FSAs) and country-specific advantages (CSAs). This takes two forms. The first is to suggest that Chinese multinationals do not possess FSAs; they rely entirely on CSAs. This includes overt state support (subsidiaries) and reliance on the scale of the Chinese market (Rugman, 1981; Rugman and Verbeke, 2003, 2004; Nguyen and Rugman, 2015). The second is to assert that Chinese FSAs are different from 'Western' FSAs and to adduce that Chinese multinationals have superior skills in dealing with bureaucracy (Ramamurti, 2009a, 2009b, 2012).

The difficulty with these FSA-based explanations is that they have problems in explaining COFDI in advanced countries. The FSA/CSA conceptual approach relies on the firms' *relative* competitiveness versus other firms – which is how FSAs are defined (arising from the resource-based view of the firm [Penrose, 1959; Barney, 1991; Peteraf, 1993; Foss, 1997] and related to the notion of dynamic capabilities [Teece et al., 1997]). Chinese firms are 'FSA deficient' when compared to leading firms in the industry, yet they still manage to invest in the home markets of these seemingly formidable competitors. Rather than drawing the conclusion that the theory is suspect, proponents of this view have declared that Chinese investment in advanced countries is not successful and will not be successful in the future, leading to failure, closure or take-over (by Western competitors) of existing COFDI (Nguyen and Rugman, 2015). The latter part of this hypothesis is untestable – as we shall have to 'wait and see', and there is little evidence on the success of COFDI because of its lack of time in existence and secrecy (and obfuscation) by the investors, but it would be an unusual outcome to see mass failure of such significant investment.

Meeting the challenge

The large amounts of COFDI in advanced countries, geographically and culturally distant from China, also make the Uppsala approach (Johanson and Vahlne, 1977, 2009; Johanson and Wiedersheim-Paul, 1975) to COFDI a theoretical non-starter. The Uppsala approach suggests that companies will venture out from their home base on a cautious, step-by-step basis. Their first investments will be in culturally (and geographically in many cases) close countries where they can negate the 'liability of foreignness' (Zaheer, 1995) or 'liability of outsidership' (Johanson and Vahlne, 2009) most easily before learning and moving on to more difficult foreign countries. This approach clearly does not fit COFDI. Chinese multinationals often go – even for their *first* foreign direct investment – to culturally and geographically AND economically different countries: the USA and Europe for market and asset-seeking purposes and Latin America and Africa for resource-seeking investments. There is little cautious step-by-step gradualism here.

The place to look for a satisfactory application of theory is internalisation theory of the multinational enterprise (Buckley and Casson, 1976, 1985, 2009). This explanation seeks as its root cause the imperfect markets that are internalised in the

MNE's growth. Classically, these are markets in information-intensive intermediate products, such as technology, although also including marketing skills and knowledge of managing quality sensitive value chains. In the case of China, this process begins by the internalisation of imperfect capital markets (Buckley et al., 2007). Crudely, this gives Chinese multinationals access to capital at below-market equilibrium rates, and this allows them to compete by purchasing assets unavailable to firms without this capital market advantage. It will be noted that this process also explains the 'buy abroad to compete in China' strategy and completely by-passes the CSA/FSA arguments. Chinese firms do not need FSAs when they can utilise cheap capital and can also leverage the benefits of the size of the home market and the associated number of domestic entrepreneurs (Hashai and Buckley, 2014).

The recent conceptual structure based on internalisation theory – 'the global factory' (Buckley and Ghauri, 2004; Buckley 2007, 2009a, 2009b, 2010, 2011a, 2011b, 2011c, 2012, 2017) – examines the orchestration of global value chains (Hinterhuber, 2002). Understanding the control of value chains helps to explain not only the difficulties of Chinese (and other emerging market firms) of penetrating sectors already controlled by MNEs, but also the process by which Chinese MNEs can build global factories under their own control underpinned by capital availability in the Chinese system. It is this next stage in the process of building companies (as suggested by Rugman and colleagues) that remains uncertain. This is the test by which the success of Chinese MNEs can be judged in the future – can they move from internalising markets in capital to internalising high-value-added links involving technology and information? This is the key issue in the question of 'can China innovate?'

New challenges

The internalisation theory approach to COFDI does throw up some interesting issues. The government policy variable in Buckley et al. (2007) is important, but this is unsurprising. The Chinese government's positive encouragement to (most) outward investment is unusual, but not unprecedented, and its impact is expected. Less expected, in a theoretical sense, is the behaviour of the country risk variable which in Buckley et al.'s (2007) analysis showed that COFDI was attracted to high country-risk locations.

A challenge to established theoretical reasoning – foreign investors prefer low-risk countries, other things being equal (as they are in a well-specified multiple regression) – leads to questioning of the theory and to different, or refined, explanation. It is thus appropriate to interrogate this variable. A number of reasons may be adduced as to why higher-risk locations were preferred to COFDI in this panel data sample (which it must be remembered ends in 2001). First, there is the explanation from the received theory – Chinese investors are risk takers because they have access to internalised cheap capital which both insures against capital losses and makes risk taking less dangerous. A second explanation is that, in this early period at least, country risk was not understood by the early pioneering investors. A third explanation is that, as most firms in the sample were SOEs, government direction overrode concerns about risk, and there is casual empirical support for this from investments in Cuba, Myanmar and several high-risk African countries. A fourth explanation is a competition argument – Chinese firms went to countries that were 'too risky' for Western firms (and sometimes these were prohibition rules in place from their parent governments), and therefore Chinese entrants faced no competition from Western MNEs. A fifth argument is that this is an artefact of the time period and that later investigations would negate this result.

The 'risk controversy' raises a further issue for theory – the role of management and governance issues in COFDI. The efficacy of international business theory in explaining what managers actually do in making foreign direct investment is itself constantly under scrutiny (e.g. Buckley et al., 2007), but the current evidence suggests that it works well where it has been tested. Unfortunately, that is rarely on Chinese managers (Buckley et al., 2016).

China's home country environment has thrown new light upon home country determinants of outward FDI. As Table 5.2 shows, the internalisation theory of

TABLE 5.2 Home country characteristics that determine internalisation decisions

	1	*2*	*3*
	The General Case	*Across National Boundaries*	*In the Specific Case of China*
(a)	**Industry-Specific Characteristics**		
	The nature of the product	Acceptability/compatibility outside the home country	'Nation-focused products' Value chain
	The structure of the external market	Specific national imperfections	'National champions' capital market
(b)	**Region-Specific Characteristics**		
	Geographical factors	Spatial and locational elements of internalisation	'Ports' – entrepôt (Hong Kong) distance connectivity Linguistic skills
	Social characteristics	Psychic distance to other nations	Psychic links communication costs
(c)	**Home-Nation-Specific Factors**		
	Political	Political links	Corruption State control
		Liability of foreignness	'Institutional voids'
	Fiscal	Differences in tax regimes (including tax havens)	Investment in tax havens
(d)	**Firm-Specific Factors**		
	Management skills to organise internal markets	Training International outlook Insularity (negative)	Unproven Idiosyncratic Learning

Source: Buckley and Casson (1976).

the MNE focuses, in general, on industry-specific, region-specific (spatial), home-nation-specific and firm-specific factors (column 1). The MNE is created when firms internalise markets across international boundaries (column 2). The case of China (column 3) has specific factors under each of these headings.

Moving from the 'general' column 1 to 'international' column 2 to factors specific to China in column 3 shows the special factors that apply to internalisation theory in a given context – in this case China. This shows the ability of the general theory of internalisation to generate 'special theories' as illustrated by the particular case of Chinese OFDI.

Conclusion

China's outward foreign direct investment is a formidable and rapidly growing phenomenon in the global economy (Buckley, 2017). Its long-term success is not yet assured, and the jury is still out on the efficiency of its direction and management. International business theory has so far been concerned with the determinants of COFDI and its distribution whilst performance data have been rare, and so its outcomes are not yet subject to definitive judgement.

As a challenge to theory, COFDI has been prominent in the explanation of emerging market multinationals, regarded by some as a 'new' phenomenon that requires 'new' theory (Mathews, 2006). This chapter has suggested that the internalisation theory of the multinational enterprise captures COFDI and EMNEs as special cases of a general theory. The mapping of those markets that are internalised by Chinese firms, notably the imperfect domestic capital market, provide a satisfactory explanation of the take-off of COFDI. The dynamics of COFDI are now to be explained by the internalisation of other markets, in knowledge, technology and information. The ability of Chinese managers to accomplish this will determine the further expansion of COFDI and the viability of Chinese multinationals as global competitors. It is possible that Chinese MNEs will largely focus on the rapidly expanding Chinese domestic market, bringing back technology to compete at home rather than globalising their activities. These strategies are now beginning to emerge, and their success across the spectrum of activities of Chinese MNEs will have a major effect on the international economy for a considerable time period ahead.

References

Barney, J 1991, 'Firm resources and sustainable competitive advantage', *Journal of Management*, vol. 17, no. 1, pp. 99–120.

Buckley, PJ 2004, 'Globalisation, economic geography and the strategy of multinational enterprises' (co-author Pervez N. Ghauri), *Journal of International Business Studies*, vol. 35, no. 2, pp. 81–98.

Buckley, PJ 2007, 'The strategy of multinational enterprises in the light of the rise of China', *Scandinavian Journal of Management*, vol. 23, no. 2, pp. 107–126.

Buckley, PJ 2009a, 'The impact of the global factory on economic development', *Journal of World Business*, vol. 44, no. 2, pp. 131–143.

Buckley, PJ 2009b, 'Internalisation thinking – from the multinational enterprise to the global factory', *International Business Review*, vol. 18, no. 3, pp. 224–235.

Buckley, PJ 2010, The role of headquarters in the global factory. In Ulf, A. & Ulf, H. (eds.) *Managing the Contemporary Multinational*, Edward Elgar, Cheltenham, pp. 60–84.

Buckley, PJ 2011a, *Globalization and the Global Factory*, Edward Elgar, Cheltenham, p. 634.

Buckley, PJ 2011b, 'The governance of the multinational enterprise: Insights from internalisation theory' (co-author Roger Strange), *Journal of Management Studies*, vol. 48, no. 2, pp. 460–470.

Buckley, PJ 2011c, 'International integration and coordination in the global factory', *Management International Review*, vol. 51, no. 2, pp. 269–283.

Buckley, PJ 2012, The multinational enterprise as a global factory. In Verbeke, A. & Merchant, H. (eds.) *Handbook of Research on International Strategic Management*, Edward Elgar, Cheltenham, pp. 77–92.

Buckley, PJ 2017, 'China goes global: Provenance, projection, performance and policy' (forthcoming 2017).

Buckley, PJ & Casson, MC 1976, *The Future of the Multinational Enterprises*, Macmillan, London.

Buckley, PJ & Casson, MC 1985, *The Economic Theory of the Multinational Enterprise*, MacMillan, London.

Buckley, PJ & Casson, MC 2009, 'The internalisation theory of the multinational enterprise – a review of the progress of a research agenda after 30 years', *Journal of International Business Studies*, vol. 40, no. 9, pp. 1563–1580.

Buckley, PJ & Ghauri, PN 2004, 'Globalisation, economic geography and the strategy of multinational enterprises', (co-author Pervez N. Ghauri), *Journal of International Business Studies*, vol. 35, no. 2, pp. 81–98.

Buckley, PJ, Chen, L, Clegg, J & Voss, H 2016, 'Experience and FDI risk-taking: A microfoundational reconceptualisation', *Journal of International Management*, vol. 22, pp. 131–146.

Buckley, PJ, Clegg, J, Cross, A, Zheng, P, Voss, H & Xin Liu, X 2007, 'The determinants of Chinese outward foreign direct investment', *Journal of International Business Studies*, vol. 38, no. 4, pp. 499–518.

Buckley, PJ, Devinney, TM & Louviere, JJ 2007, 'Do managers behave the way theory suggests? A choice theoretic examination of foreign direct investment location decision making', *Journal of International Business Studies*, vol. 38, no. 7, pp. 1069–1094.

Buckley, PJ, Sutherland, D, Voss, H & El-Gohari, A 2014, 'The economic geography of offshore incorporation in tax havens and offshore financial centres: The case of Chinese MNEs', *Journal of Economic Geography*, vol. 14, no. 6, pp. 1–26.

Dunning, JH 1979, 'Explaining changing patterns of international production: In defence of the eclectic theory', *Oxford Bulletin of Economics and Statistics*, vol. 41, no. 4, pp. 269–295.

Foss, NJ 1997, *Resources, Firms, and Strategies: A Reader in the Resource-Based Perspective*, Oxford University Press, Oxford.

Hashai, N & Buckley, PJ 2014, 'Is competitive advantage a necessary condition for the emergence of the multinational enterprise?' *Global Strategy Journal*, vol. 4, no. 1, pp. 35–48.

Hinterhuber, A 2002, 'Value chain orchestration in action and the case of the global agrochemical industry', *Long Range Planning*, vol. 35, no. 6, pp. 615–635.

Hymer, SA 1960, *The International Operations of National Firms: A Study of Direct Foreign Investment*, MIT Press, Cambridge, MA, Boston.

Hymer, SA 1976, *The International Operations of National Firms: A Study of Direct Foreign Investment*, MIT Press, Cambridge, MA.

Johanson, J & Vahlne, J-E 1977, 'The internationalization process of the firm: A model of knowledge development and increasing foreign market commitments', *Journal of International Business Studies*, vol. 8, no. 1, pp. 23–32.

Johanson, J & Vahlne, J-E 2009, 'The Uppsala internationalization process model revisited: From liability of foreignness to liability of outsidership', *Journal of International Business Studies*, vol. 40, no. 9, pp. 1411–1431.

Johanson, J & Wiedersheim-Paul, F 1975, 'The internationalisation process of the firm: Four Swedish cases', *Journal of Management Studies*, vol. 12, no. 3, pp. 305–322.

Kindleberger, CP 1970, *American Business Abroad*, Yale University Press, New Haven, CT.

Mathews, JA 2006, 'Dragon multinationals: New players in 21st century globalization', *Asia Pacific Journal of Management*, vol. 23, no. 1, pp. 5–27.

Nguyen, QTK & Rugman, AM 2015, 'Multinational subsidiary sales and performance in South East Asia', *International Business Review*, vol. 24, no. 1, pp. 115–123.

Penrose, ET 1959, *The Theory of the Growth of the Firm*, Basil Blackwell, Oxford.

Peteraf, M 1993, 'The cornerstones of competitive advantage: A resource-based view', *Strategic Management Journal*, vol. 14, no. 5, pp. 179–191.

Ramamurti, R 2009a, What have we learned about emerging-market MNEs? In Ramamurti, R. & Singh, J. (eds.) *Emerging Multinationals in Emerging Markets*, Cambridge University Press, Cambridge, UK, pp. 399–426.

Ramamurti, R 2009b, Why study emerging country multinationals? In Ramamurti, R. & Singh, V.S. (eds.) *Emerging Multinationals in Emerging Markets*, Cambridge University Press, Cambridge, UK, pp. 3–22.

Ramamurti, R 2012, 'What is really different about emerging market multinationals?', *Global Strategy Journal*, vol. 2, no. 1, pp. 41–47.

Rugman, AM 1981, *Inside the Multinationals: The Economics of Internal Markets*, Columbia University Press, New York.

Rugman, AM & Verbeke, A 2003, 'Extending the theory of the multinational enterprise and strategic management perspectives', *Journal of International Business Studies*, vol. 34, no. 2, pp. 125–137.

Rugman, AM & Verbeke, A 2004, 'A perspective on regional and global strategies of multinational enterprises', *Journal of International Business Studies*, vol. 35, no. 1, pp. 3–18.

Teece, DJ, Pisano, G & Shuen, A 1997, 'Dynamic capabilities and strategic management', *Strategic Management Journal*, vol. 18, no. 7, pp. 509–533.

Vernon, R 1966, 'International trade and international investment in the product cycle', *Quarterly Journal of Economics*, vol. 80, pp. 190–207.

Witt, MA & Lewin, AY 2007, 'Outward foreign direct investment as escape response to home country institutional constraints', *Journal of International Business Studies*, vol. 38, no. 4, pp. 579–594.

Zaheer, S 1995, 'Overcoming the liability of foreignness', *Academy of Management Journal*, vol. 38, no. 2, pp. 341–363.

PART II

Policy development and implications

6

RECENT CHANGES IN CHINA'S OUTBOUND INVESTMENT POLICIES AND THEIR IMPLICATIONS

Zucai Hu

Overview of China's outbound investments

The 'Going Out' policy was an important decision made by the Chinese government at the turn of the century that has had tremendous influence on the long-term overall economic and social development of China. It encourages enterprises to participate in international economic and technological cooperation of various forms, including outbound investment (overseas investment), international EPC (engineering, procurement and construction) projects, and labour service cooperation. Among these forms, outbound investment is an essential one. From the perspective of international balance of payments, capital gains generated from outbound investment flow through the capital and financial account, while revenues from EPC projects or service cooperation flow through the current account, which is different from the former by nature. Outbound investment, as defined by official sources, refers to activities where investors invest in currencies, securities, intellectual property rights or technologies, equity interest, debt interest and other assets, or provide guarantee to acquire foreign ownership, operational and management rights, and other related rights and interests.

During quite a long period of time since China's reform and opening up, China's cross-border direct capital flows have been mainly composed of capital inflow, while the size of direct outbound investment was quite small. Generally speaking, Chinese overseas investment experienced three phases of development.

The start-up phase refers to the period from the beginning of reform and opening up to the 1990s. In this period, China's overseas investment was mainly made by small-sized service providers as well as trade companies and a small number of primary processing businesses that grew on the basis of international trade. The size of investments was relatively small. In 2000, the Chinese government announced an initiative to encourage its enterprises to 'go abroad', opening the chapter of rapid expansion for outbound investment. In 2002, China officially set up a statistics system for overseas investment, which stood at USD 2.7 billion for that year. The number exceeded USD 10 billion for the first time in 2005, reaching USD 12.26 billion, and further increased to USD 68.8 billion in 2010. During the 'Eleventh Five-Year Plan' period, aggregate overseas investment amounted to USD 228.92 billion, with an average annual growth rate of 34.3%, approximately 3.3 times GDP growth in the same period.

From 2012, China's overseas investment entered into a 'ramp-up period' of greater significance. Businesses had more demand, willingness and capabilities to go outward to participate in international cooperation and competition of a higher degree. The 'three-phase' evolution is in line with the historical experiences of other economies.

Overseas investment maintained high-speed growth. During the 'Twelfth Five-Year Plan' period, China's overseas investment grew at an annual rate of 16.2%, amounting to USD 145.67 billion in 2015 and exceeding the size of inward foreign direct investment, with a net stock of outward FDI of over USD 1 trillion by the end of 2015. According to the latest statistics, outward direct investment in 2016 reached USD 170.11 billion, up 44.1% year-on-year. Investment activities ranged across every major industry and covered over 180 countries and regions; a number of commodity production and processing bases were built up; the quantity and quality of investment in high-tech and advanced manufacturing industries both increased; and the capacity and level of financial services export improved steadily.

Global production capacity cooperation was carried forward steadily. In May 2015, Beijing issued the State Council's Guiding Opinions on Boosting International Production Capacity and Equipment Manufacturing Cooperation, which clarified the Chinese government's guiding opinions and key tasks of boosting international production capacity cooperation. A policy framework will be gradually built up on such basis. China has entered into multi-lateral and bilateral capacity cooperation arrangements with multiple countries and international organizations. Chinese manufacturers have pushed their production capacity to 'go outward' by investing in production facilities abroad, gained access to cutting-edge proprietary technologies by acquiring foreign patents, and built up international marketing networks.

Breakthroughs have been made in improving connectivity. Since the implementation of the 'Twelfth Five-Year Plan', the Chinese government has proactively supported domestic entrepreneurs to participate in major foreign railway and harbour construction projects so as to bring China-made infrastructure and equipment abroad. A number of large-scale railway and harbour projects have made substantial progress, including the China-Laos Railway, Thailand Railway, Hungary-Serbia Railway, Jakarta-Bandung High-Speed Railway in Indonesia, Moscow-Kazan High-Speed Railway in Russia, Ethiopia-Djibouti Railway, Mombasa-Nairobi Railway in Kenya, and China-Europe Adriatic-Baltic-Black Sea Seaport projects. All these projects have made positive progress and played a significant role in promoting interconnectivity between China and its neighbouring countries.

Substantial outcomes have been achieved in key fields of outbound investment. Chinese corporations have participated in a large number of overseas oil and gas exploration and development projects through green field direct investment, merger and acquisition, and equity participation, which resulted in an increase in overseas interest in oil and gas reserves and output, creating substantial results from overseas energy and mineral resources development. They invested in mineral resources that were short of domestic supply and heavily reliant on import from Australia, South Africa, Peru and Brazil, which greatly contributed to the expansion of global mineral resources supply. Investment in the foreign agricultural sector was also carried forward steadily. Chinese enterprises initiated a number of influential cross-border mergers and acquisitions in this sector, which turned out to be quite fruitful. Chinese companies also carried out plantation of soybeans, corns, wheat and rubber in more than 50 countries and gradually expanded to processing and trade areas in the meantime.

Chinese enterprises operate more globally. In recent years, the number of Chinese multinationals has expanded rapidly. More companies have moved up on the global value chain, with enhanced international competitiveness and industry influence. To date, the number of offshore-registered enterprises of Chinese investors has exceeded 30,000, creating over 1.225 million job opportunities for foreign residents, 0.39 million more than the end of the previous year. From 2015 to 2016, Chinese enterprises paid over USD 60 billion of taxes to the foreign jurisdictions in which they operated.

China's overseas investment administration framework and progress of reform

Under the current framework, the regulation of overseas investment by domestic corporations and institutions mainly involves three government departments, namely the development and reform departments (including the National Development and Reform Commission, referred to as 'NDRC', and its provincial bureaus), the business and commerce departments (including the Ministry of Commerce, referred to as 'MOFCOM', and its provincial bureaus) and the foreign exchange departments (including the State Administration of Foreign Exchange, referred to as 'SAFE', and its provincial bureaus).

The development and reform departments are responsible for placing overseas investment projects on record and reviewing. According to regulations published by the NDRC in 2014, it has been adopting a new management system under which overseas investment projects generally need only to be placed on record, with government review required for only a limited number of projects in sensitive industries or in sensitive countries and regions.

The business and commerce departments are responsible for placing China-invested overseas enterprises on record and reviewing. The newly amended Administrative Measures regarding Overseas Investment of MOFCOM has been implemented since October 6, 2014. Accordingly, the regulation system of the

TABLE 6.1 History of simplifying administrative procedures for overseas investment projects

Time	*Approach*	*Administration Authority*
Before 2004	Review and approval	Investments of over USD 1 million by Chinese investors should be reported for government approval
July 2004	Review	Non-resources development projects of over USD 10 million and resources development projects of over USD 30 million require review by the NDRC or the State Council
February 2011	Review	Non-resources development projects of over USD 100 million and resources development projects of over USD 300 million require review by the NDRC and then the State Council
December 2013	Record-filing and review	Projects of over USD 1 billion and sensitive projects require review by the NDRC and then the State Council, while others need only to be placed on record
October 2014	Record-filing and review	Except for sensitive projects, all other projects only need to be placed on record

business and commerce departments has been shifted to a system under which China-invested overseas enterprises need only to be placed on record, with government review required for a limited number of enterprises in sensitive industries or in sensitive countries or regions. The relevant procedures have also been significantly streamlined.

Procedures of foreign exchange management have been reformed. According to the Notice of the SAFE on Further Simplifying and Improving the Foreign Exchange Management Policy on Direct Investment released by the SAFE on February 28, 2015, administrative approval on outward direct investment by domestic enterprises was abolished from June 1, 2015, replaced by the approach of 'handled by banks, supervised by SAFE'. Based on this notice, banks would replace the role of the state foreign exchange administration authorities in handling relevant foreign exchange registration procedures for outward direct investments by domestic enterprises through the capital account information system of the SAFE. Meanwhile, the focus of the SAFE has been shifted to post-investment supervision and management. From June 1, 2015, domestic institutions are permitted, at their own discretion, to select banks in the area in which they are registered to acquire services related to outward direct investment, such as foreign exchange registration, account opening and remittance of funds. In the meantime, the foreign exchange record-filing system for overseas reinvestment and the annual inspection system for outward direct investment were replaced by the registration and reporting system through banks.

By streamlining administration and delegating power to lower levels while strengthening post-investment management and optimizing services, reform of the overseas investment administration system was deepened, substantially facilitating overseas investment. Generally speaking, China has accomplished a shift from the review system to the record-filing system in regulation on outward direct investment. Investment facilitation mainly resides in the following aspects:

First, autonomy of enterprises is fully recognized. The government only reviews the authenticity and compliance of investment, while enterprises are given full autonomy in decision-making and are held accountable for profit or loss, which affirms commercial orientation in overseas investment.

Second, the record-filing requirements have been dramatically simplified. Enterprises only need to fill in the application form for project record-filing.

Third, with efficiency substantially improved, enterprises can complete the record-filing process within seven working days.

Fourth, online registration has become fully operational. Currently, more than 98% of overseas investment projects were placed on record and managed online, significantly improving the efficiency and facilitating overseas investment. Businesses can fill in the electronic registration form and check progress in real time through the online system.

Fifth, the foreign exchange management procedures for outward direct investment have been further simplified and improved. Due to this reform, it has become much easier for domestic players to 'go outward'.

Continue to improve the policy environment for enterprises to invest abroad

In addition to the measures mentioned above, the Chinese government has put forward various initiatives to encourage and support enterprises to invest abroad.

First, actively expand the financing channels that support the internationalization of Chinese enterprises. Recently, China has established the China-Latin America Production Capacity Cooperation Fund and the China-Africa Production Capacity Cooperation Fund, and it has promoted the building of several other multilateral and bilateral funds such as China-Europe Mutual Fund in order to lower the financing cost of key projects. In order to deepen foreign debt management reform so as to help enterprises gain access to low-cost capital abroad, optimize the debt structure of enterprises, and explore stable overseas funding sources for companies, the government initiated the reform on foreign debt filing and registration system in September 2015. In 2016, the government received filings for offshore debt offerings of USD 193.2 billion. In addition, national policy-based financial institutions such as China Development Bank, Export-Import Bank of China, China Export and Credit Insurance Corporation, and other commercial financial institutions have also strengthened financial support in various ways.

Second, strengthen fiscal and taxation support. For instance, resident enterprises that have paid income taxes offshore are allowed to deduct the equivalent amount from the income tax payables onshore. Zero VAT rate and tax exemptions are applied to selected cross-border taxable activities such as export of R&D and design services, export goods insurance, and export credit insurance. VAT export rebate policies are applied to selected duty-free goods. In the meantime, China has entered into international tax treaties to avoid double taxation with over 100 countries and regions.

Third, improve the service platform. Twelve industry associations – including associations of steel, non-ferrous metals, electric power and chemical industries – have been supporting Chinese enterprises to seek international industrial collaboration. As bridges in their industries, these associations have promoted the establishment of business alliances. In 2016, the Central China International Production Capacity Cooperation Forum was held in Hubei Province; the Western China International Production Capacity Cooperation Forum was held in Gansu Province; China Overseas Development Association hosted the International Production Capacity Cooperation Forum and Corporation Outbound Investment Fair. The large number of international expos and forums has provided Chinese entrepreneurs with the opportunities to reach out to their prospective international partners for pragmatic business cooperation.

The direction of reform of outbound investment administration in the next period

Looking ahead, during the coming 'Thirteenth Five-Year Plan' period, the global economy will still be in a period of profound adjustment, with investment, trade and financial rules to be rewritten; cross-border investment on the rise; and restructuring of the industrial landscape to speed up. The Chinese economy has entered a new phase, concluded as the 'new normal'. In this phase, the One Belt One Road (OBOR) Initiative has been widely implemented; international production capacity cooperation has gotten off to a good start; Chinese enterprises have become more competitive internationally yet are also facing the challenge of preventing investment risks in a more complicated global environment. Against such a backdrop, the authorities overseeing outbound investment will continue to adhere to the new development philosophies by focusing on China's overall goal of building a prosperous society in all respects while highlighting the major task of supply-side structural reform. The focus will be placed on providing investment guidance, support and services for enterprises under the OBOR Initiative, so that enterprises can make overseas investment in a well-regulated manner and more diverse ways, enhance investment quality and efficiency, and effectively prevent risks. Hopefully, remarkable results will be achieved in outbound investment in the key sectors.

Further enhance national guidance on outbound investment. The government will further improve the mid- and long-term plan for overseas investment on the basis of the overall national economic and social development plan and the world-oriented economic policies focusing on the OBOR Initiative and international production capacity cooperation. Following the 'business-centred, market-oriented, rule-based and government-led' principle, the Chinese government will continue to provide guidance in the form of national plan, policy support and investment facilitation services for enterprises to 'go outward'. It will formulate laws and regulations on overseas investment to provide a solid legal framework under which enterprises will orderly make overseas investments. Businesses are encouraged to pursue overseas expansion in a proactive and prudent manner based on their actual conditions and capacity, in their own near-term and long-term interests. They should operate by law and fulfil their corporate social responsibilities so as to establish a sound public image abroad. Industry associations are encouraged to make their own international development plans, taking into consideration the actual industry situation, to facilitate and support the overseas operations of industrial players.

Further optimize management of overseas investment. The government will further streamline administration and delegate more power to lower levels, improve the registration-based overseas investment administration mechanism, optimize the online record-filing system and strengthen inter-agency coordination to facilitate overseas investment. Efforts will be made to strengthen authenticity management on overseas investment and enhance oversight when investments are made and subsequently. The government will exercise all-round management over inward and outward investment, improve the national online investment supervision platform and build a more effective public service platform for 'going out' enterprises. It will establish a regulatory system on illegal activities and misconduct of Chinese enterprises abroad, promote inter-agency information sharing and joint enforcement, and further penalize the illegal operations of Chinese businesses in foreign jurisdictions, including false investment, forgery and infringement, bribery, and environmental pollution. Relevant government authorities, overseas commercial agencies, industry associations and Chinese chambers of commerce shall play a coordinated role in promoting fair and orderly competition. The foreign exchange registration system for outward direct investment shall be further improved to allow more efficient registration. The negative checklist for foreign exchange management shall be gradually built up.

Improve the overseas investment service system. The government will accelerate negotiation and signing of multilateral and bilateral agreements on investment protection with the relevant countries and regions and improve the consular protection system to provide more services including interest and rights protection, investment promotion and risk alert. The role of commercial agencies shall be brought into full play with the rising of a number of international agencies specialized in design consultation, asset appraisal, credit rating or legal services. The government will establish a sophisticated overseas state-owned asset supervision and management system, auditing system, performance evaluation system and accountability system. A comprehensive financial support system shall also be established, where policy-directed financial institutions and commercial financial institutions shall be fully utilized to combine the support for outbound investment with RMB internationalization, so as to promote the mutual development of industrial and financial sectors.

Improve the risk control system. First, the Chinese government will improve the risk warning system for major countries. By regularly issuing risk evaluation reports by nation, it will strengthen risk guidance and warning for investment in high-risk countries or regions, report timely on major risks in relevant countries and take precautions and mitigating measures accordingly. The government will resort to diplomatic, economic and legal means to properly deal with major national risks and emergencies to protect the legitimate interests and rights of Chinese enterprises abroad. Second, it is essential to improve the overseas investment risk control mechanism. Enterprises of all sectors will be guided to improve their internal risk control mechanism and, at the same time, conduct their overseas operations under stronger supervision and regulation to prevent and manage potential risks. The government will urge SOEs to strengthen decision-making monitoring and financial control relating to outbound investment, and tighten regulation on the overseas auditing and business operations of SOEs and increase the value of SOEs' assets. Third, the government will enhance protection of overseas personal safety and property security. It will improve the offshore safety and risk warning mechanism and emergency management mechanism; encourage and guide domestic security service providers to provide professional services for domestic corporations and institutions operating offshore; and strengthen the prevention and control of epidemic diseases and the training of overseas personnel on security knowledge and knowhow to enhance their awareness and capability of self-protection.

The administrative system of outbound investment is a major component of the new and open economy that China is currently constructing. The Chinese government will combine institutional building in the medium to long term with well-timed regulation in the near term, promote the facilitation of outbound investment, and in the meantime prevent potential investment risks, while regulating and improving market order to promote outbound investment in a healthy and orderly manner.

7

CHINA BUILDS UP FREE TRADE AREAS TO FACILITATE OFDI

Xiangchen Zhang

Chinese enterprises' outward foreign direct investment (OFDI) is going through three development stages simultaneously

Currently, OFDI by Chinese enterprises has moved into a period combining three development stages: OFDI itself is growing rapidly, while still in its infancy; transforming and upgrading are also underway. This situation is in line with the road taken by the Chinese economy in the past few decades, in other words 'compressed' development.[1] It is also the conclusion of the development of Chinese enterprises' OFDI in terms of speed, level and mode.

From the perspective of development speed, Chinese enterprises' OFDI is at a stage of rapid growth. From 2002 to 2015, the average annual growth rate of Chinese outbound investment was as high, at nearly 35.9%. It far surpassed that of advanced economies and other emerging economies during the same period, and it was also significantly higher than the level of those economies in their high-growth phrases (Figure 7.1). In 2015, China ranked second globally in terms of OFDI flows. With an ever-expanding base, it is possible for the growth rate to fluctuate within an acceptable range. However, considering China's developing economy and its increasingly competitive enterprises, OFDI by Chinese enterprises will continue to snowball in the long run.

From the perspective of development level, Chinese enterprises' OFDI is still at the initial stage. This is demonstrated by the relatively small size and imbalanced structure of OFDI stock, as well as the overall low international competitiveness of Chinese enterprises. By the end of 2015, Chinese OFDI stock recorded USD 1.0979 trillion, ranking eighth in the world, only 18% of that of the US (USD 5.9828 trillion) (Figure 7.2) and 4.4% of the global stock (USD 25 trillion), which is much lower than China's GDP contribution to the global total (15.5%).

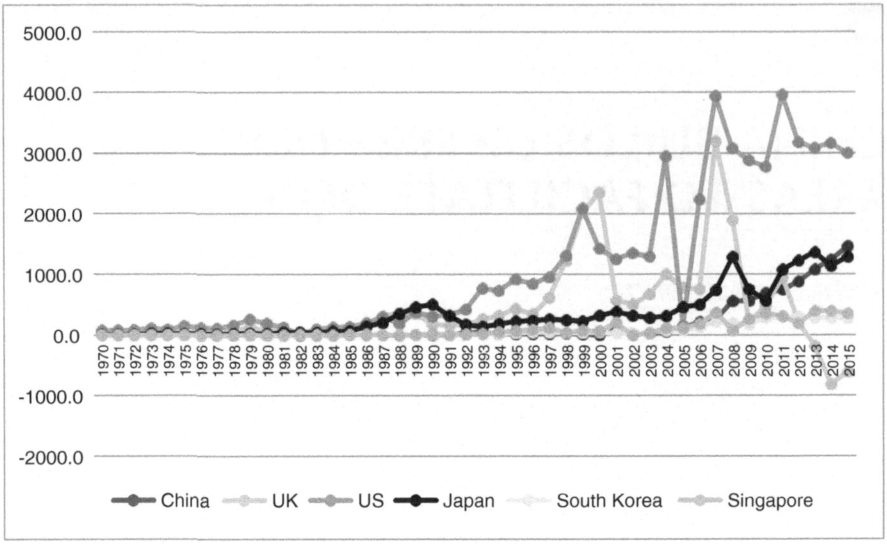

FIGURE 7.1 OFDI flows from selected economies, 1970 to 2015 (USD 100 million)

Source: United Nations Conference on Trade and Development (UNCTAD) data centre, the *2015 Statistical Bulletin of China's Outward Foreign Direct Investment* issued by the MOFCOM, the National Bureau of Statistics of China and the State Administration of Foreign Exchange.

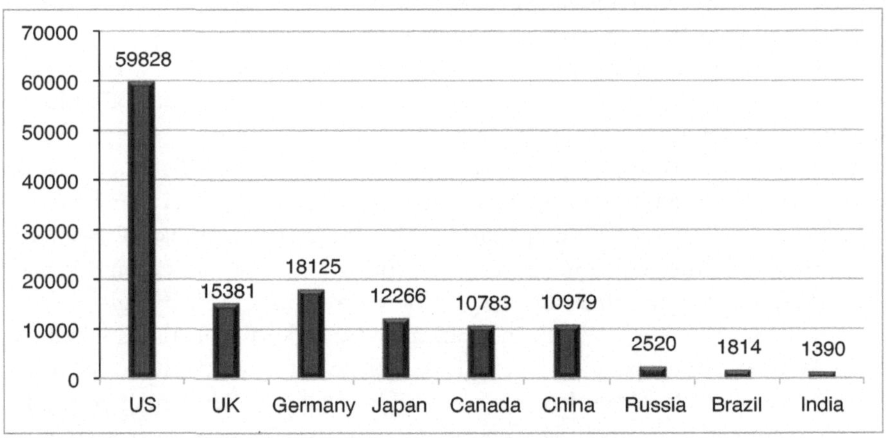

FIGURE 7.2 OFDI stock of major countries in 2015

Source: the *2015 Statistical Bulletin of China's Outward Foreign Direct Investment* issued by the MOFCOM, the National Bureau of Statistics of China and the State Administration of Foreign Exchange.

Investments from the resource and energy industries take a larger proportion of Chinese OFDI stock, while investments from the manufacturing industry account for a smaller stake. By the end of 2015, OFDI stock in the Chinese manufacturing industry totalled USD 78.53 billion, only 7.2% of China's total stock. By contrast,

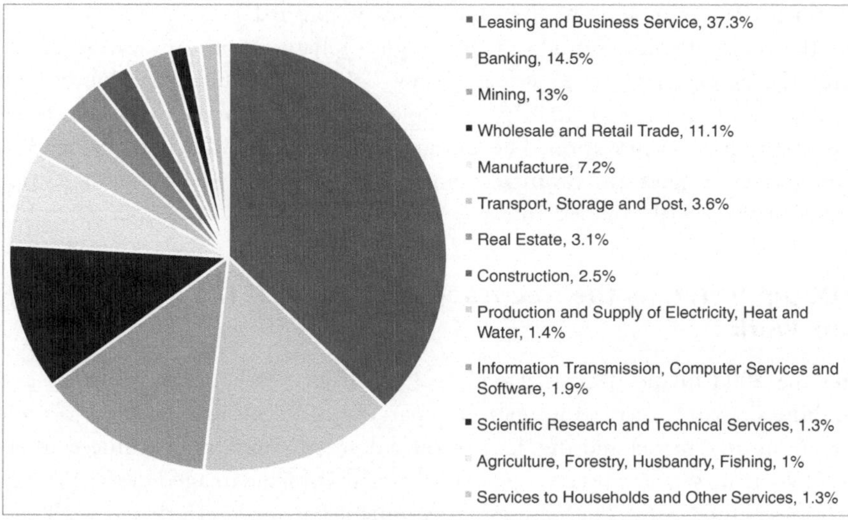

FIGURE 7.3 Breakdown of China's OFDI stock by industry as of the end of 2015

Source: the *2015 Statistical Bulletin of China's Outward Foreign Direct Investment* issued by the MOFCOM, the National Bureau of Statistics of China and the State Administration of Foreign Exchange.

manufacturing powers such as the US, Japan and Germany enjoy much higher proportions. In particular, South Korea has maintained a high level of more than 50% since 1990 (Figure 7.3).

This indicates that most Chinese manufacturing enterprises have not achieved the 'special monopolistic advantages' defined by the general theory of investment, including technology, patent, brand, management, resource integration, presence in global value chains etc. They are still at the lower end of global value chains, without the ability to take the initiative in drawing a global layout. The good news is that in recent years, OFDI by the Chinese manufacturing industry has been on the rise and exceeded that of the resource and energy industry in 2015.

From the perspective of development mode, Chinese enterprises' OFDI is at the upgrading stage. China now faces a formidable task to transform itself into a major power in the OFDI field. In today's world, outbound investment represents an extension of the whole systematic industrial chain rather than a specific move by any single enterprise. Chinese enterprises start overseas investment with engineering contracting, but, due to the increasing material and labour costs in the domestic market, they are losing their traditional advantages. Given the experiences of successful enterprises from other countries, Chinese players should expand the scope of service export to all parts of the industrial value chain, ranging from capital, technology, standard-setting, design, construction and consultation to operation, maintenance and management service. They should also equip their engineer contracting activities with high-value-added services, such as project financing, design consultation and operation and management, so as to establish a comprehensive advantage.

Information technology has become firmly established globally, and the world is on the verge of a new round of technological renewal, with innovation in full swing. For enterprises, 'going abroad' is not only about acquiring resources but also about bringing in cutting-edge technologies from the outside world in order to realize high-end innovation. The 'going abroad' policy will help to foster additional growth triggers and promote domestic innovation, thereby moving China further up the global value chain.

OFDI supported by the free trade agreement (FTA) framework

After the 2008 financial crisis, facing a sluggish global economic recovery and shrinking demands in the international market, some countries turned to trade protectionism. They closed the door of their domestic markets to Chinese enterprises by setting security review and entry barriers, which damaged the legal rights of Chinese enterprises. The Chinese government has made efforts to sign bilateral and multilateral FTAs in order to protect the rights and interests of domestic enterprises by improving the international trade and investment system, removing explicit or implicit entry barriers, and properly settling investment disputes.

Overview of FTAs signed by China

By now, China has entered into and implemented 14 FTAs, which cover 22 countries and regions from Asia, Latin America, Oceania and Europe. Specifically, China has signed FTAs with ASEAN, South Korea, Singapore, Pakistan, Australia, New Zealand, Chile, Peru, Costa Rica, Iceland and Switzerland; the Chinese mainland has entered into the Closer Economic Partnership Arrangement (CEPA) with Hong Kong and Macao as well as the Cross Strait Economic Cooperation Framework Agreement (ECFA) with Taiwan. China is now in negotiations of 12 free trade areas, including free trade area negotiations on the Regional Comprehensive Economic Partnership (RCEP) and China-Japan-ROK Free Trade Area and negotiations with the Gulf Cooperation Council (GCC), Sri Lanka, Maldives, Israel, Georgia and Norway; upgrade negotiations with New Zealand, Chile and Singapore; as well as second-phase negotiations with Pakistan. Moreover, China is also conducting eight free trade area joint researches, including the free trade area joint feasibility researches with Canada, Columbia, Nepal, Bangladesh, Fiji, Papua New Guinea and Mauritius, as well as free trade area upgrade joint research with Peru. As of the end of 2016, China has accomplished or is negotiating with 25 of the 65 countries (nearly 40%) regarding the establishment of free trade areas along the Belt and Road region.

FTAs facilitate the 'going abroad' of Chinese enterprises

Traditionally, international investment rules were mainly shaped by bilateral investment treaties (BIT). However, in recent years, FTAs have encompassed an expanding scope of economic activities, including investment liberalization. Issues concerning investment often make up an independent chapter in the FTAs that China has signed with other economies.

The FTAs have made it easier for Chinese enterprises to invest overseas. On the one hand, international trade and investment can be mutually reinforcing: free trade has deepened Chinese enterprises' understanding of host country markets and equipped them with experience for investment activities. Many of the major OFDI destinations of Chinese enterprises are also China's close trade partners. Since 2008 when the China–New Zealand FTA came into force, China's exports to New Zealand have soared. The rate of export growth from 2011 to 2012 reached as high as 34%. Over the same period, Chinese enterprises' investment in New Zealand also picked up speed: the year-on-year growth rate stood at 607%, 237% and 102% in 2010, 2012 and 2013, respectively. After the China-Switzerland FTA came into force in 2014, Chinese enterprises were allowed to export semi-finished products to Switzerland and reprocess them there, and then sell the products to Europe. In this way, they can avoid trade barriers and expand in the European market. Attracted by the favourable treatment, more and more Chinese enterprises have set up branches in Switzerland. In 2015, China's direct investment in Switzerland was USD 0.25 billion, up 634% over the previous year.

On the other hand, the investment terms in FTAs effectively lower the barriers for Chinese enterprises to enter local markets and provide them with all-round legal protection. These terms cover issues such as investment entry, investor treatment, investment protection and dispute settlement mechanisms, which protect Chinese enterprises' interests and rights at all stages of investment. As a result, they have effectively promoted multilateral and bilateral transnational investment and bring opportunities to both sides. For example, in the China-Australia FTA, the two countries grant Most Favoured Nation (MFN) treatment to each other. Australia has increased the investment quota for Chinese private enterprises, under which they can enjoy a waiver, from AUD 252 million to AUD 1.094 billion. This allows Chinese investors to enjoy the same benefits as those of investors from the US and New Zealand. The favourable conditions have led to broader cooperation between China and Australia in agriculture and mining. China's investment in Australia has increased rapidly, especially in the energy and mining fields. Many large enterprises – such as Baosteel, Sinosteel, PetroChina, Sinopec and CNOOC – have invested and set up permanent offices in Australia. Another example is the China-ASEAN Free Trade Area. Under the free trade area framework, a free, convenient, transparent and fair investment system has been built. Both countries grant national treatment, MFN status as well as fair and equitable investment opportunities to each other. Related laws and regulations have also been made more transparent to provide more favourable investment conditions. In 2015, China's direct investment in ASEAN reached USD 14.6 billion, accounting for 12.4% of China's total OFDI that year.

Moreover, with the signing of FTAs, most of the economies involved adopt supporting policies to facilitate foreign enterprises' entry into their local market. In

2015, the Ministry of Trade, Industry and Energy (MOTIE) in South Korea rolled out three schemes to attract foreign investment, covering adjustments of preferential policies, deregulation, and establishment of free economic zones. Not long after the execution of the China-ROK FTA, South Korea introduced the Scheme of Utilizing Free Trade Agreement to Attract Foreign Investment as well as specific measures to attract Chinese investment through the FTA. According to South Korea's statistics, in 2015, Chinese investment in South Korea hit a record high of USD 1.978 billion, which surpassed that of Japan (USD 1.665 billion) for the first time.

China's considerations on FTAs in the future

In recent years, economic globalization has suffered several setbacks, such as Brexit, the election of pro-protectionist President Donald Trump in the US, and the ascendance of right-wing political forces and rising populism in Europe, all adding to the appeal of investment protectionism. The free flow of capital and other factors are blocked, hindering the integration of global capital and industries. The global economic recovery faces new uncertainties and is negatively affected. China – as a supporter, defender and practitioner of economic globalization – will strive for an open world economy and promote trade and investment liberalization and facilitation in an open environment. At the G20 Hangzhou Summit in 2016, the G20 Guiding Principles for Global Investment Policymaking formulated by China was approved by all leaders. It urged governments not to employ protectionism in relation to cross-border investment but to create open, non-discriminatory, transparent and predictable conditions for investment and provide legal protection such as dispute settlement mechanisms for investors. In future negotiations on FTAs, the Chinese government will make continuous efforts to uphold the relevant rules, further facilitate regional investment, improve global trade and investment governance, and give a greater role to transnational investment in promoting global economic growth and industrial integration.

In recent years, the Chinese government has accelerated existing free trade area negotiations in order to further liberalize trade activities in free trade areas and continue establishing free trade areas with the majority of its neighbouring countries and regions. Hopefully, the trade volume between China and its free trade partners as a proportion of China's total could reach or even exceed that in most developed countries and other emerging economies. In the medium to long term, China will continue to build high-level free trade areas, undertake the model of 'pre-establishment national treatment (PENT) with a negative list' in investment fields, and incorporate new issues into free trade negotiations such as the environment, intellectual property rights, e-commerce and competition policy. During the negotiations and signing process, China is committed to having the market play a decisive role in resources allocation and government to do a better job. Going forward, China will gradually build up a high-level global free trade network based on neighbouring countries and regions, while covering those along the Belt and Road area.

Suggestions for Chinese enterprises on OFDI

Under the principle of conducting 'business-centred, market-oriented, rule-based and government-led' investment, MOFCOM has been supporting qualified enterprises to make outbound investments in an honest and law-abiding way. It has strived to improve the regulatory system, policy framework and service system to guide enterprises to 'go abroad' in an orderly fashion. The Outbound Investment and Cooperation Guidelines by Countries (Regions) issued by MOFCOM annually, covering 171 countries and regions, has obtained more than 100 million annual hits and been highly recognized by enterprises. In recent years, MOFCOM has also provided greater support to overseas economic and trade cooperation zones and encouraged Chinese enterprises to share their experience with local people to promote the development of local industries and economy.

Currently, while the overall performance of China's outbound investment and cooperation is satisfactory, enterprises still need to rationally analyse the present situation and identify better opportunities. As the principal decision-maker, it should choose where and what to invest in, based on a full consideration of its needs and advantages. It also needs to ensure the feasibility and sustainability of outbound investments by utilizing markets and resources both at home and abroad. Efforts can be made in the following areas:

First, businesses should be motivated to improve their own capabilities. As 'students' in the OFDI field, Chinese enterprises still have a long way to go to catch up with world-class multinational enterprises in terms of global investment information network, investment model design and operation, integration of assets, overseas asset management, media and public relations. Chinese enterprises should benchmark themselves against best practices that are suitable for their particular stages, enhance the capability to participate in global capital and industrial cooperation, and explore win-win modes for overseas investment.

Second, businesses should aspire to upgrade their OFDIs. Without quick and effective initiatives, they could lose the upper hand in competition. Chinese enterprises should explore new business models (such as PPP), enhance their technological capabilities and indigenous innovation, better adapt to business environments in different countries and regions, and make active efforts to expand markets in developed countries. They should seize the opportunities offered by the global technological revolution and industrial integration, and expand investment in manufacturing and high-end service industries in order to move up the global industrial value chain.

Third, businesses should pursue inclusive and open cooperation. As a late mover in global investment, Chinese enterprises have not yet developed their own network of cooperation in the global market. Participating in global asset integration alone is of high cost, with great economic and social risks. Chinese enterprises should seek win-win outcomes, deepen their understanding of local markets as well as the international market, expand networks for further cooperation, and enhance their ability to cooperate with international partners with a more confident and open attitude, so that they can share risks and benefits with local and third-country partners.

Fourth, businesses should become committed local citizens. Since different countries have different political, legal, social and cultural systems and customs, to invest in a foreign country, Chinese enterprises should comply with local laws and regulations, take on social responsibilities, project a favourable public image, and contribute to local development. Many Chinese enterprises are already aware of this and have begun their work in this regard. After the Nepal earthquake in April 2015, Chinese enterprises in Nepal volunteered to repair roads for free. During the battle against the Ebola virus in Africa, Chinese enterprises in Sierra Leone delivered free laboratory equipment to local communities despite various difficulties. Chinese enterprises have come a long way in this regard, but they still need to improve communication skills and build better public images so as to gain recognition from the local community.

Fifth, businesses should make full preparations to fend off risks. To deal with the security risks faced by overseas institutions and personnel, in addition to governmental coordination, enterprises should also adopt the necessary preventive and precautionary measures, and formulate an internal security and risk prevention system. With the world undergoing political and economic adjustments, uncertainties and instability are increasing. Chinese enterprises should therefore be well prepared before they get started. They should make full use of the public services provided by MOFCOM, such as outbound investment guidance, in order to fully understand the essential situation as well as the policies and legal environments in host countries. They should also thoroughly analyse the feasibilities as well as the risks. Preparations should cover legal consultation, accounting, risk assessment and insurance. When necessary, they should turn to local laws in order to protect their legitimate rights and interests.

Note

1 'Compressed' development refers to the fact that China took only 30 years to accomplish urbanization and industrialization, while developed countries took 100 years. This rapid development, however, has left many problems and put greater pressure on structural adjustment and reform.

8

ASIAN INFRASTRUCTURE INVESTMENT BANK (AIIB)

A new mechanism for global financial cooperation

Yaobin Shi

AIIB was established at the right time and is therefore endowed with far-reaching effects

In October 2013, Chinese President Xi Jinping and Prime Minister Li Keqiang flagged the important initiative of establishing the Asian Infrastructure Investment Bank (AIIB) during their respective visits to Southeast Asia. Establishing AIIB is a constructive move by China to undertake greater international responsibilities, help refine current international economic governance and produce more international public goods. It will surely inject more 'positive energy' into the development undertakings of Asia and the world.

Bridging infrastructure funding gap in Asia and related areas

An analysis carried out by the Organization for Economic Co-operation and Development (OECD) shows that global annual demand for infrastructure funding is USD 3.8 trillion, of which only USD 2.7 trillion can be met. In addition, based on the statistics of the Asian Development Bank (ADB), the infrastructure financing gap in Asia during 2010–2020 stands at USD 8 trillion. Currently, infrastructure investment in Asia by existing multilateral development banks such as the World Bank and the ADB remains limited and is far from enough to meet the actual needs. Meanwhile, in terms of public sector investment, many countries in Asia have accumulated great shortfalls in infrastructure sector investment, due to fiscal constraints. In countries where national revenues undulate greatly in line with price fluctuations of bulk commodities such as energy resources, public funding in infrastructure can hardly be sustainable and stable. In the private sector, although countries within the Asian region, especially East

Asian countries, have relatively high household savings rates, projects such as construction of railways, highways and ports; energy resources exploration; and urban infrastructure construction still remain unattractive to private capital due to their large investment size, long investment horizon and uncertain return, together with an unstable market environment and an unsophisticated investment and financing mechanism.

Thus, to tackle the bottleneck in Asia's infrastructure financing, we need not only a large amount of funds but also an effective financing mechanism and platform to channel private investment into infrastructure construction and inter-connectivity development. As a newly founded multilateral development bank, AIIB provides the perfect platform for achieving this.

Contributing to the global economic recovery

Since the 2008 global financial crisis, the global economy has experienced sluggish growth and been slow to recover. An important means to stimulate economic recovery and growth is to increase investment, while increased investment in infrastructure is a cornerstone for long-term sustainable economic growth. However, the current shortfalls in global infrastructure investment are too huge to drive growth. As a result of the quantitative easing policies of major developed countries, global liquidity remains satisfactory. What are lacking are mechanisms and capabilities for mobilizing greater investment in the infrastructure sector. With the protracted global economic downturn, the establishment of AIIB can channel greater governmental and social investment into infrastructure construction and inter-connectivity development, which will drive investment growth, expand total global demand, create more job opportunities and accelerate the pace of the global economic recovery.

Enriching current international economic governance

The current international economic governance system is dominated by developed countries, while developing countries do not enjoy sufficiently balanced representation and a voice. With the development of emerging market countries, this imbalance is becoming increasingly severe. Driven by developing countries, including China, in 2010 the voting reform of the World Bank increased the share of developing members (3.13 percentage points were transferred from developed countries to developing countries, enabling developing countries to enjoy an increase in their share of total votes from 44.06% to 47.19%; China saw its share increase from 2.77% to 4.42%, lifting it from the sixth to the third shareholder in the bank). Despite this increase, the representation of developing countries still hardly reflects the true proportion of their economic power – especially China – within the global economy. Setting up AIIB will further strengthen the voice of developing countries including China. The competition brought about by AIIB can also help MDBs including World Bank and ADB to improve their operational efficiency and lending performance, by strengthening internal reforms and better addressing the concerns of developing countries.

AIIB is built to be an open and inclusive multilateral institution

Chinese President Xi Jinping has pointed out that AIIB shall remain committed to open regionalism and welcome all countries for win-win cooperation. Based on the 'open and inclusive' principle, China started consultation with all interested countries – regional followed by non-regional – with parallel discussions on both the bilateral and the multilateral fronts. Since early 2014, interested countries have convened five times for multilateral consultation meetings and reached consensus over issues of the AIIB's mandate, strategic focus, capital size, governance structure and headquarters location, which are included in the *Memorandum of Understanding on Establishing the Asian Infrastructure Investment Bank* (MOU). In October 2014, the first group of 22 prospective founding members signed the MOU in Beijing and jointly decided to set up the AIIB. Since then, the AIIB initiative further attracted worldwide attention and active participation from developed countries outside Asia. From mid-March 2015, the UK, Germany, France and Italy applied to join AIIB respectively. By April 15, 2015, the prospective founding members of AIIB reached 57, more than that of the World Bank and the ADB. Of these 57 countries, 37 are Asian countries, and 20 are non-regional countries, covering Asia, Oceania, Europe, Africa and South America, thus showing the broad representation. Four countries of the G7, 14 of the G20, and all the BRICS countries have joined AIIB. A crucial reason that AIIB has attracted major countries to join within a short period is because it responds rightly to the needs of the era and reflects as far as possible the interests of all parties. A quote from George Osborne, the former UK Chancellor of the Exchequer, may better explain why Western powers were attracted by AIIB: 'Joining AIIB at the founding stage will create an unrivalled opportunity for the UK and Asia to invest and grow together'.

The Articles of Agreement of the Asian Infrastructure Investment Bank (AOA) are a 'mini-constitution' observed at the founding of AIIB and during its operational stage. After signing the MOU, all parties agreed that meetings of the chief negotiators composed of finance deputies would be the main negotiation channel of the Bank's AOA. As the initiator – in line with the democratization trend in international relations, abiding by the principles of openness, inclusiveness and transparency, and with full respect to the concerns and appeals of all prospective founding members – China successfully co-chaired the Chief Negotiators Meetings with many other countries, including India, Kazakhstan and Singapore. By adopting multilateral principles that are acceptable to all, the negotiation process has been greatly accelerated. Thanks to the strong dedication and collaboration of all the prospective founding members, negotiation of the agreement was advanced efficiently. On 22 May 2015, 57 prospective founding members agreed on a high-quality text of the Articles of Agreement of AIIB, which laid a solid foundation of legislation for the official founding and early operation of the bank. On 29 June, the agreement-signing ceremony was held in Beijing, on which 50 prospective founding members including China signed the Articles of Agreement of AIIB. By the end of 2015, all 57 prospective founding members had signed.

In line with the AOA of AIIB, the bank aims to promote the sustainable development of the Asian economy, creating wealth and improving infrastructure inter-connectivity through investment in infrastructure and other productive sectors. It also intends to cooperate closely with other multilateral and bilateral development institutions and to promote regional cooperation and partnerships so as to address development challenges. The authorized capital stock of AIIB is USD 100 billion, with USD 20 billion paid in and USD 80 billion as callable shares. The ratio of capital stock contributed by regional members should not fall below 75% of the total subscribed capital stock unless otherwise agreed by a supermajority of the Board of Governors (more than two-thirds of the total number of governors representing not less than 75% of the total votes). With a supermajority, the Board of Governors can decide to increase the bank's authorized capital and reduce the capital ratio of regional countries, on the condition that the capital proportion of regional countries should be no less than 70% of the total. Within the ratio of 75 to 25, capital stock subscriptions of members within and beyond the region will be distributed mainly based on their GDP (calculated as a weighted average of market exchange rate [60%] and purchasing power parity [40%]). The total votes consist of share votes, basic votes and founding member votes exclusive to the founding members. The number of share votes held by every member is equal to the number of shares it holds in AIIB. Basic votes take up 12% of the total votes, distributed evenly among all members (including the founding members and ordinary members that join at a later stage). Each founding member is granted 600 founding member votes. Founding member votes together with basic votes take up about 15% of the total votes.

The official founding of AIIB marks a milestone and a major innovation in international development

On 25 December 2015, as the 17 prospective founding members ratified the AOA of AIIB and submitted their instruments of ratification, the legal threshold for the AOA to enter force was satisfied, and AIIB was officially founded. The official founding and operation of AIIB marks an important milestone in the process of reforming the international economic governance system and a major innovation in international development.

First, it is an innovation of the international economic governance model. Emerging economies contribute a great deal to the global economic recovery. But it is still hard for them to enjoy a voice consistent with their economic scale in international affairs. The international economic governance structure is in urgent need of reform, and progress in this regard has been slow. The establishment of AIIB – as an institution in which developing members hold more shares (67%)

than developed members, enjoying a bigger say – has not only complied with the evolving trend of the global economic landscape but demonstrated the resolution and determination of developing countries in working together to advance Asian regional development and improve the international economic governance model. As for its management structure, AIIB adopted a new mechanism – a non-resident Board of Directors, with the aim of reducing operational costs and improving the efficiency of daily administration and decision-making processes by management. In addition, by allowing constituencies with more than five member states to appoint two alternate directors, it further enhances the representation of its Board of Directors.

Second, it is an innovation of the development concept and business model. A persistent stance of AIIB is to seek common ground while acknowledging differences, to remain open and inclusive, and to pursue mutual benefits and win-win results. Being both practical and objective, AIIB solves the developmental problems faced by countries through concrete projects and therefore supports countries in building development patterns with their own characteristics. The bank enjoys a 'late-mover' advantage, which enables it to learn from other existing multilateral institutions. On this basis, AIIB can combine new trends in international development with the diversified demands of its developing member countries, expand investment and financing channels, create new business patterns and financing tools, and enhance investment efficiency. These abilities make it possible for AIIB to provide emerging and developing countries with individually tailored, high-quality infrastructure financing services at low cost and to offer financial support and guidance to even more nations in order to promote sustainable economic development and achieve common prosperity through infrastructure investment.

Third, it is an innovation of partnership. AIIB is committed to open regionalism, and, with the purpose of accomplishing mutual benefits, the institution and other multilateral development banks complement each other. With its inherent advantages and unique features, AIIB makes the current multilateral system more dynamic and promotes the common development of all multilateral institutions. Throughout history, the establishment of similar regional multilateral development banks such as the ADB and the EBRD did not weaken the influence of existing multilateral development banks like the World Bank. Instead, these newly built banks enhanced the overall strength of multilateral development finance. Being open, inclusive and win-win, AIIB builds closer cooperation partnerships with existing multilateral development banks, bilateral development agencies and private sectors. It explores various business patterns including joint financing as well as governmental and social capital cooperation. Joining hands with other agencies, the bank advances the infrastructure investment and financing level of emerging and developing countries, and it drives sustainable development and the recovery of the global economy. While developing countries make up the mainstay of AIIB membership, the bank has also attracted a large number of developed members. Such a unique strength makes it a bridge and a bond for facilitating both South-South and North-South cooperation.

Adhering to the principle of being international, rule-based and high-standard, AIIB stands as a professional, efficient and clean platform for infrastructure related financing

AIIB is the first multilateral development bank initiated by China. It follows the general operational pattern and principles of multilateral development banks and draws lessons from the experiences and best practices of existing multilateral development banks. Mutual learning and sharing helps AIIB operate at high standards. Since its opening, China, along with other member countries, has proactively participated in system-building and regulation creation via meetings of the Board of Governors, the Board of Directors and its subordinate committees. These efforts were aimed at ensuring that AIIB got off to a good start, gained a firm footing, and became an international, rule-based and high-standard institution.

With regard to establishment of the governance structure and inner organs, AIIB follows the modern governance pattern and has put in place a three-layer management system including the Board of Governors, the Board of Directors and management. The Board of Governors enjoys supreme authority. Besides the strategy, personnel, treasury and business operation departments, AIIB has also built a standardized and efficient anti-corruption unit of compliance, effectiveness, and integrity with multiple functions to offer a systematic guarantee for supervision, anti-corruption and effective operation. Under the creative governance structure featuring a non-resident Board of Directors, the bank has established a Policy and Strategy Committee and a Budget and Human Resources Committee of the Board to strengthen policy-related communication and exchanges among directors and between directors and the bank. AIIB also receives guidance from directors through meetings on theoretical matters and briefings on business, which enhances the understanding and trust of directors in the AIIB management.

With regard to operational policy and project loans, AIIB fully respects and draws on the successful experiences and practices of existing multilateral development banks in terms of environmental and social frameworks, procurement policies, project management and debt sustainability assessment. The bank draws up strict, practical and high-standard business policies. In 2016, the AIIB Board of Directors ratified more than ten business policies, and it launched the planning and discussion work of energy strategy, which was AIIB's first sectoral strategy. In the meantime, in order to build a clear and unique brand and allocate resources reasonably as soon as possible, AIIB proposed three strategic priorities: sustainable infrastructure, cross-border connectivity and mobilization of private resources. During the first year, the Board of Directors approved nine projects. The total of committed loans reached USD 1.73 billion.

With regard to human resource management, the AIIB members require management to strictly control the formulation of human resource policies and staff selection procedures and standards. This is to ensure that the bank can undertake global recruitment of its staff at all levels (including management) based on open and transparent multilateral procedures. By the end of 2016, the institution had employed 78 professionals, including the president and five vice presidents, from 24 countries and regions.

In 2016, AIIB signed a co-financing framework agreement with the World Bank and memorandums of understanding with ADB and EBRD. This became a strong support for the institution to expand its business with existing resources, as well as its influence, in its preliminary stage of operation. Six of the nine approved projects were co-financing projects, and the amount of loans accounted for about 73% of the total. The operational efficiency and growth prospects of the bank are highly regarded by the international community. Apart from its 57 founding members, by the end of 2016, there were around 30 economies from within and outside the Asian region that had officially applied to join AIIB. With this infusion of new blood, the bank will move further along the path toward becoming a global multilateral development bank.

AIIB has enjoyed a strong and steady start, but this is only the first step on a long journey. To be an international financial institution at the highest standard, persistent efforts will be needed. China believes that with the joint endeavours of all members, AIIB will become the model for a new type of multilateral development bank in the twenty-first century and will actively contribute to both infrastructure construction and sustainable development in Asia and the world at large.

9

RMB INTERNATIONALIZATION

History and outlook

Jun Ma and Huaizhu Xie

International use of the renminbi (RMB) maintained strong growth momentum between 2009 and mid-2015, although its pace has slowed since then. As of October 2016, the RMB ranked third in trade financing and sixth as a payment currency in the world. We expect RMB internationalization to regain momentum when the market's expectation of the RMB exchange rate stabilizes. This chapter reviews the developments in RMB internationalization, its policy framework and its market infrastructure, and discusses its outlook over the medium term.

Role of the RMB as an international currency

RMB for trade settlement and trade financing

International use of the RMB experienced rapid growth between 2009 and mid-2015. The proportion of cross-border payments and receipts between the Chinese Mainland and overseas parties settled in RMB increased to 28.7% in 2015, up from 2% in 2010. At the same time, the offshore RMB markets also grew rapidly, and international cooperation on RMB usage has continued to deepen. In 2016, the ratio of RMB cross-border payments declined to 28.2%, due partly to the depreciation of RMB against USD.

According to SWIFT statistics, in October 2016 the RMB ranked third for trade financing, with a global market share of 4.61%. The RMB ranked sixth for payments, with a market share of 1.67%, following the USD (40.55%), Euro (32.26%), GBP (7.61%), JPY (3.38%) and CAD (1.82%). According to data from the BIS, the RMB ranked eighth in foreign exchange (FX) transaction and international bond issuance, with a share of 2%, following the USD (43.8%), Euro (15.7%), JPY (10.8%), GBP (6.4%), AUD (3.5%), CAD (2.6%) and CHF (2.4%).

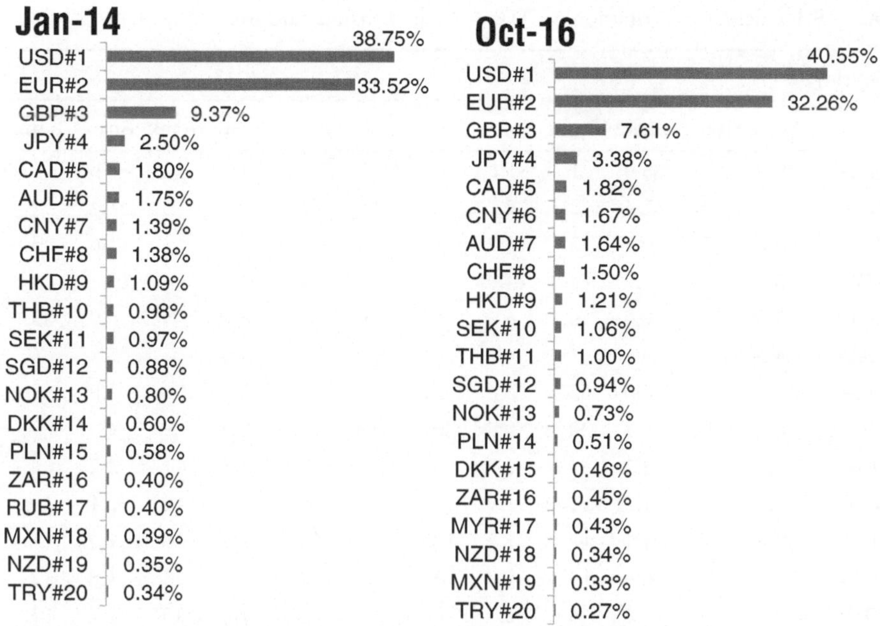

FIGURE 9.1 RMB's share as an international payments currency

Note: customer-initiated and institutional payments messages exchanged on SWIFT.

Source: SWIFT.

RMB as a reserve currency and investment currency

From the perspective of a reserve currency, as of the end of 2015, the balance of RMB assets held by foreign central banks or monetary authorities was about RMB 864.70 billion. These assets include bonds, stocks, deposits and other financial products denominated in RMB. Although this is equivalent to less than 1% of total global reserve assets[1] at the end of 2015, we believe that the potential for the RMB as a reserve currency is huge in the longer term.

The international holding of RMB assets by the private sector also expanded gradually. For instance, RMB assets held by non-residents (offshore institutions and individuals) in the onshore market amounted to RMB 3,225 billion by the end of November 2016. These included RMB 709 billion in stocks, RMB 835 billion in bonds, RMB 655 billion in loans to onshore entities, and RMB 1,027 billion in onshore RMB deposits. Note that the RMB assets held by non-residents in the offshore market were not included in these statistics.

RMB as an invoice currency

In the business world, an invoice currency is a currency that a firm uses to charge its customers. A buyer agrees to an invoice currency when signing a purchase agreement or placing an order. In either case, the invoice currency represents the way of

TABLE 9.1 Currency distribution of OTC foreign exchange turnover

Currency	*2001*		*2004*		*2007*		*2010*		*2013*		*2016*	
	Share	Rank	Share	Rank	Share	Rank	Share	Rank	Share	Rank	Share	Rank
USD	89.9	1	88.0	1	85.6	1	84.9	1	87	1	87.6	1
EUR	37.9	2	37.4	2	37	2	39.0	2	33.4	2	31.4	2
JPY	23.5	3	20.8	3	17.2	3	19.0	3	23	3	21.6	3
GBP	13.0	4	16.5	4	14.9	4	12.9	4	11.8	4	12.8	4
AUD	4.3	7	6.0	6	6.6	6	7.6	5	8.6	5	6.9	5
CAD	4.5	6	4.2	7	4.3	7	5.3	7	4.6	7	5.1	6
CHF	6.0	5	6.0	5	6.8	5	6.3	6	5.2	6	4.8	7
CNY	0.0	35	0.1	20	0.5	20	0.9	17	2.2	9	4	8
SEK	2.5	8	2.2	9	2.7	9	2.2	9	1.8	11	2.2	9
NZD	0.6	16	1.1	11	1.9	11	1.6	10	2	10	2.1	10
MXN	0.8	14	1.1	12	1.3	12	1.3	14	2.5	8	1.9	11
SGD	1.1	12	0.9	13	1.2	13	1.4	12	1.4	15	1.8	12
HKD	2.2	9	1.8	8	2.7	8	2.4	8	1.4	13	1.7	13
NOK	1.5	10	1.4	10	2.1	10	1.3	13	1.4	14	1.7	14
KRW	0.8	15	1.1	14	1.2	14	1.5	11	1.2	17	1.7	15
TRY	0.0	30	0.1	26	0.2	26	0.7	19	1.3	16	1.4	16
RUB	0.3	19	0.6	18	0.7	18	0.9	16	1.6	12	1.1	17
INR	0.2	21	0.3	19	0.7	19	0.9	15	1	20	1.1	18
BRL	0.5	17	0.3	21	0.4	21	0.7	21	1.1	19	1	19
ZAR	0.9	13	0.7	16	0.9	15	0.7	20	1.1	18	1	20
DKK	1.2	11	0.9	15	0.8	16	0.6	22	0.8	21	0.8	21
PLN	0.5	18	0.4	19	0.8	17	0.8	18	0.7	22	0.7	22
TWD	0.3	20	0.4	18	0.4	22	0.5	23	0.5	23	0.6	23
THB	0.2	24	0.2	22	0.2	25	0.2	26	0.3	27	0.4	24
MYR	0.1	26	0.1	30	0.1	28	0.3	25	0.4	25	0.4	25
HUF	0.0	33	0.2	23	0.3	23	0.4	24	0.4	24	0.3	26
SAR	0.1	27	0.0	32	0.1	32	0.1	34	0.1	34	0.3	27
CZK	0.2	22	0.2	24	0.2	24	0.2	27	0.4	26	0.3	28
ILS	0.1	25	0.1	26	0.2	27	0.2	31	0.2	29	0.3	29
CLP	0.2	23	0.1	25	0.1	30	0.2	29	0.3	28	0.2	30

Note: net-net basis, percentage shares of average daily turnover in April.

Source: BIS.

TABLE 9.2 RMB assets held onshore by non-residents

Unit: billion yuan

Instrument	*Dec 2013*	*Mar 2014*	*June 2014*	*Sept 2014*	*Dec 2014* ★	*Mar 2015*	*June 2015*	*Sept 2015*	*Dec 2015*	*Nov 2016*
Stocks	344.8	319.3	364.2	462.5	642.0	738.5	784.4	528.52.	598.67	709.25
Bonds	399.0	512.3	559.3	634.1	671.6	712.8	764.1	764.58	751.71	834.76
Loans	531.0	746.8	893.8	860.5	819.0	876.9	924.2	935.71	851.56	654.47
Deposits	1,604.9	1,984.0	2,045.1	2,237.2	2,372.2	2,024.8	2,120.4	1,664.18	1,538.07	1,027.10
Total	2,879.7	3,562.5	3,862.5	4,194.3	4,504.8	4,353.0	4,593.1	3,892.98	3,740.00	3,225.58

*From November 2014, stocks held by non-residents through Shanghai Stock Connect were included in the above statistics.

Source: People's Bank of China, China Securities Regulatory Commission, China Government Securities Depository Trust & Clearing, Shanghai Clearing House, China Securities Depository and Clearing Co.

measuring the price (unit of account) for an order. The invoice currency and amount are fixed at the time a firm issues the invoice. The invoice currency for a product can affect the price for the buyer if the exchange rate between the buyer's currency and the invoice currency changes during the sales process. In most cross-border trade transactions, invoice currencies are the same as the settlement currencies.

Along with growing RMB usage in international trade settlement, the role of the RMB in trade invoicing also grew significantly. In addition, the role of RMB as an invoice currency in financial transactions has expanded due to the development of offshore RMB financial products, such as bonds, stocks, futures and insurance policies.

On 24 July 2015, the People's Bank of China (PBC) released an announcement on Issues Concerning RMB Cross-Border Settlement of Crude Oil Futures Trading on Onshore Market (PBC Public Announcement [2015] No.19), regarding the use of the RMB as the invoice currency for crude oil futures traded on the onshore market. On 20 October 2015, the PBC issued RMB 5 billion of one-year central bank bills in London, with a coupon rate of 3.1%. It was the first time for the PBC to issue RMB-denominated central bank bills outside mainland China, which is conducive to expanding high credit rating RMB-denominated financial products in the offshore market.

The government has also promoted the role of the RMB as an invoice currency through reporting requirements. For example, the major statistical reports released by the General Administration of Customs (GAC) are now denominated mainly in RMB; the Ministry of Commerce (MOC) reports ODI and FDI statistics denominated in both US dollars and RMB; and the State Administration of Foreign Exchange (SAFE) publishes Balance of Payments and foreign debt statistics both in RMB and US dollars. Adopting the RMB as the invoicing currency in reporting of external economic activities by government agencies plays a guiding role in facilitating market participants to use the RMB as the invoice currency.

RMB's inclusion in the Special Drawing Right (SDR) basket

On 30 November 2015, the Executive Board of the IMF decided to include the RMB in the SDR currency basket as the fifth currency along with the US dollar (USD), Euro, Japanese yen (JPY) and British pound (GBP). The weight of the RMB in the SDR basket is 10.92%, whereas the weights of the USD, Euro, JPY and GBP are 41.73%, 30.93%, 8.33% and 8.09%, respectively. The new SDR basket became effective on 1 October 2016.

The inclusion of the RMB in the SDR currency basket is an acknowledgement of the international status of the RMB by the international community and is an important milestone in the integration of the Chinese economy into the global financial system. It demonstrates the belief of the international community that the continuation and deepening of China's financial reforms will contribute positively to a more robust international monetary and financial system.

We believe that the inclusion of the RMB in the SDR currency basket will increase the representativeness and attractiveness of the SDR. It will also further boost the confidence of market participants in its use for international transactions and in the holding of RMB denominated assets, including by foreign central banks. Domestically, the inclusion of the RMB in the SDR basket will serve as a stimulus for China to continue its market-oriented financial reforms and further open up its capital account.

The use of RMB in trade and direct investment

This section presents some recent statistics on the use of RMB for current account transactions and for FDI and ODI.

RMB settlement under the current account

In 2016, RMB settlement for cross-border transactions amounted to RMB 9.205 trillion, a decrease of 12.9% year-on-year, of which total receipts were RMB 3.45 trillion and total payments were RMB 5.75 trillion. This resulted in a net outflow of RMB 2.30 trillion, and a receipt-to-payment ratio of 1:1.67.

From January to November 2016, RMB settlement under the current account amounted to RMB 4.85 trillion, a decrease of 24.7% year-on-year. In this period, RMB settlement of goods trade was RMB 3.82 trillion, down 33% year-on-year. RMB settlement accounted for 28.7% of China's total merchandise imports and exports for January through November 2016, while the ratio was only 6% in 2011 and 2% in 2010. RMB settlement of cross-border services trade and other items under the current account was RMB 1.03 trillion in January through November 2016, up 39.6% year-on-year.

Geographically, by the end of November 2016, 192 countries and regions had conducted RMB settlement transactions with Mainland China. The following

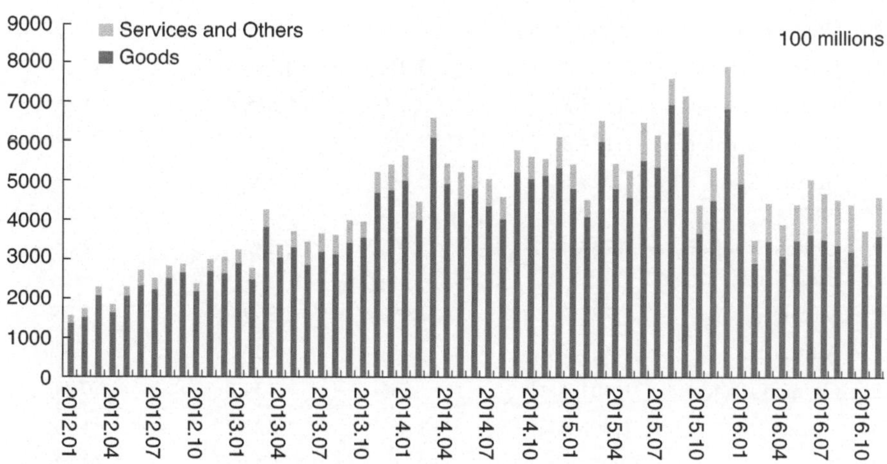

FIGURE 9.2 Monthly RMB settlement under the current account

Source: PBC.

TABLE 9.3 RMB settlement under the current account

			Unit: billion yuan
Period	*Goods Trade*	*Services Trade and Other Items*	*Total*
2009	1.95	0.61	2.56
2010	303.40	46.70	350.10
2011	1,387.07	207.86	1,588.93
2012	2,603.98	275.75	2,879.73
2013	4,136.84	499.94	4,636.78
2014	5,894.65	656.37	6,551.02
2015	6,391.14	843.22	7,234.36
2016.01–11	3,824.11	1,030.54	4,854.65

Source: PBC.

TABLE 9.4 Geographical distribution of cross-border RMB receipts and payments (2016)

	Country/Jurisdiction	*Jan–Nov 2016*		*2015*	
		Amount of Receipts (100 Millions)	*Percentage*	*Amount of Payments (100 Millions)*	*Percentage*
1	Hong Kong	49,546.9	53.8%	64,246.0	52.9%
2	Singapore	7,591.3	8.2%	13,012.2	10.7%
3	Germany	3,821.7	4.1%	3,655.1	3.0%
4	Chinese Taipei	3,800.6	4.1%	8,135.2	6.7%
5	Japan	3,634.9	3.9%	3,526.9	2.9%
6	South Korea	2,277.8	2.5%	1,838.4	1.5%
7	United Kingdom	2,174.5	2.4%	2,904.0	2.4%
8	British Virgin Islands	1,829.6	2.0%	2,402.5	2.0%
9	United States of America	1,733.4	1.9%	2,387.8	2.0%
10	Macau	1,720.7	1.9%	2,269.4	1.9%
11	Australia	1,439.1	1.6%	1,687.2	1.4%
12	Cayman Islands	1,401.4	1.5%	434.8	0.4%
13	Vietnam	1,305.8	1.4%	1,323.7	1.1%
14	Total	82,277.8	89.3%	107,823.3	88.8%

Source: PBC.

TABLE 9.5 RMB settlement of cross-border direct investment

Unit: billion yuan

Period	*ODI*	*FDI*	*Total*
2010	5.68	22.36	28.03
2011	26.59	100.68	127.27
2012	31.19	259.20	290.39
2013	86.68	457.09	543.76
2014	224.41	960.55	1,184.96
2015	736.17	1,587.10	2,323.27
Jan–Nov 2016	1,031.36	1,296.08	2,327.44

Source: PBC.

table lists those countries and regions with the highest RMB transactions with mainland China.

RMB settlement under capital and financial account

From January to November 2016, RMB settlement under the capital and financial account amounted to RMB 4.35 trillion, up 5.4% year-on-year, of which China's total receipts were RMB 1.47 trillion and total payments were RMB 2.88 trillion. This resulted in a net outflow of RMB 1.41 trillion, and the receipt-to-payment ratio was 1:1.96.

Outward direct investment (ODI). In January through November 2016, the volume of RMB settlement of ODI transactions reached RMB 1,031.36 billion, with YoY growth of 76.6%.

Foreign direct investment (FDI). In January through November 2016, the volume of RMB settlement of FDI transactions reached RMB 1,296.08 billion, a decline of 2.9% year-on-year.

Policies promoting RMB internationalization

Since 2009, the PBC has adopted a range of policies aimed at creating an enabling policy environment by removing the restrictions on RMB settlement of cross-border transactions. This section reviews these policies.

Policies supporting cross-border RMB settlement for current account transactions

The pilot programs for RMB settlement of cross-border trade transactions were initiated in July 2009, and their coverage was expanded to the whole country in

August 2011. In June 2014, the PBC allowed individuals and corporates to conduct RMB settlement of cross-border goods and services trade, and it provided support for banking institutions to cooperate with payment institutions in conducting cross-border RMB settlement businesses. The permission for RMB settlement helped to reduce currency risks and hedging costs for trading companies and individuals. In November 2014, the PBC further permitted multinational corporations (MNCs) to centralize their cross-border RMB payments and receipts under the current account. As a result, the transaction costs of RMB settlement were materially reduced, and currency mismatch was mitigated.

Policies supporting cross-border RMB transactions under the capital account

Direct investment

As the Chinese economy matures, its outward direct investment has begun to grow more rapidly compared with inward foreign direct investment. To enhance the role of RMB in direct investment, policies have been rolled out since 2011 to enable RMB settlement for ODI and FDI. From 2011, domestic institutions were allowed to use RMB to settle their ODI transactions, and RMB settlement of FDI transactions was also permitted. In September 2013, foreign investors were permitted to use RMB to establish, merge and acquire or take a stake in financial institutions in China. In June 2014, the procedures of RMB settlement in direct investment business were further simplified.

In November 2014, qualified MNCs were authorized to conduct two-way cross-border RMB cash-pooling business. By cash pooling, MNCs can centralize their RMB cash holdings in one account and freely use the cash in the pool according to business needs. As a consequence, internal RMB flows inside these qualified MNCs, inbound to and/or outbound from China, are less constrained by cross-border RMB regulations. This policy improved the cash management efficiency of MNCs. In September 2015, the PBC further amended the two-way cross-border RMB cash pooling framework for MNCs. The minimum requirements for qualification were reduced, and the cap on net RMB capital inflows was raised. These policy changes allowed more MNCs to participate in RMB cash pooling.

Cross-border RMB financing

As an international currency, the RMB should also be used as a funding currency (i.e. securing RMB funding in the form of loans and bonds), in addition to its role as an asset class. To develop the financing role of the RMB, the PBC has removed many policy restrictions since 2011, as follows:

- Since October 2011, domestic banks have been allowed to provide RMB loans for overseas projects. In July 2013, domestic banks were allowed to sell cross-border RMB trade finance assets. Domestic non-financial institutions were authorized to provide RMB guarantees to overseas projects and enterprises. Furthermore, in order to provide enough liquidity to the offshore market through overseas participating banks, the PBC relaxed the terms and quotas of their RMB financing account. As a result, the amount of financing from domestic correspondent banks (the agent conduit to the onshore money market) to participating banks has been substantially increased.

- In September 2014, the PBC allowed overseas non-financial institutions to issue RMB bonds (also called panda bonds) in the Chinese inter-bank bond market.
- In January 2016, the cross-border RMB financing policy framework was upgraded once again in accordance with the newly introduced PBC macro-prudential policy scheme. For qualified corporates and financial institutions in the pilot areas, the traditional ex-ante approval procedure for foreign debt administrated by the PBC and the State Administration of Foreign Exchange was replaced by a set of macro-prudential rules, which allowed banks and firms to borrow internationally based on ratios of their capital or net assets.
- In May 2016, the pilot scheme for macro-prudential management of cross-border financing was extended to the whole country. Domestic non-financial enterprises (excluding local government financing platform and real-estate corporations) and financial institutions whose establishments were approved by the PBC, China Banking Regulatory Commission (CBRC), China Securities Regulatory Commission (CSRC) and China Insurance Regulatory Commission (CIRC) had the discretion to raise financing from offshore markets, denominated in RMB as well as in foreign currency, within the caps calculated based on borrowing entities' capital or net assets.

Portfolio investment

Opening of the onshore bond market:

- In August 2010, the PBC allowed three types of overseas institutions (overseas central banks or monetary authorities, overseas RMB clearing banks and participating banks) to invest in the onshore interbank bond market. In May 2015, all overseas RMB clearing banks and participating banks were allowed to enter the interbank bond market to conduct repo transactions against the RMB bonds they hold, including pledged-style repo and outright repo.
- In July 2015, the PBC further improved the access of foreign central banks (monetary authorities), international financial institutions and sovereign wealth funds with RMB funds to the Chinese interbank bond market. This new policy removed the quota control on these foreign institutions and expanded the range of authorized investments to interest rate instruments, including cash bonds, repos, securities lending, bond forwards and interest-rate swaps. The above-mentioned institutions are also given the right to select their onshore agents as well as more flexible settlement channels.

- In September 2015, the PBC granted access to foreign central banks and similar institutions to enter the onshore inter-bank FX market. Foreign central banks and similar institutions were able to conduct trading in all listed FX products through bilateral or automatic matching (anonymous) trading mode, without any quota limits.
- In January 2016, the trading time of the Chinese interbank FX market was extended to 23:30, and more qualified overseas institutions were granted access. Qualified overseas participating banks could apply to China Foreign Exchange Trade System (CFETS) for China interbank FX market membership and conduct trading of all FX products on CFETS.
- In February 2016, the PBC allowed other (non-central-bank) qualified overseas institutional investors – including banks, insurance companies, pension funds and other asset managers – to make investments in the China interbank bond market without quota restrictions and any lock-up requirements.
- In February 2017, the State Administration of Foreign Exchange (SAFE) issued a circular permitting other (non-central-bank) qualified overseas investors to access the domestic FX hedging markets. This initiative could potentially reduce FX hedging costs for foreign investors that invest in the Chinese bond market.

Following these new initiatives, China's bond market is now largely open to international investors.

Opening of the onshore equity market:

- The RMB Qualified Foreign Institutional Investor (RQFII) pilot program was launched in December 2011, while the scope of the pilot program was expanded and the restrictions on the investment portfolio were relaxed in March 2013.
- The RMB Qualified Domestic Institutional Investors (RQDII) pilot program was introduced in November 2014, and, in the same month, the Shanghai–Hong Kong Stock Connect program was launched, which allowed overseas investors to invest in the Shanghai stock market without the need to go through onshore registration and account opening.
- In July 2015, the PBC clarified the rules concerning the RMB as the invoicing and settlement currency for domestic crude oil futures. Overseas traders and brokers have been allowed to participate in domestic crude oil futures trading since then.

Market infrastructure for RMB internationalization

To provide required RMB liquidity to the offshore market and to enhance clearing and settlement efficiency, the PBC has made substantial efforts in developing the infrastructure for RMB internationalization in recent years. These efforts include the establishment of the bilateral RMB swap programs, RMB clearing networks and the cross-border RMB payment system.

RMB swap agreements with other central banks

By the end of 2015, 33 central banks or monetary authorities had signed bilateral local currency swap agreements with the People's Bank of China (PBC). The total size of these agreements reached approximately RMB 3.31 trillion, and the actual usage of the swap lines has increased significantly in recent years. Bilateral swap agreements could become an important channel for foreign central banks to obtain RMB liquidity for many purposes: providing RMB liquidity to their domestic banks to facilitate trade and investment settled in RMB, conducting investment in RMB assets such as RMB bonds and, in extreme cases (such as in the case of Pakistan in 2013), providing balance of payments support for the country.

RMB clearing network

Over the past eight years, offshore RMB clearing centres have been established in 23 countries and regions, covering Southeast Asia, Western Europe, the Middle East, North America, South America, Oceania and Africa. The key element of such clearing systems was the appointment of a clearing bank in each centre. Clearing banks serve the functions of clearing cross-border RMB payments, providing RMB liquidity and offering various RMB financial products to local clients. The following table lists the overseas RMB clearing banks as of December 2016.

Cross-border Interbank Payment System (CIPS)

Phase One of CIPS launched on 8 October 2015. As an important financial infrastructure, CIPS provides clearing and payment services for financial institutions conducting cross-border and offshore RMB transactions. CIPS is designed to be built in two phases. CIPS Phase One adopts a gross settlement mechanism, facilitates processing of cross-border RMB business and supports settlement of cross-border trade in goods and services, cross-border direct investment and financing activities. CIPS Phase Two will adopt a mixed settlement model, which will be more efficient in the use of liquidity.

CIPS Phase One currently has the following features: real-time gross settlement for fund transfers by both individual customers and financial institutions; one-point entry by all direct participants for centralized clearing through a shortened route of clearing to achieve efficiency; operation hours that cover the time zones of Europe, Asia, Africa and Oceania.

The first batch of direct participants in CIPS includes 19 banks. In addition, 38 domestic banks and 138 overseas banks located in Asia, Europe, Oceania and Africa have participated in the system as indirect participants.

Outlook

Over the past eight years, the international role of the RMB has grown substantially. This has been fuelled by China's strong economic growth, its dominant

TABLE 9.6 Overseas RMB clearing banks

	Country or Region	*Time of Designation*	*Name of RMB Clearing Bank*
1	Hong Kong	Dec 2003	Bank of China (Hong Kong) Co. Ltd
2	Macau	Sept 2004	Macau Branch, Bank of China
3	Chinese Taipei	Dec 2012	Taipei Branch, Bank of China
4	Singapore	Feb 2013	Singapore Branch, Industrial and Commercial Bank of China
5	United Kingdom	June 2014	China Construction Bank (London) Co. Ltd
6	Germany	June 2014	Frankfurt Branch, Bank of China
7	South Korea	July 2014	Seoul Branch, Bank of Communications
8	France	Sept 2014	Paris Branch, Bank of China
9	Luxembourg	Sept 2014	Luxembourg Branch, Industrial and Commercial Bank of China
10	Qatar	Nov 2014	Doha Branch, Industrial and Commercial Bank of China
11	Canada	Nov 2014	Industrial and Commercial Bank of China (Canada) Co. Ltd
12	Australia	Nov 2014	Sydney Branch, Bank of China
13	Malaysia	Jan 2015	Bank Of China (Malaysia) Co. Ltd
14	Thailand	Jan 2015	Industrial and Commercial Bank of China (Thailand) Co. Ltd
15	Chile	May 2015	Chile Branch, China Construction Bank
16	Hungary	June 2015	Bank of China Limited Hungarian Branch
17	South Africa	July 2015	Bank of China Johannesburg Branch
18	Argentina	Sept 2015	Industrial and Commercial Bank of China (Argentina) Co. Ltd
19	Zambia	Sept 2015	Zambia Branch, Bank of China
20	Switzerland	Nov 2015	Zurich Branch, China Construction Bank
21	United States of America	Sept 2016	New York Branch, Bank of China
22	Russia	Sept 2016	Industrial and Commercial Bank of China (Moscow) Co. Ltd
23	United Arab Emirates	Dec 2016	Dubai Branch, Agricultural Bank of China

Source: PBC.

position in the global value chain and trade, its growing status as an exporter of capital as well as the various policy efforts by the government and the PBC. However, between mid-2015 and the end of 2016, the RMB depreciated against the USD due to a number of factors, including the rapid strengthening of the USD index, China's domestic stock market volatility and a decline in corporate profitability, although the CNY basket remained relatively stable during this period. As a result, offshore RMB market activities contracted accordingly. This contraction was partly due to the decline in offshore interest in holding RMB assets due to currency depreciation and partly related to the increase in offshore RMB interest rate volatility which dampened fundraising activities in the offshore RMB market. Some provisional measures to control cross-border RMB flows for disguised speculative moves also contributed to the decline in offshore RMB liquidity.

We believe that the contraction in offshore use of RMB during the past two years is a temporary setback and that RMB internationalization will resume its long-term trend when the market's expectation for the RMB exchange rate begins to stabilize. This long-term trend is fundamentally supported by China's economic scale (including GDP, trade and FDI) as a proportion of the global economy, its relatively stronger potential growth compared with most other economies and the country's long-term strategy of financial liberalization and opening of its capital account. Note that China contributes about 12% of global GDP and 30% of global growth, its share in global merchandize trade is roughly 15%, and it is the third-largest source of global FDI, but the RMB remains only about 1% of the global reserve system. This comparison shows that the RMB will eventually assume a more important role in the global financial system.

In the coming few years, a number of factors could help stabilize the market's expectation of the RMB exchange rate. First, the USD index may not continue its aggressive appreciation as in the past few years, given that it has risen by more than 25% in the past four years and over 40% in the past ten years. A reversal of the USD trend could remove the most important source of depreciation pressure on the RMB.

Second, China will continue to reform its exchange rate formation system over the medium term, with a view to allowing market forces to play a decisive role in exchange rate determination. When exchange rate formation becomes fully market based, there will no longer be any one-sided expectation for the RMB exchange rate (either appreciation or depreciation). By then, the absence of one-way betting by the market on the exchange rate will enable use of the RMB for international transactions to expand again and will facilitate the rise of the RMB as a reserve currency.

Third, China's capital account will eventually become more open, which will permit free capital flows, including cross-border RMB flows. In particular, China will further improve market access to the China Interbank Bond Market (CIBM) for global investors, by allowing foreign investors to access the local FX hedging market, extending trading hours and settlement dates, clarifying tax treatment on interest income and capital gains from bond investing, and allowing easier access to the CIBM by international collaboration on market infrastructure including custodian, clearing and settlement. As the third-largest bond market in the world, China's RMB 60 trillion bond market could become a very important asset class for global investors.

Fourth, China's One Belt One Road (OBOR) Initiative will create tremendous opportunities for Chinese companies to invest in the destination countries, and will also facilitate RMB usage in these countries. Many of these ODI projects will involve the purchase of equipment, raw materials, and services (such as engineering and construction services) from Chinese companies. Therefore, a substantial part of ODI in the OBOR countries could be settled in RMB, in order to reduce exchange rate conversion and hedging costs. The OBOR Initiative should enable financial institutions to extend more RMB loans, issue more RMB bonds and provide more RMB payments/clearing/settlement and cash management services.

In the past decade, significant progress has been made in the international usage of the RMB as a global clearing and settlement currency. We believe that other aspects of RMB internationalization, for instance the RMB as a reserve currency and an investment/funding currency, will also advance more visibly in the coming decade, due to capital account liberalization, the RMB's inclusion in the SDR basket, and the firm establishment of the OBOR Initiative. In addition, the rising demand for global diversification of financial assets (including by global institutional and individual investors) may also provide an impetus for the creation of more RMB-denominated assets in the overseas market.

Note

1 According to statistics from IMF Currency Composition of Official Foreign Exchange Reserves, total global reserve assets at the end of 2015 amounted to roughly USD 10,926 billion.

10

JAPAN'S EXPERIENCE OF FOREIGN INVESTMENT AND CHINA'S POLICY OPTIONS

Wenling Chen and Guanqun Mei

The Chinese economy has experienced rapid growth for almost 40 consecutive years since its reform and opening-up, becoming the second-largest economy in the world. Over the past decade or two, China's foreign investment has also continued expanding. Throughout the development of Chinese foreign investment in various countries, rather than being exclusive, the investment development mode has actually been similar to that of many countries at certain phases, especially to the path taken by Japan since the mid-1980s. At that time, Japan adopted a series of effective measures to facilitate its companies' efforts to 'go global', which serve as worthwhile lessons for China and also provide guidance for China in formulating its foreign investment policies.

Comparison of China and Japan's foreign investment development phase

After World War II, Japan restarted its industrialization process, and this eventually resulted in the fast rebound of its industrial production capacity and rapid economic growth. On the basis of the capital accumulated in this period, Japan started to invest overseas at the beginning of the 1970s. In 1985, the US, Japan, Germany, France and the UK signed the Plaza Accord, leading to the sharp appreciation of the Japanese yen. This dealt a heavy blow to Japan's export-oriented economic structure, and a huge volume of excessive domestic capital began to 'go global' in search of new markets. As a result, from 1985 to 1990, the average annual growth of foreign investment in Japan hit 51.1%. Despite the bursting of the economic bubble in the 1990s and the 2009–2010 global financial crisis, Japan's foreign investment, by and large, has continued to grow rapidly over the long term. The development process of China's foreign investment

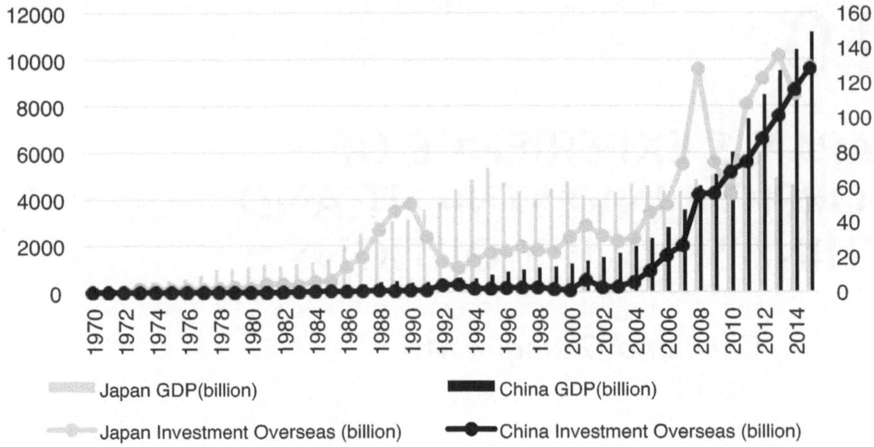

FIGURE 10.1 Comparison of investment overseas between China and Japan
Source: UNCTAD.

followed, and the trend it presents is very similar to that of Japan (Figure 10.1). China has been pushing ahead with reform and opening-up since the end of the 1970s, shifting its economic system from a planned to a market economy and thereby realizing significant economic growth and accumulating capital for foreign investment. This is akin to the rapid development of Japan's foreign investment only after its economic growth achieved during the period 1945–1985. China's entry into the WTO in 2001 was a major turning point for its foreign investment. Since 2002, China's foreign investment has been rapidly increasing, similar to the development track of Japan after 1985 (Feng, 2009). From 2002 to 2015, the average growth rate of China's foreign investment amounted to 24%, and the 'price scissors' between the foreign investments China received and invested abroad continued to narrow. As shown in Figure 10.2, China has gradually transformed from being merely a destination of foreign investment to an advanced player that allocates resources both at home and abroad, with balanced two-way investment.

Experience and lessons from Japan of promoting foreign investment

Official Development Assistance (ODA) plays the leading role in promoting outbound investment

Japan invests around the globe, and so it is of great significance for the security and risk control of its outbound investments to ensure that Japanese companies are welcomed in a favourable environment provided by the host country. The market environments and legal systems of developed countries in Europe and the

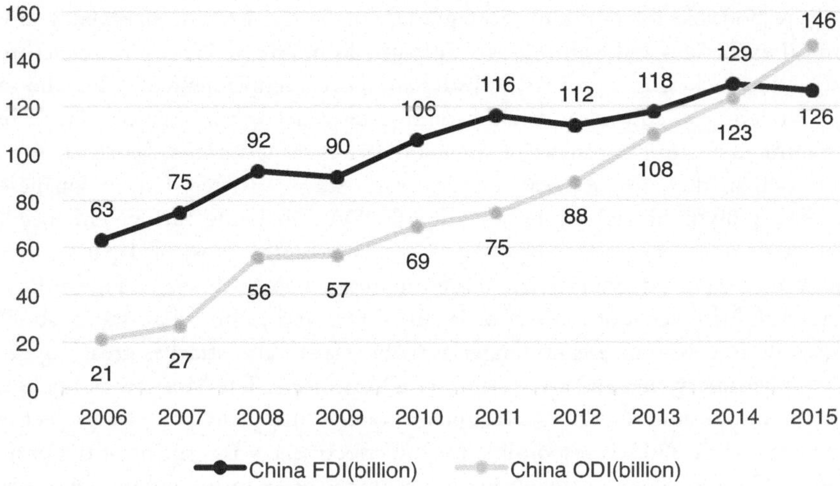

FIGURE 10.2 Comparison of Chinese FDI and ODI
Source: National Bureau of Statistics of China.

US are sound, with lower risks for investment. However, for key foreign investment destinations such as certain Southeast Asian and African countries, given their relatively poor business conditions, Japan has brought ODA into full play in steering its companies to 'go global'. By providing assistance to infrastructure construction and livelihood projects in the host countries, not only has it established mutual trust mechanisms at the governmental level with the host countries, deepened bilateral cooperation and won support and even preferential policies for Japanese companies from local governments, but it has also won recognition and support from the general public for Japan's national image and investments by Japanese companies. From 1970 to 1980, Japan's ODA grew from USD 458 million to USD 3.34 billion, ranking fourth globally only after that of the US, France and West Germany. In 1989, Japan surpassed the US for the first time and became the largest donor country in the world (Liu, 1997). And from 1993 to 2000, it remained the biggest donor for eight consecutive years. At present, Japan remains among the top five countries for providing foreign aid on a global scale.

Drawing in almost half of Japan's ODA, the Southeast Asia region is a key destination for Japan's outbound investment. Indonesia, Vietnam and the Philippines are the countries that have received the most assistance, absorbing 40%, 30% and 10% of the regional total, respectively (Zhang, 2014). Africa is another major region for Japan's ODA. In 2006, aid flowing into Africa even exceeded that of Southeast Asia. At the same time, these countries and regions are also important destinations for Japan's foreign investment. The Japanese government is only responsible for handling a small part of the ODA directly, and, for the rest, governmental economic cooperation organizations such as the Japan International Cooperation Agency are the main operators. JICA was established in 1974 and is mainly responsible for providing foreign aid, preferential loans, emergency aid, technical exchanges and training, etc. Foreign aid mainly refers to infrastructure construction including highways, railways and ports complemented by livelihood projects relating to education, healthcare, disaster relief and other areas. Japanese aid for infrastructure construction in Southeast Asia accounted for about 60% of the total in this area. Assistance at the early stage was free, but, as Japanese economic growth slowed while the role of ODA was being further enhanced, preferential loans gradually replaced free aid. Currently, most of Japan's ODA projects are supported by preferential low-interest loans. As shown in Figure 10.3, low-interest loans account for 85% of Japan's ODA, and technical assistance about 15%, while free assistance is no longer available. Japan also attaches great importance to the supervision and assessment of ODA projects. The Ministry of Foreign Affairs is responsible for the assessment of policies and plans before a project is conducted, while JICA is responsible for the effectiveness assessment of the project after it is complete and the evaluation report is open to the public. ODA has made a very positive impact on improving the national image of Japan as well as that of Japanese companies. JICA's survey of Southeast Asia showed that local people did not accept exchanges with Japan at the beginning due to the disasters imposed on them during World War II. However, as ODA came into effect and Japan began to invest in education in Myanmar and other Southeast Asian countries, Japan was more widely welcomed. About 90% of local people think that the relationship between their countries and Japan was 'friendly' and that Japan was a 'trustworthy' neighbour; 93% thought Japanese investment came with goodwill and had played an active role in promoting the economic development of the host countries.

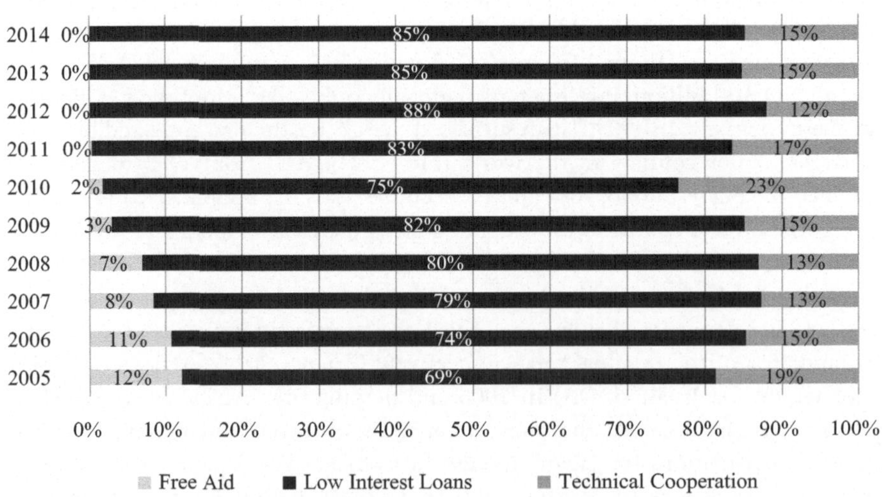

FIGURE 10.3 Structure of Japan's ODA

Source: Japan International Cooperation Agency.

Removing financing barriers in foreign investment for companies through policy finance

Financing is a key to foreign investment. Domestic financing is easier to accomplish as companies investing in their home countries are more familiar with the relevant laws and regulations and have developed close relationships with local financing partners. However, when investing overseas, companies need to get to know various capital partners, as the systems and environment are different. Financing difficulties caused by inconsistencies in mortgage, guarantee and rating standards become a major bottleneck during investment. To help companies deal with such problems, Japan has invested great efforts in developing policy financial tools that have been truly effective. At the early stage of Japan's foreign investment after World War II, typical policy financial institutions included the Export-Import Bank of Japan (JEXIM), which provided long-term credit support for export-oriented Japanese companies, and the Overseas Economic Cooperation Fund (OECF), which offered financial support to private Japanese companies when they invested in developing countries. In 1995, the two institutions merged into the Japan Bank for International Cooperation (JBIC), a major policy bank in Japan to support foreign investment. JBIC, through its cooperation with banks of the host countries or the branches of Japanese banks, transfers the capital to Japanese companies as credit in the form of two-step loans (TSL). In terms of supporting Japanese companies to 'go global', JBIC provides long-term low-interest loans to companies through overseas investment lending projects. Besides Japanese companies and overseas affiliates, prospective borrowers also include cooperation partners with equity investments in Japanese companies. As to direct loans, JBIC pays high attention to small and medium enterprises (SMEs), overseas strategic resource projects, and overseas merger and acquisition (M&A) projects including those of large companies. JBIC is funded fully by the government, and the source of the funding is mainly comprised of capital contributed by the Japanese government as well as government debts and JBIC bonds. Under special circumstance, the Japanese government can grant loans to JBIC through the Foreign Exchange Fund Special Account to support Japanese companies in investing abroad.

Supporting Japanese SMEs to invest abroad by improving the administrative screening and approval system, removing financing barriers, and providing information training services

The challenges and risks faced by SMEs are more daunting as compared with foreign investment by large companies. In order to assist the 'go global' efforts of SMEs, the Japanese government has provided them with support by improving the administrative screening and approval system, removing financing barriers and providing information training services.

In an effort to make SMEs more motivated to invest overseas, Japan has pushed forward with reform of the administrative screening and approval system step by

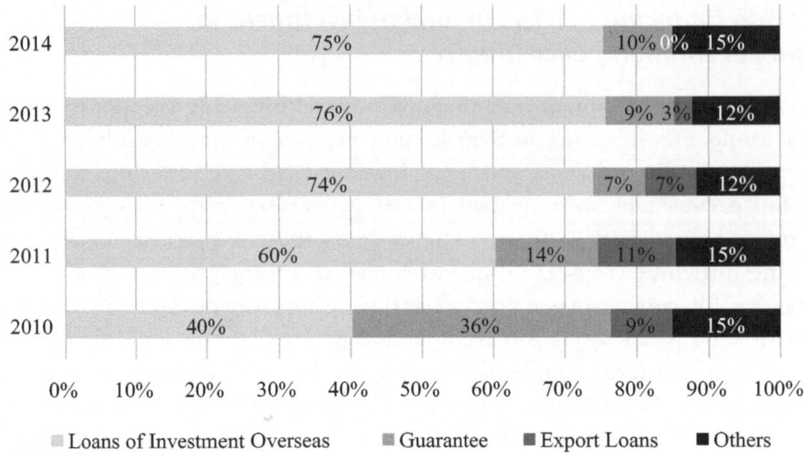

FIGURE 10.4 Structure of spending of JBIC

Source: Japan Bank for International Cooperation.

step. In the 1950s, the administrative system adopted by the Japanese government was on a deal-by-deal basis, and SMEs had to go through prolonged approval procedures when investing overseas. After bold reforms, a new management system was adopted under which foreign investments were divided into three categories: investments with special permission, investments for which prior application was required and investments that needed to be reported only after being conducted. Except for special industries and projects requiring government permission or approval, most investments by SMEs need only to be reported, and this has dramatically streamlined the foreign investment administrative process for SMEs.

Large companies are more capable of raising capital, either through direct financing including issuing shares and bonds or indirectly through bank credits. However, due to problems such as lack of mortgage assets and low credit rating, it is more difficult for SMEs to gain access to financing. In order to support SMEs' foreign investment efforts, the Japanese government has provided credit guarantees to SMEs. Since the 1950s, a two-tier credit guarantee system has been established, in which SMEs in each region receive guarantees from regional credit guarantee commissions (CGCs), while these CGCs are guaranteed by Japan Finance Corporation for Small and Medium Enterprise (JASME). Currently, about half of the SMEs in Japan have used such service. On the other hand, policy financial support is also given to the SMEs. As mentioned previously, JBIC has set up policy financial support projects targeted at SMEs. As well as JBIC, other policy financial institutions – including PPP Investment Fund, JASME, NLFC and Shoko Chukin Bank – also provide SMEs with special loans at low interest rates.

To enhance the risk management capability of SMEs, Japan has invested great efforts in training them. The Japanese government set up the Small and Medium Enterprise Agency under the Ministry of International Trade and Industry, the top organizational institution for managing SMEs, to enhance services and administration for overseas investors among SMEs. Promoted by the agency, the Japanese government has funded a host of private organizations – such as SMRJ, SME Diagnosis Organization, SME Revitalization Organization and JETRO – to provide investment training, information consultation, legal assistance and other services, in order to help SMEs with objective and comprehensive evaluation on investment conditions and projects at the early stage. Japan also established investment promotion organizations with the participation of governments of both sides and economic groups, which are dedicated to deepening SMEs' understanding of the host country investment environment, assisting in project-matching for SMEs and protecting as well as promoting investment activities of the SMEs in these countries. The Japan-China Investment Promotion Organization, established in June 1991, is a perfect example.

Establishment of the Overseas Investment Insurance System to help Japanese companies mitigate risk and develop markets

To cope with the various risks faced by companies in outbound investment, the Japanese government set up the Overseas Investment Insurance System in 1956, making Japan the second country with such a system following the US. In 1957, Overseas Investment Profit Insurance was set up, and in 1972 the Overseas Mineral Resource Investment Insurance System was established. Japan's overseas investment insurance covers deprivation of income, property ownership and the right for use, war, force majeure and so on. Japanese natural and legal persons can apply for the insurance when investing abroad. The total volume of claims settlement is quite considerable. For example, according to the overseas investment loss reserves system, Japanese companies that invest in the overseas resources, manufacturing and agricultural sectors can enjoy subsidies as high as 12% of the accumulative investment if they suffer losses abroad. In addition, companies can claim back 95% of losses due to war, social unrest and other risks induced by force majeure, and 40% of losses induced by the credit bankruptcy of their overseas partners.

Lessons from Japan: the hollowing-out of domestic industries and the bursting of the domestic asset bubble resulting from large-scale outbound investment

In 1985, five developed countries (the US, Japan, Germany, France and the UK) reached the Plaza Accord, which stipulated that the exchange rate of the US dollar to the Japanese yen, Deutschmark and other major currencies should be lowered in an orderly approach so as to cope with huge trade deficits with the US. Following the accord, the Japanese yen appreciated sharply, which on the one hand resulted in a large increase of paper wealth for the Japanese yen against the US dollar and the acceleration of foreign investment. On the other hand, the appreciation of the yen led to a rise in Japan's export costs, forcing some manufacturing companies to move to Southeast Asia and China, resulting in huge capital outflows. The rapid expansion of foreign investment took its toll on Japan's domestic economy in many ways, among which the most obvious challenge was that the domestic manufacturing industry was hollowing out. As shown in the figure below, since the execution of the Plaza Accord, the ratio of value added in Japanese manufacturing to GDP has continued to decrease by more than 10% compared with that of 1985. The manufacturing industry is the pillar industry in major countries, and the hollowing-out of the manufacturing industry is one of the root causes of Japan's two 'lost decades'. Furthermore, during the initial five-year period following the Plaza Accord, rapid capital outflows from Japan gave rise to a domestic liquidity shortage. Together with an ill-timed tight monetary policy introduced by the Bank of Japan, the domestic economic bubble that emerged during the period of high economic growth burst in the early 1990s. Property prices in Tokyo plummeted by two-thirds, and the country's financial system also suffered a heavy blow. The expansion of foreign investment in Japan is the inevitable result of its economic growth and the upgrading of its industrial structure. However, in the mid- to late 1980s, Japan poorly managed the relationship between foreign investment and domestic economic development while promoting foreign investment, and there was little coordination between foreign investment and domestic industrial upgrading. As a result, the large-scale capital outflow eventually had a detrimental impact on the domestic economy. This was a valuable lesson for Japan in the process of promoting foreign investment.

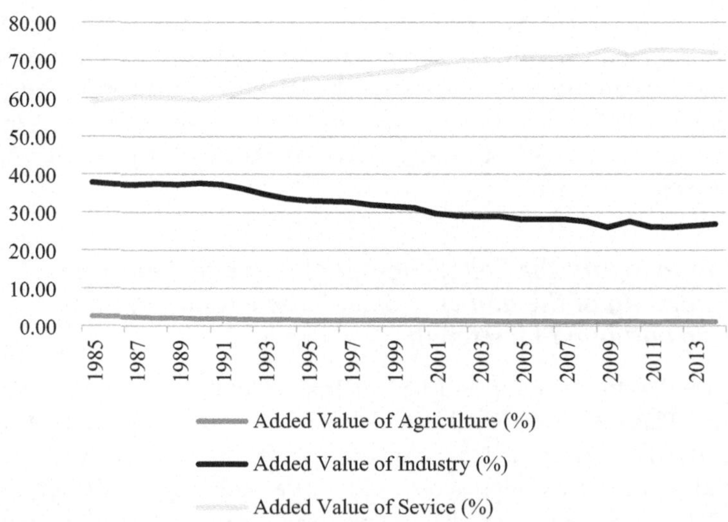

FIGURE 10.5 Change of Japan's industrial structure

Source: World Bank.

Implications for China's foreign investment policy options

Reforming the methods of utilizing foreign aid capital to facilitate the overseas operations of Chinese companies

Currently, many Chinese companies invest in developing regions such as Southeast Asia and Africa, and even in underdeveloped areas with poor infrastructure. As a result, enterprises often encounter problems in production and operation as well as product sales. In addition, social issues such as healthcare and education are pervasive in these regions and have restricted the development of consumption in host countries and the supply of high-quality labour forces. When faced with similar situations, Japan chose to use foreign aid capital to promote infrastructure construction and improve living conditions in the host countries, which merits China's attention. To date, China has been an important contributor to foreign aid globally. However, problems such as low efficiency, the singular aid model and scattered aid projects with unsatisfactory effects are still prominent. China should learn from Japan's experience and reform its methods of using capital for foreign aid, so as to bring money into full play and pave the way for foreign investment by Chinese companies. For example, free assistance and direct investment could be reduced or replaced by expanding the scale of preferential loans with low- or zero-interest rates, and the free assistance could be used to subsidize the interest of loans. Priority should be given to key infrastructure construction and livelihood projects that can strengthen local economic development, rather than investing indiscriminately in too many projects to maximize the utilization of funds. Third-party project evaluation – including project selection and feasibility studies at the early stage, progress follow-up at the medium phase, and quality checks and effectiveness evaluation at the later phase – should also be enhanced with the help of professional institutions. China's national image may be improved through foreign assistance and thus benefit the investment activities of Chinese companies.

Improving domestic as well as international capital channels to further develop policy finance and reduce financing difficulties

Financing difficulties are the most daunting challenge for Chinese companies when investing overseas. With about 30,000 Chinese companies operating in 185 countries and regions, there are around 150 Chinese financial enterprises in only 41 countries and just 90 in such key 'go global' regions as Asia, Africa, Latin America, Central Europe and Eastern Europe. The pace of internationalization of Chinese financial enterprises falls far behind actual demand. Chinese companies are also faced with problems when financing through foreign financial institutions, as they have just only started to go global and thus do not have large fixed assets which enable them to acquire mortgage loans. Policy barriers still exist for China to open its financial market, and it is often hard to obtain offshore financing against domestic guarantee via companies' domestic assets. Measures adopted by Japan in coping with financing difficulties for its 'go global' companies can be borrowed, such as the establishment of development financial institutions. On the one hand, China should actively promote its financial marketization and liberalization process, eliminate policy barriers relating to offshore financing against domestic guarantees, and improve the domestic as well as overseas circulation channels of capital. On the other hand, the significant role of policy finance should be brought into better play. Currently, policy financial institutions such as the China Development Bank and the Export-Import Bank of China have played a key role in China's foreign investment. In the future, the JBIC model can be borrowed. Differences between the role of policy and commercial finance should be further identified so as to make better use of important tools such as concessional loans and preferential loans for foreign aid, in order to provide stronger support to 'go global' SMEs and key M&A projects. Meanwhile, more encouragement should be given to China's financial institutions to 'go global' and establish overseas branches and service networks to provide financing services to Chinese companies that invest abroad.

Streamlining foreign investment administrative approval procedures and facilitating the 'go global' efforts of companies

In the past, companies needed to go through time-consuming and complicated procedures due to the conventional Chinese foreign investment screening and approval system. 'Go global' companies encountered great inconvenience in foreign exchange management, equipment and materials export, and port entry and exit. The investment management system fell short of foreign investment requirements. Since 2013, the Chinese government has invested great efforts in streamlining administration and delegating powers, as well as promoting reform of the administrative screening and approval system. Measures include reform of the means of foreign investment management, including amendment of the *Offshore Investment Management Approach*, which has switched the administrative mode for comprehensive offshore investment approvals to 'record-filing first with management as a supplement' to reduce the scope of screening to the minimum and improve overseas investment facilitation. However, the management efficiency of capital outflow and foreign exchange utilization by Chinese companies is still low. In the future, such problems will be resolved incrementally with the improvement of offshore investment administration and China's more open financial system.

Further improvement of the risk management system to ensure sound development of foreign investment

Similar to Japan, Chinese companies are faced with various political, social and security risks in host countries. For example, the Myitsone Hydropower Station, sponsored by the State Power Investment Corporation, came to a halt as Myanmar ceased construction unilaterally, resulting in a heavy loss to the Chinese side.

CITIC Pacific Limited suffered a forex loss as high as HKD 15.9 billion due to exchange rate fluctuations in 2008 when the company acquired the iron ore project in Australia. Due to the war in Libya and turmoil in Syria, Chinese companies with investments in those regions also suffered disastrous losses. There is much that points to the need for China to set up a sound risk control system as soon as possible. One of the key factors causing the failure of many Chinese companies when investing overseas is their lack of understanding of local circumstances and rules, regulations and policies, as well as of religions, people and culture. The Chinese government, industry associations and think tanks should provide better information services and make efforts to offer country-specific investment guidance, establish information-sharing platforms, and provide legal services and risk warnings. Companies should also be encouraged to utilize third-party investment consultations and assessments before investing, so as to minimise the risks. China could also set up a proper foreign investment insurance system like that of Japan. Although it has established policy insurance institutions such as Sinosure, the scale, types and services of insurance cannot meet the actual demand and scope in the area of foreign investment.

Continuing to promote internationalization of the RMB and properly handling the relationship between foreign investment and domestic development

With growth in China's economic power, the increased proportion of foreign trade in global trade volume and the scale of bilateral investment, the RMB has been enjoying an ever-rising status in the international monetary system, gradually becoming an important currency for global trade settlement, investment and reserves. The internationalization of the RMB has made significant achievements. China has also actively promoted interest-rate marketization reform and established a more open and transparent financial system in order to create more favourable conditions for overseas investors and boost the 'go global' efforts of Chinese companies. In this process, China must draw lessons from the experience of Japan in the 1980s, when the revaluation of the Japanese yen and large-scale foreign investment led to the hollowing-out of domestic industries. The relationship between the 'go global' efforts of industry and capital and stable, sustainable domestic economic development should be properly handled. The internationalization process of the RMB needs to be promoted step by step. The capability of the Central Bank to regulate and control the capital market should be enhanced to keep the RMB exchange rate fluctuating steadily at the market equilibrium level and ensure proper management of short-term cross-border speculative capital flows.

A call for creative solutions

Although the development features of Chinese and Japanese foreign investment are similar, China faces many problems that Japan has never or seldom encountered, as the situation of the two countries and the international environment in which they operate are different. The Japanese experience is not a panacea for all the problems faced by China, and China must explore more creative and innovative solutions. For example, Japan was faced with rapidly expanding globalization and promotion of the WTO at the initial stage of overseas investment. Nowadays, China is faced with a new environment characterised by regional integration that is on track to surpass the globalization trend. China's foreign investment has been challenged by a higher standard and protectionism. China needs to sign FTAs with more countries and regions and establish a bilateral and multi-lateral free trade system on a global scale to deepen the connections between itself and the global economy. For instance, the shift of China's labour-intensive industries to Southeast Asia, South Asia, Africa and other regions requires it to enhance economic and trade partnerships with these areas. However, due to their relatively slow economic development, less advanced infrastructure and different cultural environments, China proposed the One Belt One Road Initiative and established the Asian Infrastructure Investment Bank, with the hope of promoting co-construction, co-sharing and win-win cooperation through the connectivity of policy, road, trade, currency and people. Chinese companies are also faced with stringent security reviews when investing abroad, and certain investments and M&A projects may still suffer great setbacks, despite being in compliance with the laws and regulations of the host countries. Japan was once mired in a similar situation, but for China the situation is even more challenging. In the future, China should enhance coordination on investment security reviews with the relevant countries.

References

Brown, K & Wood, P 2009, 'Chinese overseas direct investment and the economic crisis: Reaching out', *The World Today*, vol. 65, no. 1, pp. 15–16.

Feng, J 2009, 'Comparative analysis on overseas direct investment liberalization between PRC and Japan', *Matsuyama University Review*, vol. 21, pp. 23–29.

Liu, C 1997, 'Historical review of investment overseas of Japan after World War II', *Japanese Studies*, vol. 13, no. 2, pp. 36–53.

Zhang, B 2014, 'Analysis and evaluation of aid from Japan to Southeast Asia countries', *International Economic Cooperation*, vol. 30, no. 4, pp. 38–42.

PART III

The dynamics of Chinese ODI

11

FROM ACTIVE BUYERS TO ACTIVE OWNERS

Gordon Orr and David Cogman

We are now a decade past Lenovo's acquisition of IBM PC – the first major outbound acquisition by a Chinese company. Since then, almost 700 deals over $100m have happened. Chinese investors have gone from rarities in the international deal market to regular participants in major auctions.

Post-2008, there was considerable discussion of the impact of outbound Chinese investment. This mostly considered the impact on sellers – whether this new capital was bidding up asset prices, whether governments should fear Chinese buyers – or looked at the role capital outflows play in China's economic development. While these are relevant questions, more important is the buyers' results. Were the investments successful? Did they create value? If not, why not?

We examine here the experience of the past decade. The track record has been mixed: most deals did not clearly accomplish their original objectives. One major reason for that is simply bad timing – something no company can fully avoid. But another is what Chinese companies did – or didn't do – after closing deals.

Historically, many Chinese acquirers had limited ability to manage acquisitions post-deal: this constrained their ability to extract synergies. With the emergence of a pool of Chinese management capable of operating internationally, that no longer has to be the case. More companies are taking a hands-on approach to integration, recognizing the importance of actively managing their acquisitions while appreciating differences in culture and operating model. We expect that soon this will become the norm rather than the exception.

The decade in review

Assessing the 'success' of an acquisition is subjective. The analysis has no 'control' – we never know what *would* have happened without the deal. Share price reactions to deals tell you whether the market liked the concept at announcement, but say nothing about the subsequent execution. To properly assess the success of a deal, one must look at the original objectives and whether they were met.

By this standard, the past decade's results look less than impressive. Around 60% of outbound investments by Chinese companies, almost 300 billion dollars, created little or no value for acquirers.

The resource curse

The deals with the worst success rate were the late 2000s' resource acquisitions. The decade preceding 2008 saw China's resource import prices rise by 18% CAGR for ten years. This was a challenge to companies' international competitiveness and a national security issue.

As a result, 43% of the deals done in the past decade (217 deals, representing 56% of total outbound investment value) involved natural resources; 80% of this happened during the run-up in commodities prices, before their peak in 2013; the remainder happened in the three years following, when a dip in prices seemed like a buying opportunity. However, commodity prices mostly remained below the prices when these deals were done. In 84% of the deals we reviewed, 89% of deal value, these deals did not create value for the acquirer, losing on average around 10% of the initial investment, in some cases as much as 25%.

Financial diversification and relationship-building

A second group with limited success is investments into listed companies that remain listed post-deal, motivated either by financial diversification or by building relationships with the target – this was 24% of the deals done (119 deals,

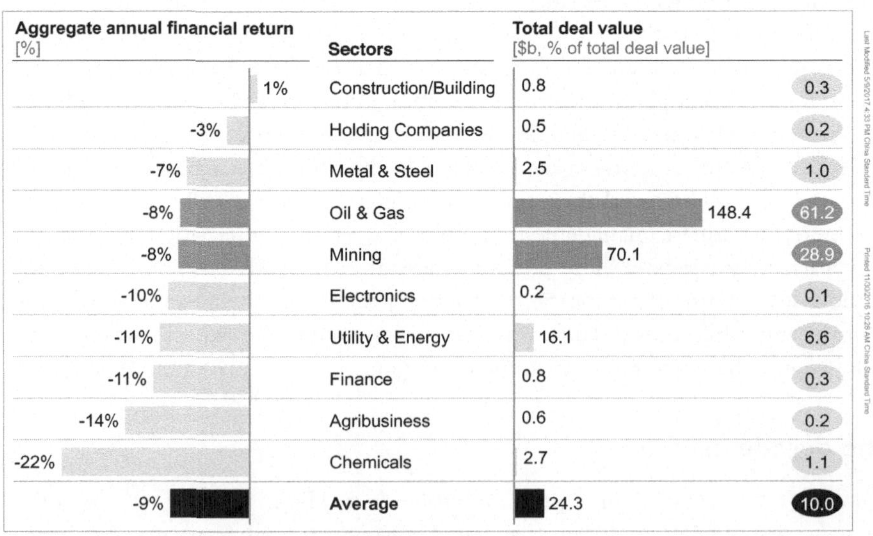

FIGURE 11.1 Investment mix for resource deals

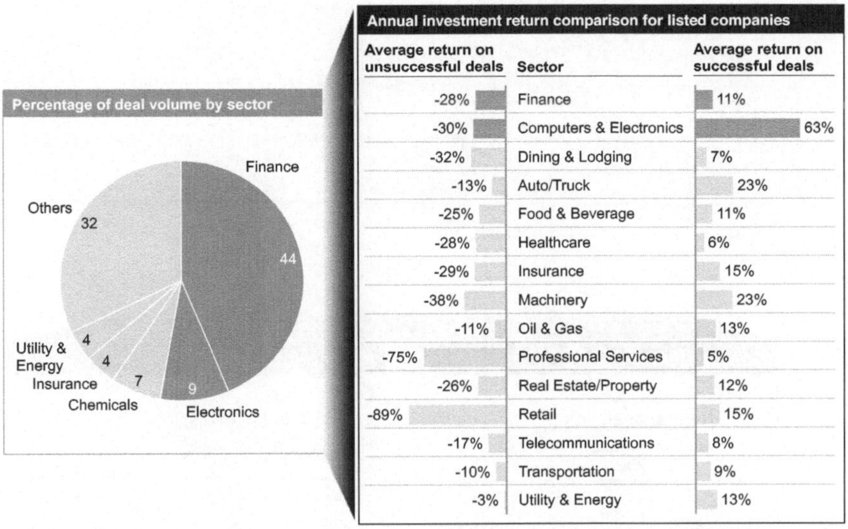

1 Others include sectors has less than 4%: Auto, Dining & Lodging, Food & Beverage, Forestry, Healthcare, Holding Companies, Leisure, Machinery, Oil& Gas, Professional Services, Property, Transportation

SOURCE: team analysis

FIGURE 11.2 Sector mix of diversification/relationship-building deals

18% of total value). These targets generally kept considerable independence post-acquisition. This approach was successful domestically, but not so abroad. On average, the companies invested lost about 7% p.a. of their value from date of investment to date. If we include opportunity cost – making a similar minority investment in Chinese equities, which rose on average 15% p.a. since 2008 – the track record looks considerably worse. Bad timing again played a major role: most of these deals were concentrated in financial services and in computers and electronics, each of which lost around 30% of their initial investments on average. The hardest-hit sectors were retail and professional services: deals there lost on average more than 70% of the initial investment.

Majority investments into listed companies did slightly better than minority investments. On average, the share prices of these deals lost around 2% per annum post-investment; however, the range was wide, with more than half of deals yielding positive returns. There is more evidence of synergies being captured by acquirers in their core business for majority control deals – bringing technology or products into the China market and creating genuine growth in the acquirer's profits.

Identifying the successes

Slightly over a quarter of the deals done do not fall into either of these categories. We analysed the stated objectives of these deals – product, technology or cost – and looked at whether these objectives had been achieved. We found that around 70% of these deals clearly did achieve their objectives. For control deals, that success rate rose to 75% vs 60% for the non-control deals.

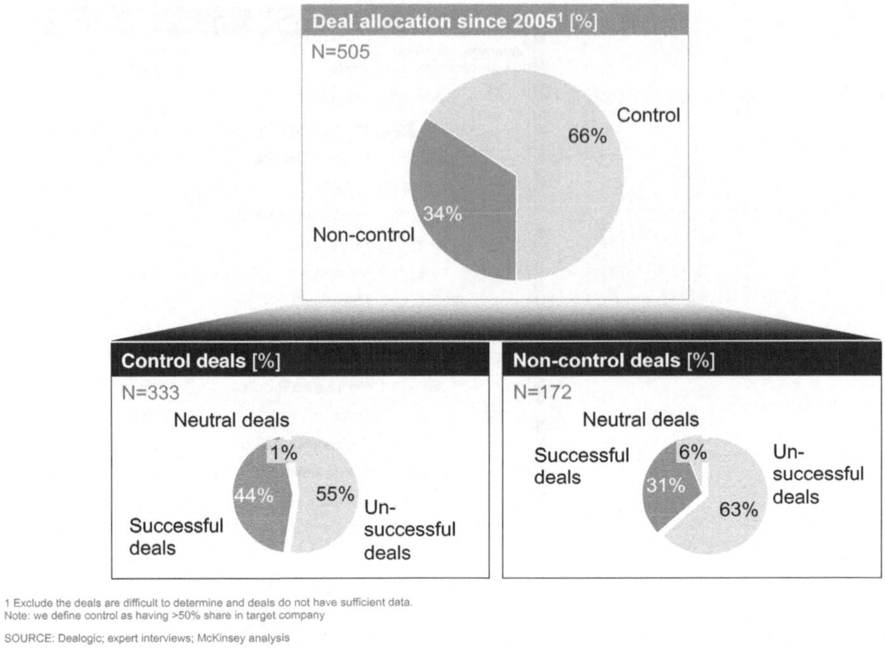

FIGURE 11.3 Non-control investments generally did worse than control investments

*1 Excluding deals that are difficult to determine and deals without sufficient data.

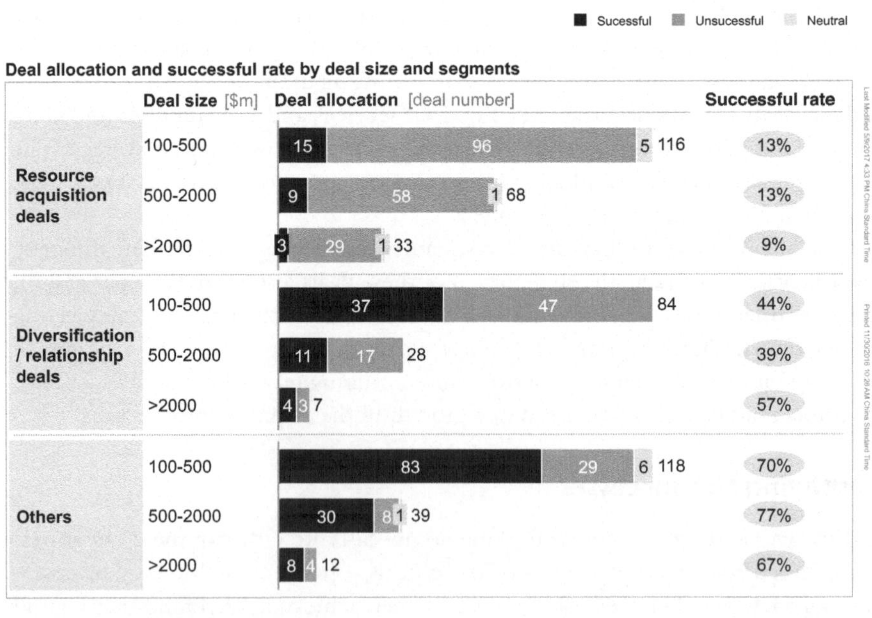

FIGURE 11.4 Success rates by deal size

Looking across the full set of deals, we see that level of control matters: 34% of the total 505 deals were non-control investments, of which only about 30% were successful. For control investments, the success rate rises to around 45%.

This paints a stark picture. Of 505 deals and $432bn of deal value, only 200, worth $146bn, clearly achieved their objectives. Moreover, this happened at a time when M&A was creating value for most companies.

In the post-2008 period, when money became historically cheap, equity markets were encouraging companies to acquire for the first time in decades, to convert cheap funding into productive assets. Asian acquirers in particular were rewarded richly by investors for acquiring. The market more consistently rewarded Asian acquirers, on average, than Western acquirers for the value their deals were expected to create. What, then, caused the problems for Chinese acquirers?

The challenge of integration

These are still early days for outbound M&A. But there is enough experience to highlight some important lessons. The primary controllable reason for failure is lack of integration post-deal. In too many cases, the Chinese acquirers were hesitant to take control post-deal.

Chinese companies do not, generally, pay a much higher premium than other buyers. Over the past year, the average premium paid by Chinese acquirers was 25% vs 32% for all cross-border deals. But the prices paid assume that they will extract some synergies, which is possible only through active management of the asset post-deal. Therein lies the challenge.

Most Chinese companies pre-2010 – and most today – had very limited ability to operate overseas assets. Their managers with international experience tended to be in sales or procurement; the cadre of experienced managers who had run businesses outside China was small, even smaller in the SOE sector where salary constraints made hiring managers returning from overseas difficult. Moreover, experience needs to be specific; managers need to operate in the language and business culture of the target's home country.

Models of integration

Chinese acquirers today are extremely diverse: there is no single 'correct' model of integration for all situations. We have seen almost every possible approach be successful in one situation and fail in another. Acquirers need to learn which to apply when.

Looking at the experience of the past decade, post-deal management fell into five broad approaches. Of these, two did not involve meaningful integration but were essentially arms-length management of an asset. Three involved actual integration, but to differing degrees:

- **'Hands-off'**, where the acquirer keeps the target's operations separate and manages primarily through the board;

- **'Turnaround'**, where the buyer uses management appointments, compensation and incentives to put pressure on a standalone asset to perform better;
- **'Full-on'** integration, where the target is as far as possible brought into the acquirer's management system, requiring restructuring of how the target functions;
- **'Selective'** integration, where the target is kept largely separate, but with closer collaboration in one or two specific areas where there are significant synergies available; and
- **'Progressive'** integration, which starts by integrating one functional area and gradually expands to others.

We discuss each below and illustrate them with specific deals. This is not intended to praise or criticize management teams: it is impossible to say how the stories would have played out under different management. However, there are useful lessons to be drawn from both successful and less-than-successful deals.

Minimalist post-deal management

Standard thinking on integration is to do it as fast and comprehensively as possible, involving both organizations extensively. This approach pervades Western business literature on the topic.

Early Chinese outbound acquisitions largely did the opposite. Managers on either side had difficulty working together, and they quickly found that the two companies' management models were incompatible. Even basic corporate processes like budgeting, planning and HR looked so different that there seemed little point trying to harmonize them: what works in a Chinese context could not be expected to work in a Western context.

They therefore focused on governance as the primary point of control. Strategy, investment and budgeting were decided at the acquiree's board. Typically there was one 'bridge' person on each side – a pair of senior managers who would often talk informally – but there was no 'pairing' of managers across functional areas such as finance and operations as is normal in post-merger integration, nor transplanting of management processes from acquirer to target.

This was a rational response to a challenging problem, and often acquirers were happy with the outcomes. State Grid exercises control of ElectraNet mainly through governance mechanisms at the board level, but with little involvement in operational decisions. Chinese managers placed into ElectraNet play liaison roles rather than direct operational management. A similar setup was used at Putzmeister after Sany's acquisition. There was little Sany involvement in the day-to-day business, and Putzmeister's management team remained largely intact. Planning and strategy are aligned with Sany management through their participation in Putzmeister's supervisory board.

This approach remains the ingoing assumption for many acquirers. In several Chinese outbound deals in 2016, including Ctrip-Skyscanner, ChemChina-

Syngenta, COFCO-Nidera and Midea-Kuka, there was explicit announcement pre-deal that targets would retain separate management and operations for several years post-deal. This was in part to reassure stakeholders but also reflects a degree of caution.

This model can be effective if value creation derives from bringing acquirers' order flow to targets, or from taking IP from targets to acquirers. But then, could the benefits have been achieved through commercial cooperation, without a full acquisition? Are these deals really more than just financial investments?

The risks, moreover, are obvious. Success is dependent on a few personal relationships. The model cuts off the acquirer from access to the 'controls' for the business. Significant operational improvements in the target are usually impossible, even if the target suffers a performance downturn.

Minimizing these risks requires establishing a 'control environment' early on in the deal – defining a set of basic management information that you see weekly, monthly and quarterly that highlights any problems early enough to take action. The information needed varies from deal to deal but is never purely financial: it includes key indicators in operations, marketing and sales, and sometimes R&D and product development. This requires deep understanding of the target business and familiarity with what could go wrong: however, companies pursuing a 'hands-off' approach to post-deal management often do so precisely because they lack this depth.

Full integration

Some Chinese acquirers attempted full integration. These were in many, but not all cases, unsuccessful – in some cases spectacularly so. Generally these were deals with large cost synergies, requiring genuine integration to capture.

One example was SAIC's acquisition of Korea's SsangYong Motor. This looked like a good deal: for half a billion dollars they acquired a complete IP and R&D platform to develop domestic Chinese products. The challenge was turning around the Korean business. Chinese managers tasked with this lacked the operating and cultural skills to make this work. Their attempts to restructure management and put in place new working practices quickly lost them the support of the Korean executives, union and workforce. Unions rallied public sentiment against SAIC: Korean media supported them. In 2009 the company entered bankruptcy, and in 2010 India's Mahindra & Mahindra acquired majority control.

The Koreans complained about illegal technology exports, but the underlying issues were more fundamental. From the outset the Koreans resented attempts to impose a foreign operating model. They felt disrespected and misunderstood by the acquirer's team. Had SAIC chosen to keep SsangYong's operations largely separate, perhaps it would have retained enough goodwill to achieve a turnaround. However, this deal left a cloud over Chinese acquirers' reputation in Korea that persists to this day.

The stand-out success from the early years was Lenovo, and in their multiple acquisitions we find a very different story on 'full' integration – of how and why it can succeed.

Lenovo's goal was to become global #1, but expanding organically beyond China was too slow. This deal in one stroke took them from domestic to global leader. However, the economics depended heavily on operational synergies. Synergies almost equal to the price paid were available through procurement, but only if the two businesses fully integrated.

To achieve this, Lenovo was willing to tear up and rebuild its own organization: without that level of commitment, the deal probably would not have worked. It accepted that many of the current Chinese management would need to step back, at least for a while, and re-learn how to operate in this new environment. It also revamped the board to bring in more international experience. It was also willing to create new management processes in which foreign and Chinese leadership could both operate, which involved some painful choices, such as exiting previously successful managers who could not adapt.

After acquiring IBM PC, Lenovo identified 200 high-potential future global leaders. They emphasized 'world-sourcing', locating functional centres where the best talent was available, meaning that many decisions were no longer made in Beijing. These were all steps that few Chinese acquirers were willing to take then: indeed even now, most would still be unwilling.

Lenovo institutionalized its approach to integration after this deal and did more than five subsequent acquisitions using a similar template. This was a significant investment of time and effort, justified only by commitment to further growth by acquisition. Today, 60% of Lenovo's top-20 leadership team are non-Chinese, all with extensive international exposure.

Many companies – Chinese and foreign – think that 'integration' means bringing the acquired company into your management model. Often that isn't the best choice: to get the best results, you may need to use what you've bought to change your own business. Lenovo went from being a Chinese company to an international company with Chinese heritage. For most Chinese acquirers, that would be unappealing: they want to become an international business without changing how they operate at home. As many foreign acquirers have found as they expanded abroad, that is difficult.

Turnarounds

One type of deal rarely seen among outbound acquisitions is the purchase of a distressed manufacturing business. Post-2008 there have been many acquisitions of financially distressed businesses, such as real estate assets or struggling mines where commodity prices had fallen. But it was unusual to see Chinese buyers purchasing manufacturing companies in or near bankruptcy with the intention of 'fixing' the business. Few Chinese companies have these skills. Turnaround of a distressed business is an unusual and special ability. In the growth-focused China market of the 1990s and 2000s, few Chinese managers ever needed to develop this particular skillset.

There were some early examples of this, such as SEC's purchase of printing equipment manufacturer Goss International in 2007, which they subsequently divested to PE firm American Industrials Partners in 2015. In recent years there have been a small but growing number of Chinese companies attempting a genuine turnaround of a foreign business. Perhaps the most notable example was Shuanghui's acquisition of Smithfield. The political and financing aspects of this deal attracted much attention – US agriculture is politically sensitive, and the deal was highly leveraged – but what happened post-deal is far more interesting.

Smithfield was very loosely organized pre-deal: it had three distinct operating centres in Kansas, Chicago and Virginia, and a large number of independent subsidiaries, resulting in considerable duplication and redundancy across their US operations. Top management were long-term veterans of the company, with high salaries but limited incentives to shake the company up.

Shuanghui saw synergies in owning a reputable US meat brand. However, it also wanted to strengthen Shuanghui's operational performance. It first consolidated the operating centres to two, aiming to eventually reduce to one. It streamlined shared services across all operating entities and reorganized into business units with primary P&L (profit and loss) responsibility, rather than the fragmented operating companies.

It introduced Shuanghui's business reporting system – transplanting all the processes and templates into Smithfield. These were much more detailed and rigorous than Smithfield's system and also required much more frequent reporting. It put in place stronger performance-based compensation than previously. Over two to three years, it retired the previous top management and installed a new team, mostly promoted from within. This 'changing of the guard' had considerable signalling value to Smithfield's staff. Shuanghui did not import managers from outside; it brought through the next generation of leadership, giving them a platform to individually prosper.

Shuanghui placed only one full-time senior manager in Smithfield. The implementation work was all done by Smithfield employees themselves. The board of Smithfield, however, is composed of three Shuanghui representatives and the new Smithfield CEO: accountability is very clear.

This model – changing management, imposing a tougher performance management system, simplifying the organization and strengthening financial incentives – is what private equity investors do to portfolio companies, though PE investors use more financial leverage and allow the management to make more personal profit if they deliver. However, the philosophy is similar. This raises the question: if Shuanghui could do this with only one manager in the company, why can't everyone else? Are turnarounds really that difficult?

Unfortunately, you need the right conditions for this sort of deal to work. These have not been seen much in recent years due to equity market valuations. Smithfield was not cheap: Shuanghui paid around 9×EBITDA (earnings before interest, tax, depreciation and administration) for the asset. At that valuation, few financial investors would be interested in a 'turnaround' deal: risks were high relative to potential rewards. Hence, Smithfield was able to operate with these inefficiencies, as few potential buyers were able to come in and fix them. Shuanghui, however, could count on significant synergies between the Smithfield brand and its Chinese operations to backstop financial performance. Even if it was not entirely successful in the turnaround, the deal would still make sense financially thanks to those synergies. It was additionally fortunate that there was an ambitious second tier of managers in Smithfield that supported change.

It is clear from this example that turnarounds are possible. If valuations cool off in the coming years, then over the next decade we should expect this to become a common part of the globalizing toolkit of Chinese acquirers.

Selective integration

In recent years, there have been an increasing number of deals where acquirers have attempted to selectively integrate one or two business areas, while managing the overall relationship with the target through a board. Under the right circumstances, this can be effective. A few examples illustrate common features of this model.

Petrochina – Ion: combining technology with market presence

When a subsidiary of Petrochina acquired geophysical survey technology company Ion in 2010, Petrochina was already one of the world's largest explorers for hydrocarbons. Ion had arguably the best 3D seismic imaging equipment in the industry. The deal's logic was compelling. However, Ion was a relatively flat, informal, entrepreneurial Houston-based company; Petrochina remains a large and complex SOE.

What Petrochina had, however, was a small group of managers with many years' experience running exploration operations outside China. These managers shared a common technical language and frame of reference with Ion's management. Hence, they became the 'bridge' between the two companies. Management of Ion was done primarily through the board, but there was extensive and close collaboration on how to rapidly deploy Ion's technology and expertise into Petrochina's exploration operations and how to integrate their R&D roadmaps. Other functional areas were left largely untouched.

CSR – Dynex: accelerating scale-up of R&D

In 2008, Dynex, a mid-sized UK semiconductor company focused on supplying the railroad sector, was 75% acquired by China state-owned CSR (one of China's largest railroad equipment producers who was then developing high-speed rail capabilities). CSR gave Dynex new capital to scale up R&D and to expand sales into new geographic markets. CSR brought Dynex products to market in China through its own channels. Dynex management now includes several executives from CSR, including the heads of R&D and sales, and the board has four Chinese members out of nine.

Making selective integration work

This approach is appealing, though hard to execute. It requires a few skills that not all companies possess.

First, the acquirer needs the ability to manage an asset through the board. This is not as simple as it sounds. Boards are cultural phenomena; their authority and role varies significantly across countries. The legal role of a board in China is quite different from the US, Germany or the UK. Some companies are skilled at doing this – for instance, this is the standard operating model for Hong Kong conglomerates such as Swire and Jardine Matheson – but many are not and treat the board as little more than a legal formality.

Second, the acquirer needs bench strength in the specific integration areas. It needs a cadre of people – maybe as few as a dozen – that have credibility and can interact at a working level with the target's management.

Third, the acquirer needs a deal team capable of negotiating arrangements that achieve a practical mutual understanding with the other side, with no confusion or ambiguity. This is harder than it sounds. In some situations, notably tightly controlled auctions where access to the target is restricted by the sale process rules, it may be outright impossible – one of many reasons why Chinese acquirers still do not like formal auction processes.

Progressive integration

Geely's acquisition of Volvo in 2010 was a milestone in the global auto industry: it made many MNC auto makers wake up and realize that domestic Chinese auto makers' international ambitions were serious. Chinese brands had not, at that point, achieved notable success in the domestic market relative to Sino-foreign JV (joint venture) brands. None had meaningful presence outside China, and none had integrated foreign operations into their business: for the Sino-foreign JVs, it was domestic operations that integrated into existing global product platforms.

Auto integrations pose unique challenges. Value lies primarily in achieving scale through consolidating product platforms and procurement. This is hard to do without full-on integration; hence, most post-merger integrations in auto are very hands-on and involve extensive restructuring.

Geely's management were aware of the risks involved. Having bought Volvo out of financial distress in 2010 at a relatively attractive price, they had more time on their side than most acquirers. They decided, sensibly, to walk before running. The easiest, highest-value task was sharing R&D and manufacturing expertise from Volvo into Geely, so this was the first priority. The next area was a significant step-up: finding operational synergies in the procurement and product roadmap. This was a multi-year effort. The next was to look at the marketing and distribution footprint and find areas for consolidation.

The pace of integration was slower than anticipated at first. Yet the company has defied the sceptics who predicted a culture clash and financial underperformance.

Geely traded off returns against risk in this approach, and, having avoided the short-term danger of becoming another SAIC-SsangYong, it had time on its side to achieve its strategic goals.

Working with partners: how can co-investors help?

The problems discussed above include mismatch between management systems and lack of experience in a foreign environment. Can a partner help with these? Numerous co-investors, primarily buyout funds, actively seek opportunities to partner with Chinese companies on outbound deals. Much of their value is in the pre-deal stage. Though helpful post-deal, they create one additional problem: orchestrating their exit from the investment.

Funds bring deep experience in deal execution. This has significant value to Chinese companies that lack proprietary dealflow, providing opportunities they otherwise would not see and helping them navigate the deal process efficiently. Partners are less consistently helpful in navigating government and other stakeholders, such as in Huawei's failed bid for 3com: even Bain Capital as co-investor was unable to get the deal through CFIUS review.

Zoomlion's 2008 investment in Cifa is a good example of how the dynamic changes from pre- to post-deal. Three financial co-investors – Hony, Goldman Sachs and Mandarin Capital Partners, a Sino-European fund with Italian roots – helped source and execute the deal. They provided heavy support on diligence, negotiation, funding, and corporate governance post-closing, without which the deal would have been much harder, perhaps even impossible.

They helped install a new CEO. However, post-deal the company struggled in operations and R&D – two areas where the PE investors could not help much. Revenues fell, and soon the PE-backed CEO was replaced by one of Zoomlion's choice. However, despite poor financial performance – revenues in 2011, only three years out from the initial investment, were less than 40% of pre-deal projections – the financial investors still exited with respectable returns. PE investors put considerable effort into the structuring of these deals to protect their downside, and typically the strategic investors take greater risk because they have greater ability to manage the asset post-deal. But it is nonetheless difficult to explain to shareholders when the strategic investor does more operationally but makes lesser returns.

In Lenovo's first outbound deal, the acquisition of IBM's PC business, two foreign funds – TPG, General Atlantic – invested alongside Lenovo and brought considerable expertise in deal execution and risk mitigation and also provided international credibility to Lenovo, who had almost no profile outside China at the time. However, their primary interest was necessarily the financial returns at exit, while Lenovo's core motivation was developing an international platform for growth over coming decades. This initial deal needed the funds' involvement to achieve success. In subsequent deals, Lenovo chose to be sole investor.

In recent years a new kind of partner has emerged: local Chinese funds, mostly private sector, who help Chinese companies execute acquisitions. Staff in these funds, particularly at the junior level, are typically Chinese nationals with international experience – people who have studied and worked in investing abroad – bringing experience that their partners lack. The limited partners are predominantly Chinese institutions, and they often do not have the pressure of the fundraising cycle that foreign funds feel, allowing them to be more relaxed on timing of the exit for investments.

It is too early to say whether these funds will behave differently from their foreign counterparts. However, they provide a middle-ground, and numbers of co-investment deals with them involved have grown very fast in the past few years. Take, for instance, Chinese retail operator Sanpower's acquisition of Brookstone Holding, a US-based retail store network. It was supported by Sailing Capital, a Shanghai-based fund set up to assist Chinese companies acquiring overseas, relying on using RMB funding but whose investment team worked previously for foreign investment firms such as PAG. Early results appear positive: it has opened three stores in China already (including a flagship in Shanghai), innovated on formats and marketed aggressively toward younger age groups.

There is clearly a role for funds in executing outbound acquisitions. However, in all the examples we studied, we found few where the fund played a meaningful role in operational improvement or restructuring.

Where next for Chinese companies?

These are still early days for outbound Chinese investment. Chinese companies spent 0.76% of GDP on outbound acquisitions in the last decade: US companies spent 1.16%, and EU companies 1.22%, investing 2.8×and 2.4×the dollar amount Chinese companies spent respectively. We are at the beginning of a long growth curve: the experience of the past decade provides lessons for future deals.

One important lesson is that success in M&A always requires luck as well as good judgement. If the resource deals had happened a few years earlier or later, many would have been successful. No manager has perfect timing. However, they can control what they do after the deal. Considerable effort is always spent on understanding the industry and projecting pricing and demand – assessing the 'luck' side of the equation. More time should go to planning how to integrate, as this is fully within management's control.

The fundamental challenges that we highlight above are mostly in three areas: historic lack of a managerial cadre that can function in foreign environments; incompatible management systems; and differences in corporate culture. Over time, these are improving. The pool of internationally experienced Chinese nationals with experience in multiple corporate cultures continues to grow, and Chinese companies' management systems become ever-more sophisticated.

That said, there are a few necessary elements to successful deals that Chinese companies will not develop unless they make the effort to do so. The first is to develop their own 'playbook' for these acquisitions. As with any corporate function, you become good at M&A by codifying and standardizing how you do it.

Lenovo did this after its purchase of IBM PC, and it has served them well in subsequent acquisitions.

The second is developing the ability to run a company in a light-touch manner primarily through the board. This is something that no company or manager has naturally, and how you do it outside China is substantially different from within China. It is a question of knowing what management information to look at, how frequently, where you need transparency into operations and how to achieve that. Most successful private equity investors acquire this skill through their careers by sitting on multiple portfolio company boards, but one cannot expect a corporate manager to know how to do this.

★ ★ ★

We remain optimistic for outbound Chinese acquirers. Chinese companies have almost limitless capacity to experiment, to take risks and to learn from their mistakes. This is precisely the ability that will make them successful as acquirers abroad. The era of learning is ending; the era of execution is about to begin.

12

EXECUTION IS THE STRATEGY

The key to Lenovo's success in IBM PC division acquisition

Chuanzhi Liu and Neng Liang

Introduction

Going global through merger and acquisition (M&A) is known to be very difficult; some studies have put the average failure rate of M&A at as high as 70%. What factors enabled Lenovo to succeed in its acquisition of the IBM PC division (PCD), which was four times its size? Or more broadly, what accounts for the success of emerging economy-based multinational companies (EMNC) – without superior technology or brand – in out-competing established developed economy multinationals (DMNC)?

These are the two questions we attempt to answer in this chapter.

Lenovo's acquisition of IBM PCD: background and update

Lenovo was founded in 1984. With an initial investment of RMB 200,000 (roughly USD 125,000 at that time) from the Chinese Academy of Sciences (CAS), eleven CAS scientists, led by the first author of this chapter, launched what eventually became known as Lenovo in a tiny guard house of CAS that was no larger than 20 square metres. The 1980s and 1990s were full of challenges for Chinese entrepreneurs. With determination, patience and perseverance, we gradually found our way to success in the Chinese market. During the early 2000s, Lenovo attempted to diversify its products beyond manufacturing and the sale of personal computers in China, but that effort largely failed. We concluded that for our long-term success, international expansion had become essential.

IBM, the 'Big Blue', had been the number-one personal computer manufacturer worldwide during the 1980s and 1990s, with a market share of 7% in the Chinese market. In 2002–2003, IBM began sourcing buyers for its PCD. Lenovo became IBM's preferred choice, partly because IBM believed that selling to Lenovo could help its service expansion into China.

Lenovo completed the acquisition of IBM PCD in May 2005 for USD 1.25 billion in stock and cash. The purchase included the ThinkPad brand, IBM PC operations in 166 countries, and a global workforce of more than 10,000.

Today, Lenovo's acquisition of IBM PCD is widely regarded as a success, despite some questions regarding Lenovo's latest performance in its non-PC lines. When Lenovo acquired IBM PCD in 2005, its global market share was less than 2.5%, with virtually no sales outside China. By second quarter of 2013, Lenovo had become the world's largest PC producer with a global market share of more than 20% (Figure 12.1), and with more than 60% of its sales outside China (Figure 12.2).

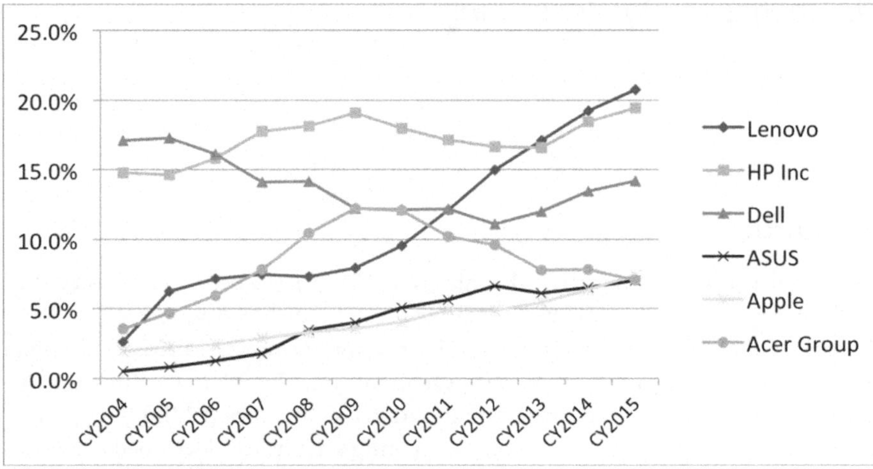

FIGURE 12.1 PC industry market share, 2004–2015

Source: IDC WW PC Tracker, 2016Q3 historical database.

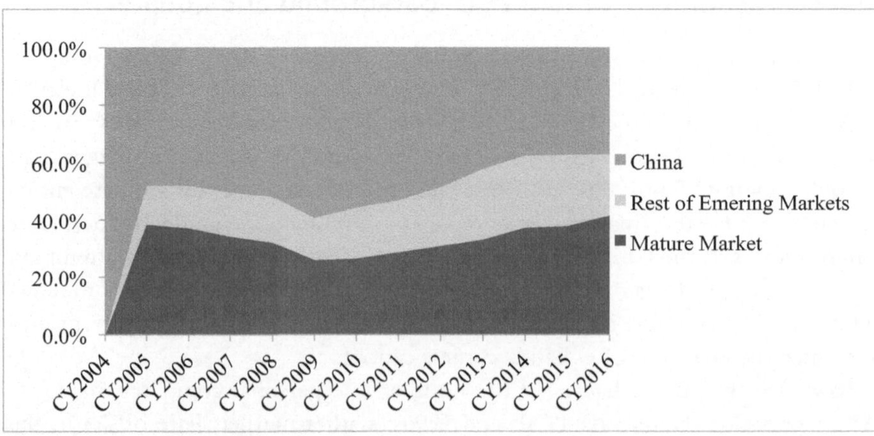

FIGURE 12.2 Lenovo sales by region

Source: Lenovo Company Records.

The challenges of mergers and acquisitions in a global context

Lenovo's success in acquiring and integrating IBM PCD did not come easy. In fact, M&A failure in the technology industry is notoriously common. During roughly the same time period that Lenovo worked to integrate Lenovo and IBM PCD into one global enterprise, seven major M&A attempts in the technology field failed.

'Matches made in hell'

In 2011, *CIO* magazine, a well-respected business magazine, published an article entitled 'Matches made in hell'.[1] It identified the seven worst M&A failures in the technology industry during the first decade of the twenty-first century (Table 12.1). For example, News Corp acquired Myspace in 2002, the hottest social media website at the time, for $583 million. It was eventually sold to a little-known ad agency for $35 million in 2011, a mere 6% of what News Corp had paid.

About the same time, several major international acquisitions by Chinese companies had also failed. For example, Shanghai Automotive Industry Corporation (SAIC) acquired a controlling stake (48.9%; later increased to 51%) in South Korea's SsangYong Motor for USD 572 million in 2004. A series of environmental shocks and poor decisions rendered the acquisition a disaster. A 25% appreciation of the Korean won after the acquisition made SsangYong's product pricing uncompetitive in the export market. It did not help that SAIC replaced all top SsangYong's Korean executives with SAIC managers with little international business experience. A series of labour disputes led to two prolonged and bitter strikes, costing the company a total of $553 million. By the time the venture was sold to an Indian company in 2010, SAIC had lost well over $1.2 billion in this acquisition.[2]

Why are M&A failures so common? Academic studies have identified many factors. We discuss three primary reasons here: (1) misjudging strategic fit in the planning stage, (2) paying too much in negotiations and (3) cultural clashes in post-merger integration.

Misjudging 'strategic fit'

'Strategic fit' refers to the business synergies to be realized between the acquirers and the target firms. The central argument is that a high fit enhances market power and productivity. Strategic fit is typically a function of the complementarity of the product, technology, market and top management team; these complementarities offer the merging firms a wide range of opportunities that neither firm could achieve alone.

Assessment of potential strategic fit, however, is difficult for many reasons. One is the environmental uncertainty. Acquisition involves considerable ambiguity in means-ends relationships, with the eventual outcome extremely uncertain. In the case of eBay's acquisition of Skype, the leading voice-over-Internet provider, the

TABLE 12.1 Matches made in hell

	Acquirer/Target	*Buying Price*	*Selling Price*	*Acquisition Rationale and Reasons for Failure as Reported by CIOs*
2000	Terra/ Lycos	12.5	–	Back in 2000, Lycos was the top search engine and the third-most visited US website. Wanting a piece of this online hotshot, Spanish telecom company Terra Networks put up $12.5 billion. The name changed to Terra Lycos, and then the dot-com bubble blew up in everyone's face.
2000	Time Warner/AOL	164 (merger)	About 1/7 original value	This $164 billion merger in 2000 was to create a perfect union between old media (Time Warner) and the Internet (AOL). By 2002, AOL Time Warner reported an astonishing $99 billion loss. In 2009, Time Warner finally sold AOL to an independent company.
2002	HP/Compaq	25	-	Hewlett Packard was then ranked number two and became number one after the acquisition. But serious disagreements on strategy led to some of the worst political board infighting in American corporate history. CEO Carlio was dismissed by the board due to the acquisition failure.
2005	Sprint/Nextel	36	shutdown	Both companies thought they would be able to quickly merge customers and catch up with Verizon and AT&T. But cultural clashes and incompatible wireless technologies made that impossible.
2005	News Corp/ Myspace	0.58	0.035	(1) Myspace stopped innovating once it became just another property of the Murdoch domain. (2) Facebook exploded as the dominant social media site.
2005	eBay/Skype	2.6	1.9	E-mail is good enough for online buyers and sellers. Nobody on eBay, it turns out, wants to talk. After four unfulfilling years, eBay sold Skype at a loss for $1.9 billion.
2006	Alcatel/Lucent	13.4	'Bleeding billions ever since'	Many problems with this merger have been cultural. Alcatel is French, and Lucent is American. When revenues started tanking, there was no organised plan to fix things. Add time differences, language barriers and different approaches to crisis management, and you have a troubled company.

Source: compiled by the authors based on data from *CIO* magazine, 2011.

benefits of providing voice communication to eBay's auction service proved elusive. It turned out that e-mail is good enough for both online buyers and sellers, and eBay lost $700 million in this failed acquisition.

Misjudging strategic fit also arises from the political nature of strategic decisions. From a political perspective, organizations are coalitions of diverse individuals and groups with enduring differences in values and preferences. It is not surprising that M&A proposals often bring to the surface deep-rooted disagreements within the top management team regarding the future direction of the company. In the case of HP's acquisition of Compaq, divergent aspirations led to vicious infighting within the board. The HP board became driven by feuds – so out of control that some directors were leaking secrets to the press while the chairman of the board was hiring private investigators to obtain their phone records (and those of reporters) to uncover the perpetrators.

In the Lenovo acquisition, there were also major concerns regarding strategic fit. One of our key objectives was to purchase the well-established 'ThinkPad' brand. But after the purchase of the brand by a Chinese company, would 'ThinkPad' still be viewed by its customers as a premium brand? If 'ThinkPad' customers had not stayed with us, much of the value of the acquisition would have been lost.

Paying too much

The second failure factor is paying too high a price for what the M&A synergy is worth. In one famous example, Campeau paid a 124% premium to acquire Federated Department Stores. One year later, Campeau declared bankruptcy, as it was unable to cover the debt it incurred for the deal.[3]

Studies have consistently showed that, with some notable exceptions, acquisitions tend to destroy value for the acquiring firms' shareholders.[4] Despite mounting evidence that the majority of acquisitions fail, many CEOs over-estimate their abilities to extract value from an acquisition and end up paying too high a premium for the acquisition targets.[5] Studies show that acquisition premiums averaged 41% between 1976 and 1990, and 55.5% and 97.4% between 1990 and 2006.[6] Everything else being equal, the higher the premium paid, the more difficult for the acquirers to generate positive returns. An exhaustive study on the topic found that shareholders of acquiring firms suffer a 10% loss over a five-year post-merger period, and a major reason for that loss is paying too high a price.[7]

Paying too much was a real concern for us as well. Why should Lenovo pay a huge price to buy a business that was losing money in IBM? When we started acquisition discussions in 2003, few people believed that we could manage such a large acquisition, let alone make money out of it.

'Cultural clash'

'Cultural clash' between the acquiring and acquired firm in post-merger integration is by far the most common cause of M&A failure.[8] For example, Myspace could not continue to innovate at the pace needed once it had become part of a traditional media company. Reuter News commented that this is what happens when a traditional media company imposes its will on a fast-growing startup.[9] News Corp's CEO Rupert Murdoch admitted himself that 'we screwed up in every way possible, learned lots of valuable expensive lessons'.[10]

Cultural clash happens in diverse ways. At the individual level, social psychology literature shows that people tend to be attracted to those whose attitudes and values are similar to their own. Shared norms, ideologies and identities facilitate the emergence of trust; conversely, the potential for conflict increases when a person or group is perceived as not sharing the same key values. In the context of mergers and acquisitions, members of the acquired firm often fiercely resist the integration effort imposed by the acquirer, especially when the out-group is perceived to be very different from the in-group. One study terms such resistance as 'the conquering army syndrome'.[11]

At the organization level, every organization has a unique culture that is shaped by its history and that defines its DNA. Firms founded in the Silicon Valley are clearly different from those based on Wall Street in terms of how they organize, plan, control and coordinate. 'Cultural distance' theory suggests that the greater the cultural difference between two organizations, the more difficult the post-merger integration.[12]

At the national level, managers from different cultures are likely to implement different control systems and use varying managerial practices in acquired firms. One research studied 40 acquisitions in the United Kingdom. The findings show that American firms, being more experienced internationally and more sophisticated in organization design, tend to adopt an 'absorption' approach and rely on policies and procedures to integrate fully the acquired UK firms. Japanese firms are more likely to be 'preservers'. Due to their lack of international experience, Japanese firms tend to take a long-term view and leave the acquired UK subsidiaries alone while providing them with significant financial support. French firms, on the other hand, tend to take a 'colonialists' approach, dictating command and control from their headquarters without attempting to absorb the subsidiaries into their corporate systems.[13] One study reported that talent turnover is much higher when US firms are acquired by foreign firms than they are by domestic firms.

Initial market reaction in December 2004

In addition to the above three common failure factors, Lenovo faced two more challenges. One is the size of the acquisition. Studies have shown that the larger the acquisition size, the more likely the M&A will fail. The Lenovo acquisition of IBM PCD was valued at $1.25 billion, the largest attempted by any Chinese firm at that time. One well-known acquisition principle of Cisco, the company best known for its acquisition success, is to limit its acquisition targets to small firms with less than 60 employees and located nearby. This is because small firms located nearby are easier to integrate. But IBM PCD is large in size and worldwide in scope.

Furthermore, not only was the acquisition target large, but it was also being acquired by the much smaller Lenovo. Lenovo was acquiring a target that was four times its size. It was a rare case of 'a snake swallowing an elephant' that could well cause indigestion.

As the above discussions made clear, the risk of failure was very high for Lenovo's IBM PCD acquisition. In fact, the global stock market reacted negatively to the news of Lenovo's acquisition of IBM PCD. After the news was released on December 8, 2004, Lenovo's stock price fell for four consecutive days, resulting in a total loss of market capitalization of 14.9%.

Seven secrets of Lenovo's success in the IBM PCD acquisition

We took a step-by-step approach in the IBM PCD acquisition and integration. We began with a programme of stabilization during 2004–2005. Initially we made few changes. For example, we moved the former IBM employees from their original office building to the Lenovo China headquarters so that both the Lenovo and the former IBM employees could get to know each other, but we made no structural changes in roles and responsibilities at that time. As reassurance to the thousands of IBM employees who now worked for Lenovo, we also promised former IBM employees that we would neither cut headcounts nor reduce salaries.

One year later, we began the second phase of the operational integration. Major organizational structural changes took place during this stage. We accelerated efforts to integrate the global supply chain of Lenovo and IBM PCD to lower cost and boost efficiency. We cut headcount by 1,100 and 1,400 in 2006 and in 2007, respectively, and moved our US head office closer to our operational centres in the US to save commuting costs.

The third stage began in February 2009, when we restructured the top management team and appointed Yang Yuanqing as CEO and founder Liu Chuanzhi as non-executive Chairman of the Board. During this stage, we rolled out our 'dual model' in full force and launched a major program to regain our strength in strategy execution by building a strong corporate culture. By the second quarter of 2013, we had surpassed both HP and Dell and became #1 in the PC industry.

Looking back now, among the many factors that contributed to our success in the IBM PCD acquisition, the following seven are the most critical.

Plan carefully before proceeding

To avoid misjudging strategic fit and paying too high a price, we planned carefully before making the final decision.

Following the Lenovo tradition of 'think carefully and clearly before taking strategic action', we set up a planning team of both senior executives and leading specialists with not only finance expertise but also operations, business development and human resource experience. This team diligently worked for 13 months in secret. We retained the service of two top professional firms to help us size up the potential and risks of the acquisition. Through careful and diligent analyses of industry trends and IBM PC division's data, we concluded that while the PC business was losing money in the IBM system, it would be profitable in our hands.

Because investment bankers and consulting firms sometime have a bias in recommending a 'go' decision, we did not take their recommendations at face value. We sought a private equity (PE) firm, General Atlantic (GA), which was very experienced in acquisitions and knowledgeable of the PC industry, as our independent advisor. Because PE firms invest with their own capital and would be potential partners in our acquisition, their advice was likely to be more objective and impartial. The willingness of three PE firms to collectively invest $350 million of their own money in this acquisition helped us to guard against the danger of misjudging strategic fit.

Take a learning approach

Given the high risk involved, we consciously decided to take a learning approach. We planned everything based on the assumption that we did not know how to lead a multinational firm and made a critical decision to not take the CEO position ourselves until after we had figured out how to manage a multinational firm.

Not taking the CEO position does not mean that we were 'hands off' or passive as was the case in the Japanese 'preserver' approach to M&A. Far from it. We placed Yang Yuanqing as 'Executive Chairman' so that he could work closely with the CEO and learn how to lead a multinational enterprise in the process. We also installed a strategy committee on the Board, with Yang and Liu on that committee. This ensured that we were fully engaged in all strategy issues and were able to learn all that we could about running such a large business.

While deliberately deciding not to take the CEO position in the first three to five years, we took measures to protect our home market in China. We shielded the China operations from our first two American CEOs, as neither knew much about the China market. It was a delicate balancing act. Four years later, when the daunting task of integrating operations had been completed, when Yang had learned the ropes of leading a multinational enterprise, and when our American CEO had proven unable to provide the strategic leadership that Lenovo needed, we then placed Yang into the CEO position with Liu Chuanzhi as Non-executive Chairman.

To ensure 360-degree learning from all angles, we set up a dual headquarters system, with the primary headquarters located in the US. Yang moved his entire family to live in the United States, and several other senior Lenovo executives moved their families to Singapore and other key international markets. We set up a special KPI (key performance indicator) for HR internationalization and required each Lenovo division to either nurture internally or recruit from outside at least two executives each year who were capable of operating on a global scale.

Reform the fundamental

From the experience of our own history, we know that sound corporate governance and a sound ownership structure are fundamental to the long-term vitality of any business, even more so for a multinational enterprise. We realized that Lenovo would not become a true global enterprise if we were to continue with our original governance structure developed inside China.

Therefore, right from the outset, we made important changes to Lenovo's governance structure. Pre-acquisition, the Chinese Academy of Sciences (CAS) was our single largest shareholder with a 37% equity stake. In the post-acquisition ownership structure, IBM owned 19%, and CAS's share was reduced to 29%. This more balanced ownership structure gave us more freedom in strategic decision-making, while the 19% equity share made IBM a partner in our globalization effort. In 2011, we also made arrangements for Yang Yuanqing to become a 7.9% owner of Lenovo.

We made significant changes in the composition of the Board. Before the acquisition, Lenovo's Board consisted primarily of insiders. After the acquisition, three private equity firms joined with us as strategic investors and received three of the 12 seats on the new Board. In 2012, when we combined the CEO and Chairman positions and had Yang Yuanqing assume both roles, we appointed a Lead Independent Director on the Lenovo Board. The Lead Independent Director has broad authority and responsibility and will call and chair meeting(s) with all independent non-executive directors without management and executive directors present at least once a year. With all these changes, Lenovo's Board became truly global and far more independent than it was before the IBM PCD acquisition.

In their globalization efforts, many entrepreneurs have made structural changes in the business organization but were reluctant to reform their boards, due to the fear of losing control. However, we view a sound governance structure as a source of competitive advantage and are willing to pay the price to have a truly world-class Board.

The first benefit of a world-class Board is the legitimacy it brings to Lenovo. It signalled to former IBM executives, PC customers, Lenovo suppliers and institutional investors worldwide that Lenovo's management was committed to becoming a global organization. The reconstituted Board has played a critical role in helping retain top talent in the IBM PC division, and it helps attract new talent into Lenovo from outside of China.

A second major benefit of having a truly global Board is the knowledge, expertise and global network that our new board members brought in with them. For example, Lenovo's first CEO from the IBM side was not the right CEO to lead the second stage of operations integration and was replaced within a year of his initial appointment. At that time, we had no experience in hiring and dismissing non-Chinese executives, although the private-equity directors had done so many times. It would have been much more difficult for us to replace a CEO and find a more suitable alternative quickly had it not been for the help of the three private-equity representatives.

A third benefit of having a truly global Board is its role as an impartial third party between Chinese and non-Chinese executives. It was inevitable that the former IBM executives would view things differently from the Chinese executives who had worked at Lenovo for 20 years. The private-equity representatives on the Board helped prevent business judgment differences from spilling over into relational conflicts between former IBM executives and pre-M&A Lenovo executives, and between Chinese executives and non-Chinese executives.

Globalize the top team

Before the IBM PCD acquisition, Lenovo was led by an all-Chinese top executive team. Today, there are six nationalities represented in Lenovo's executive committee, the highest decision-making body of Lenovo, and over 20 nationalities are represented among the top-100 executives.

Nevertheless, globalizing a top management team is by no means an easy task. On the one hand, Lenovo's Chinese executives were truly talented and outstanding, although they lacked some of the requisite experience to serve immediately in senior executive roles in a multinational firm. They were the people who had built Lenovo to a level at which it could acquire IBM PCD. Naturally, many of them were anticipating promotion and taking on greater responsibility now that Lenovo had become a global enterprise.

On the other hand, IBM was one of the greatest companies in the world with many super-talented executives and professionals. They were extremely valuable to our dream of becoming a truly global institution. It was imperative that we make the former IBM executives feel respected, trusted, and welcomed, and give them the opportunities and responsibilities to further their careers and make greater contributions to the new Lenovo.

We made major efforts to develop a global top management team. In the first stage of stabilization, we split the 180 senior executive positions 50/50: half of the 180 executive positions went to former IBM executives, and the other half went to Lenovo's Chinese executives.

We decided from the very beginning to make the new Lenovo a truly global organization. We made English the official language, and we did not want people from the IBM side to have a feeling of being taken over by a Chinese company. We wanted an integration process that did not involve which part takes over which part.

Beginning in 2006, we added quite a few former Dell executives to Lenovo's top management team. Later on, we also recruited top executives from other firms to join us. For example, in 2012, former CEO of Acer, Gianfranco Lanci, joined us and is now our president and COO. The former chairman of Sony also joined our board.

Of course, globalizing a top management team requires much more than membership diversity. Starting from late 2005, we developed a work routine whereby the entire top management team would fly to one city on a monthly basis, usually in a key market of ours, and meet face-to-face for two to three days. Such frequent and close interactions, plus an open mind and a common goal to succeed, gradually bonded our executives into one team.

As an indication of both our determination and success in building a top global team, we did not send Chinese executives as expatriates, as was common in many international acquisitions, to head our operations in other countries. We have always chosen a local executive from the specific country to head the operations in that region.

Embrace and leverage diversity

Just as studies of interpersonal trust and relational conflicts reviewed earlier in this chapter predicted, we encountered many difficulties when we brought together an ethnically and culturally diverse workforce from geographically distant countries.

First is the language issue. Executives from the former IBM PCD spoke English but no Mandarin; the Chinese executives spoke Chinese and virtually no English. Language barriers combined with the time zone differences made even the simple routine of having a meeting a major challenge. Meetings became long and ineffective, causing frustrations and stress for all participants, and delayed business decisions.

Dealing with these challenges became even more complicated, as we had to work not only with two completely different corporate cultures but also with two markedly different national cultures and worldviews. Misunderstandings inevitably arise. What was perfectly appropriate in the eyes of former IBM executives could come across as insensitive or even offensive to our Chinese executives and vice versa. For example, IBM executives were accustomed to laying all issues open on the table and argued their views at meetings. Lenovo executives, on the other hand, followed the Chinese cultural norm of not openly contradicting or challenging the views of their American colleagues at meetings for the sake of 'saving face' for all involved. Such well-intentioned 'politeness', however, actually added to the confusion about what was or was not agreed upon at these meetings.

We also had to deal with the heightened level of anxiety and the feeling of lack of control from the members of the acquired company, which is typical in an M&A situation. Some of our non-Chinese executives believe that the success of Lenovo in China was a result of the under-developed market environment and the protection of the Chinese government. They had no confidence that Lenovo could possibly lead in the world market.

The lack of understanding and trust, and the differences in values and perspectives, caused many difficulties, but we were determined to make the acquisition work. Chairman Yang Yuanqing proposed three key words as guiding principles from the very beginning: Trust, Respect and Compromise. We implemented a wide-ranging strategy to build trust among our culturally and geographically diverse workforce.

The first step was simply to learn about the cultures and history of other ethnic groups, starting with language. Immediately after the acquisition, then-CEO Stephen Ward and his American executives began taking Chinese lessons, and Chairman Yang Yuanqing and his fellow Chinese executives began to take English lessons. We organized weekly lunchtime cultural-understanding seminars in the US and China, including a class exploring how different cultures regard silence in conversations. We started a 'knowledge exchange' program that sends employees on short-term international assignments so that they could 'seed the organization' with wider perspectives of local customs and cultures while expanding employees' skill sets.

On an operations level, we made changes in communication rules to remove barriers and enhance understanding. We made it an official requirement that meeting agendas and related information must be shared 24 hours in advance so that everyone could be well prepared. We asked our American colleagues to speak more slowly and encouraged our Chinese colleagues to voice their opinions more readily at meetings. To ensure that different opinions were fully vetted at meetings, we made it our standard operation procedure to remove all non-essential items from meeting agendas. We also changed our tele-conference meeting schedule to morning time in Beijing, which allowed our Chinese executives to participate in the meeting physically together in the same room so that they could discuss among themselves and help those colleagues who may not fully understand the point being discussed, rather than taking tele-conference calls at home alone at night.

We formalized our diversity efforts in the organizational structure. In 2007, we appointed a Chief Diversity Officer, a black female executive from Dell, to focus on trust-building and cultural inclusion. Chairman Yang Yuanqing himself served as executive diversity sponsor. To embrace diversity, we know it is important for people to get out of their comfort zone and reach out to others. Our top management led the way by 'walking the talk' themselves. Chairman Yang Yuanqing and SVP Gina Qiao, for example, began giving English speeches to Lenovo's American employees about one year into the acquisition. Although their English was far from perfect at that time, their determination and willingness to reach out sent clear signals to all employees about the importance of building understanding and trust within the company.[14]

Gradually, we built trust among our diverse employees, and an open-minded atmosphere developed thereafter.

Build a winning culture

After the 'ease in' period passed and we started to make major structural changes, deep-rooted differences in assumptions, preferences, perspectives and unconscious, ingrained routines began to emerge as a major problem within the organization.

Nurtured in Lenovo's strong corporate culture of team spirit, Yang had developed great faith in the collective wisdom of the top management team. In pre-acquisition Lenovo, major decisions were made by the top management team as a group, not by the CEO alone. Senior managers would vet focal issues thoroughly before a final decision was made. And once the company had reached a decision, the entire team would go all out in its execution. They had been part of the decision-making process, and they understood and owned the objectives and rationale behind the decision. Our American CEO, on the other hand, had a quite different leadership style. Groomed in the American culture of individual responsibility and fast action, he instructed regional and functional managers to report to him directly and individually – for the sake of faster decision-making.

The corporate cultures also differed. At that time, most of our executives derived from three corporations: the pre-acquisition Lenovo, IBM and Dell. Lenovo's Chinese managers emphasized group spirit and building a strong leadership team, while IBM managers placed great value on 'respect for the individual'. The culture at Dell had been described as being 'mercenary', and employees described it as a 'sink or swim' environment.[15] With a mix of Lenovo legacy here, a touch of Dell there, and some of IBM as well, Lenovo's execution capability was eroded. Agreed-upon performance targets were often adjusted downwards, with responsible executives offering one excuse after another. In February 2009, we launched a major programme to build a winning culture for the new Lenovo.

How would we build a strong culture for the new Lenovo? The first step was to define it. Back in 2007, Lenovo's Human Resources Department worked hard to define the corporate culture of the new Lenovo. They worked out four core values: (1) serving customers, (2) entrepreneurship and innovation, (3) trustworthiness and integrity and (4) diversity and win-win relationship.

After resuming the chairman's role in 2009, Liu Chuanzhi asked everyone to rethink Lenovo's culture: 'Were these the four core values of Lenovo? If these were the core values and we were actually practising them, why did we have such significant problems in our performance?' This question triggered a soul-searching process for the entire executive committee. After extensive discussions and reflections, we finally decided on a single-sentence statement of our core value: *We do what we say and we own what we do.*

This 'Lenovo Way' was later elaborated upon using four P's:

We **PLAN** before we pledge.
We **PERFORM** as we promise.
We **PRIORITIZE** the company first.
We **PRACTISE** improving every day.
Later on, we added a fifth P: we **PIONEER** new ideas.

After the 'Lenovo Way' value had been articulated within the organization, Liu made personal trips to visit Lenovo executives in key international markets. In his talks to European executives, Liu first took responsibility for Lenovo's loss, then talked about Lenovo's commitment to its employees and his confidence in Lenovo's strategy and Yang's team, and implored just one simple thing to the audience: 'Do what you have promised and meet your planned target'. This simple requirement crystalized all the problems at that time. With this simple requirement, corporate culture was no longer a fussy-messy concept but a down-to-earth, life-and-blood issue of company survival.

Our second step in building a strong culture was to 'walk the talk'. To make the 'Lenovo Way' take root and become embodied in each person's actions, we begin at the very top, the CEO. Yang had a meeting with his executives, and he publically stated what target he would meet in the year and asked everyone to monitor him. He then asked every executive to do the same. This sent a powerful message throughout the entire company.

The third step of building a strong culture for the new Lenovo was to put the money where our mouth was. We designed a special cash-bonus scheme tied directly to performance targets. Some of our Board members expressed reservations to this cash-bonus scheme, pointing to the fact that Lenovo already had a well-developed stock option plan in place. However, facing the largest loss in Lenovo's history, many executives were doubtful as to whether Lenovo could really survive the 2009 global financial crisis. Under such conditions, when people did not have confidence in the long-term perspective of Lenovo, incentivizing by stock ownership or options was unlikely to be effective. The Board eventually approved the cash-bonus scheme. It proved to be very effective, and most executives met their pledged performance targets.

Compromise anything but strategy

Acquisition is the merging of two previously independent, and different, organizations. Since the interests of the two organizations are unlikely to be identical, conflicts are inevitable. In order for the two entities to work together, the willingness to make compromises is a must. At the same time, both companies will insist on certain things they consider fundamental. The dilemma is deciding what to compromise and what to insist upon.

We know we face many constraints and have to make compromises if we are to develop as a successful company. On the other hand, we also know we have to stick firmly to our fundamental goals and should never waiver in this regard. It is critical to think clearly about what we must insist upon, and what we can compromise on.

In this regard, our experience in the IBM PCD acquisition can be summarized as follows: 'Compromise on anything, but hold firm on strategy'. We made many compromises during the acquisition process. For example, we made compromises in CEO positions in the first four years, even though our ultimate dream was to be able to lead a top multinational firm ourselves. On quite a few issues during the first four years, our judgments differed from those of our two American CEOs. In most situations, after making efforts to communicate and reason with the CEO in office, if he was not convinced, we compromised in order to support our CEO.

In one instance, our second CEO wanted to replace a Lenovo executive that both Yang and Liu personally knew to be well qualified and outstanding; however, we compromised in this situation to support the CEO's authority.

But one thing that we never compromised was our strategy of rolling out a 'dual model' to the global market, because this was fundamental to our long-term viability. 'Dual model' refers to the application of distinct strategies to two different market segments: a 'relationship model' targeting large-enterprise clientele and a 'transactional model' targeting consumers and small to medium-sized enterprises (SMEs). Though conceptually simple, the use of both strategies at the same time had proven too complex for many companies, but we have managed to make it work. It is a model unique to Lenovo, as no other company has found a way to do it successfully. Lenovo's dual business model approach was developed and refined in China. Based on different customer needs and preferences in products, service and buying channels in China, we first segmented customers into two types – relational and transactional – and then built complementary business models accordingly. The success of Lenovo's dual model in China lies in the end-to-end integration of product development, marketing, sales, manufacturing and customer service, allowing fast, yet disciplined, response to market shifts, enabling Lenovo to operate efficiently on an optimized cost structure.

Towards the end of 2005, Yang began to explore ways to replicate our successful 'Dual Model' in international markets. After the dual model had succeeded in India, our then-CEO and many of our non-Chinese executives still did not believe in the dual model. They pointed to the fact that India was very similar to China and speculated that the dual model was suitable only to developing countries and would not work in developed economies. There was considerable resistance internally, both at the Board level and within the top management team, to organizing the new Lenovo structurally according to the dual model and to implement this model globally.

We persisted in this endeavour but took a step-by-step approach. After the initial trial in India, we next chose a well-developed market, Germany, for our dual model programme, with Yang personally leading the way. It worked again. This raised eyebrows throughout our company; people became more receptive to the dual model. We then rolled it out in France, followed by the Middle East, Africa and North America. It worked in all these markets.

The dual model enabled us to ride the wave of growth opportunities in PCs: small- and medium-sized businesses (SMBs) and emerging markets. It is not an overstatement to say that the dual model was a key success factor for Lenovo becoming #1 in the PC industry by 2013.

Discussions

We now return to the general question: what factors enable emerging economy-based multinational companies (EMNC) – initially without superior technology or brand – to out-compete established developed economy multinationals (DMNC)?

The conventional theories of multinational companies (MNCs) posit that multinational firms go international to take advantage of their superior technologies or brand developed in their home countries. Possession of superior technology and brand is necessary, as the MNCs need such valuable assets to compensate for the additional costs and risks involved in going abroad and competing on the home turf of their rivals. The global expansion of General Electric and Proctor & Gamble attest to the ownership advantage of superior technology and brand names.

Contrary to the predictions of the conventional theory of multinational firms, many successful EMNCs start from behind and overcome their deficiencies to emerge as industry leaders, and they do so without initial resources, without advanced skills and knowledge, and without the social capital that is to be found in high-tech regions like Silicon Valley.[16]

In the case of Lenovo's globalization success, we began in 2004 with a global market share of less than 2.5%, with virtually no operations outside of China. This raises an intriguing question: how can EMNCs like Lenovo – without superior technology or brand – out-compete well-established multinationals from technologically and managerially advanced developed economies such as Dell and HP?

We believe there are both external and internal factors. The external factor is a fundamental change in the PC industry structure, which provided latecomers like Lenovo an opportunity to surpass incumbent industry leaders. As Figure 12.3 shows, the PC industry entered a period of consolidation around 2002. The top-four firm concentration ratio, a typically used measure of industry structure, was about 40% in the late 1990s. This ratio started to rise around 2002 and eventually reached 60% in 2016 (Figure 12.3).

Structural change also happened on the demand side. The SME and transactional customers in the emerging economies were becoming increasingly more important. The percentage of sales from emerging markets in the PC industry

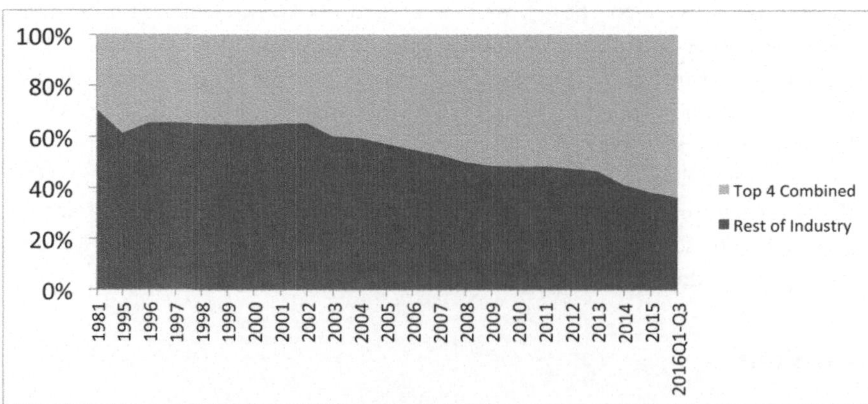

FIGURE 12.3 PC industry structure by concentration ratio

Source: compiled by authors based on IDG data.

increased from an average of 24% between 1997 and 2001 to an average of 54% between 2011 and 2015. This significant structural change represented a window of opportunity for Lenovo to surpass the incumbent industry leaders.

Structural change itself, however, is not a sufficient condition for the success of EMNCs. We believe that three internal factors have been critical to Lenovo's success. They are all organizational capabilities, rather than technology or brand. The first is our understanding of a unique business model. Although our 'dual model' was developed and refined in China, it was tested and proven effective in our direct and head-on competition with Dell. It prepared us to compete in the global market and allowed us to ride the wave of the rising demands of transactional-type customers while simultaneously maintaining strong and close relationships with corporate users worldwide. In a sense, it is our secret weapon; we would not have succeeded in the IBM PCD acquisition if we had not possessed this critical advantage of a superior business model.

The second factor that enables us to out-compete incumbent DMNCs is Lenovo's organizational capability to learn.[17] Possession of a superb business model is one thing; being able to replicate and apply this on a global scale, across different host country environments in a newly acquired company that is four times our size, is a totally different story. It is the speed and effectiveness of learning that is the most important success factor during a period of global industry shakeup, rather than the static advantage of product technology or brand equity.

Studies have shown that breadth or variety of experience has a major impact on executives' learning and innovation capability.[18] As a consequence of operating in China's fast-growing economy with primitive market institutions and high-velocity policy change, Lenovo developed a strong learning capability; this was because we have had to learn how to do almost everything on our own. In the words of Lenovo's founder, the first author of this paper, Lenovo had developed the ability 'to write its own cooking recipe', rather than relying on recipes developed by others. In contrast, well established multinationals from the West function within a mature and relatively stable environment; thus, their learning experience is comparatively more limited. They are superbly positioned to exploit their existing technology and brand advantage but less well equipped to explore new business models in a fast-changing environment.

In short, when the rules of the game are fast changing, it is the capability of developing a suitable new 'recipe', rather than the capability of cooking the old recipe better, that counts. This also explains why EMNCs' approach to globalization is different.

DMNCs traditionally take a gradual approach to internationalization. They typically enter one foreign market at a time and start from nearby, familiar neighbouring countries. They tend to rely on a low-commitment entry mode of export in their initial international expansion, and, once they have gained enough experience, they gradually move up the commitment/risk scale to foreign direct investment in the target market. This pattern has characterized the historical development of most DMNCs.

In contrast, EMNCs often take the M&A approach as the entry mode to international markets and globalize rapidly. In the Lenovo case, we became a multinational firm almost overnight. Such an entry model is not only necessary during rapid industry structure change but has also enabled us to better leverage our advantage in organizational learning capability.

A third critical factor is Lenovo's core competency in execution. Of course, we made the right strategic choice of acquiring IBM PCD in 2004. But that was actually the easy part. The hard part is to make the strategy work.

Making strategy work requires taking thousands of operational decisions correctly, performing millions of tasks to a level of excellence, and achieving seamless coordination across all functions and organizational sub-units. For this kind of execution to happen, the entire Lenovo workforce has to be willing and capable of, and passionate about, winning the acquisition and integration battle. Fortunately, Lenovo has developed the core competency of execution in its DNA, and we have raised this to a new height in our journey following the IBM PCD acquisition. We have won the support of the whole management team and the entire Lenovo workforce all over the world, regardless of their demographic, ethnic, personal and corporate background and cultural differences. It is for this reason that we give this chapter the title 'Execution is the strategy'.

We hope that this paper can help executives to better understand the conditions and requirements for successful international M&A and help MNCs from other emerging economies to better plan their globalization journey.

Notes

1 O'Neill, S 2011, 'Match made in hell: 7 worst tech mergers and acquisitions', *CIO*, July 27, https://www.cio.com/article/2405907/mergers-acquisitions/match-made-in-hell--7-worst-tech-mergers-and-acquisitions.html.

2 White, S & Xu, R 2011, 'Shanghai Automotive and SsangYong Motor: A tale of two dragons', *Asian Case Research Journal*, vol. 16, no. 1, pp. 1–37.

3 Hauncschild, P 1994, 'How much is that company worth? Interorganizational relationships, uncertainty and acquisition premiums', *Administrative Science Quarterly*, vol. 39, pp. 391–411.

4 King, DR, Dan, RD, Daily, CM & Covin, JG 2004, 'Meta-analyses of post-acquisition performance', *Strategic Management Journal*, vol. 25, pp. 187–200.

5 Acquisition premiums are typically defined as the ratio of the ultimate price paid per target shares divided by the price prior to takeover news.

6 Gu, F & Lev, B 2011, 'Overpriced shares, ill-advised acquisitions, and goodwill impairment', *The Accounting Review*, vol. 86, no. 6, pp. 1995–2022.

7 Jaffe, A & Manderlkar, G 1992, 'The post-merger performance of acquiring firms: A re-examination of an anomaly', *Journal of Finance*, vol. 47, pp. 1605–1621.

8 Weber, Y 1996, 'Corporate cultural fit and performance I mergers and acquisitions', *Human Relations*, vol. 49, no. 9, pp. 1181–1202.

9 Adegoke, Y 2011 'Special report: How news corp got lost in MySpace' 2011, *Reuter, Technology News*, April 7.

10 O'Brien, SA 2014, 'Murdoch: MySpace failure was my fault', *CNN Money*, October 29.

11 Faulker, D, Child, J & Pitkethly, R 2003, 'Organizational change processes in international acquisitions', *Advances in Mergers and Acquisitions*, vol. 2, pp. 59–80.

12 Deepak, KD 1991, 'Organizational fit and acquisition performance: Effects of post-acquisition integration', *Strategic Management Journal*, vol. 12, pp. 281–297.
13 Shimizu, K, Hitt, MA, Vaidyanath, D & Pisano 2004, 'Theoretical foundations of cross-border mergers and acquisitions: A review of current research and recommendations for the future', *Journal of International Management,* vol. 10, no. 3, pp. 307–353.
14 Giao, G & Conyers, Y 2015, *The Lenovo Way*, Beijing: China Machine Press.
15 Lowther, R 2006, 'Embracing and managing diversity at dell', *Strategic HR Review*, vol. Sep/Oct, pp. 16–19.
16 Mathews, JA 2006, 'Dragon multinationals: New players in 21st century globalization', *Asia Pacific Journal of Management*, vol. 23, no. 1, pp. 5–27.
17 Useem, M, Singh, H, Liang, N & Cappelli, P 2017, *Fortune Makers: The Leaders Creating China's Great Global Companies*, New York: Public Affairs, Hachette Book Group.
18 Crossl, C, Zyung, J, Hiller, NJ & Hambrick, DC 2014, 'CEO career variety: Effects on firm-level strategic and social novelty', *Academy of Management Journal*, vol. 57, no. 3, pp. 652–674.

13

WHY GO GLOBAL? THE LOGIC BEHIND INVESTING OVERSEAS

John Zhao

Introduction

Chinese businesses going global face an unprecedented situation – although the rate of growth of the Chinese economy has slowed down, it continues to lead the world, and the country's contribution to the global economy has never been higher. At the same time, the structure of the Chinese economy is undergoing profound changes. The consumer services industry, a market worth USD 6 trillion, is replacing manufacturing as the country's new economic engine.

This huge market has bred a number of large Chinese companies, including a considerable number of which now rank in the global Fortune 500. However, it is also worth noting that many of those companies remain vulnerable in terms of competitiveness. In the eyes of many Chinese entrepreneurs, their businesses must grow internationally, expand their market share and build up their own capabilities and competitiveness by taking on their international counterparts. This is the force which inevitably drives Chinese companies to explore opportunities overseas. Meanwhile, over the last three decades of reform and opening up, China has attracted huge FDI inflows through preferential policies and low costs, which in turn has made China the world's factory of producing low-priced products for the global marketplace. This has, however, also brought about excess production capacity, against which high-end production capacity must be re-balanced to meet the world's demands as well as requirements for domestic economic structural adjustment.

While being the world's factory, China has also become the world's market – the consumption capacity of Chinese consumers has proven itself beyond doubt, and the country's consumption structure is rapidly catching up with that of developed economies. There is a need for investment in leading international businesses in order to bring global leading products, brands and services to serve the rapidly growing Chinese market and the ever-changing needs of Chinese consumers.

This evolutionary trend of Chinese economic transactions has driven Chinese businesses to expand overseas, while also attracting top-rank international businesses to establish a presence in the Chinese market. This is a reflection of increasing integration between China and the world economy: the internationalization of Chinese businesses and the localization of international businesses. As part of this process, capital in the form of private equity combined with China's awareness and global experience has played an irreplaceable role in helping Chinese businesses with their internationalization process.

Going global for Chinese businesses

'Going global' is a historical proposition for Chinese enterprises. Having long relied on the huge domestic market which has delivered rapid development, large scale, strong capabilities and leading talent, they must now continue this expansion on the world stage. As China continues its transformation into a capital-exporting nation, the participation of market-oriented capital in this globalization process is allowing Chinese companies to take flight even further. The routes taken by Chinese hotel industry leader Jinjiang Hotels and global fiberglass industry giant China Jushi are typical examples.

Jinjiang Hotels: going global through cross-border M&A activities

As China's leading listed hotel and restaurant chain, Jinjiang Hotels is also one of the most successful state-owned enterprises in Shanghai, China's most economically developed city. Jinjiang Inns, as a subsidiary of Jinjiang Hotels, is one of the big four budget hotels in China.

We invested in Jinjiang Hotels for several reasons. First, Jinjiang Hotels enjoys strong competitive advantages in terms of industrial position, operational management and domestic brand impact, and it is in an urgent need of expansion in scale and a transition to a mobile Internet-driven hotel chain. Second, China's middle class is expanding, and the number of outbound travellers is increasing steadily, generating new development opportunities for the hotel industry abroad. Third, 'going global' has been a major theme in the development of Shanghai SOEs. Jinjiang Hotels has a wealth of cross-border experience, outstanding team expertise, and a scale suited to the hotel industry, making it well-positioned to explore cross-border M&A opportunities.

The senior management of Jinjiang Hotels holds a strong conviction to build Jinjiang Hotels into an international hotel group with a global presence, multinational management, international competitiveness and strong global brand impact. The first thing we did once we had invested in Jinjiang Hotels was to assist the company to introduce a more market-oriented management approach and adopt the best practices of the industry. First, we tailored the management incentives scheme based on better defined KPIs, so that management performance was more directly linked with the performance of the company. Second, the company recruited new senior international talent to facilitate and strengthen post M&A integration. Third, the company launched the WeHotel direct sales platform, which enabled Jinjiang Hotels to consolidate separate booking channels into a unified point of entry, thereby facilitating cross-selling of products and services. Fourth, there was further integration of back-end functions including brand management, procurement, IT, finance and human resources infrastructure in order to increase operational efficiency and further enhance overall economies of scale.

At the start of 2015, Jinjiang Hotels took the lead in completing its wholly owned acquisition of the Louvre Hotel Group, the third-largest hotel group in Europe. With its global presence taking shape, it also completed acquisitions of China's second-largest economy brand hotel chain, Plateno, and China's largest mid-range brand, Vienna Hotels. Recently, Jinjiang Hotels also entered into an agreement with a major Indian hotel group, Sarovar, and became its controlling shareholder.

Jinjiang Hotels has relied on its organic growth as well as domestic and foreign M&A to increase the number of rooms from 110,000 to 550,000, ranking fifth worldwide and achieving a corresponding increase in market value. The company is now China's largest and the world's fifth-largest hotel group in terms of scale, but now is by no means a harvest season. With the joint efforts of its investors, Jinjiang Hotels will move forward to become the world's third-largest international hotel group, with solid international competitiveness and strong brand impact.

China Jushi: serving overseas markets using local resources

In 2006, Hony invested USD 75 million to become the third-largest shareholder in Jushi Group (the operating entity of Jushi's fiberglass business) and subsequently took the lead in the reorganization of the company's assets. In 2011, Hony became the third-largest shareholder in China Jushi, a listed company, holding approximately 10% interest. In 2016, Hony Capital participated in Jushi's investment in the construction of an 80,000-ton fiberglass production line in South Carolina, US, which marked the first green field investment in the US by any China fiberglass business.

Since investing in Jushi, Hony Capital has helped the group improve corporate governance, in particular to keep a good balance and adeptly manage the interests of different shareholders including SOEs, the management team and private investors. Based on our in-depth understanding of the fiberglass industry as well as Jushi's business, we assisted the company in optimizing its development plans, supporting the implementation of its internationalization strategy and completing two strategically positioned fiberglass plants in Egypt and the US, making it the first Chinese fiberglass company to establish a global presence. In Egypt and the US, we actively provided the company with a range of value-added services including strategic decision-making, governmental communications, competitor analysis and global supply chain structure development. As a result, Jushi has benefited from preferential tax rates from local government and sophisticated trade union infrastructure support, allowing it to build a global network for supply chain procurement, logistics and distribution. Meanwhile, we actively supported China Fiberglass to merge with Jushi Group through a share swap and assisted Jushi in expansion of its network and cooperation with international financial institutions, which in turn not only provided more diversified sources of capital but also contributed greatly to Jushi's foreign market entry.

Ten years of rapid growth has made China Jushi a global industry leader. Its annual production capacity rose from 320,000 tons during the global financial crisis to 1.2 million tons in 2015. The company set up the world's largest (700,000-ton) fiberglass production plant in Tongxiang, as well as a foreign production plant in Egypt. The production capacity of these two locations totalled 160,000 tons. Jushi's status in the industry is rising rapidly, gradually overtaking overseas giants and far outstripping its domestic Chinese competitors.

China's cost advantages are fading away due to the increasing costs of labour, raw materials and other factors. With effective strategic measures, Jushi has transformed itself from a pure fiberglass distributor to a global business operator by setting up plants overseas. In 2014, China Jushi successfully established its first overseas production plant in Egypt, where supply and demand are currently booming. The establishment of the plant in the US in 2016 marks another step towards allocating resources more efficiently worldwide and generating income at home.

The kick-off of Jushi's US project not only helped the company make full use of the US technology and human resources but also represents a breakthrough in going global for Chinese businesses. In the past, the Chinese government relied on preferential policies to attract foreign investment to build factories in China, a typical model of combining Chinese workers and US capital and technology. Jushi's US project, on the other hand, represents a new internationalization business model by using Chinese equipment, capital and technologies in combination with foreign land, workers and markets to deepen global industry integration.

Inbound investments by international enterprises

China is transitioning from being the world's factory to the world's market. Its middle-income population is expanding, and the rise of mobile Internet technologies is fundamentally changing China's consumer market. Bringing foreign high-quality service and innovation to serve China's increasingly active consumers is another important motive for Chinese companies to invest abroad. The following cases show how PizzaExpress and WeWork are already benefiting from such a business rationale.

PizzaExpress: a Chinese touch on a well-established British brand

PizzaExpress has a long history and is beloved by consumers in the UK. PizzaExpress was established in 1965. By the time it was acquired by Hony Capital in 2014, PizzaExpress had 435 directly operated outlets across the UK, making it the country's largest and one of the best-known restaurant chain brands. It had also built up an excellent reputation abroad, with 70 outlets in regions including China, Southeast Asia, the Middle East and India.

The rationale behind our acquisition lies in the robustness of the British local business and the huge upside potential in the Chinese market. In 2013, our analysis concluded that the business would be a particularly valuable target for overseas investment. First, as the UK's largest chain catering business, it was a market leader in terms of size and profitability, which supports the sound growth of the business in its British home market. Second, there is huge market penetration potential in China. PizzaExpress had been operating in the Greater China region for close to 15 years and had already established a strong reputation as well as a sophisticated operating model. The profitability of its outlets in Chinese first-tier cities even exceeded that of its British businesses. Compared to its competitors, PizzaExpress had fewer outlets in China, a mere 30 locations versus Pizza Hut's 1,300 – indicating remarkable potential for further expansion.

In July 2014, we took over PizzaExpress. In the following six months, we brought in a number of strong investors as minority shareholders, including China's largest hotel management group, Jinjiang Group, the Bank of China, Taiwan's Fubon Financial Holdings and well-known Chinese restaurant chain operator Hai Di Lao. These industrial partners and financial investors provided not only financial support but more importantly rich resources from different fields to support business expansion in China.

Within one year after the acquisition, PizzaExpress made a quick buyback of its Chinese franchising rights. The PizzaExpress China team was established with members carefully selected, laying a solid foundation for further development. PizzaExpress quickly locked in a number of high-quality outlet locations in major Chinese cities. By the end of 2016, PizzaExpress had gained a larger presence in China by operating almost 50 outlets in major cities such as Beijing, Shanghai, Guangzhou, Shenzhen, Nanjing and Hong Kong. PizzaExpress will expand aggressively into the China market, with the aim of making the country its home market second to the UK. Over the longer term, it looks poised to outgrow even the scale of its British counterpart.

WeWork: embracing the millennial generation to create a global community

WeWork pioneered the concept of shared office areas. Founded in New York in 2010, WeWork has established over 100 office locations in 32 cities across 12 countries worldwide and is regarded as one of the world's largest unicorn start-ups. As the originator of the concept of shared office areas, it provides office space and a full range of business development services. The company's business model reduces operating costs for small and medium-sized businesses, entrepreneurs and freelancers, and it injects a unique business culture of global community and a spirit of sharing into the daily working environment. For example, with freshly brewed beer offered at any time, WeWork members enjoy the opportunity to exchange information and stories with people from different professional backgrounds and to participate in various thematic social events to expand their personal networks and meet potential customers and investors. This unique community experience makes WeWork distinct from traditional office operators. From tenants' perspective, they discover that WeWork's unique community culture helps them to attract and retain young talent, to improve work efficiency and creativity, and furthermore to reduce operating costs by up to 30% to 40% compared to traditional office environments.

In 2014, the Chinese government announced an initiative to encourage start-ups and innovation. Since then, entrepreneurs and freelancers have exploded in number, leading to a spurt in demand for shared office space. By 2015, the floor space of shared offices in China increased tenfold, with supply in central areas of first-tier cities unable to keep up with demand. The traditional cubicle arrangements of major companies are increasingly unable to satisfy the working requirements of the millennial generation who want independence, communication and to work and live in a truly global social network, marking a unique opportunity for WeWork and the office space that it represents to expand in China.

In March 2016, WeWork completed its first round of financing, led by Legend Holdings and Hony Capital. Other investors included Jinjiang, China Oceanwide and Greenland Holdings. The investor group brought in significant strategic resources and branding support for WeWork's expansion into the Chinese market. Four months after this investment in July 2016, WeWork opened its first office space in China, on Yanping Road in Shanghai. Tenant occupancy reached 100% within only one month, making the premises one of WeWork's best-performing areas worldwide. By September 2016, more offices were opened in Hong Kong and Seoul. In November 2016, its Asian flagship store opened on Weihai Road in Shanghai, and the company later announced that it would open its seventh Chinese office space in seven months, at the prime location of Shanghai's commercial district on Huaihai Road. The company also announced plans to cooperate with Sino-Ocean Group in the opening of two venues in Beijing in 2017.

With its unique competitiveness in working environment development drawn from its in-depth understanding of the millennial generation, WeWork has redefined working style. So far, China has a millennial workforce of over 400 million. In response to this huge market, WeWork is well positioned to become market leader by localizing its activities and making a further global impact. With its experience in exploring opportunities in the world's second-largest economy, its next mission is to replicate such success in the rest of the world.

Conclusion: as a business partner, private equity funds can help enterprises become multinational companies

As China has grown from the world's factory to the world's market, it has also transformed from a capital importer into a capital exporter. During this transformation, China's capital and production capacity have both been channelled overseas, while (high value added) services and products have been drawn in. Through such an exchange, it can be seen that an increasing number of Chinese MNEs are quickly growing up. Jushi and Jinjiang have travelled outwards, while PizzaExpress and WeWork have found new roots in China, all following the trend of the internationalization of Chinese companies, and the localization of international companies. Bi-directional capital flows are reflected in the ongoing phenomenon of China's integration with the rest of the world. Importantly, during such a process, Chinese companies and investors can act as a bridge between different markets.

The interaction between the Chinese economy and the global economy is accompanied by both economies learning from each other. On the one hand, Chinese companies going global need to learn to adopt the best practices and play by the rules of the international game. On the other hand, the world is also becoming accustomed to the rise of Chinese enterprises. With China being the world's second-largest economy, Chinese companies are positioned to play a more important role on the world stage: this is not simply about learning from the world's experience and applying it in China as before, but rather about taking initiatives and becoming an inseparable part of the global economy, leading and innovating in new areas and industries (such as Internet technology) and having a strong voice in shaping the rules for the new world economy.

In this process, Chinese private equity funds will continue to play an important role. With resource advantages and experience in cross-border investment, they will be vital players in the internationalization of Chinese enterprises and the localization of international companies.

14

THE DYNAMICS OF CHINESE OUTBOUND INVESTMENT – CHALLENGES AND CASE STUDIES

Andrew Wood and Yu Cao[1]

Introduction

Opportunity exists alongside risk in the world of outward direct investment (ODI). This is especially true for Chinese investors, being often relatively new to global mergers and acquisitions (M&A). In this section, we explore some of the key hurdles Chinese companies currently face in outbound M&A. We also look at a handful of case studies from recent years in order to understand better some of the complex dynamics at play.

Setting the scene – common challenges facing Chinese outbound investors

Chinese companies are enjoying an unprecedented buying spree internationally off the back of many positive factors both at home and abroad – from the relaxation of economic policies within China to the slowdown of major Western economies in the aftermath of the global financial crisis. However rosy things may appear on the surface, recent statistics prepared by Boston Consulting Group (BCG) paint a somewhat sobering picture. On average, only 67% of outbound deals by Chinese investors are actually completed – a number that lags behind equivalent data for Western outbound activities. Further, only 32% of China outbound deals were described by those surveyed by BCG as 'trouble-free' (Willers et al., 2015).

Something is clearly hindering the efforts of many ambitious investors looking to expand their reach abroad. Based on our experience, we see the following key issues as those most commonly faced.

Not having a well thought-out international acquisition strategy

Attempts at opportunistic acquisitions without a stress-tested rationale become more evident at times like this, when external macroeconomic factors make large swathes of the international market appear 'good value'. However, not having a coherent investment strategy and lacking a clear understanding of why a deal is being done can fatally undermine the M&A process. It can, for example, make it extremely challenging to convince a seller of the benefits of what is being offered by a bidder, even in a non-competitive bid scenario. Even if an acquisition is ultimately successful, critical opportunities for synergy and cost efficiencies can be overlooked if the target company cannot be easily placed into the larger context of a company's expansion plans.

Too often, outbound investors launch bids with a focus on short-term financial return, without giving due attention to the longer-term aspects of the transaction. A desire for a quick return on investment above all else can lead to an undue fixation on purchase price in negotiations, to the detriment of other, perhaps more subtle (but important), terms.

Deal management and timing

As in the world of project management, the ability to successfully implement a deal is inextricably linked with the amount of early preparation carried out. Preparation is key to understanding a deal's likely time and personnel demands, as well as a company's knowledge and gaps in expertise that need filling by external advisers. Embarking upon a transaction without having adequately considered these factors and without having allocated sufficient – and the right – internal resources is likely to result in a missed opportunity. Being on the back foot hinders a company's ability to anticipate the ebb and flow of a deal, which in turn can lead to timing slips which jeopardise the deal – particularly in a competitive bid context.

We see professional advisers often brought on board quite late in deals. Attempting to execute a deal without the requisite expertise – or without giving advisers the necessary time to complete due diligence and properly advise their clients – not only exposes the investor to unknown potential financial, legal and reputational risks but also risks frustrating the seller and its team and undermining the investor's credibility and sincerity at the negotiating table.

Deals frequently fail due to a poor grasp not only of what needs to be delivered by when but also what needs to be done by whom in order to be able to deliver. Advance internal stakeholder management and involving the right people early is essential to avoid internal timing roadblocks, particularly in organisations where the decision-making process may be relatively stratified or complicated. We have seen examples of deal teams negotiating transactions largely autonomously until the last minute and then struggling to obtain the necessary internal approvals to proceed on the terms agreed by them – not only can this create internal tensions as a result of not keeping the necessary people 'in the loop', but it also runs the risk of internal decision-makers not agreeing with the terms of the deal struck and the deal team needing to go back to the negotiating table at a late stage. This is a good way to lose goodwill with a seller.

Difficulties with effective cross-cultural communication

Failure to communicate effectively over geographical and cultural boundaries can put a wall between buyer and seller that does not need to exist, and it can undermine rapport and seller confidence as well as make it difficult for a buyer to sell its bid properly.

The right advisers, with local and international experience and insight, can be instrumental in helping to bridge not only linguistic but also cultural gaps. Used properly, they can also help give context to the unique traits of doing business in the relevant territory that may otherwise be missed.

As mentioned above, it is not uncommon for advisers to be brought into a deal quite late. Chinese buyers need to be cognizant of their own abilities to deal with cross-cultural communications, so they can bring in appropriate advisers at the right time. Spending insufficient time upfront with advisers in trying to understand the cultural aspects of a deal – including very practically what is or is not the 'market norm' in the territory – can readily lead to expectation mismatches between buyer and seller and unnecessary tensions. We know, for example, of a relatively recent situation where a Chinese bidder expressed strong resistance to the manner in which purchase consideration was being calculated in a competitive auction abroad because it was not consistent with the bidder's experience in China. It was however consistent with both the territory and the industry in which the target company operated. While the bidder ultimately relented on the point, it was not asked to proceed to the final round of the auction even though the general terms of its offer were largely competitive relative to the ultimate winner.

Chinese investors often place significance on the value of 'principal to principal' meetings in facilitating knotty commercial negotiations. Advisers are frequently not invited to such meetings (or if they attend they may be asked not to actively contribute). While the active involvement of advisers may create a different dynamic to that of a strict 'principal to principal' meeting, the right advisers will be able not only to help facilitate discussions from a practical linguistic perspective but also to pick up on non-verbal nuances that may otherwise be missed.

Effective cross-cultural communication is also vitally important for post-acquisition integration. Whereas the buyer and the seller will likely only be 'ships that pass in the night' and will have no ongoing dealings post-acquisition, the buyer will be adopting the target company into its family. Taking steps to manage that relationship early and establishing rapport across geographical and cultural boundaries with those key managers of the target company who will be retained post-acquisition will be instrumental in effectively implementing a post-acquisition integration plan. We have seen instances where target management have been wary of – and even hostile to – their Chinese acquirers due to their concerns around job continuity and business strategy not being adequately dealt with early on. This made obtaining their buy-in post-acquisition an uphill struggle.

The legal and regulatory landscape – the (in)ability to offer certainty

Overseas sellers often express some level of concern around the execution certainty of a deal with a Chinese buyer, due to what some see as a relatively opaque regulatory approval process in China. In recent years, the Chinese government has responded to these concerns by significantly streamlining the ODI approval process, which has been very well received globally. Nevertheless, the fact that multiple regulators are involved and that each has the power to effectively veto a deal is still viewed as a significant deterrent. Recent highly publicized regulatory scrutiny in obtaining foreign exchange control approvals in China and talks in November 2016 of potential capital controls have also been considered by some as examples of regulatory opaqueness. Reportedly, 30 outbound deals in Europe and the US – worth almost US$75 billion – were cancelled in 2016 (Jones and Espinosa, 2017). Obviously, the Chinese government will not close any 'window' that has already been opened, which the market should have more confidence in. Nevertheless, it is possible that overseas sellers will tend to favour prospective purchasers from jurisdictions with fewer regulatory hurdles if the deal terms being offered by them are otherwise substantially the same as those offered by Chinese bidders.

It is not just domestic factors that have created an atmosphere of regulatory uncertainty. As we will see further in the section below entitled 'European high-tech acquisitions – a new headwind?', European regulatory and political sentiment towards Chinese investment is in certain areas becoming more cautious and conservative. There are also concerns that under Donald Trump, Chinese investments into the US may become subject to even greater national security scrutiny by CFIUS. All of this only adds further to the wariness of overseas sellers.

The natural response to these factors has in many cases been for Chinese bidders to compensate for this uncertainty with a higher price or to give in to demands for cash deposits and heavy break fees for failure to obtain regulatory clearances (as was seen in the case of HNA Group's US$6 billion acquisition of Ingram Micro). While this has been attractive to certain sellers, many still view the damage (in terms of economics and publicity) that can arise from a failed sale as too great a risk. For example, few would want to risk experiencing the pain felt by the shareholders of German chip equipment manufacturer Aixtron when its shares fell by 13% in the immediate aftermath of the German government withdrawing its approval for the company's takeover by a Chinese consortium towards the end of 2016 (Reuters, 2016). Chinese companies looking overseas will increasingly need to engage with these issues head on in their discussions with sellers and be clear in their plans to address uncertainties. To do this, they will need to further frontload their regulatory and political stakeholder management and planning.

Tax exposure

Tax issues are often instrumental in structuring an overseas transaction and can be easily ignored by smaller and/or relatively inexperienced investors. Tax planning at an early stage is essential to ensure that an investor will be able to extract the maximum value from its overseas investment – whether in the form of dividends, service fees, interest or even sale price on any future exit.

Usually, tax-efficient structures involve setting up intermediate holding companies. In doing so, investors must usually consider commonly, among other things, the following:

- whether there is an advantageous tax treaty between the intermediate holding company's jurisdiction and the investment target's jurisdiction;
- whether corporate income tax in the intermediate holding company's jurisdiction is low or can even be exempted;
- the cost of setting up and maintaining the intermediate holding company;
- the ease of building business substance in the intermediate holding company's jurisdiction for tax purposes; and
- whether there is any foreign exchange control in the intermediate holding company's jurisdiction.

Chinese investors also need to separately consider the effect of tax residency rules in China as well as the tax rules on controlled foreign companies and foreign income tax credits as stipulated by China's tax laws and regulations.

Professional advisers can provide vital support to Chinese investors in navigating through this highly complex and technical area, and they should be engaged early in a deal to provide the maximum benefit.

Difficulties in post-acquisition integration

Cultural factors influencing the ability to successfully integrate a target business post-acquisition have already been discussed above. This assumes that there is in fact a clear and coherent post-acquisition integration plan to implement – too often this is not the case for Chinese investors. It is not uncommon to see insufficient time being spent in the preparation stage of a deal to map out how best to fit the target business into the buyer's existing operations and to identify where possible cost and revenue synergies lie.

Operational governance structures vary globally. Many Chinese groups operate, at this time, in a relatively decentralised manner, with subsidiary businesses having a high degree of day-to-day autonomy within the parameters of performance targets set by the head office. Decision-making in overseas businesses in Europe and the US can frequently be more centralised. This is all the more reason for Chinese buyers to ensure not only that they have the complete buy-in and confidence of the post-acquisition management team overseas (who need to be given clear and coherent objectives for their integration efforts) but also that the overseas management team is equipped with the necessary skills and expertise to deliver. Without these elements, a Chinese buyer may struggle in practice to guide the governance and strategy of its new acquisition.

Labour challenges

We frequently see insufficient time being spent early on in a transaction to identify key personnel who are instrumental to the continued success of a business. Without taking the necessary steps to engage with such key individuals at the outset and obtain comfort that they will remain post-acquisition (whether through revised compensation packages or otherwise), Chinese buyers have been caught short in the past by finding themselves with a shell of a business and a lack of the right people to operate it.

Additionally, post-acquisition integration often involves some streamlining of a target company's workforce, in order to remove overlaps and redundancies. While Chinese companies will already be used to operating in a relatively employee-friendly legal jurisdiction, the costs and logistics associated with downsizing overseas have caught certain Chinese investors by surprise. Heavy redundancy packages required by law may push a deal's costs well beyond expectations if not budgeted for at the outset and can in extreme scenarios render a deal simply not cost-effective.

Even where significant changes to the workforce are not anticipated, in certain countries – France for example – employee unions and/or works councils will commonly be heavily involved in approving the terms of an acquisition. Failure to successfully engage with these bodies at an early stage can not only slow down a deal but derail a deal completely. Experienced local advisers are critical to predicting and negotiating such challenges, which have been the downfall of deals in the past.

European high-tech acquisitions – a new headwind?

China outbound M&A in Europe has increasingly become the focus of regulatory and political scrutiny and concern over the last year (China Venture, 2016). While this has been particularly pronounced in the technology industry, it appears symptomatic of a more general disquiet around the increase in China's appetite for outbound investments and the unsolicited nature of many Chinese investors' offers.

The controversy of Kuka

After quietly amassing a 13.5% stake over the course of almost a year, Midea Group, the home appliance manufacturer, launched an unsolicited EUR 5 billion bid for the German robotics company Kuka AG in May 2016 (Financial China, 2016). Midea's senior management cited perceived opportunities for business synergies – particularly in the areas of robotics development – and increased efficiencies as key reasons for the approach. Reading between the lines, Chinese media has reported this as suggesting that the proposed acquisition was part of a strategy to foster new growth and product diversity in efforts to hedge against a potential recession in the home appliances industry and to expand access to international markets.[2]

This is a move similar to that of one of Midea's competitors, Gree, which earlier in 2016 took steps towards diversifying into the electric vehicle market with the announcement of its acquisition of Zhuhai Yinlong New Energy Co.

International media was quick to pick up on Midea's offer, with the *Wall Street Journal* among others identifying it as part of a surge in unsolicited bids from Chinese companies and as evidence of how brash the Chinese had become in their global mission to buy the best assets available internationally.

Midea's approach also raised the spectre of European protectionism, as Germany's economy minister Sigmar Gabriel quickly remarked that he would welcome an alternative offer for the robotics company from Europe given the company's importance in Germany's car industry (Heller and Georgina, 2016).

While the German government committed to scrutinising the role played by Kuka in the digitisation of the country's industry and the effects of transferring it into Chinese hands, it finally decided not to intervene, and the deal ultimately proceeded. Midea was however required to preserve jobs and factories for seven and a half years and to not delist or otherwise restructure the company during this time.

Aixtron – upping the ante

Approval of the Kuka acquisition did not silence the concerns raised in the corridors of the Bundestag or elsewhere in Europe's political capitals. The European Union's digital economy commissioner Günther Oettinger was reported in a newspaper interview in October 2016 as saying that Europe's high-tech industry 'should not just be sold off' and that other key players in the EU such as Italy and France also backed a 'stronger industrial policy' to protect home-grown technology businesses (Chazan, 2016b). This echoed a similar sentiment coming out of the US, which earlier in 2016 saw Go Scale Capital's proposed acquisition of Philips' lighting business Lumileds terminated due to unspecified CFIUS concerns (Tencent Technology, 2016).

Matters came to a head in Germany shortly thereafter when the German government withdrew its approval for the takeover of Aixtron by a Chinese consortium following its receipt of 'previously unknown security-related information' (Reuters, 2016).

Osram – ever stronger backlash

Tentative approaches to the shareholders of lighting company Osram by both San'an Optoelectronics and Go Scale Capital (bruised but not beaten after Lumileds) towards the end of 2016 triggered the powerful German labour union IG Metall to publicly undertake to block any takeover of the company. The labour union went on record to state that a takeover of the company would bring with it 'significant risks in terms of outflow of critical know-how and the cancellation of projects by customers' and that there was a real concern that any Chinese acquirer would want to 'siphon off Osram's technology' and move production out of Germany (Chazan, 2016a).

Spreading disquiet throughout Europe

Fast forward to early 2017. In the latest sign of increasing protectionism, February saw the governments of Germany, France and Italy write to the European Commissioner for Trade Cecilia Malmström to ask for a right of veto over Chinese high-tech takeovers out of concern for a loss of control over important technology assets. Foreign companies 'must show that their investments in Germany are not driven by the state, and that financing for their deals is in keeping with the market', Germany's deputy economy minister Matthias Machnig was reported as saying (Chazan, 2017).

Our view – what do we think is really underpinning this resistance?

There seem to be at least two key factors at play here. One is the international community's wariness around the motives of Chinese outbound investment in light of the 'Made in China 2025' plan announced in 2015 – as exemplified by deputy economy minister Machnig's desire to see that acquisitions are not driven by the perceived state mandate in China to either beat high-tech companies in the rest of the world or, if that fails, acquire the competition (Gordon, 2016).

Another factor is the allegedly one-sided nature of acquisition opportunities and market access that some in the international community perceive. At the time Midea was courting Kuka's shareholders, German Chancellor Angela Merkel was reported to have expressed frustration at what she saw to be a lack of reciprocity shown toward foreign investors in the Chinese market (Rettman, 2017). She has not been alone in doing so. Foreign media has remarked on several occasions in recent years of the practical and regulatory difficulties they believe foreign companies encounter when looking to invest in certain high-tech industries in China. The OECD has also taken a similar view in placing China almost at the bottom of a list of 59 countries in its assessment of restrictiveness towards foreign direct investment (OECD, 2017). While it is widely accepted that investment restrictions were imposed in certain industries in China for legitimate policy reasons in order to protect national interests, some outside of China have argued that the relaxation of these restrictions over the years have not kept pace with China's economic development and growing strength and independence (Prasad, 2017).

Clear steps have however recently been made in liberalising the regulatory framework around foreign investments into China. In October 2016, the Chinese government rolled out a significant reform of its foreign direct investment regime, under which a 'filing-for-record' system replaced the former 'approval' process for foreign investments other than those covered by a negative control list. It is estimated that following this reform, over 90% of foreign investments will no longer need to go through an approval in advance process (HAIWEN and PARTNERS, 2016). In January 2017, the State Council further issued the 'Notice on the Several Measures for Expansion of China's Opening Up to the Outside World and Active Use of Foreign Capital', which, among other things, mandates the further relaxation of foreign ownership restrictions in certain key financial and manufacturing sectors and clarifies that the strategy, policy and measure of 'Made in China 2025' apply to foreign-invested enterprises and domestic-funded enterprises equally (The State Council, 2017).

For so long as there remains a vocal element outside of China who perceive there to be an unfair lack of reciprocity in investment opportunities, Europe's political backlash against Chinese investment and the territory's growing protectionism are unlikely to see much change for the better. That said, the Chinese government's clear commitment towards simplifying the foreign direct investment process and relaxing foreign investment restrictions should go a long way to assuaging the concerns of this vocal element over time.

Complexity of cross-border tax matters

What follows is a brief case study to demonstrate, among other things, the complexity of tax issues that may arise in a cross-border transaction and, consequently, the importance of having the awareness to plan – and engage experienced advisers – early.

The transaction in question was, on the face of it, relatively straightforward. Company A, a Chinese investor, needed to invest in certain talented US citizens for the purpose of producing commercially valuable intellectual property products. These products were expected to then be sold and exploited worldwide to generate revenues in the nature of, essentially, royalties. The parties together decided to form a joint venture through which to conduct all production, sales and licensing activities.

The initial – and quite logical – inclination of the parties was to form the joint venture in the US, as the development and production activities for the products were to largely take place there. This, however, would not have been tax efficient. Revenues from the US would have been subject to US federal and state income taxes and then withholding taxes before Company A's share of the revenues could have been remitted back to China. Also, revenues from outside the US, if travelling through the US joint venture, would have been subject to taxes levied by the repatriating country, then US federal and state income tax, and then the US withholding tax. The aggregate effective tax rate would have defeated the purpose of the transaction.

Naturally, the next route that was explored was to move the joint venture to a tax-free jurisdiction. What if the joint venture were set up in the British Virgin Islands (BVI), for example, with a production entity in the US? The parties studied the possibility of forming a limited partnership in the BVI, which would have been a so-called 'pass-through' entity. While income generated would not have been subject to US corporate income tax for the US production entity or foreign entity withholding income tax for the BVI partnership, it quickly became apparent that the royalty revenues from the US and many other foreign jurisdictions would have been subject to significant other withholding taxes when being paid into the BVI. More importantly, given the nature of the transaction, the BVI joint venture principals would have needed to constantly carry out business activities in the US, which would likely have made the US-sourced income constitute so-called 'effectively connected income', rendering the joint venture subject to US corporate income taxes regardless.

The parties finally realised that they needed to consider setting up more than one joint venture to handle all of these challenges. With the same equity ratio, the parties now proposed to set up three limited partnerships to conduct sales and licensing activities for the products and to receive revenues from, separately, the US, China and the rest of the world. It was agreed that the US joint venture would be located in the US, the China joint venture would be located in China, and the 'rest of the world' joint venture would be located somewhere that was most tax-efficient in light of the available double-taxation treaties. All three joint ventures were to be structured as pass-through entities.

This siloed investment structure looked very different from what was originally expected, but it was substantially more tax efficient. It was not perfect however – if Company A were to act as the direct investor into the US joint venture, then after US corporate income tax there would have still been US withholding tax levied on Company A's share of the revenue.

This then led to the introduction of a so-called 'double blocker' structure for Company A. In this structure, Company A would establish a wholly owned subsidiary in the US (Sub 1). Sub 1 would then in turn establish its own wholly owned subsidiary in the US (Sub 2). Sub 2 would act as the direct investor in the proposed US joint venture. Conceptually, given current US tax law practices, if Company A wanted to take back the first round of royalty income, after US enterprise income taxes were levied, it would be able to dissolve Sub 1, and the money residing within Sub 1 could be taken back by Company A as Sub 1's parent free from US withholding tax due to the dissolution. Because royalty income (hopefully) continues for a long term, after a certain amount of time Company A would be able to dissolve Sub 2 as well, allowing it to again save on the withholding tax that would otherwise be applicable.

Our view – what does this example tell us?

All the above structures and complexities are depicted in only a very brief and conceptual manner here, but they do demonstrate the importance of investors bringing in experienced tax advisers early, as tax structuring alone can take months.

Competing with the dual track phenomenon – a case study

Dual track processes – where sellers run an IPO process for their target business simultaneously with a sale process – have in recent years become increasingly common around the world, as they allow sellers to keep their exit options open until late in the day. Inevitably, Chinese investors come across these structures in their outbound investment activities.

The following case study is anonymised but is a good example of how cross-cultural dynamics, questions of bidder sophistication in international deal-doing and regulatory uncertainty can undermine the competitiveness of a Chinese outbound offer in a foreign dual-track process.

The target company, based in Europe, was majority-owned by investors who were looking for an exit opportunity. The decision was made to find the most appropriate exit through a dual track process, simultaneously pursuing a listing on a major international exchange and a retail sale through a public auction process.

A consortium of Chinese state-owned enterprises put forward a bid for the target company. The shareholders of the target company continued to test the market while engaging with the consortium. The consortium's bid was ultimately unsuccessful, and the target's shareholders decided to proceed with the IPO process instead.

Why the consortium failed – a question of value and flexibility

The IPO gave the shareholders the opportunity for a partial sell-down only, as opposed to the full exit expected under the auction sale route. A partial sale was ultimately favoured, as the robust financial performance of the target company to date meant that the shareholders had confidence in future share price increases (which they wanted to be able to enjoy).

The Chinese consortium became hamstrung internally on the subject of price given the investment return requirements of certain consortium members, which meant that it was unable to offer pricing flexibility. This firm stance on pricing during negotiations meant that the price it offered for a full buy-out – while not necessarily unreasonable – was not sufficiently attractive to the shareholders to compensate for them having to give up the possibility for future capital growth on at least part of their respective stakes.

Why the consortium failed – a question of certainty and credibility

Also instrumental in the shareholders choosing to proceed with the IPO was the issue of certainty. The Chinese consortium's bid was made subject to confirmatory due diligence, which meant that the consortium could potentially pull out of the sale process at a later date if it was not satisfied with the results of its further investigations into the target company. The shareholders decided this was an unacceptable risk.

Additionally, the shareholders were concerned about the level of regulatory approval the consortium would require and the execution uncertainty this introduced. Of concern were not only the National Development and Reform Commission, Ministry of Commerce, China Securities Regulatory Commission and State Administration of Foreign Exchange filing requirements within China – and certain disagreements within the consortium as to what precisely these would be – but also the perceived need for anti-trust filings in a number of jurisdictions including the US, EU and China. It was also agreed that CFIUS clearance in the US would be required before the sale could complete, which in light of the regulatory body's approach to approvals described elsewhere in this book was seen as a variable not entirely within the parties' control.

The shareholders also expressed concern around the make-up and credibility of the consortium itself following the introduction of a third consortium member, which had been strongly opposed by the shareholders from the beginning of negotiations and which weakened the consortium's perceived strength.

The consortium further damaged its credibility in the eyes of the target's shareholders by not engaging with the draft sale documentation provided to it – instead, it responded with an entirely new draft share purchase agreement. This also raised further concerns around the ability to reach a binding agreement on the transaction in a timely manner – or at all.

Conclusion

As we can see from the above analysis, the road to overseas investment by Chinese companies is littered with a handful of potential obstacles for prospective investors to overcome. Some – such as deficiencies in strategic planning and project management and difficulties with effective cross-cultural communication – are more micro in nature and are within the power of Chinese investors to ultimately take charge of with the help of seasoned professional advisers. Others, however – such as the impact on deal certainty of applicable laws and regulations and the regulatory, political and commercial sentiment abroad towards investment from China – are part of a more macro investment landscape that Chinese investors must be cognizant of and factor into their investment decision-making. Time will tell whether the continued commitments made by the Chinese government to improve both legal and regulatory transparency and foreign access to certain key industries in China will help address the headwinds that Chinese investors are experiencing in this landscape. Our hope is that such moves will eventually yield positive results in this regard and that Chinese investors when going abroad will be able to compete on an even footing with other international investors.

Notes

1 The authors would like to thank their colleagues at Haiwen & Partners for their invaluable assistance in preparing this analysis.

2 As indicated by Kuafo Consulting chief adviser Liu Buchen in his interview with the Xinhua news network on 20 May 2016 (Xinhua-China Focus, 2016).

References

'Approval upon Chinese company's acquisition of Axitron withdrawn' 2016, *Reuters*, 24 October. Available from: http://cn.reuters.com/article/china-fgc-aixtron-idCNKCS12O0MW. [19 February 2017].

Chazan, G 2016a, 'German labour union warns Chinese suitors over Osram bid', *Financial Times*, 15 November, 2016. Available from: www.ft.com/content/ed463896-aa74-11e6-9cb3-bb8207902122. [19 February 2017].

Chazan, G 2016b, 'Germany withdraws approval for Chinese takeover of tech group', *Financial Times*, 24 October. Available from: www.ft.com/content/f1b3e52e-99b0-11e6-8f9b-70e3cabccfae. [19 February 2017].

Chazan, G 2017, 'EU countries seek stronger right of veto on Chinese takeovers', *Australian Financial Review*, 15 February. Available from: www.afr.com/news/world/eu-countries-seek-stronger-right-of-veto-on-chinese-takeovers-20170215-gudfca. [19 February 2017].

'China's Midea taps new business with Kuka bid' 2016, *Xinhua-China Focus*, 20 May. Available from: http://news.xinhuanet.com/english/2016-05/20/c_135374502.htm. [19 February 2017].

'Chinese syndicate's acquisition of Philips being blocked by the US Government' 2016, *Tencent Technology*, 22 January. Available from: http://tech.qq.com/a/20160122/046288.htm. [19 February 2017].

'Data report on Chinese ODI in Europe' 2016, *China Venture*, 11 October. Available from: www.chinaventure.com.cn/cmsmodel/news/detail/303474.shtml. [19 February 2017].

'Germany withdrew approval of Aixtron deal on new security-related information' 2016, *Reuters*, 24 October. Available from: http://finance.yahoo.com/news/germany-withdr-approval-aixtron-deal-130219113.html. [19 February 2017].

Gordon, G 2016, 'U.S., EU say "no" to China buying the world', *Forbes*, 30 October. Available from: www.forbes.com/sites/gordonchang/2016/10/30/u-s-eu-say-no-to-china-buying-the-world/#3fb42d5922b8. [19 February 2017].

Haiwen & Partners 2016, 'Haiwen alert: China amends its foreign investment approvals', 12 October. Available from: http://mp.weixin.qq.com/s?src=3&timestamp=1487502474&ver=1&signature=9f*VHSGOQXvy-3nXeI5Z3NHWbZhIE-hipx59lwwfrEBxKkkclyBKA2vUaGxzxj7NBVTaGAI94UeMxeuVdSB6oTCYWzCKWYhdYCDX9NYvB8yUoq5a0XPfgk5YXDZUnk12u1YPSVF-xxOeWox2bpKBbgUzh9Xc73wP-wdtSkyNYCA=. [19 February 2017].

Heller, G & Georgina, P 2016, 'German economy minister says would welcome European bid for Kuka', *Reuters*, 1 June. Available from: http://finance.yahoo.com/news/german-economy-minister-says-welcome-225916762.html. [19 February 2017].

Jones, C & Espinosa, J 2017, 'Overseas Chinese acquisitions worth $75bn cancelled last year', *Financial Times*, 6 February. [19 February 2017], www.ft.com/content/b0ff426c-eabe-11e6-930f-061b01e23655.

'Midea group's TOB on 56.79% of Kuka's equity' 2016, *Financial China*, 14 July. Available from: http://finance.china.com.cn/news/20160714/3811930.shtml. [19 February 2017].

OECD 2017, *FDI Regulatory Restrictiveness Index*. Available from: www.oecd.org/investment/fdiindex.htm. [19 February 2017].

Prasad, E 2017, 'Colomn: Is China's economy a house of cards?', *PBS Newshour*, 13 January. Available from: www.pbs.org/newshour/making-sense/column-chinas-economy-house-cards/. [19 February 2017].

Rettman, A 2017, 'EU states seek protection for high-end technology', *EU Observer*, 15 February. Available from: https://euobserver.com/economic/136914. [19 February 2017].

The State Council 2017, 'Notice on the several measures for expansion of China's opening up to the outside world and active use of foreign capital'. Available from: http://law.wkinfo.com.cn/document/show?aid=MTAwMTA0NTAyMTk%3D&bid=&collection=legislation&language=%E4%B8%AD%E6%96%87&tokens=&modules=&showType=1. [19 February 2017].

Willers, Y, Li, J, Luo, Y, Yuan, S & Yang, L 2015, *Welcome to the New Era of Chinese Enterprises' ODI*. Available from: www.bcg.com.cn/export/sites/default/cn/files/publications/reports_pdf/BCG-Gearing-Up-New-Era-China-Outbound-MandA-Sep-2015-CHN.pdf. [19 February 2017].

15

CAPITALIZING ON OPPORTUNITIES AND TACKLING MAJOR LEGAL CHALLENGES AND RISKS

A practitioner's perspective

Joseph C. Shenker, Chun Wei and Jordan H. Oreck

Introduction

In this era of globalization, companies commonly seek to expand through investments outside of their home country. Cross-border transactions provide companies with opportunities that are unavailable when operating solely domestically; however, they also present challenges and risks not present in the domestic setting. While Chinese investors have an array of particular advantages in cross-border investments, they are also subject to several unique obstacles relating to the transaction execution process, obtaining of regulatory approvals required for the transaction, and integrating the target's business after closing. It is therefore imperative for Chinese investors to adequately prepare for these challenges in order to ensure that each transaction has the highest chance of coming to fruition and yielding its anticipated benefits.

Managing key transaction execution issues

The annual number of overseas acquisitions by Chinese investors increased from less than ten in 2004 to 154 in 2014 (Willers et al., 2015b). Despite this increase, 'the deal completion rate for outbound M&A by Chinese [acquirers] is just 67 percent, still behind more developed peers such as in America, Europe, and Japan', according to a report published by the Boston Consulting Group in 2015 (Willers et al., 2015a). Why is it that Chinese investors complete such a relatively low number of transactions?

One reason is a relative lack of experience in cross-border transactions compared to investors from some other countries. 'An [acquirer] that has successful experience with overseas [acquisitions] is more likely to complete a deal than one without experience' (Zhang and Ebbers, 2010, pp. 117–118, 122–124), and it has only been in recent years that Chinese investors have become actively involved in large-scale cross-border transactions.

In China, the conduct of business has traditionally relied heavily on relationships, and investment opportunities and the process of executing transactions in China depend on such connections to a larger degree than in international investments. Outside of China, fiduciary duties of directors in evaluating and executing transactions often override considerations of relationships, and competition amongst bidders is commonplace. It is paramount for Chinese investors to understand these issues and how they affect the deal execution process in order to facilitate a successful transaction.

Fiduciary duties and the potential for litigation

Fiduciary duties of directors (and the related risk of transaction-based litigation) form one of the foundations for the transaction process in international deals. In common law jurisdictions, directors generally have fiduciary duties to do what is in the best interests of a company and its shareholders. A given transaction, particularly a company sale, may or may not be in the best interests of a company and its shareholders. A variety of factors, including (importantly) the price the investor offers and the target's forecast, must be carefully evaluated by directors in concluding whether a transaction is advisable and how to manage the transaction execution process.

Directors' duties are taken particularly seriously in transactions involving listed companies because of the scrutiny around the actions of listed companies' directors, and each of the target itself, the directors of the target that approve the transaction, and the buyer may be sued by former shareholders if a proper process is not followed. Illustratively, 84% of deals valued over $100 million involving US public companies were litigated in 2015, and 64% were litigated in the first half of 2016 (Sinha, 2016).

A primary driver for the high amount of litigation in the US is class-action lawsuits, through which a dispersed number of individuals – none of whom likely have a claim sufficient in magnitude to warrant a suit on their own – can file a suit together seeking a large judgment against the company, its directors and/or the buyer either for a breach of fiduciary duty or for disclosure deficiencies. In the US, certain law firms specialize in monitoring transactions, seeking out individuals to represent a 'class' of plaintiffs for such lawsuits (usually former shareholders of the target) and commencing suit against the defendants in order to obtain a substantial contingency fee or costs; even where amounts awarded to the actual plaintiffs are relatively *de minimis* or the only remedy is corrective disclosure. These suits are launched even where the likelihood of success is low, as defendants often find it more convenient and cost-efficient to settle rather than litigate. For example, 'from 2009 to 2014, between 74 and 78 percent of M&A litigation was resolved before the deal closed', and although this declined to 56% in the first half of 2016 (Sinha, 2016), largely because of enhanced judicial scrutiny of proposed settlements and their benefits to the plaintiffs, it still remains high.

In light of their duties and the potential for litigation, directors of target companies are required to follow an often proscriptive process to ensure not only that the sale price is fair to shareholders but also that the deal execution process properly safeguards the interests of the company and its shareholders. This requires directors to stay informed during a transaction with respect to its progress and terms, carefully evaluate and compare the price offered by buyers to the target's prospects on a standalone basis or after an alternate transaction, and vigorously negotiate to obtain the best deal for shareholders. During litigation, facts regarding deal execution are reviewed in hindsight, and therefore directors must not only follow the aforementioned process but also ensure that written records and communications – such as meeting minutes and presentations made to directors – properly document it.

Chinese investors must appreciate these considerations when undertaking international transactions. They may query why a seller is so adamant on certain terms or compliance with certain timing deadlines or, alternatively, why it cannot conclude negotiations more quickly. For example, in discharging their duties, directors of selling companies often conduct a 'market check', which can take several weeks, in an attempt to find additional bidders that may offer better deal terms. By understanding the duties and potential liability of directors, Chinese investors will be better prepared to execute transactions and proactively engage with the target in a positive and constructive manner. For instance, where the investor has a strong desire to sign quickly, instead of a pre-signing 'market check', the investor could suggest a post-signing 'go shop' period, allowing the seller to seek competing proposals for an agreed amount of time after signing. Although this may seem to interfere with an acquirer's desire to close a transaction, it may be necessary to ensure that the target's directors have complied with their fiduciary duties, therefore reducing the chance or costs of litigation.

Chinese investors should also encourage sellers to follow a proper process not only out of empathy for the target and its directors in light of the possibility of litigation but also because of the potential liability that the investor itself may be subject to. If the target is the defendant of post-closing litigation, it will be the buyer that suffers the consequences. This is frequently the case in lawsuits where the plaintiffs allege that the disclosure provided to shareholders in connection with a transaction was somehow deficient, depriving shareholders of information they were entitled to when voting on a transaction. Therefore, in addition to allowing the seller to properly prepare deal-related disclosure, buyers should be involved in the drafting process to limit the chances of inheriting litigation resulting from the target's non-compliance with disclosure requirements. Following a proper process also helps ensure, although it does not guarantee, that shareholders receive fair value for their shares. This reduces the likelihood of a successful 'appraisal suit' post-closing, which could require the buyer to pay a higher purchase price to shareholders who dissented from the transaction.

Competitive bidding environments and the consequences of failing to follow the sale process

In addition to fiduciary duties, a competitive bidding environment or an auction is also a foundation for the development of a sale process which in turn must be followed by all parties. The typical auction process in cross-border transactions commences when the seller sends a process letter to multiple interested parties, together with initial drafts of transaction documents, requesting comments or conditions to be met by a specified date. In the past, inexperienced PRC bidders have prejudiced, and even lost, opportunities by failing to follow the process guidelines.

PRC bidders may be particularly disadvantaged in auctions due to factors within China, such as the failure to obtain approval (or pre-approval) from domestic regulators prior to submitting an offer. For example, in 2011, Bright Food's bid for 50% of Yoplait was rejected in favour of a competing offer from General Mills – despite Bright Food offering a higher price – in part due to Bright Food's late bid submission. It was reported that while General Mills and the seller were progressing with negotiations, Bright Food was still evaluating the transaction internally, as well as waiting for the National Development and Reform Commission's approval to submit its bid (Tse et al., 2011).

CNOOC's attempt to acquire Unocal in 2005, although some time ago, is a notable example of how a proposed buyer's difficulty in following the sale process can result in lost opportunities. As a result of CNOOC's own board processes, it was unable to submit its offer by the deadline set by Unocal. This allowed Chevron, a competing bidder, to reach an agreement with Unocal only a few days later (Pottinger et al., 2005). Although CNOOC did improve the price of its offer in response to Chevron's bid, CNOOC's revised proposal provided that it would no longer pay a previously agreed US$500 million termination fee, which represented a significant, last-minute change to an important economic term (Guerrera, 2005). This request and CNOOC's failure to react before the deadline set by the seller in the sale process, coupled with difficulties and uncertainties in obtaining regulatory approvals in the United States, resulted in CNOOC ultimately withdrawing its proposal and losing the transaction to Chevron – despite Chevron offering a lower purchase price (Pottinger et al., 2005).

These cases illustrate the importance of following the seller's process, how essential it is for Chinese investors to consider the timing implications of various work streams that must be completed prior to submitting a bid, and how Chinese investors cannot assume that because they are offering the highest price that they will secure an investment opportunity. It is of paramount importance to follow and respect the sale process in order to maximize the chances of signing and closing a transaction.

Navigating the regulatory approval process

In any cross-border transaction, assessment and management of the regulatory approval process is critical. Common examples of important regulatory approvals include those from relevant antitrust authorities, industry-specific regulators and national security review bodies. However, several factors (including the background of government ownership of, and other connections the government has with, Chinese companies; the target country's views towards foreign investments, particularly in sensitive industries; and the perception that Chinese companies are 'taking over' through their acquisitions in recent years) have all created challenges for Chinese investors in obtaining foreign regulatory approvals. Although each transaction presents its own set of required regulatory approvals and related issues, there are certain approvals which best illustrate some of the issues unique to Chinese investors: namely, national security review in the United States and competition approval in Europe.

United States national security review

When purchasing or investing in a company that is based or does business in the United States, one critical area for Chinese investors is the process for national security review of foreign investment in the United States. The Committee on Foreign Investment in the United States, or CFIUS, reviews 'transactions that could result in control of a US business by a foreign person in order to determine the effect of such transactions on the national security of the United States' (US Department of the Treasury, 2012). 'Control' is a very broad concept and may include various transactions short of the acquisition of majority control. If a transaction 'presents national security risks and other provisions of law do not provide adequate authority to address the risks, then CFIUS may enter into an agreement with, or impose conditions on, parties to mitigate such risks or may refer the case to the President for action' (US Department of the Treasury, 2010). In general, very few transactions are referred to the President; if the parties are not able to clear their transaction at the CFIUS level, through mitigation agreements or otherwise, they typically abandon the transaction.

According to the most recent CFIUS Annual Report to Congress, acquisitions by investors from China accounted for the largest number of CFIUS notices filed for the three-year period from 2012 to 2014 (19%) and in each of the three individual years (CFIUS, 2016, p. 19). Increasing numbers of attempts by Chinese investors to acquire US companies, particularly in industries deemed essential to national security, have led to concerns of US policymakers due to the potential for leakage of American technology, intellectual property and sensitive information pertaining to critical infrastructure (Saha, 2012, pp. 205–206).

The CFIUS review process is 'voluntary', in that it is not unlawful to close a transaction without obtaining CFIUS approval; however, CFIUS can review a transaction on its own initiative, and its jurisdiction is not cut off by the closing of the transaction or the passage of time. Indeed, there are recent, high-profile examples of CFIUS revisiting transactions involving Chinese acquirers post-closing. For example, in 2011, Huawei – despite already having transactions with 3Com, 2Wire and Motorola derailed due to CFIUS objections – purchased $2 million of intellectual property rights from 3Leaf Systems without filing for CFIUS review. CFIUS ultimately required divestment of the acquired assets after reviewing the transaction on its own initiative post-closing (Flicker and Parsons, 2011). Similarly, in 2012, Ralls was ordered to divest wind farms located near a US naval base that it had acquired without obtaining pre-approval from CFIUS (Cooper, 2012).

Therefore, the CFIUS review process is a vital regulatory hurdle to clear in advance when the US business implicates US national security. Potential national security concerns associated with any proposed transaction should be considered early in the process whenever a Chinese investor seeks to acquire or invest in a US company or asset or in a company doing business in the United States. If it appears that the transaction is one which implicates national security, given the potentially grave consequences of a post-closing review by CFIUS, voluntary filings are generally advisable. CFIUS encourages parties to consult with it prior to making filings to help aid CFIUS in understanding the transaction and allow it to request that the parties include specific information in the filing (US Department of the Treasury, 2014) – all of which may help facilitate the review process. As it can be difficult to determine whether US national security is implicated, investors should consider hiring consultants with expertise in this area to provide assistance.

Partnering with co-investors that do not usually raise national security concerns with CFIUS may also help in politically sensitive transactions, as can engaging public relations specialists to assist with local communications and outreach to various interest groups. For example, in connection with CNOOC's acquisition of Nexen, CNOOC engaged lobbying and public relations firms in Canada and the United States to facilitate obtaining approvals from regulators (Spegele, 2012), and the transaction did ultimately obtain CFIUS approval and close.

Chinese investors should note that the potential for CFIUS to block a transaction may be sufficient for the seller to proceed with an alternate buyer (particularly where multiple potential buyers are involved), even where the Chinese investor offers the most attractive price. For example, in February 2016, Fairchild Semiconductor sold itself to US-based ON Semiconductor, even in light of a higher competing bid from a Chinese consortium, due to the CFIUS approval risk associated with the Chinese investors (Bartz and Baker, 2016). The next month, in March 2016, Affymetrix rejected a topping bid from a Chinese investor in favour of a lower-valued transaction, similarly citing a lack of certainty about the CFIUS approval process as a reason for its decision (Merced, 2016).

Therefore, Chinese investors must appreciate this risk when negotiating with US targets and show the target that they are sensitive to the potentially lowered level of closing certainty that they present. Where a buyer may be seen to introduce heightened regulatory and completion risk, the requirement to pay a 'reverse break-fee' (an agreed percentage of the transaction value payable by the buyer if specified regulatory obstacles materialize) may be requested by the seller. A target that would otherwise be unwilling to forego an alternative transaction with a higher chance of completion may be willing to take on the risk of CFIUS not approving a deal if, in the event that risk materializes, they are compensated for their costs and lost opportunity.

Nevertheless, it is important to highlight that many transactions involving Chinese investors have been cleared by CFIUS. Notably, in August 2016, CFIUS approved ChemChina's $43 billion acquisition of Syngenta, a global biotechnology company. Often, CFIUS may approve a transaction through agreeing on mitigation arrangements with the parties, such as the divestment of certain assets either simultaneously with closing or within an agreed amount of time after closing (which may require placing the assets to be divested in a trust pending disposition); however, in this case, although Syngenta did not disclose any details of CFIUS clearance, it indicated that any mitigation measures it was required to take were 'not material to [its] business' (Revill, 2016). The Syngenta transaction also illustrates the important points that the target need not be a US company for CFIUS review to apply (substantial operations in, and sales to, the United States may be sufficient) and that a voluntary filing coupled with general cooperation with CFIUS can ultimately result in a positive outcome.

Chinese investors should also proactively consider potential mitigation arrangements where US national security is likely to be an issue, and deliberate on how a deal can be structured in light of potential national security review. If an acquisition of 100% of the target would create regulatory uncertainty, the buyer can consider whether purchasing only key assets, divisions, subsidiaries or less than 100% of the target would alleviate risk or, alternatively, if assets that are likely to cause regulatory concern can be divested pre- or post-closing.

European commission competition review

Outside of the United States, one critical regulatory approval process is antitrust review by the European Commission. A recent landmark decision by the European Commission is likely to have a substantial effect on the Commission's review of antitrust filings where Chinese SOEs are involved, and it illustrates an issue that is unique to Chinese SOEs making investments in Europe.

In its decision for 'EDF/CGN/NNB Group of Companies', the European Commission concluded that China General Nuclear Power Corporation and other Chinese SOEs in the energy sector 'should not be deemed to have an independent power of decision from Central SASAC' and that the 'turnover of all companies controlled by Central SASAC that are active in the energy industry should therefore be aggregated' in determining whether the thresholds of the EU Merger Regulation are met (*EDF/CGN/NNB Group of Companies* [Case M.7850] Commission Decision 32016M7850 [2016], para 49).

The ramifications of this decision are significant. Although the decision covered parties in the energy sector, it suggests that the turnover of Chinese SOEs in other sectors could be aggregated in determining whether the thresholds are met. Therefore, Chinese SOEs that previously did not anticipate having to obtain clearance from European antitrust authorities may need to do so if they, together with other SOEs in the relevant sector, generate substantial turnover in Europe. An acquiring SOE would need to gather operating data from other SOEs in order to determine what regulatory filings are required prior to signing, which may create logistical delays and decrease closing certainty. This is in addition to the general competition approval process in Europe, which may require approvals from several individual member states, in addition to the European Commission itself.

Transitional services, post-closing integration and operations

Although signing and closing a transaction is important, it is what comes after closing that will ultimately determine the success or failure of a transaction. Successfully transitioning into a new business line, integrating an acquired business into existing operations, and effectively operating a business post-closing are other areas in which Chinese investors in particular have struggled in the past.

As Chinese companies may not be accustomed to operating in foreign environments (in particular, the types of market economies in Western countries), planning and preparation become critical to the post-closing success of their transactions. Although they may have a thorough understanding of the PRC's systems, Chinese investors cannot expect governments, business frameworks, legal systems and operating environments to function the same way elsewhere. In particular, the laws of the target's jurisdiction may thwart an intended development or operating plan, and, therefore, Chinese investors must be sure that they understand the legal environment of the target jurisdiction prior to committing substantial resources to an investment. For example, after CITIC Pacific launched the Sino Iron Project in Western Australia, it found it had to modify its original plan to bring in lower-wage workers from China. This was because Australian law requires that imported workers possess a specific degree of English-language skill and local professional qualifications and that all workers (local and imported alike) be paid the same wage. CITIC Pacific ultimately had to hire most workers locally (Pu, 2014).

Understanding the target jurisdiction is particularly important in emerging markets, where attractive investment opportunities may exist, but where legal and business environments are often undeveloped. For example, ZTE International planned to develop a large palm-oil plantation in the Democratic Republic of Congo, but the project disappeared after ZTE found out that 'there were no roads, the river was barely navigable, and villagers were hostile', in addition to crops being stolen quickly after being planted (*The Economist*, 2015, p. 55). Partnering with a co-investor that has experience in the target jurisdiction can be invaluable in these circumstances, as such investors will be familiar with the environment and can help identify jurisdiction-specific risks and related solutions.

However, in all markets outside of China, it is equally as important to understand the culture of companies and individuals in the target jurisdiction. One example of an issue in this respect is the acquisition by Shanghai Automotive Industry Corporation of a 49% interest in the South Korean automaker SsangYong in 2004. Due to various factors, including that 'because of cultural reasons, Chinese and Korean executives could not agree on how to improve performance', the investment did not succeed, and 'SsangYong filed for bankruptcy protection in January 2009' (Williamson and Raman, 2011).

Chinese investors have, however, successfully integrated and operated acquisition targets in the past, and lessons can be learned from how they have done so. Lenovo's acquisition of IBM's personal computing business in 2005 has been cited as 'a business case for how [the integration of a US company] should be done' (Bajarin, 2015). One of the primary ways Lenovo was able to successfully integrate the IBM business was by hiring former IBM employees, thereby allowing it to maintain relationships with customers and overcome differences in culture (Bajarin, 2015). This illustrates the principle that identifying and retaining key management is often an integral part of transaction planning and execution. It is important to have at least preliminary discussions with senior members of the target's management relatively early in the process to understand their strengths and weaknesses and to gauge their interest in remaining with the target post-acquisition (and on what terms). If management are not so interested, the investor will need to seriously consider whether and how it should proceed.

Preparing an integration plan, which takes into account and provides solutions for expected issues and difficulties, is also imperative to facilitate a successful transaction. Integrating a target's business and operations on a granular level allows synergies to be created, redundancies to be removed, and greater value to be generated for shareholders; however, this integration is anything but automatic and must be considered in detail at a practical level through the transaction process. Lenovo's acquisition of Medion in 2011 is a prime example of successful detailed integration planning. In this transaction, Lenovo and Medion 'created a professional project management office (PMO) whose sole purpose was to drive integration without the distractions of any daily business responsibilities' (Ping et al., 2014). The PMO was created early and helped guide additional integration teams who developed further detailed integration plans throughout the process. These tactics have been cited as a reason that 'Lenovo was able to integrate Median relatively smoothly within a year and significantly increase its European market share' (Ping et al., 2014). Additionally, having a detailed integration plan can help bridge cultural gaps that may otherwise interfere with a successful acquisition. In connection with Geely's purchase of Volvo, the chairman of Geely acknowledged, 'As two firms located in two continents geographically far apart, it's no doubt that [Geely and Volvo] have differences in culture', but 'as long as the strategy is clear enough and all the plans are implemented earnestly, the so-called cultural gap could be conquered' (*Global Times*, 2015), which indeed it was.

Conclusion

Cross-border investments present Chinese investors with both attractive opportunities and difficult challenges. Through proper planning and preparation, and learning from past experiences, Chinese investors will continue to improve their success rate in completing international transactions by capitalizing on the unique advantages they have, which in turn will provide them with invaluable experience and the confidence to undertake similar transactions in the future. Although international transactions contain an array of risks and challenges for Chinese investors, they are hopefully not insurmountable, and the benefits that arise from successfully closing cross-border transactions will surely encourage Chinese investors to pursue international investment adventures for years to come.

References

Bajarin, T 2015, '10 years later, looking back at the IBM-Lenovo PC deal', *PC Magazine*, 4 May. Available from: www.pcmag.com/article2/0,2817,2483557,00.asp. [21 November 2016].

Bartz, D & Baker, L 2016, 'Fairchild rejects Chinese offer on U.S. regulatory fears', *Reuters*, 16 February. Available from: www.reuters.com/article/us-fairchild-semico-m-a-idUSKCN0VP1O8. [21 November 2016].

'Chinese investment in Africa: Not as easy as it looks' 2015, *The Economist*, 21 November, pp. 55–56.

Committee on Foreign Investment in the United States 2016, *Committee on Foreign Investment in the United States Annual Report to Congress*, US Department of the Treasury. Available from: www.treasury.gov/resource-center/international/foreign-investment/Documents/Annual%20Report%20to%20Congress%20for%20CY2014.pdf. [21 November 2016].

Cooper, H 2012, 'Obama orders Chinese company to end investment at sites near drone base', *The New York Times*, 28 September. Available from: http://nyti.ms/QLhR7o. [21 November 2016].

EDF/CGN/NNB Group of Companies (Case M.7850) Commission Decision 32016M7850 2016. Available from: http://ec.europa.eu/competition/mergers/cases/decisions/m7850_429_3.pdf. [21 November 2016].

Flicker, S & Parsons, D 2011, 'Huawei – CFIUS Redux: Now it gets interesting, Paul Hastings LLP'. Available from: www.paulhastings.com/docs/default-source/PDFs/1868.pdf. [21 November 2016].

Guerrera, F 2005, 'CNOOC at odds with Congress over Unocal deal', *Financial Times*, 26 July. Available from: www.ft.com/content/07ca91da-fdfc-11d9-a289-00000e2511c8. [21 November 2016].

'Li Shufu commenting on Geely's strategy towards Volvo: Setting free the tiger back to the mountains' 2015, *Global Times*, 5 January. Available from: www.globaltimes.cn/content/899971.shtml. [21 November 2016].

Merced, M 2016, 'Affymetrix rejects $1.5 billion takeover bid', *The New York Times*, 20 March. Available from: http://nyti.ms/25eixdt. [21 November 2016].

Ping, Y, Yeung, S, Neuner, C & Chen, C 2014, 'How to integrate overseas acquisitions successfully', *Roland Berger*. Available from: www.rolandberger.com/publications/publication_pdf/roland_berger_tac_chinese_overseas_pmi_20140401.pdf. [21 November 2016].

Pottinger, M, Gold, R, Phillips, M & Linebaugh, K 2005, 'CNOOC drops offer for Unocal, exposing U.S.-Chinese tensions', *The Wall Street Journal*, 3 August. Available from: www.wsj.com/articles/SB112295744495102393. [21 November 2016].

Pu, J 2014, 'Can Sino Iron dig out of its investment hole', *Caixin Online*, 16 January. Available from: http://english.caixin.com/2014-01-16/100629880.html. [21 November 2016].

Revill, J 2016, 'Syngenta says won't disclose details of CFIUS clearance, any mitigation measures not material to its business', *Reuters*, 22 August. Available from: www.reuters.com/

article/syngenta-ag-ma-chemchina-measureschina-n-idUSZ8N135028. [21 November 2016].

Saha, S 2012, 'CFIUS now made in China: Dueling national security review frameworks as a countermeasure to economic espionage in the age of globalization', *Northwestern Journal of International Law and Business*, vol. 33, no. 1, pp. 199–235.

Sinha, R 2016, 'Shareholder litigation involving acquisitions of public companies: Review of 2015 and 1H 2016 M&A litigation', *Cornerstone Research*. Available from: www.cornerstone.com/Publications/Reports/Shareholder-Litigation-Involving-Acquisitions-2016. [21 November 2016].

Spegele, B 2012, 'CNOOC's new tack shows in oil deal', *The Wall Street Journal*, 27 December. Available from: www.wsj.com/articles/SB1000142412788732473130457819288314 0076040. [21 November 2016].

Tse, D, Pang, F, Xu, A & Sun, A 2011, 'Before going overseas, what do Chinese enterprises need to pay attention to', *PwC Strategy &*. Available from: www.strategyand.pwc.com/media/file/Going_Overseas_CN.pdf. [21 November 2016]. (In Chinese).

US Department of the Treasury 2010, 'Process overview'. Available from: www.treasury.gov/resource-center/international/foreign-investment/Pages/cfius-overview.aspx. [21 November 2016].

US Department of the Treasury 2012, 'The Committee on Foreign Investment in the United States (CFIUS)'. Available from: www.treasury.gov/resource-center/international/Pages/Committee-on-Foreign-Investment-in-US.aspx. [21 November 2016].

US Department of the Treasury 2014, 'Filing instructions'. Available from: www.treasury.gov/resource-center/international/foreign-investment/Pages/cfius-filing-instructions.aspx. [21 November 2016].

Willers, Y, Lee, D, Luo, Y & Yuan, S 2015a, 'Catching the next wave of outbound M&A', *The Boston Consulting Group*. Available from: www.bcg.com.cn/export/sites/default/en/files/publications/reports_pdf/Catching_the_Next_Wave_of_Outbound_M_and_A.pdf. [21 November 2016].

Willers, Y, Lee, D, Luo, Y, Yuan, S & Yang, V 2015b, 'Gearing up for the new era of China's outbound M&A', *The Boston Consulting Group*. Available from: www.bcg.com.cn/export/sites/default/en/files/publications/reports_pdf/BCG-Gearing-Up-New-Era-China-Outbound-MandA-Sep-2015.pdf. [21 November 2016].

Williamson, P & Raman, A 2011, 'The globe: How China reset its global acquisition agenda', *Harvard Business Review*. Available from: https://hbr.org/2011/04/the-globe-how-china-reset-its-global-acquisition-agenda. [21 November 2016].

Zhang, J & Ebbers, H 2010, 'Why half of China's overseas acquisitions could not be completed', *Journal of Current Chinese Affairs*, vol. 39, no. 2, pp. 101–131.

PART IV

Chinese ODI in a global context

16

POLICY IMPLICATIONS OF FDI ON FINANCIAL SECTOR DEVELOPMENT

Andrew Sheng[1]

Introduction

China has moved from being a net receiver of foreign direct investment (FDI) to a major provider of FDI, with the annual value of Chinese outward FDI (ODI) estimated to exceed total inward FDI by 2017. However, in terms of China's stock of FDI, the net international investment position (NIIP) was US$3.0 trillion at the end of September 2016, compared to US$1.3 trillion for ODI.[2]

This chapter looks at the impact of FDI, both outward and inward, on host and home country financial sector development. Foreign direct investment stimulates economic growth and assists job creation, innovation and upgrading of skills and infrastructure. FDI brings in new foreign exchange resources to supplement domestic savings, especially when the domestic capital market development is still relatively immature. Relatively few studies have been made on the positive and negative impacts of FDI on home and host country financial sector development.

Section I looks at the strategic considerations of FDI on financial sector development. Section II examines the lessons from Malaysia's FDI from a host country perspective. Section III uses national balance sheet data to compare and contrast how FDI stocks and flows have affected financial structure. Section IV considers how the One Belt One Road (OBOR) strategy is likely to impact on Chinese ODI into emerging market economies (EMEs). Section V concludes.

Strategic policy issues in FDI

Conventional thinking argues that FDI is beneficial for the host country, since it brings new financial resources, technology, access to foreign markets and job opportunities, including new funding for infrastructure and investment in higher quality manufacturing and services sectors, which cannot be financed domestically. The typical argument against FDI is usually political, in that FDI may bring polluting industries and low-quality jobs that are dangerous, dirty and degrading; that are exploitative of domestic labour and natural resources; and that displace domestic industries.

Financial sector development is considered useful for economic growth in four key aspects – improved resource allocation, better price discovery, sounder risk management and upgrading of corporate governance. Indeed, despite recent lessons from global financial crises, most academics consider that FDI is positive and less risky than short-term portfolio flows. Given its long-term nature, FDI is also considered more desirable than short-term foreign portfolio investment (FPI) since speculative flows can be withdrawn rapidly, causing liquidity and domestic market stresses.

There is technically very little difference in risks between FDI and FPI, particularly if the investor hedges the foreign exchange risk. By doing so, the hedge actually depletes foreign exchange and is considered a capital outflow.[3] In practice, however, FPI is more sensitive to FX volatility than FDI, unless FX volatility increases significantly, which forces the home country head office to hedge its currency exposure, thus putting further pressure on capital outflows.

The functions of finance, including considerations of pollution/environmental degradation and inequality/job creation issues, are discussed below.

(1) Resource Allocation – Inward FDI adds to national progress if it improves productivity, long-term investments and job creation, while importing new technology and also opening access to new markets. It would be detrimental to the host country if the FDI worsens pollution/natural resource degradation and social inequality. Indeed, if the FDI increases only domestic consumption without export potential, the economy could become over-reliant on imports in the long-run.

(2) Price Discovery – Inward FDI is helpful to national progress if it lowers the transaction costs of trade and also improves market mechanisms and price transparency. The entry of foreign participants into local markets actually helps competition, innovation and price formation.

(3) Risk Management – All FDI projects should be considered from the potential risks associated with maturity, foreign exchange and debt/equity mismatches. Ideally, there should be long-term funding for long-term investments, export income to fund foreign debt and a sufficient equity cushion to avoid excess leverage that would subject the project to both interest rate and liquidity shocks. Two major risks for all FDI projects are political risk and implementation risk, both of which are intertwined. Political risk needs to be managed because it is easy to blame the foreigner for everything that local people feel insecure about. The messages and delivery of FDI promises should be executed carefully and sensitively in order to gain local buy-in and ensure that social stability is not adversely impacted, and to avoid any pushback on FDI projects. Implementation risk is high because many infrastructure projects are long-term, with uncer-

tain payback and high risks. Given complex local laws and conditions, many projects are subject to implementation delays, and yield lower-than-expected returns. Projects with high leverage are vulnerable to shocks and global financial volatility, arising from technical, political, cultural and legal sources, mainly due to lack of understanding and insufficient preparatory research concerning the project conditions by the project investors on the ground. What works in the home country does not always work in the host country, due to the different laws, cultural behaviour, social norms and perceptions.

(4) Corporate Governance – The FDI project should have a proper governance structure to ensure that the project is professionally managed and accountable to all stakeholders, including the local population. It is important to include local partners, professional consultants and senior management at all levels to ensure a better appreciation of operating conditions and laws in the host country.

(5) Pollution/Environmental Degradation – In many countries, rejection of or protests against FDI occur when the local community suffers from pollution or disruption concerns. For example, Malaysians protested against a Japanese project that was alleged to create radiation risks, and Papua New Guinea protested against an Australian gold mining project. Pollution or de-forestation could also have longer term climate change implications, with carbon emissions or toxic impacts on water, air and soil conditions, particularly where local communities need to be resettled and lifestyle disturbed. Small local protests can put a stop to very large projects.

(6) Social Inequality – Brexit and the rise of populism are direct consequences of insufficient policy attention to rising social inequalities in income, wealth and job opportunities or risks. FDI projects need to consider how FDI can help alleviate or address social inequality issues. Experience has shown that community projects that create jobs and a sense of ownership can alleviate such concerns.

Country case study – Malaysia

Malaysia is a multi-racial middle-income nation with a population of 30 million and per capita income of US$9,768, with a land area of 330,800 sq. km.[4] The country has a highly trade-oriented GDP of US$296 billion in 2015, with an export/GDP ratio of 70.9%.[5,6] Since the 1960s, Malaysia has upgraded its economy from being a primary producer of tin and rubber to a diversified oil and gas producer, the second-largest palm oil producer and an integral part of the Asian global supply chain in electronics, light engineering components, foodstuffs and low-tech consumer/commodity-based products.

Malaysia has a fairly deep financial system with a large banking system (183.8% of GDP in assets in 2016), equity market (122.5% of GDP) and bond market (115.4% of GDP in Q2 2016).[7,8,9] The ringgit (MYR), the national currency, is based on a managed floating regime but subject to some macroprudential exchange controls. From 1998 to June 2005, it was pegged to the US dollar at MYR3.8 to US$1, but floated at the same time as the RMB in June 2005 and was MYR4.45 to US$1 in March 2017.

China is now Malaysia's largest trading partner. Direct exports to China accounted for 13.4% of Malaysia's total exports in 2013, with a larger portion re-exported through Singapore. Malaysia's imports from China accounted for 16.4% of total 2013 imports. Bilateral trade with China was estimated to total nearly US$60 billion in 2015, making Malaysia China's eighth largest trading partner. As 80% of Malaysia's exports to China are in commodities (such as palm oil, timber and rubber) and intermediate products (56%), Malaysia is highly exposed to any slowdown in China's manufacturing activity. Moreover, as China has upgraded its value added production, especially in sophisticated consumer products and capital goods (cars, engines, cranes), Malaysia has run a larger trade deficit with China in recent years, even though the country has a healthy current account surplus overall.

In recent years, China's ODI into Malaysia has risen progressively to around MYR5 billion, compared with Malaysian FDI into China of around MYR3 billion annually. China is now simultaneously a supplier, buyer and investor with Malaysian producers. While most of this is welcome, a large influx of Chinese tourists and a major Chinese land reclamation and property investment in the Iskandar project in Johor, opposite Singapore, have raised local political concerns about there being too much Chinese influence. Chinese developers and project contractors need to be sensitive to the cultural, racial and social dimensions of investing in a country with different political, language and business cultures.

Most Malaysian business and community leaders understand and welcome Chinese ODI and FPI in Malaysia, which bring new opportunities for business, jobs and markets. But the rise of populism everywhere means that the political narrative needs to be managed carefully and sensitively to avoid pushback or resistance to Chinese investments.

An example is steel production, where the scale of China's production today sets the global steel price, with many countries complaining of dumping. Even though Malaysian steel manufacturers are fairly sophisticated and efficient, they cannot compete on cost alone. Rising Chinese steel imports threaten domestic de-industrialization in Malaysia, which must be addressed.

For example, Malaysia's electrical and engineering (E&E) exports fell from 60% of total exports in the early 2000s to just over 30% today, partly due to Chinese competition. This caused Malaysia to shift in the last decade from manufacturing to commodities (e.g. crude oil, palm oil) and services exports (e.g. healthcare, education, tourism).

Many Malaysian businessmen point towards the experience of Japanese manufacturing in ASEAN, where Japanese car and electronic producers manufacture and assemble throughout ASEAN in order to share the business and avoid concentration risk.

Because of its middle-income status, Malaysia is aware that it cannot rely on cheap labour and must compete on superior infrastructure and technology upgrading. With robotization, 3D printing and de-industrialization even in China, the

Asian supply chain is changing rapidly. Internet distribution platforms are adding artificial intelligence and digitization is changing Asian supply and distribution. Such upgrading can lead to job disruption, with political consequences. This requires very different types of policy response, such as higher education input, skill upgrading, social welfare, export diversification, migrant-led wage suppression and the like.

Fortunately, many Malaysian leaders recognize that restructuring of the Malaysian economy within the changing international supply chain and monetary order cannot be achieved by Malaysia alone. This has to be a cooperative venture that recognizes that as the West begins to turn inwards and becomes more protectionist, Asia possesses the savings, consumer markets and productive capacity to make it on its own as a region. In this regard, China can assume leadership in partnership with all.

Asia should be able to achieve greater regional integration (but not political integration) along a multi-level path. With 48.1% of the world's population, 21.0% of global GDP and 17.6% of global trade in 2015, Asia is already trading primarily within the region, rather than focusing on the US and European markets as was the case previously.[10,11,12,13] South–South trade between emerging markets has already reached parity with North–North trade between advanced economies (Figure 16.1).

At the same time, while advanced countries are still in a state of low growth, Asian economies remain the fastest growing, with China and India registering growth of more than 6% annually, while ASEAN economies are growing around

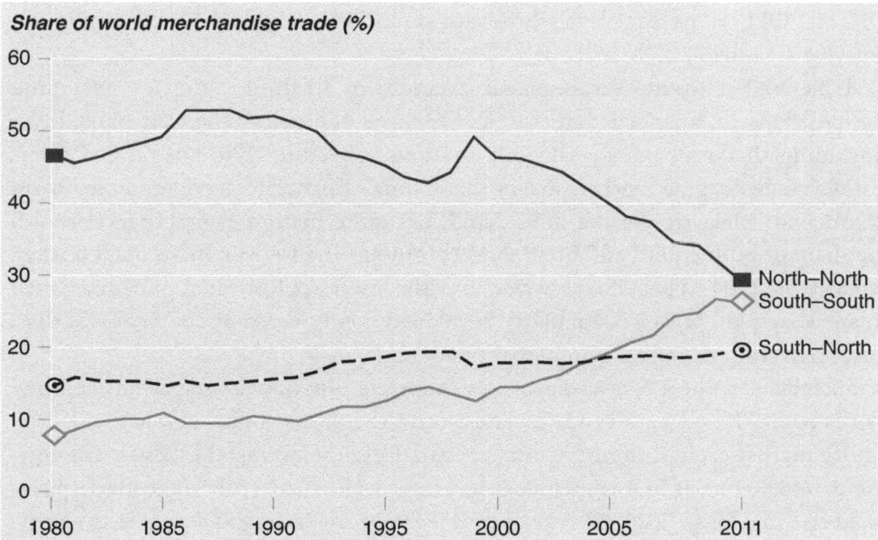

FIGURE 16.1 South–South trade already equal to North–North trade

Note: North in 1980 refers to Australia, Canada, Japan, New Zealand, US and Western Europe.

Source: Ortiz-Ospina & Max Roser. 2016. *International Trade.*

5% per annum. With very young populations and substantial natural resources, the ASEAN economies would be able to raise productivity and income levels given higher investments in better infrastructure, as proposed by the OBOR Initiative.

Impact of FDI on financial structure

Consumption and investments are *flows*, but, over time, these cumulative flows end up as *stock* or balance sheet items. The nature of how these flows and stocks are financed can be examined from recently published NIIP statistics.

Table 16.1 shows that China, Malaysia and the US all used FDI and FPI to fund their domestic economies. In 2004, FDI stock was as much as 37.0% of GDP for Malaysia and 25.3% for the US. Like all export-based EMEs, China relied on FDI to fund domestic investments to the extent of 18.9% of GDP in 2004, but not FPI (2.9%). In contrast, both Malaysia and the US used FPI to fund domestic growth to the extent of 40.8% and 53.9% of GDP, respectively.

By 2016, as China rapidly grew from a US$2 trillion to a US$11 trillion economy, the level of FDI and FPI rose moderately, but China switched to becoming a major investor overseas of ODI, with stock amounting to 11.9% of GDP. Malaysia has also moved towards becoming a large foreign investor regionally, with ODI of 48.1% of GDP and OFI of 23.4% of GDP. As the largest source of ODI (40.7%) and OFI (56.2%), the US was also the largest recipient of FDI (39.9%) and FPI (97.1% of GDP). This is because the US acts as the world's investment banker, receiving large capital inflows to fund its current account deficit, but also to fund its investments overseas. The point is that the US makes substantial returns (around 12%) on its ODI and OPI but pays relatively little cost on its FPI (roughly 2.5% per annum on ten-year treasuries).

Table 16.2 illustrates the financial structure in all three countries, excluding the positions in financial derivatives. All three countries relied on bank loans (including shadow bank loans) with amounts exceeding 100% of GDP. China's less developed capital markets meant that China's financial system remained bank dominated. Malaysia, on the other hand, has quite mature capital markets, with the share of both equity and bond markets amounting to over 100% of GDP even as early as 2004. The US, however, has the most sophisticated and diversified financial system, with a particularly developed bond market at 208.5% of GDP in 2016, reflecting its reliance on global financing.

Such balance sheet data also provides an insight into how leveraged an economy can become. Based on a crude leverage ratio (bank loans plus bonds divided by equity market capitalization), China appeared highly leveraged in 2004, amounting to 748%, but, if FDI is included, leverage declines to 410%. Indeed, despite a rapid rise in debt to 2016, China's overall leverage, including FDI as part of equity, would have declined to 348%, reflecting also the growing size of China's equity markets.

The conclusion is that the structure of inward and outward foreign investments affects the shape of the real economy and financial system. As the

TABLE 16.1 China, Malaysia and US – NIIP, 2004 vs 2016 (US$ billion)

Country	*2004*								
	GDP	*NIIP Assets*[2]				*NIIP Liabilities*			
		Direct investment (ODI)	*ODI as % GDP*	*Portfolio investment (OPI)*	*OPI as % GDP*	*Direct investment (FDI)*	*FDI as % GDP*	*Portfolio investment (FPI)*	*FPI as % GDP*
China	1,955.3	52.7	2.7%	92.0	4.7%	369.0	18.9%	56.6	2.9%
M'sia	124.7	15.8	12.7%	2.5	2.0%	46.1	37.0%	50.9	40.8%
US	12,274.9	3,746.9	30.5%	3,828.3	31.2%	3,101.5	25.3%	6,621.2	53.9%
	2016								
China	11,007.7	1,310.1	11.9%	340.6	3.1%	2,961.0	26.9%	794.6	7.2%
M'sia	296.3	142.6	48.1%	69.2	23.4%	139.4	47.0%	144.5	48.8%
US	18,036.6	7,349.3	40.7%	10,137.1	56.2%	7,193.6	39.9%	17,514.0	97.1%

TABLE 16.2 China, Malaysia and US – crude leverage ratio, 2004 vs 2016

Country	*2004*					
	(1)	*(2)*	*(3)*	*(4)*	*(1+3)/2*	*(1+3)/4*
	Bank loans as % GDP[3]	*Equities (Eq.) as % GDP*[4]	*Bonds as % GDP*[5]	*(Eq. + FDI) as % GDP*	*Crude Leverage Ratio*	
					(Loans+Bonds)/ Eq.	*(Loans+Bonds)/ (Eq.+FDI)*
China	138.7%	22.9%	32.6%	41.8%	747.9%	410.0%
M'sia	11.9%	145.6%	99.1%	180.1%	163.1%	131.9%
US	51.45%	133.0%	181.9%	158.3%	175.5%	147.4%
	2016					
China	251.4%	66.5%	73.3%	93.4%	488.3%	347.7%
M'sia	112.8%	122.5%	115.4%	169.6%	219.3%	158.5%
US	56.7%	151.6%	208.5%	191.5%	174.9%	138.5%

Sources: World Bank; Bank for International Settlements (BIS); World Federation of Exchanges (WFE); People's Bank of China (PBoC); State Administration of Foreign Exchange (SAFE); Bank Negara Malaysia (BNM); International Monetary Fund (IMF); Board of Governors of the Federal Reserve System; and US Bureau of Economic Analysis.

economy matures, there is greater outward investment in order to diversify the income and business structure. Japan, the largest net international investor in the world, is increasingly relying on income from its FDI and FPI to sustain household and corporate incomes (Bank of Japan, 2016). As the Japanese population ages, it will rely less on manufacturing exports and more on investment income. China is also going down this path, with the OBOR Initiative to deepen globalization in order to create a win-win scenario for China and its trading partners.

OBOR Initiative and impact on host countries

After its phenomenal growth into the world's second largest economy, China has had to change its strategy, from being an exporter to a major stakeholder in globalization. China has more trading partners around the world than the United States and is now emerging as a major source of FDI.

The OBOR concept was first raised by Chinese President Xi Jinping in 2013 involving both the historic land and the maritime Silk Road routes. The land route comprises two road/rail routes from China to Europe via Russia and the Baltic states, and another via the Persian Gulf and Mediterranean Sea. The Maritime Silk Road leads through the South China Sea to Europe via the Malacca Straits and Indian Ocean, and also to Oceania/South Pacific.

The OBOR region involves roughly 58 countries, accounting for nearly 64% of the world's population, 37% of global GDP and 31% of global consumption.

The OBOR Initiative comprises five connected areas:

(a) Policy Coordination – aligning development strategies to improve transport, infrastructure and trade
(b) Capacity Building – improving connectivity in ports, roads and rail
(c) Liberalization and Facilitation of Trade and Investment – information exchange, mutual recognition of regulations and mutual assistance in law enforcement
(d) Financial Cooperation – increasing efforts to build currency stability systems, investment and financing systems and credit information systems
(e) People – China offers 10,000 scholarships to countries along OBOR every year.

China has set up several flagship financial institutions (AIIB, New Silk Road Fund, New Development Bank), in addition to existing policy banks such as China Development Bank and the Export-Import Bank of China, to fund OBOR projects. The initial capital of US$240 billion is substantial but would meet less than 30% of Asia's infrastructure funding needs (US$750 billion by 2020 according to ADB). Hence, alternative funding sources would have to come from traditional banking and debt or equity markets, perhaps from the development of more sophisticated Asian financial markets.

The OBOR Initiative is designed to entrench Asia's growth potential. By 2030, Asia will account for two-thirds of the world's middle class, leading to large increases in regional tourism, notably from China and India. The acceleration of business connections will be helped by the widespread use of technology platforms, such as Alibaba and Tencent (WeChat), which will facilitate SME trade between OBOR countries and China. As part of the OBOR Initiative, China will open up its capital account in phases to encourage greater RMB usage globally.

There are, however, financial sector inadequacies that impede on FDI and regional trade:

- Due to legacy reasons and financial under-development within Asia, Asia still relies on USD funding, creating a fundamental currency mismatch between USD funding and local currency usage.
- Going forward, China could play a critical leadership role in the region. Currently, Asian excess savings are essentially saved in dollars and Euros in New York and London (mostly in foreign exchange reserves). These savings return to Asia in the form of trade credit, FDI and FPI, yielding high returns for the investment banks and fund managers for New York and London. However, as the dollar strengthens and major US and European banks are restricted in their funding of emerging markets by new banking regulations, emerging market trade and credit are slowing. The excess savings economies of North Asia, especially China, could help address the currency mismatch problem by

> promoting RMB as an alternative to USD as the key currency for Asian liquidity. This could be achieved through the promotion of RMB/Asian currency clearing and settlement for the facilitation of Asian trade and investments. In the yen internationalization phase of the 1990s, a mistake was made in selling in US dollars and lending in yen. This meant that Japan's trading partners in Asia had yen liabilities but dollar income, which caused volatility in the yen when it began to appreciate. If the Chinese were to buy, sell and lend in RMB, the bilateral trade would be naturally hedged.

The strategic issues regarding FDI in OBOR projects involve both implementation and financing issues.

Chinese companies, irrespective of whether they are state-owned or private, lack experience of operating in foreign markets, and they are only beginning to learn the complexity of implementing large-scale projects overseas, which typically involve multiple stakeholders of different languages and cultures, applying local laws, tax regulations and customs. Executing such complex projects requires specialized local expertise and experience that can bridge different cultures. Even private-public partnership projects involving only two nations face implementation obstacles, let alone multiple countries and coordination of different projects, such as those envisaged under OBOR.

For OBOR projects to succeed, there must be much greater investment in human skills, including in-depth understanding of local practices, customs and culture, which require local partnerships and buy-in. Very often, local partners or advisory groups can alleviate some of these concerns. But the credibility of OBOR projects – a win-win proposition not only at the national level, but also at local levels – is critical to their success.

In this regard, the role of government is fundamental, since many OBOR projects may not initially have high commercial returns, requiring long-term commitment in order to obtain higher social returns. OBOR participating governments must structure the projects so that the commercially viable parts are separated from those projects that are less commercially viable. The credibility of projects can be enhanced by using sovereign wealth funds or professional asset managers such as Khazanah Nasional Berhad Malaysia or the China Investment Corporation, which can assess the commercial viability of OBOR projects from a sovereign perspective. Where necessary, public guarantees can be provided, but not on a blanket basis.

Currency arrangements

A major obstacle to the deepening of trade and investment in OBOR countries lies in currency arrangements. The use of the dollar as the intermediary currency helps as a standard of value and unit of account, but, when the USD exchange rate strengthens against local currencies, tighter liquidity can deter trade and investments. For example, despite the fact that the central banks of China and Malaysia have signed a bilateral swap arrangement to facilitate bilateral trade, over 80% of Malaysia-China trade is denominated in USD.

There are several practical obstacles to using RMB as the currency for trade and investments:

- **High spread costs:** If RMB-USD spreads are 3% either way, and MYR-USD spreads are 5% either way, then the two trading or investment parties may have to pay a difference in spreads of up to 8% in order to conduct business. Since the current profitability of trade may be less than 5%, this would make the trade non-viable. These costs become greater in long-term investment projects, adding to cost uncertainties and affecting both implementation and funding risks.
- **Bias towards USD:** Since most companies are used to USD, their accounting, banking and legal documentation and processes are all based on USD pricing. Changing this would require persuasion and incentives not only by financial institutions and governments but also by chambers of commerce.
- **Liquidity issues:** Until recently, USD liquidity was never a problem. However, as US and European banks begin to face liquidity issues due to new and tighter banking regulations, FX liquidity has become a major issue. Businesses and households will not adopt RMB usage if it remains expensive, inconvenient or inefficient. Ready funding for RMB and local currencies must be made available to address this.

Solution: The People's Bank of China announced the launch of the China International Payment System (CIPS) in October 2015, which provides one-point entry by participants and a central location for clearing renminbi payments. Because it is linked with the China National Automated Payment System (CNAPS), and utilizes the ISO20022 messaging standard, it will facilitate inter-bank clearing of RMB transactions. However, CIPS does not yet address the issues of RMB funding and transactions for small and medium enterprises (SMEs), as currently its participants only involve banks. In future, when cross-border e-commerce becomes more prevalent through platforms such as AliPay, then transactions will have to involve more FX transactions.

By designating FDI in RMB, China could increase depth in the swap curve, improve liquidity, and lower spread costs. Furthermore, China should consider establishing a special trade payment infrastructure for SMEs that is synchronized with CIPS. This would encourage small transactions (e.g. less than US$10 million) that are denominated in RMB, with short-term fixed exchange rates that would limit transaction costs and currency risks. This could create the critical mass and trigger the momentum for wider usage of RMB in larger transactions in the future.

Just as Alibaba created a simple-to-use and convenient platform for SME trading, it should be feasible to construct a clearing arrangement and special platform for SMEs to facilitate trade and transactions in RMB, building on OBOR. Most SMEs in China or OBOR countries do not understand the complex trade, licensing and customs arrangements in China that inhibit the access to trade that is now increasingly available through financial-technology-type (FinTech) platforms such as Alibaba.

This could be achieved through a pilot city-to-city platform project, using local partners, which could be the prototype that would reveal the on-the-ground barriers to trade and investments faced by SMEs. Removing the barriers for OBOR country SMEs to participate in OBOR trade and projects would help build support for OBOR objectives of wider political and social stability and foster regional growth.

Mapping of OBOR opportunities

As in any large project, a lack of understanding of the opportunities and risks can impede success. Hence, one of the priorities of promoting FDI and OBOR must be to increase awareness among OBOR companies and business regarding the need for better alignment of business models with new opportunities and risks. This could be achieved by the mapping of opportunities and risks between China and OBOR countries, so that the supply and distribution chain will be as efficient as current supply chains. China can be a major catalyst in the adaptation of new technology for the upgrading of OBOR partner country productivity.

There should be more frequent conferences and business meetings to ensure that Chinese enterprises understand OBOR risks and opportunities, and OBOR enterprises understand the benefits and risks of working in OBOR projects. Such meetings between chambers of commerce, cities, universities etc. will have the key objective of upgrading business and supply chain technology. OBOR governments will complement this effort by tailoring laws, taxes and rules to facilitate growing trade and FDI.

In short, the facilitation of OBOR and FDI objectives will require specialized skills in the OBOR financial and commercial sectors. OBOR financial institutions will have to step up to the mark to meet these critical objectives. Given modern information technology to do this, financial institutions will have to apply FinTech in order to rise to the occasion and deliver such services with speed and convenience, at low cost. In short, financial sector development must incorporate FinTech and cyber-currencies in future design.

Conclusions

This short survey suggests that the objectives of FDI can be met by shifting financial policy and systems to create new markets, jobs and a win-win strategy for all. Financial markets cannot be for the benefit of the few at the expense of the many. The old model of financial intermediation created feelings of inequality, rather than fostering inclusion, leading eventually to populism, anti-globalization, anti-trade and Brexit/Trumpism.

Given the different stages of development in different OBOR countries and languages, culture and institutional arrangements, there is no one-size-fits-all standard, process or project template that can work uniformly across all OBOR countries at all times.

Since the overarching philosophy of OBOR is to achieve a win-win scenario for both China and the region, its success will hinge on winning hearts and minds at the grassroots level. Governments and public institutions should adopt the soft power approach and leverage various platforms such as social media and civil society to market OBOR to the public.

Specifically, because of the higher risks involved, an equity-based solution involving asset managers, private equity and key investment intermediaries will be critical. There is no substitute to developing strong investment banking and project management expertise within the OBOR region itself. This would include the emergence of larger regional investment banks and fund managers.

Such development is consistent with not only the micro-objective of institutional strengthening to embedding the financial labour force with ethical values and professional expertise but also the macro-objective of overall financial system stability, founded on macro-social stability. New systems require new technology and a new mindset. This is the right time to re-think the role of FDI and its overall impact on both financial sector and social development.

Notes

1 The author is grateful to Ms Jillian Ng for research assistance in preparing this paper, and Dr Chen Meng of CIC and Mr Ng Chow Soon for helpful comments. All errors and opinions are the author's own.
2 China State Administration of Foreign Exchange (SAFE) 2016, *The Time-Series Data of International Investment Position of China*. [10 February 2017].
3 An FX hedge involves borrowing local currency and buying foreign currency forward, which ultimately will reduce official foreign exchange reserves (equivalent to a capital outflow).
4 World Bank 2017, *GDP per capita (current US$)*. Available from: http://data.worldbank.org/indicator/NY.GDP.PCAP.CD?locations=MY. [10 February 2017].
5 World Bank 2017, *GDP (current US$)*. Available from: http://data.worldbank.org/indicator/NY.GDP.MKTP.CD. [10 February 2017].
6 World Bank 2017, *Exports of goods and services (% of GDP)*. Available from: http://data.worldbank.org/indicator/NE.EXP.GNFS.ZS. [10 February 2017].
7 BNM 2016, *Monthly statistical bulletin December 2016*. Table 1.7: Banking System: Statement of Assets. Author's calculation. Available from: www.bnm.gov.my/index.php?ch=en_publication&pg=en_msb&ac=238&en&uc=2. [10 February 2017].
8 WFE 2016, *December 2016 monthly report*. Author's calculation. Available from: www.world-exchanges.org/home/. [10 February 2017].
9 BIS 2016, *Summary of debt securities outstanding*. Author's calculation. Available from: http://stats.bis.org/statx/srs/table/c1. [10 February 2017].
10 World Bank 2017, *Population, total*. Author's calculation. Available from: http://data.worldbank.org/indicator/SP.POP.TOTL. [10 February 2017].
11 World Bank 2017, *GDP (current US$)*. Author's calculation. Available from: http://data.worldbank.org/indicator/NY.GDP.MKTP.CD. [10 February 2017].

12 World Bank 2017, *Exports of goods and services (BoP, current US$)*. Author's calculation. Available from: http://data.worldbank.org/indicator/BX.GSR.GNFS.CD. [10 February 2017].

13 World Bank 2017, *Imports of goods and services (BoP, current US$)*. Author's calculation. Available from: http://data.worldbank.org/indicator/BM.GSR.GNFS.CD. [10 February 2017].

References

Bank for International Settlements (BIS) 2016, *Summary of Debt Securities Outstanding*. Available from: http://stats.bis.org/statx/srs/table/c1. [10 February 2017].

Bank Negara Malaysia 2016, *Monthly Statistical Bulletin December 2016*. Table 1.7: Banking System: Statement of Assets. Available from: www.bnm.gov.my/index.php?ch=en_publication&pg=en_msb&ac=238&en&uc=2. [10 February 2017].

Bank of Japan 2016, *Japan's Balance of Payments Statistics for 2015 and International Investment Position at Year-End 2015*. August, International Department, Bank of Japan. Available from: www.boj.or.jp/en/research/brp/ron_2016/data/ron160815a.pdf. [12 February 2017].

China State Administration of Foreign Exchange (SAFE) 2016, *The Time-Series Data of International Investment Position of China*. Available from: www.safe.gov.cn/wps/portal/!ut/p/c5/04_SB8K8xLLM9MSSzPy8xBz9CP0os3gPZxdnX293QwP30FAnA8_AEBc3C1NjIxNHQ6B8JG75YGMKdLubGRDQHQ5yLX7b8ciDzQfJG-AAjgb-6fh75uan6BbmhEQaZAekAYS-UDA!!/dl3/d3/L2dJQSEvUUt3QS9ZQnZ3LzZfSENEQ01LRzEwT085RTBJNkE1U1NDRzNMTDQ!/?WCM_GLO. [10 February 2017].

Ortiz-Ospina & Roser M 2016, International Trade. *Our World in Data Organization*. Available from: https://ourworldindata.org/international-trade.

World Bank 2017a, *Exports of Goods and Services (% of GDP)*. Available from: http://data.worldbank.org/indicator/NE.EXP.GNFS.ZS. [10 February 2017].

World Bank 2017b, *Exports of Goods and Services (BoP, Current US$)*. Available from: http://data.worldbank.org/indicator/BX.GSR.GNFS.CD. [10 February 2017].

World Bank 2017c, *GDP (Current US$)*. Available from: http://data.worldbank.org/indicator/NY.GDP.MKTP.CD. [10 February 2017].

World Bank 2017d, *GDP per Capita (Current US$)*. Available from: http://data.worldbank.org/indicator/NY.GDP.PCAP.CD?locations=MY. [10 February 2017].

World Bank 2017e, *Imports of Goods and Services (BoP, Current US$)*. Available from: http://data.worldbank.org/indicator/BM.GSR.GNFS.CD. [10 February 2017].

World Bank 2017f, *Population, Total*. Available from: http://data.worldbank.org/indicator/SP.POP.TOTL. [10 February 2017].

World Federation of Exchanges 2016, *December 2016 Monthly Report*. Available from: www.world-exchanges.org/home/. [10 February 2017].

17

THE HISTORY AND EVOLUTION OF CHINESE COMPANIES GOING GLOBAL

What to expect in the years ahead

Yibing Wu

When Lenovo announced its acquisition of IBM's personal computer (PC) business in December 2004, the deal, and others like it, inspired a decade of frenzied mergers and acquisitions (M&A) activity by Chinese companies seeking to go global. The use of M&A as a globalization strategy unfolded in three phases. We first saw a burst of acquisitions to establish a presence in foreign markets. However, the results fell well short of expectations, hindered by post-merger integration challenges exacerbated by the inexperience of Chinese companies in global commerce. In a second phase, Chinese companies trained their sights on deals involving natural resources and tangible assets that did not rely on post-merger integration for success. However, this strategy was vulnerable to swings in commodity prices and operational obstacles that caused many deals to miss profitability goals. In a third, more recent phase, Chinese companies have sought to acquire intangible assets, notably talent and intellectual property (IP) – the lifeblood of innovation and, for many companies, the key to survival.

During the most recent phase, Chinese companies have become much more sophisticated in their use of M&A. Executives have absorbed the lessons from unsuccessful acquisitions to refine their M&A approach for both strategy and management. Nowhere was this progression more evident than in Lenovo's acquisition of IBM's x86 server business in 2014. The deal put Lenovo into the top tier of suppliers and positioned them to compete against the likes of Dell and Hewlett Packard Enterprise (HPE). Within ten years, Lenovo had gone from a neophyte taking its first steps onto the world stage to the number-one computer maker in the world, with $45 billion in annual revenues. Lenovo has been joined by scores of Chinese companies that have carried out their own acquisitions in an effort to reach new foreign markets and become more competitive domestically.

What can we expect from Chinese companies in the coming years? Will they focus more on the domestic market and burgeoning consumer class or continue their push outward? Will the bulk of M&A activity be concentrated in specific sectors such as technology or consumer goods? And have Chinese companies found new ways to use strategic acquisitions to complement their strengths in manufacturing and engineering? The answers to these questions, informed in large measure by the past decade, can shed light on where they will place their bets and what it could mean for China's ability to shape the global economy.

We believe that by gaining a better understanding of the evolution of M&A in China, investors can obtain a clearer picture of the growth strategies that Chinese companies might pursue in the years ahead.

China pushes beyond its borders

The seeds of China's global M&A push were sown more than two decades ago. Foreign direct investment began to flow into China in the early 1990s, as global companies sought to take advantage of the country's low-cost manufacturing. This investment, which reached more than $40 billion annually by 1996, helped domestic companies achieve the necessary scale to test the waters of international commerce.[1] However, it was not until 11 December 2001, when China joined the World Trade Organization, that the country's private companies and state-owned enterprises accelerated their efforts to transition from domestic champions to global organizations. M&A activity expanded quickly: from outbound foreign direct investment (FDI) of just $915 million in 2000, Chinese companies ramped up total international investments to $12.2 billion by 2005.[2] The Chinese government supported these undertakings with state financing for M&A.

The globalization effort addressed two priorities. The first was aspirational: after years of being viewed as primarily a low-cost manufacturer for the world's top brands, China was eager to showcase its engineering talent, depth of production expertise and ability to satisfy global consumers. The second priority was more practical: expansion into other markets would help diversify business risk in the event of a slowdown at home. The strategies that Chinese companies would pursue to achieve these goals evolved significantly over the ensuing decade.

Phase 1 (2004–2008) – acquisitions of global companies and divisions to gain market entry

In the first phase of M&A, Chinese companies that had achieved sufficient scale as domestic brands or low-cost manufacturers sought to expand into foreign markets by purchasing the divisions of established global brands. This strategy seemed a natural fit; Chinese companies had mastered the engineering, design, and production of high-quality goods that were in the homes of domestic consumers. In some cases, Chinese companies were the producers of white-label goods for leading global brands, reinforcing their belief that they were ready for expansion.

What they lacked, and what these acquisitions could provide, was a direct line to markets outside of China.

Strategic acquisitions also held the potential to address another crucial issue: despite the success of Chinese companies domestically, their brands were virtually unknown in developed markets. When consumers did think of Chinese goods, the perception was often negative – low cost, poorly made and lacking in cutting-edge features. So by using established brands as a platform in developed markets, China would gain greater access to consumers.

However, Chinese companies were generally unprepared for the difficulties of integration with a global brand. Such arrangements highlighted organizational differences, from divergent cultures and management styles to governance and compensation structures. TCL offers a cautionary tale: In 2003, it was the second-largest television maker in China, with annual revenues of more than $4 billion. Encouraged by the initial overseas success of its products, the company spent $560 million in 2004 to merge its TV and DVD businesses with France-based Thomson Multimedia. On paper, the deal made sense: Thomson was well-established in Europe and also commanded 18% of the US television market. TCL's chairman said at the time that the 'deal fulfils our objective of being one of the top five players in multimedia electronic devices in the global marketplace'.[3]

The Thomson brand was struggling, something TCL's pre-merger due diligence did not detect. In the years preceding the merger, it had seen its sales plummet while incurring heavy losses in Europe. The joint venture was also late to address the shift in consumer tastes to flat-screen TVs, saddling the brand with a reputation for outdated products. From 2005 to 2006, the venture recorded total losses of $680 million, leading TCL to eliminate the Thomson brand and close five of its seven EU distribution centres.

By contrast, Lenovo's global journey demonstrates the rewards for getting it right. In 2004, the company (born as Legend) was at a crossroads. After a meteoric rise over two decades marked by annual revenue growth of 20%, the company had captured nearly 30% of the Chinese computer market. Yet its growth had slowed in 2002 and 2003, leading Lenovo's executives to explore ways to jump-start expansion. One tantalizing prospect was the acquisition of IBM's PC business. Though a leader in China, Lenovo was not widely known beyond its borders, so IBM's preeminent brand and global reach could open up coveted developed markets such as the European Union and the United States. As part of the deal, Lenovo also gained ownership of the ThinkPad brand of PCs, a product line with an established reputation.

The merger posed challenges for the company, including that of integrating disparate cultures. Over several years, however, Lenovo began to unlock the potential of its acquisition. For example, Lenovo established headquarters in both China and the United States and launched several cultural-integration initiatives. Such measures helped the company to smooth the ownership transition and emerge as the world's biggest manufacturer of PCs by units sold.

Phase 2 (2009–2012) – a focus on natural resources and tangible assets

Several failed deals revealed the inexperience of Chinese companies in managing post-merger integration, especially when buying divisions of global companies. In response, the Chinese government encouraged state-owned enterprises to shift their focus to amassing natural resources – oil, natural gas and mineral deposits. The rationale was that such acquisitions could support the growth of the Chinese economy while requiring little integration, thus removing the operational and cultural challenges that had plagued companies in phase 1. As important, while the rest of the world struggled in the aftermath of the economic downturn, the Chinese government had more than $2 trillion in foreign exchange reserves in 2009, providing its companies with the funds to pursue M&A aggressively.[4] Indeed, from 2009 to 2013, the country's largest oil and gas companies made acquisitions totalling almost $119 billion.[5] However, these deals were undermined by fluctuating commodity prices and management challenges that hindered value creation.

In 2010, for example, China Petrochemical Corporation (Sinopec) paid $4.65 billion to purchase ConocoPhillips' share of Syncrude, a joint venture to extract petroleum from the Canadian oil sands. Despite optimistic projections, Sinopec experienced rising costs, delays and falling production. By the time it opted to sell its stake in 2016, it had spent more than $10 billion on the project. The Chinese National Offshore Oil Corporation (CNOOC) encountered similar challenges when it purchased the Canadian energy producer Nexen in 2012 for $15.1 billion. At the time, oil prices were around $89 a barrel, making the 61% premium that CNOOC paid seem justified.[6] In the aftermath of the merger, however, oil prices declined significantly. CNOOC was also confronted with lower-than-expected production from the Canadian oil sands, the forced divestment of operations in the Gulf of Mexico, and a pipeline rupture, among other challenges.

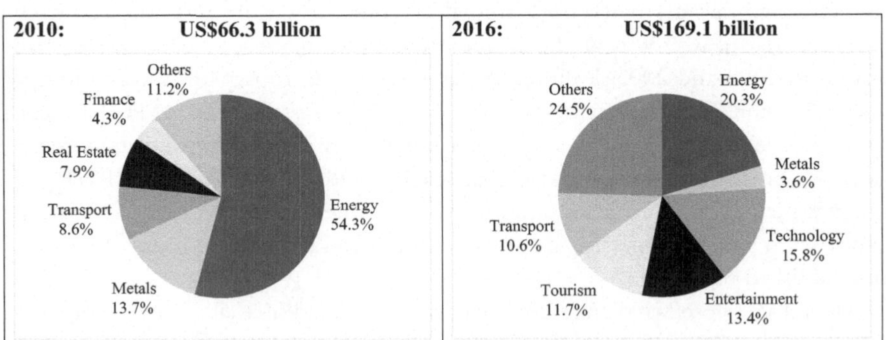

FIGURE 17.1 Total resources deals have declined as a percentage of China's outward direct investment

Source: China Global Investment Tracker, American Enterprise Institute and Heritage Foundation, January 2017 (www.aei.org/china-global-investment-tracker/).

During this period, Chinese mining companies such as Citic Pacific, which spent more than $10 billion to develop an iron ore mine in Australia, also encountered a range of difficulties, from cost overruns to labour regulations that prevented the company from using Chinese labourers. Such challenges led China Mining Association Executive Vice President Wang Jiahua to estimate in 2013 that as much as 80% of mining investments had failed.[7] These losses resulted in a recalibration of Chinese M&A away from such a heavy emphasis on energy and natural resources to a more diversified approach. The share of Chinese M&A involving energy and metals dropped from nearly 80% in 2008 to 63% in 2013.

Phase 3 (2012–present) – the evolution of Chinese M&A

China's robust economic growth, exploding middle class and rapid urbanization have made it the most attractive consumer market in the world. Indeed, today China's maturity and competitiveness mean that its leading companies often see M&A not simply as a door to foreign markets but also as a direct way to gain a competitive advantage within China.

The types of deals have changed accordingly. Since 2012, the leading Chinese companies across industries have increasingly pursued M&A with the goal of securing intangible assets – intellectual property, top talent, or management skills – to steer innovation. Several factors spurred this shift: first, a company's ability to reinvent itself and develop new products and offerings will be a key indicator of its growth prospects. Second, although China is awash with engineering talent, executives recognize that they must augment this deep pool with top innovators and technologists to create products that can compare favourably with those emerging from innovation hubs such as Silicon Valley and Israel. Third, as global conglomerates have understood for years, the acquisition of more innovative and nimble start-ups is a necessity once companies achieve a certain scale.

Many Chinese companies have adopted a two-pronged M&A strategy as they seek to acquire a capability that will provide a boost in China while also achieving greater global market share. This 'pulling in' while 'pushing out' essentially makes the global benefits of M&A a by-product of greater competitiveness at home. The following three strategies illustrate how companies have integrated this mind-set into their approach to M&A.

Gaining access to proprietary intellectual property

Some of the most successful Chinese companies have acquired IP rather than enter new foreign markets. Sany, one of the world's largest construction machinery manufacturers, highlights the benefits of this approach. Founded in 1994 and listed on the Shanghai Stock Exchange in 2003, it had $7.5 billion in annual revenues and over 34,000 employees in 2012.[8] The company made its mark in manufacturing with its stationary concrete pump, a critical piece of equipment for constructing high-rise buildings. In 2012, Sany generated the bulk of its revenues (81.3%) from the Chinese market.[9] The company's management viewed globalization as its third strategic stage (after its founding and initial public offering) and began investing overseas in 2006.

As its first major acquisition, Sany pursued the German Mittlestand manufacturer Putzmeister. The company was ripe for acquisition: Putzmeister had earned a reputation for technological excellence and high-quality products, but the European debt crisis had halved its annual revenues in just a few years. In addition, its owner had no succession plan in place and was eager to find a buyer. Sany obliged, acquiring Putzmeister in 2012 for $402 million.[10] Sany was hopeful that Putzmeister's IP would help it gain a technological edge over its domestic rivals and improve the performance of its manufacturing sites. The deal's announcement was met with trepidation in Germany, which feared losing an industrial linchpin to China as well as the prospect of layoffs.

Sany's sophisticated approach to post-merger integration has enabled it to address issues adeptly while ensuring that the merger amounts to much more than the sum of its parts. Sany has kept its headquarters in China while agreeing to maintain Putzmeister employment levels in Germany through 2020. It also granted Putzmeister's executives a large degree of autonomy in the EU market. In other areas, the merged entity has focused on coordination and knowledge sharing: Sany and Putzmeister collaborate on annual planning and long-term strategy and share IP.

After the acquisition, Sany's overseas revenue in fiscal year 2012 reached $1.7 billion (equal to year-on-year growth of 155.6%). It has maintained its position as the most successful heavy machinery industry player in China, with operating revenue of $3.49 billion and an annual profit of $20.7 million in 2015. Meanwhile, Putzmeister has enjoyed similar success in Germany: sales are up by nearly a third, the brand is still intact, established relationships with suppliers are still in place, and no layoffs have occurred.

Other Chinese companies have followed Sany's lead. The appliance maker Midea, for example, acquired Kuka, a German robot maker. Midea hopes to use the German company's expertise in production to overhaul its manufacturing, boosting efficiency through automation and cutting its workforce by one-fifth.[11] In a still-pending deal, China National Chemical Corp. (ChemChina) committed to spend nearly $43 billion for Switzerland-based Syngenta, a seed and pesticide company that boasts a large number of patents.

Using M&A to expand digital offerings

For companies that have achieved success and scale by serving Chinese consumers, the challenge can be sustaining a pipeline of fresh and innovative products for a market with shifting tastes. To maintain customer loyalty, the sprawling Internet company Tencent has used M&A to expand its gaming division and broaden its base of game developers. Founded as a mobile messenger service in Shenzhen in

1998, Tencent has developed into the leading provider of Internet, mobile and telecom value-added services in China. Its products offer communication, information, entertainment and financial services to Chinese consumers. Tencent now has more than 38,000 employees, many based in China, and in 2016 it generated revenues of $22 billion, more than half from online games.[12]

Despite its success to date, Tencent was locked in competition with Alibaba and Baidu for the attention of Chinese consumers. Its executives decided to focus on its gaming division, deeming it the ripest for global expansion among its many businesses. Tencent has been expanding its overall mobile gaming pipeline by developing its own titles, working with partners to convert strong video game titles for PCs to mobile games, and licensing popular PC titles from other Chinese gaming companies such as Changyou, Giant, and Shanda. Tencent's M&A strategy also includes acquiring promising game development companies and gaming franchises.

According to a Tencent senior executive, 'When we started building our gaming business 10 years ago, we understood that the relationship between publishers and developers should address the interests of both sides. So we started investing in development companies, and we have had great success with this strategy'. In 2011, Tencent became a global e-sports player with its purchase of Riot Games, the developer of the popular combat game 'League of Legends', which generated $1.63 billion in revenue in 2015 to make it the world's top-grossing PC game.[13]

To exploit its position as the world's largest gaming publisher by revenues and reach inside China (more than 800 million users on its dominant mobile social platform Weixin and WeChat), in June 2016 Tencent spent $8.6 billion to acquire Supercell, a distinctive global mobile game developer responsible for the 'Clash of the Clans' franchise. The deal was beneficial for both parties: Tencent gained access to Supercell's pipeline of hot new mobile games, while Supercell expanded its reach into the Chinese market via Tencent's platforms. While Tencent isn't involved in creating the games, it does provide expertise on how to roll out games to Chinese consumers to maximize returns (for example, by localizing some ad content). The senior executive at Tencent notes, 'We have learned from Supercell how they manage their creative and product teams, which have generated two top-five games. Their productivity is off the charts, and that inspires our studio leaders to approach things in new ways'.

The deal's financial impact was immediate: during the third quarter of 2016, Supercell climbed two places to become the fourth-largest global mobile gaming company by revenues. The success of Tencent's gaming business could provide a template for its other offerings to expand globally. The senior executive at Tencent admits, 'Gaming is the one vertical that we have a very clear global expansion agenda. For our other businesses, we're still at the exploration stage'.

Other Chinese companies are making similar investments in an effort to augment their offerings. Alibaba has spent more than $30 billion on acquisitions and stakes in smaller companies since 2010, all in an effort to create a multifaceted online world to cater to every possible consumer need. In 2016, Alibaba paid $794 million for a stake in Magic Leap, a US-based company that produces virtual reality goggles. Alibaba intends to integrate this technology into its platforms in the future.[14] As digital companies seek to strengthen their connections with customers, such acquisitions are likely to continue.

Accessing talent and intangible assets (such as brand, technology and design) through phased investment

Even as Chinese companies have evolved from manufacturers of goods for global corporations to fast-growing industry leaders in their own right, one constant – and a key to their rise – has been the country's deep pool of engineering talent compared with the rest of the world. Chinese executives who understand that they can supercharge their output by complementing this foundational asset with established, top-tier expertise from around the world can not only develop new technologies and attract talent but also elevate their brand.

Accordingly, we have seen many Chinese companies evolve their approach to M&A and investment into the following three-phase strategy:

(1) *Build out R&D centres in overseas markets to access top talent.* A slew of Chinese companies are setting up offices in tech hubs around the world to support the recruitment and acquisition of global talent.[15] Baidu, for example, invested $300 million in an R&D centre in Silicon Valley in 2014 and lured Andrew Ng, formerly head of Stanford University's artificial intelligence (AI) lab, to set it up.[16] Although Ng departed Baidu in March 2017, his tenure helped the company develop a deep bench of AI experts.

(2) *Use small investments to acquire key technologies and talent.* Established organizations have been acquiring innovative start-ups to augment their current offerings, expand into new product areas, and benefit from a new source of research and expertise. Over the past several years, Baidu has made acquisitions to complement its core business, including Brazilian online discount company Peixe Urbano, Japanese online advertiser PopIn, and US-based xPerception, which makes visual recognition software.

(3) *Collaborate with global brands.* The lure of access to the Chinese market has helped foster joint ventures and strategic partnerships between China's leading companies and some of the world's iconic brands. Huawei has been at the vanguard of using this strategy to attract talent and strengthen its position at home and in global markets.

As a leader in infrastructure application software and devices with wireline, wireless, and IP technologies, Huawei relies on top global talent to develop new solutions and services. The company has served 45 of the world's leading 50 telecom operators and maintains a presence in more than 170 countries. In 2016, Huawei's revenue reached $75.1 billion, with net profits of $5.3 billion. Throughout its history, Huawei has made relatively few deals; instead, its rapid ascent to become one of the world's largest providers of telecom equipment has been organic, fuelled by investments in R&D. More recently, Huawei has made targeted acquisitions to secure technologies, often as a complement to previous investments in foreign R&D centres.

Huawei's Consumer Business Group (CBG) has greatly benefited from these strategies. In 2011, its leaders made the decision to transition the company from being a device manufacturer for other companies to being a consumer brand in its own right. They recognized that R&D would be a critical differentiator and made a sustained commitment to develop its capabilities. Yu Chengdong, director and CEO of CBG, noted, 'Out of CBG's 20,000 employees, 14,000 are R&D staff, with around 1,400 employees located in overseas offices and R&D centres'.

Over the past several years, Huawei has completed more than ten smaller deals (ranging from $2 million to $50 million) to secure technology in areas such as telecom equipment, the Internet of things (IoT), and software-defined networking technology. In 2014, it spent $25 million to acquire Neul, an innovator in IoT technologies.[17] A year later, it purchased software-defined networking technology from Ireland's Amartus for an undisclosed sum, acquiring the company's senior team and product staff in the deal.[18] This technology will enable Huawei to make remote adjustments to its telecom equipment and accelerate its move to cloud-based networks.

As far as the big picture is concerned, Yu said, 'CBG's strategy has shifted to collaborations and partnerships that can support brand building'. In early 2016, it announced a strategic partnership with German camera maker Leica. The two companies collaborated on Huawei's flagship model P9, which pioneered a dual-lens camera – a breakthrough in smartphones' photo capabilities ahead of its competitor Apple. CBG also entered into a partnership with Porsche Design to develop a limited-edition Mate 9 smartphone. On the strength of such innovations, Huawei's CBG sold more than 139 million smartphones in 2016, an increase of 29% over the previous year.[19] Its flagship model P9 was the company's first device to surpass 10 million units shipped.

To build on the initial success of this strategic partnership, in September 2016 Huawei and Leica announced the establishment of a joint research centre in Germany to focus on optical systems and imaging software.[20] According to Yu, 'These partnerships greatly enhanced Huawei's brand and played a role in the success of the P9 and P10 models in attracting high-end consumers'. Collectively, these moves have cemented Huawei as the world's third-largest smartphone maker.

What to expect in the years ahead

At the 2014 meeting of Asia-Pacific Economic Cooperation (APEC) leaders, President Xi Jinping announced China's goal of increasing outbound investment to a total of $1.25 trillion over the next decade.[21] With outbound FDI of more than $161 billion in 2016, Chinese companies are on track to comfortably exceed that goal.[22] However, they face a pushback from foreign governments to deals, particularly in tech-heavy industries where acquisitions involving IP can be construed as a security threat. For instance, political leaders in the United States have shown an interest in halting proposed mergers by invoking the US Treasury's Committee on Foreign Investment.

The Chinese government has also exerted its influence by restricting the flow of its currency out of the country and implementing more stringent screening on proposed deals. Regulators are monitoring several types of M&A activities, including newly established firms that invest overseas without existing real businesses, investments that substantially outweigh a company's registered capital, M&A that is very different from or unrelated to the Chinese company's core businesses, and investment capital in renminbi coming from abnormal sources – the last of which may be a sign of illegal asset transfers and underground lending. Rather than having a chilling effect on future deals, we see this policy change as a positive and rational development that is likely to ensure more fundamentally sound Chinese outbound M&A.

We expect Chinese companies in certain industries to still be on the lookout for more traditional M&A opportunities. Haier's 2016 purchase of GE Appliances, for example, took a page out of Lenovo's book, as Haier sought to gain access to established distribution networks and brands.[23] However, Lenovo's recent difficulty with US-based Motorola Mobility, which it purchased in 2014, reinforces the inherent challenges in traditional M&A on a global level.[24] Those obstacles aren't unique to Chinese companies, but a clear strategy and laser-like focus on post-merger integration are requirements to ensure such deals meet and exceed expectations.

That's why we expect to see more Chinese companies building on the strategies from phase 3 while tailoring them to their industries and market conditions. The recognition that talent, innovation and IP are the keys to growth and viability means that expertise, ideas and the development of new technologies will be top priorities. Increasingly fierce competition among leading players within China could mean that the battlefield focus will be on the domestic market rather than on foreign countries. We believe that Chinese companies will continue to use M&A to wage this fight.

Notes

1 United Nations Conference on Trade and Development (UNCTAD).
2 Ibid.
3 Tagliabue, J 2003, 'Thomson and TCL to join TV units', *New York Times*, Available from: www.nytimes.com/2003/11/04/business/thomson-and-tcl-to-join-tv-units.html.
4 Prasad, E & Sorkin, I 2009, 'Sky's the limit: National and global implications of China's reserve accumulation', Brookings Institution. Available from: www.brookings.edu/articles/skys-the-limit-national-and-global-implications-of-chinas-reserve-accumulation/.
5 Goodman, D & Kondom, M 2017, 'Sinopec shifts assets to global oil assets to state buyers amid downturn'. Available from: www.bloomberg.com/news/articles/2017-01-15/pound-drops-to-3-month-low-as-may-reported-to-seek-hard-brexit.
6 *Crude Oil Prices – 70 Year Historical Chart.* Available from: Macrotrends, www.macrotrends.net/1369/crude-oil-price-history-chart.

7 CIFIT 2013, '80% of Chinese companies' overseas mining investments fail'. Available from: www.chinafair.org.cn/english/news/43180_1100.html.
8 Sany annual reports, http://file.ws.126.net/quotes/pdf/sh/2013/2013-4/2013-04-27/1121106.pdf.
9 Nin-Hai Sang 2013, 'Sany's bold U.S. move', *Fortune*, June 17. Available from: http://fortune.com/2013/06/17/sanys-bold-u-s-move/.
10 Caroline Copley 2016, 'As China shops for German firms, one early example reassures', *Reuters*, June 3. Available from: www.reuters.com/article/us-putzmeister-sany-insight-idUSKCN0YO2IA.
11 Wei, D & Matthews, S 2016, *China's Midea to become largest investor in Germany's Kuka*. Available from: www.bloomberg.com/news/articles/2016-07-03/voith-sells-kuka-stake-to-china-s-midea-for-about-1–3-billion.
12 Osawa, J & Needleman, SE 2016, 'Tencent seals deal to buy "clash of clans" developer supercell for $8.6 billion'. Available from: www.wsj.com/articles/tencent-agrees-to-acquire-clash-of-clans-maker-supercell-1466493612.
13 Mueller, S 2016, *Report: League of legends made $1.6 billion in revenue last year*. Available from: https://dotesports.com/league-of-legends/league-of-legends-2015-revenue-2839.
14 Yun-Hee Kim 2017, 'Alibaba's six biggest overseas deals', *Wall Street Journal*. Available from: www.wsj.com/video/alibabas-six-biggest-overseas-deals/CE156715-48E7-4977-8F4E-CA59F6F9550E.html.
15 Dettoni, J 2016, 'Chinese R&D goes global', *Financial Times*, www.ft.com/content/ded25056-6f64-11e6-9ac1-1055824ca907.
16 Molzer, P & Winkler, R 2014, 'Baidu to open artificial-intelligence center in Silicon Valley', *The Wall Street Journal*, May 16. Available from: www.wsj.com/articles/SB1000142 4052702304908304579565950123054242.
17 Moore, M 2014, 'Huawei buys up UK IoT Pioneer Neul', *Silicon*. Available from: www.silicon.co.uk/workspace/huawei-buys-uk-iot-pioneer-neul-152690.
18 Essers, L 2015, 'Huawei buys software networking tech from Irish Amartus', *PC World*, July 13. Available from: www.pcworld.com/article/2947552/huawei-buys-software-networking-tech-from-irish-amartus.html.
19 Huawei 2016 annual report, p. 34, http://www-file.huawei.com/-/media/CORPO RATE/PDF/annual-report/AnnualReport2016_en.pdf?la=en.
20 'Huawei and Leica Camera establish new research and innovation center', Huawei. Available from: www.huawei.com/en/news/2016/9/Huawei-Leica-New-Research-Innovation-Center [23 Septermber 2016].
21 With assistance by Hamlin, K 2014, 'Xi Dangles $1.25 trillion as China counters U.S. refocus', *Bloomberg*, November 8. Available from: www.bloomberg.com/news/articles/2014-11-09/president-xi-says-7-percent-gdp-growth-makes-china-top-performer.
22 Beijing Monitoring Desk, Glenn, E & Yao, K 2016, 'China's outward investment tops $161 billion in 2016: Minister', *Reuters*, December 26. Available from: www.reuters.com/article/us-china-economy-investment-idUSKBN14F07R.
23 Ajmera, A 2016, 'GE to sell appliances business to China's haier for $5.4 billion', *Reuters*, January 15. Available from: www.reuters.com/article/us-ge-divestiture-haier-elec-idUSKCN0UT0AG.
24 Whitwam, R 2016, 'Motorola almost completely gutted by Lenovo following new round of layoffs', *Extreme Tech*, September 28. Available from: www.extremetech.com/mobile/236421-motorola-almost-completely-gutted-by-lenovo-following-new-round-of-layoffs.

18

CHINESE INVESTMENT IN THE UK

Great expectations?

Lord Sassoon and Giles Blackburne

Introduction

Mindful of the rising trend in Chinese outward foreign investment, the UK has always sought to position itself as the preferred destination in Europe for Chinese investors. Some key drivers for China's overseas investment – such as seeking technologies to address domestic challenges, acquiring brands with market prospects in China and identifying property development opportunities with steady returns – have played well to the UK's strengths. Moreover, the London factor, in terms of its status as a global financial centre and hot spot for prestigious property development, has proved highly attractive to Chinese banks and state-owned enterprises seeking a European HQ and to private enterprises seeking a safe place to invest.

Then, on 23 June 2016 the UK voted to leave the European Union ('Brexit'). It is now expected that the UK will leave the European Union in March 2019. How does this leave the prospects for Chinese investment not only in London but across the UK? The trajectory of Chinese investment into the UK during the last decade, along with the 'going out' of Chinese enterprises encouraged by the Chinese government, has heightened expectations in the UK about the scale of future investment. Can investment from China live up to the UK's needs and expectations? This chapter will examine the current expectations of the UK towards Chinese investment. Supported by interviews, it will also seek to ascertain the confidence of Chinese investors in post-Brexit UK. It will conclude with a discussion on the implications for policymakers, for those promoting British investment projects and for Chinese investors.

The current state of Chinese investment into the UK

Figures generated by the American Enterprise Institute and the Heritage Foundation report on China's global investment and construction activity across the

TABLE 18.1 Chinese investment into the UK by sector, 2005–2016*

Sector	*$ billion*	*% of total*
Real Estate	12.66	33.2
Energy	6.67	17.5
Finance	4.85	12.7
Agriculture	3.85	10.1
Transport	2.8	7.3
Metals	1.79	4.7
Technology	1.41	3.7
Entertainment	1.03	2.7
Tourism	0.4	1.0
Other	2.64	6.9
Total	**38.1**	

*Source: China Global Investment Tracker, American Enterprise Institute and the Heritage Foundation (*until end June 2016).*

world. For the period from 2005 until June 2016, the pattern of Chinese investment into the UK is shown in Table 18.1.

According to Table 18.1, real estate has dominated the flow of Chinese investment into the UK since 2005, followed by energy, finance and food/agriculture. However, such figures do little to convey the diversity of Chinese investment into the UK. For example, there has been wide variety in both investment size and destination – from sovereign wealth funds, where SAFE invested more than $2 billion into British oil and gas company BP, to investments into ownership or part-ownership of household names, such as Pizza Express (Hony Capital), House of Fraser (Sanpower), Weetabix (Everbright) and Sunseeker Yachts (Wanda). A 15% depreciation of the pound sterling following the Brexit referendum most likely influenced the timing of private enterprise Wanda buying the Odeon cinema chain for £920 million ($1.15 billion) and Creat Group making an £800 million ($1 billion) investment in UK healthcare firm BPL. More recently, Chinese online travel firm Ctrip also acquired UK travel search business Skyscanner for £1.4 billion ($1.75 billion) (Davies, 2016) in order to benefit from complementarities that will help it become a global company.

A number of recent investment deals also reflect how Chinese firms are attaching importance to issues closer to home, such as clean energy. For example, in 2015 UK automotive firm Aston Martin concluded a £50 million ($62.5 million) deal with private equity firm China Equity to develop an electric sports car, while Zhejiang Geely Holding Group invested a further £50 million ($62.5 billion) into Manganese Bronze in order to fund research and development into hybrid black cabs capable of zero emissions (Inman et al., 2015). China's admiration for

TABLE 18.2 Chinese investment into the UK and Europe, 2005–2016

Chinese Investment into UK (US$)						
2005	*2006*	*2007*	*2008*	*2009*	*2010*	
0.1 Billion*	0.8	3.04	2.01	1.7	1.13	
2011	*2012*	*2013*	*2014*	*2015*	*2016***	*Total*
0.51	7.12	4.22	8.68	5.0	3.79	**38.1**
Chinese Investment into Europe (US$)						
2005	*2006*	*2007*	*2008*	*2009*	*2010*	
0.1 Billion*	1.38	7.5	12.18	10.3	9.28	
2011	*2012*	*2013*	*2014*	*2015*	*2016***	*Total*
23.18	19.11	13.57	33.81	37.73	34.82	**202.96**

*USD **(Jan–June) *Source: China Global Investment Tracker, American Enterprise Institute and the Heritage Foundation.*

the UK's history, culture and education should also not be underestimated as an attraction for Chinese investors already pre-disposed towards investing in the UK, but still requiring a business case.

There has been a dramatic increase in Chinese investment into the UK over the last ten years (Table 18.2) although volumes have been volatile year-on-year. The figures also show that the UK has performed well within a European context, accounting for nearly 20% of total investment from China.

According to a report by legal firm Baker McKenzie (2016), if *completed* rather than agreed FDI is taken into account, the UK currently sits in third place as China's European destination of choice. In 2015, the top-five EU countries by investment value were Italy ($7.8 billion), France ($3.6 billion), the UK ($3.3 billion), the Netherlands ($2.5 billion) and Germany ($1.3 billion). However, both Italy and France enjoyed particular mega investments from China in 2015 – for example, ChemChina's investment into Pirelli ($7.7 billion).

Nevertheless, the UK needs to increase its efforts to maintain its position as China's preferred location for investment into Europe. The rewards could be considerable. A report by legal firm Pinsent Masons estimated that over £105 billion ($131.25 billion) of Chinese investment could flow into UK infrastructure and real estate by 2025 (Masons, 2014).

The UK-China context for investment

In October 2015, the UK government strengthened its relationship with China through a successful state visit to the UK by President Xi Jinping. A joint statement between the UK's Prime Minister David Cameron and China's President Xi Jinping committed to creating a global comprehensive strategic partnership for the twenty-first century and to developing a 'golden era' of increased cooperation (CCTV, 2016). This has set the scene for how China and the UK are seeking to maintain momentum for their partnership since the referendum.

The current context for Chinese investment into the UK is reflected in the outcomes of the eighth UK-China Economic and Financial Dialogue (EFD) which took place in London on 10 November 2016 (HM Treasury, 2016). These include, for example, a closer partnership between the London and Shanghai stock exchanges, mutual recognition of funds, improved China market access for UK financial services and co-operation on green finance, Belt and Road financing and FinTech. It was also announced that more Chinese financial institutions, such as China Life, China Foreign Exchange Trade System and Shanghai Clearing House, would set up a presence in London, whilst China Investment Corporation and China Banking Association reiterated commitments to establish their European headquarters in the capital.

In relation to the UK's decision to leave the European Union, the UK re-affirmed its commitment to a strong economy that is open for business, while China committed to encouraging Chinese firms to strengthen their investment in the UK. Furthermore, China highlighted the UK as being the world's leading financial services centre and committed to supporting London's development as the world's leading offshore RMB centre. A framework for discussing options for a future post-Brexit trading relationship was also agreed through a new 'trade working group' under the existing UK-China Joint Economic and Trade Commission.

The EFD also announced collaboration on infrastructure development and capacity building via a UK-China Infrastructure Alliance, not only in China and in the UK, but also in third countries via multilateral development banks including the Asian Infrastructure Investment Bank. High-speed rail, clean energy (offshore wind, marine) and nuclear energy were highlighted as areas where the UK would welcome Chinese investment. Indeed, the 'Final Investment Decision' and signing of the contractual documentation for the UK's Hinkley Point C nuclear power station was also announced, confirming a minority investment from China General Nuclear in the project along with the company's role in future UK nuclear projects. This signified the intent of both governments to put infrastructure at the centre of Chinese investment into the UK and also signalled the openness of the UK, compared with other developed countries, to accepting investment from China into sensitive areas of the economy.

At the conclusion of the EFD, the UK's Minister of State for International Trade Greg Hands stressed the need to maintain momentum in furthering the bilateral UK-China 'golden era', stating that the UK wanted China to become its second-largest foreign investor by 2020. In return, China's Vice-Premier Ma Kai was keen to underline the strength of the UK-China relationship, dismissing concerns about the UK's decision to leave the European Union and re-affirming China's commitment to the 'golden era' and deepening bilateral trade and investment.

Insights from UK regional inward investment agencies

Regions across the UK are now taking direct and proactive measures to attract Chinese investment into infrastructure, regeneration and housing – especially within the context of the UK's new regional economic development policies for the 'Northern Powerhouse' and 'Midlands Engine' (see Box 1). This section now reports on the views of inward investment professionals from four UK regions about the current and future outlook for Chinese investment.

London

London & Partners is the official promotional organisation for London. It runs promotional campaigns in China to promote opportunities in the capital's property and technology sectors, promotes London directly to potential Chinese investors and provides services to Chinese companies. Chinese investment is increasingly important for London. According to official figures for the period 2005 to 2015 (London and Partners, 2016), Chinese investment accounted for 13% of all London investment projects, contributing to 216 projects and creating 2,424 jobs. 2015 saw a record level of Chinese investment with 36 projects. China has now become the third-largest investor in London. According to EY's European Investment Monitor (2016), London attracted 13.2 % of all Chinese foreign direct investment into Europe (2004–2014) ahead of Düsseldorf/Neuss (9.1% of projects), Frankfurt (3.9 %) and Paris (2%).

BOX 1: THE NORTHERN POWERHOUSE AND MIDLANDS ENGINE CASE STUDY

The Northern Powerhouse and Midlands Engine are regions designated by the UK government to receive a programme of long-term investment that will stimulate economic growth. The long-term objective is to reduce regional disparities in the UK and rebalance the UK's economy away from London and the South East. The regions are expected to benefit from urban agglomeration and regional industrial synergies, which will be further enhanced by improved transport links, investment in science and innovation and devolution of economic development decisions.

With the Northern Powerhouse and Midlands Engine regions making annual GVA (gross value added) contributions of £304 billion ($380 billion) – 19% of the UK total – and £222 billion ($277.5 billion) – 14.6% of UK's total – to the UK economy and having combined populations of 10.7 million and 11.5 million respectively, it is anticipated that these regions will attract more attention from foreign investors, compared to when using the economic indicators of disparate cities (HM Government 2016a, 2016b).

From 2005 to 2015, financial services (19%), creative industries (17%), business services including real estate (16%) and technology (13%) accounted for nearly two-thirds of Chinese investment, while sales and marketing (44%), HQ (37%) and service (10%) accounted for over 90% of designated functions. However, Chinese investors are now looking beyond the traditional sectors of financial and business services towards the technology (see Box 2), creative and life science sectors. According to London & Partners, merger and acquisition and equity investments are now the main methods of investment, while Chinese investors are showing increased interest in start-ups and scale-ups for accessing capital and teaming up with world-leading technologies. London is also positioning itself as a Western hub for Chinese finance, an aspiration supported by China Construction Bank in London assuming a position as the first clearing bank outside Greater China for the RMB and also by the announcement that the Chinese government intends to make London the first overseas location for a sovereign debt market for the RMB. Overall, uncertainty surrounding Brexit aside, the prospects for further Chinese investment are seen as bright. Chinese investment into London property is still strong. On the one hand this is viewed as taking advantage of the weak pound, but on the other as showing confidence in the market.

BOX 2: HUAWEI CASE STUDY

Founded in 1987 in China, Huawei is a leading information and communications technology (ICT) company with global sales of more than $20 billion in 2015. It employs 150,000 people in more than 140 countries, supplying 45 out of the world's 50 top telecommunications companies and the majority of the UK telecoms market. Huawei set up in London in 2001 and has offices in Paddington, the City and Westminster, and its headquarters in Reading.

During London's Olympic year (2012), Huawei announced a plan to invest $1.9 billion in the UK. The company is on track to increase its UK workforce from 890 in 2013 to 1,500 in 2017–2018. This will include highly skilled engineers and sales staff. Since 2012, Huawei has acquired the Cambridge-based Internet of things company Neul, opened an R&D centre in Bristol, helped roll out 4G and broadband networks around the UK for customers including EE and BT, started to pioneer the development of 5G technologies, and increased its UK workforce from 781 to 1,030 people. The company now has a presence at 15 locations across the UK and currently supports 7,400 jobs directly and through its supply chain.

After the EU referendum Huawei reaffirmed its 2012 investment plan for the UK and commitment to create a further 500 jobs in the UK (*China Daily*, 2016). Huawei has established a reputation in the UK for being a technology provider, developer and investor, while at the same time accessing the UK's innovation resource to develop its capabilities back in China and across the world.

However, according to London & Partners there is still work to do. Chinese investors appear unfamiliar with the breadth of opportunity both in London and across the UK. There are information gaps about UK regulations and about how to assess investment risk. There can also be lack of flexibility from Chinese investors, especially in terms of their speed of reaction to M&A opportunities. London & Partners advise Chinese investors to seek advice from the city's professional services sector in order to minimise the risk of failure.

Birmingham

Birmingham is situated in the Midlands region of the UK and is an integral part of plans for the Midlands Engine. Established in 2010, Marketing Birmingham is the city's strategic marketing partnership responsible for delivering the city's inward investment strategy. Chinese investment into Birmingham first became noteworthy during the disposal of the UK automotive company MG Rover, which went into administration in late 2005 and was acquired by what is now Shanghai Automotive Industries Corporation. The company still has a presence in the city, where it is now developing European research and development capacity. There have been 23 FDI projects from China and Hong Kong since 2005, creating over 1,500 jobs. However, Chinese projects are viewed as being slower to come to fruition compared to those from top FDI markets such as the USA and Europe (especially Germany). In turn, more promotional resource has been allocated to those markets.

For Birmingham, early engagement with Chinese enterprises tended to be with large state-owned enterprises seeking to add value to existing products or processes in China, for example in research and development (see Box 3). The city views itself as being able to offer such benefits to Chinese enterprises, especially in the advanced engineering, automotive, aerospace and rail sectors. Recent years, however, have seen interest from smaller, privately owned Chinese companies in acquiring UK companies in sectors where China is still considered to be relatively under-developed, such as bio-medicine, FinTech and gaming.

Marketing Birmingham distinguishes between three investment types from China: first, 'classic FDI' (for example a Chinese enterprise setting up an R&D centre creating high skilled jobs); second, M&A (leading to outright acquisition or transfer of equity); and third, 'capital attraction' (covering capital flows into property and large-scale regeneration). In the short term, and in light of Brexit uncertainty, it is anticipated that there may be a slow-down in Chinese FDI (perhaps with fewer, larger projects that are slower to come to fruition) but an increase in capital flows from Chinese private wealth, family offices and institutions, particularly into property. The city is also hoping to attract Chinese investors willing to forward fund capital intensive investment into large scale regeneration and able to bring direct project delivery experience from China. Capital attraction is generally favoured since the city is a growing economy requiring more residential, office and commercial property.

BOX 3: CHANGAN UK R&D CENTRE CASE STUDY

With five domestic R&D centres in China and four overseas, Changan Automobile has formed a global R&D footprint covering China, Italy, Japan, UK and USA. The company has 12 global production bases, 32 vehicle and engine plants and over 6,000 sale and service stations in 60 countries, comprising nearly 50,000 employees, selling 2.7 million vehicles a year and generating an annual turnover of RMB 243 billion ($36.45 billion). The company also has joint ventures with Ford, PSA, Mazda, Suzuki and JMC.

Changan UK R&D Centre Ltd (CAUK) was set up in Nottingham UK by Changan Automobile in June 2010, focusing on powertrain design and development for the company's next generation of vehicles. In October 2015, CAUK relocated to Birmingham where it has ambitious expansion plans to build its own test facility and recruit more R&D roles. CAUK aims to become a world-class powertrain R&D centre, as well as a promoter and practitioner of green technologies.

Changan is now incorporating advanced engineering processes and techniques developed in the UK into its manufacturing in China, enabling the company to reach advanced levels of manufacturing.

Marketing Birmingham views the difference in business environments as a key challenge to landing Chinese investment. A spokesperson explained:

> The sense of opportunity is certainly there, but sometimes the reality is different. It requires hard work in a complex and uncertain business and political environment compared to the US and Europe. So why would we spend so much time on this, when we could perhaps pick up the phone and ask the Americans to do something?

The implication is that, until these gaps in mutual understanding narrow, Chinese enterprises will lose out on investment opportunities to culturally closer competitors from the US and Europe. Chinese investors are also observed as being less familiar with the UK business environment:

> Sometimes when you speak to some wealthy Chinese investors about the way some sectors in this country work and the regulations related to it, they find it very difficult to adapt and their expectations are sometimes a lot different to the reality or the deliverability of the UK market. There is also sometimes an expectation that government will help them financially, but we are not allowed to do that.

Manchester

Manchester is situated in the North West of the UK and is an integral part of plans for the Northern Powerhouse. Momentum for Chinese investment in Manchester came in 2012 when Beijing Construction Engineering Group (BCEG) took a partnership position with UK investors to develop the Airport City enterprise zone (see Box 4). Manchester's visibility in China was boosted by being included in the itinerary for President Xi Jinping's state visit to the UK in October 2015 and further enhanced by the establishment of a direct air route between Manchester and Beijing operated by Hainan Airlines.

Manchester's inward investment agency, MIDAS, takes a two-pronged approach to raising the city's profile in China: first, via premiership football, where matches in China and Hong Kong are used as platforms to showcase investment opportunities to wealthy investors; second, through sector led initiatives, where opportunities, for example, around life sciences or technology sectors related to manufacturing are targeted directly towards large Chinese companies. The city sees benefits from being marketed as a key centre in the UK's Northern Powerhouse, a concept which Chinese enterprises appreciate for being a government initiative that can offer them opportunities to invest in UK infrastructure and energy projects of significant scale and profile.

BOX 4: BCEGI CONSTRUCTION CASE STUDY

Beijing Construction Engineering Group was founded in 1953 and has offices in Equatorial Guinea, Libya, the United Arab Emirates, Saudi Arabia, Togo, Mongolia, Kazakhstan, Malaysia, Singapore, Thailand, Vietnam and the Philippines, where it undertakes local housing construction, roads and bridge construction, municipal works, airport construction, power plant and other projects.

Through its UK subsidiary BCEGI, it has invested in an £800 million ($1 billion) joint venture with Manchester Airports Group, the Greater Manchester Pension Fund and UK construction firm Carillion, in the development of the Airport City enterprise zone. BCEGI has also pursued further investment opportunities in Manchester, such as St Michael's, an integrated hotel/residential/office building with a value of some £220 million ($275 million).

The company is now working with local partners to promote the 'China Cluster' in the region, which aims to be a hub for Chinese businesses to invest in the North of England. BCEGI has more than 40 full time staff, of whom eight are from China. The company is creating high-level jobs in the UK via its investment and construction programme.

The work of BCEGI is a tangible example of how Chinese investment is revolutionising the UK's Northern infrastructure. The UK also offers an opportunity for BCEGI to develop and absorb new expertise which can be applied back in China and in other markets around the world.

For its part, MIDAS is optimistic about the future, observing that while investment to date has largely been into real estate, there is an appetite from Chinese firms to invest strategically, particularly into research and development and co-development, as opposed to simply making products. For example, Chinese information and communications technology company Huawei has invested in the development of graphene in the city.

The main challenge for Chinese enterprises is viewed as the steep learning curve in understanding planning and tendering processes, which affects their ability to engage with UK opportunities effectively. Overall, the objective of MIDAS is to develop and maintain a balanced portfolio of foreign investors, not one dominated by Chinese or any other nationality.

Scotland

Scottish Development International (SDI) is the investment and trade promotion agency of the Scottish Government. The organisation has had a presence in China for over 20 years focusing on trade and, increasingly, the inward investment agenda.

Chinese investment in Scotland has mainly been in the oil and gas sector, where it now accounts for over a quarter of the oil and gas infrastructure. Chinese interests also own or part-own three out of the four offshore wind projects being promoted in Scotland, each with a capital value of several billion dollars (see Box 5). However, in recent years SDI has witnessed greater diversity in the interest from Chinese investors, both in terms of sectors and investment typology – in particular moving from financial investment more into collaboration, M&A and green field projects. Some 'second phase' green field investments from London or other UK locations are expected, along with further instances where Chinese firms might establish a foothold in a company, then grow the business to fit their strategic needs.

SDI's view is that Chinese firms will not view the Brexit issue as being as important as those factors which continue to favour the UK and Scotland – such as the size of the economy, along with other assets and attributes which will continue to remain attractive. While the UK will be leaving the European Union, it will not be leaving Europe per se; therefore, opportunities will continue to arise from economic cooperation between European countries. Feedback about Brexit from Chinese investors has, on the whole, been more relaxed and more positive compared to that from other foreign investors.

SDI expects that in time, Chinese investments can play as strong a role in Scotland's economy as investments from other countries. For example, Scotland is the UK's number-one region for attracting research and development projects. There is an expectation that China will also become active in this sector. It may be some time before Chinese investments can match those of the US in terms of job creation, but over time SDI views the UK government's aspiration for China to become the UK's no. 2 investor as being realistic.

According to SDI, the main challenge for Chinese investors is to work effectively within the fiercely commercial forces at play within the UK market.

BOX 5: RED ROCK POWER LIMITED CASE STUDY

China's State Development & Investment Corporation (SDIC), a state-owned investment holdings company, has invested in Scotland's growing offshore wind sector by acquiring Spanish energy company Repsol's offshore wind power business for US$262 million in 2016. This followed Chinese developer China Three Gorges' 2015 acquisition of a 30% stake in another Scottish offshore project from Portuguese developer EDP Renovaveis.

For SDIC, in its first exposure to the European offshore wind market, this acquisition also gives it a 25% share of the £2.6bn Beatrice Offshore Windfarm Ltd (BOWL) – one of the largest private investments ever made in Scottish infrastructure.

Aiming to further increase its investment into Scotland's renewables sector and build on its offshore wind projects, SDIC's subsidiary Red Rock Power Limited has opened an office in Edinburgh. At the office launch, SDIC Chairman Wang Huishen was keen to stress SDIC's intention to be a responsible investor.

'SDIC is keen to find more investment opportunities in Scotland and will try to be an excellent model in terms of the enterprise development, the cooperation between China and the West, good employee-employer relations and the good relationship between the government and businesses . . . We are looking forward to participating in more areas of Scottish economic development and contributing more to the prosperity of Scotland'.

Chinese firms contemplating investment in the UK or Scotland, especially when it is their first investment in the West, face a steep learning curve in terms of skills, culture and business practice and are therefore at risk of business failure, which in turn could ultimately damage Scotland's attempt to attract further investment from China.

For SDI's inward investment promotion efforts, the main challenge is viewed as the supply of investable propositions from Scotland. As a spokesperson said:

> There is no shortage of interest in talking about investable propositions and there is no shortage of financial backing for them once they have been clearly articulated and presented, but the supply of those investable propositions is the biggest constraint.

The views of Chinese investors

During China-Britain Business Council's China Outbound Conference which took place in Shanghai on 3 November 2016, a panel of five senior executives from top Chinese enterprises were interviewed about their reasons for investing in the UK.

According to a senior manager from China Equity Group, the UK is already recognised by Chinese enterprises as having advantages in creative ideas, products and services and also in sectors supported by technology, such as bio-tech, FinTech, clean-tech and new materials. Indeed, China Equity Group is partnering with Chinese technology and investment group Cocoon Networks to launch a London-based venture capital fund aimed at investing in UK and European tech start-ups. A representative from Chinese investment banking firm China International Capital Corporation (CICC) also observed that the UK is more open-minded to Chinese investments compared to other jurisdictions and, furthermore, that London in particular offers connectivity with like-minded investors and an existing investment community.

As an advisor to Chinese investors, CICC highlighted a strategic logic that often lies behind a decision to invest in the UK, manifesting itself in the potential for a UK brand in China or the transferability of UK design capabilities, fashion brands or management skills to China. Chinese investment in real estate or property is not exempt from such a 'China angle' and could be viewed, for example, from the perspective of accommodating Chinese outbound tourists in hotels or Chinese tenants in commercial property or enterprise zones. The implication is that even profitable and growing UK businesses are less attractive to Chinese investors if they lack a China angle.

Two examples of a China angle were brought out during the panel discussion. First, with strengths in property, infrastructure, health, commerce and design, Nanjing based Sanpower Group acquired House of Fraser along with its 59 stores across the UK in 2014. Sanpower already owned a department store called Nanjing Xin Bai but saw House of Fraser's merchandising and buying functions, along with its European supply chain, as a means to upgrade and restructure its own systems and become more competitive. A senior executive explained, '[B]uying know-how from an international brand is a fast and efficient way to acquire the necessary capability and make ourselves more competitive in [the Chinese] market'. A flagship House of Fraser store was opened in Nanjing at the end of 2016. Later, Sanpower and its strategic partner C.banner jointly acquired British toy store Hamleys, which opened its first Nanjing store in October 2016. The popularity of the new store has now attracted the attention of other Chinese property developers and shopping malls looking for collaboration opportunities in China, thus bringing further business development opportunities for Sanpower Group. Second, Chinese property and business district developer ABP noticed that London did not possess a business district for Chinese companies wishing to go global and so decided to build a dedicated business district in the capital for Chinese companies in partnership with Chinese firm CITIC Construction.

From a strategic perspective, institutional investor Fosun focuses on 'happiness, health and fashion' related fields. A senior executive explained that Fosun's investment model is to co-operate with overseas partners and identify areas where there is a demand or a shortfall in China, from advanced bio-technology through to sports and leisure. The logic for Fosun in buying the UK's Wolverhampton

Wanderers Football Club in 2016 was that Chinese football is weak and therefore an English Club could be leveraged in China. (Fosun applied the same logic to luxury brands, investing in UK heritage nursery brand Silver Cross in 2015.) The senior executive added, 'We use our investment to set up an equity relationship with our partner. Then we rely on our strengths in China, to help the business develop the Chinese market'.

Chinese investor views on Brexit

In the week following the EU Referendum, London & Partners contacted current and potential Chinese FDI Clients, key stakeholders and partners to gauge business sentiment about the implications of Brexit. The survey included a total of 45 Chinese companies regarding 50 projects in London, of which 18 projects were underway, 31 were in discussion and one project was on hold. Business services was the dominant sector (11), followed by ICT (8) and financial services (6).

The survey found that the general sentiment was 'neutral': 67% of companies said that they were carrying on business as usual while monitoring the overall situation. Only 18% of companies expressed negative sentiment, while 15% saw positive new opportunities. In terms of future intentions, 75% of those surveyed planned to carry on with business as usual while monitoring the situation closely; 11% did not see Brexit affecting their business at all (most of these companies serviced the UK market only), while 7% put decisions on hold for now until there was more clarity. Another 7% of Chinese companies admitted to looking at alternative bases in Europe. Other concerns highlighted by those companies surveyed included the period of uncertainty, financial instability, recruiting and retaining staff and accessing key markets in Europe.

Concerning investors' reaction to the UK's decision to leave the European Union, a spokesperson for Marketing Birmingham observed that Chinese investors appeared to be initially taking a 'hold position' and believed that Chinese investors would probably come to a conclusion that the fundamentals of the UK economy are strong and that, regardless of Brexit, Birmingham remains a manufacturer of high value-added products for the automotive industry. Moreover, Brexit has not deterred Chinese investors already in discussion with Birmingham, since the investment logic remains unchanged: '[I]f you are looking at building houses here, we still have that demand'. Manchester's MIDAS also sees little prospect for disruption in the momentum of Chinese investment – especially for UK-focused infrastructure projects: '[T]here has been more concern from Chinese investors about the future of the Northern Powerhouse than about Brexit per se'. This contrasts with the views of Japanese investors, who may be more concerned with how Brexit will affect the UK as a gateway to Europe. This difference reflects the fact that Japan, unlike China, owns very large manufacturing businesses in the UK.

As for the views about Brexit from Chinese investors interviewed at CBBC's China Outbound Conference, according to China Equity a short- versus long-term view can be applied. In the short term, uncertainty about the value of sterling might delay an investment decision, but the long-term logic for investing – namely, that China has a huge potential market driven by a rise in consumption and an up-grade of technology – remains sound. So, according to China Equity, UK and Chinese companies should continue to make alliances in order to identify and exploit the potential of the Chinese market.

For its part, investment banking firm CICC sees an opportunity not only to maintain the current UK-China business relationship but also to grow it. Their straight-forward logic is that Europe is the destination for a growing proportion of China's global investment and that the UK occupies a significant proportion of Chinese investment into Europe. This indicates a momentum that will not stop.

Policy implications and recommendations

We conclude with a short discussion about the implications for policymakers, Chinese investors and those promoting British investment projects.

The recent Economic and Financial Dialogue between the UK and China, along with other ongoing government to government dialogues, show that the current UK-China relationship remains very positive. Despite the uncertainty arising from the UK's decision to leave the Europe Union, there is now an opportunity to strengthen further the trade and investment relationship between China and the UK, most importantly but not exclusively under a free trade and investment agreement.

However, if the UK wishes China to become its second-largest investor, further effort will be required to raise Chinese investors' awareness of the breadth and depth of the UK investment opportunity. The UK's competitor countries can be more adept at promoting investment opportunities to Chinese investors and, importantly, explicitly conveying the value of their projects, along with any China angles. Furthermore, the knowledge gap between Chinese investors and the UK investment environment indicates that more work is needed to assist Chinese investors in their learning, increase their confidence and ensure a greater likelihood for landing investments.

In a similar manner, UK regional government needs be proactive in conveying local opportunities and investable propositions. Project owners seeking Chinese investment should not wait for Chinese investors to come to the UK, but should prepare suitable materials and travel to China in order to build relationships with potential investors. Promotional work needs to progress from the general promotional approach to the targeting of specific investors. Different investor types may require different messaging and, aside from traditional FDI and capital flows, the UK needs to become more comfortable with acquisition scenarios and the potential benefits they can bring in terms of business development, employment and access to the Chinese market. Relations need to be maintained with existing Chinese investors in the UK in order to ensure their success and also to encourage further, second stage investments.

Finally, UK regions engage with many markets when seeking investment, some of which are viewed as being easier and having more predictable outcomes. Chinese investors risk missing out on investment opportunities or experiencing business failure unless they actively seek to learn about the UK business environment and engage appropriate professional advice at an early stage in assessing a particular opportunity.

Conclusions

This article has explored the current state of Chinese investment in the UK. In light of the UK's decision to leave the European Union, we believe that the current relationship between the UK and China shows resilience and offers further opportunity to develop two-way trade and investment. In particular, the logic for Chinese investment into the UK remains unchanged.

The 'China angle' will remain an important driver for some Chinese investors, while the prospect of returns on infrastructure, energy and property projects of scale will be important to others. Despite the UK being a popular destination for Chinese investment, it must not rest on its laurels. Promotional work must focus on engaging directly with investors and providing support in the form of investment opportunity awareness, knowledge about the UK business environment, strategic advice, training and after-sales support. UK regions must adopt more sophisticated messages, build relationships in China and respond flexibly to offers from competing locations in Europe. Chinese investors must also become more knowledgeable and flexible to avoid missing out on investment opportunities in a competitive environment.

References

American Enterprise Institute and the Heritage Foundation, *China Global Investment Tracker*. Available from: www.aei.org/china-global-investment-tracker/. [1 December 2016].

CCTV 2016, 'Full text of China-UK joint declaration', *CCTV-America*. Available from: http://china.cctv-america.com/2015/10/22/full-text-of-china-uk-joint-declaration/. [1 December 2016].

Davies, R 2016, 'Skyscanner sold to China's Ctrip in £1.4bn deal', *The Guardian* [Online]. Available from: www.theguardian.com/business/2016/nov/24/skyscanner-sold-to-chinas-ctrip-in-14bn-deal. [1 December 2016].

EY's European Investment Monitor 2016. Available from: www.eyeim.com.

HM Government 2016a, *Midlands Engine for Growth Prospectus*. Available from: www.gov.uk/government/uploads/system/uploads/attachment_data/file/482247/midlands-engine-for-growth.pdf. [1 December 2016].

HM Government 2016b, *Northern Powerhouse Strategy*. Available from: www.gov.uk/government/uploads/system/uploads/attachment_data/file/571562/NPH_strategy_web.pdf. [1 December 2016].

HM Treasury 2016, *Policy Outcomes of the 8th UK-China Economic and Financial Dialogue UK- China Global Comprehensive Strategic Partnership for the 21st Century*. Available from:

www.gov.uk/government/uploads/system/uploads/attachment_data/file/567521/UK-China_8th_EFD_policy_outcomes_paper.pdf. [1 December 2016].

'Huawei's $1.73b investment in UK to go ahead despite Brexit vote' 2016, *China Daily [Online]*. Available from: www.chinadaily.com.cn/business/tech/2016-06/29/content_25899074.htm. [1 December 2016].

Inman, P, Macalister, T, Topham, G & Sweney, M 2015, 'The UK's deals worth billions with China: What do they really mean?', *The Guardian [Online]*. Available from: www.theguardian.com/business/2015/oct/24/britains-deals-with-china-billions-what-do-they-mean. [1 December 2016].

London & Partners 2016, Foreign Direct Investment Report, 2005–2015, *China Review*. Available from: http://files.londonandpartners.com/l-and-p/assets/fdi_report_2005_2015_web.pdf. [1 December 2016].

Masons, P 2014, *China Invests West: Can Chinese investment be a game-changer for UK infrastructure?* Available from: www.pinsentmasons.com/PDF/pageturner/ChinaInvestsWest/files/assets/common/downloads/page0001.pdf. [1 December 2016].

McKenzie, B 2016, 'Chinese FDI hits USD 40 billion in 2015 for Europe and North America', *Baker Mckenzie*. Available from: www.bakermckenzie.com/en/newsroom/2016/03/chinese-fdi-hits-usd40-billion/. [1 December 2016].

19

THE 'NEW NORMAL' AND ITS IMPLICATIONS FOR CHINESE INVESTMENT IN AFRICA

Jacko J. H. Maree and Jeremy J. Stevens

Introduction

In the early 2000s when the African continent was being ignored by most, China embraced Africa – first politically and then, increasingly, commercially. Fast forward a decade and a half later, and many cities across Africa are virtually unrecognisable from just a decade ago, in large part because of this reinvigorated partnership with China.

Even in the aftermath of the global financial crisis, ties have been reinforced. By vigorously responding to the global financial crisis and launching a set of policy measures designed to boost demand, China has supported commodity demand. Faced with soft demand in mature economies, Chinese exporters have also increasingly looked to alternative markets, particularly in Africa. Meanwhile, the regulators have supported outbound investment by easing requirements, decentralising regulatory procedures and broadening financing channels.

Meanwhile, since the turn of the century, across the continent some important internal reforms have been complemented by internal changes and better macroeconomic management. Simultaneously, African governments have built up institutional credibility, diversified economies and invested in physical and social infrastructure. The rewards of this are clear: African economic growth more than doubled to 5.0% p.a. from the previous decade, and more African countries have experienced faster economic growth.

The confluence of this policy mosaic is that China has become Africa's main trading partner, increasing its share of total African trade from under 10% in 2008 to 15% last year. Moreover, China established itself as an important source of capital – foreign direct investment (FDI), as well as concessional and non-concessional loans.

Looking ahead, for any serious-minded, ambitious firm, of which China has many, Africa is a compelling proposition. In the next phase – which as this chapter explores has already started – many Chinese corporates, now including some of the largest companies in the world that have built up huge capacity and competitiveness in recent decades in their home market, will be looking to find opportunities abroad. However, for Africa to attract a larger share of Chinese capital and corporate externalisation, and benefit from this important partnership, work needs to be done to differentiate Africa from the emerging market herd.

The 'New Normal' and Africa

China's partnership with Africa – reflected in both trade and investment – has flourished in recent years. By vigorously responding to the global financial crisis and launching a set of policy measures designed to boost demand, China has supported commodity demand. Faced with soft demand in mature economies, Chinese exporters have also increasingly looked to alternative markets, particularly in Africa. Indeed, many local governmental authorities in China introduced preferential loan programs to aid export-oriented companies. Meanwhile, regulators have supported outbound investment by easing requirements, decentralising regulatory procedures and broadening financing channels.

The important question, then, is to what extent economic spill-overs from China's own domestic transformation will impact on Chinese investments in Africa. Indeed, African leaders, regulators, businesses and so on, are alive to the fact that the Chinese domestic economy has started to face headwinds. To some extent, the investment-led and credit-fuelled response to the global financial crisis – whilst justified at the time – has exacerbated resource misallocations, further distorting incentives across the economy. Realising that the economy needed to change its shape and structure, in 2014 the Chinese President Xi Jingping described a 'New Normal'. Envisioned here: a Chinese economy that is expanding more slowly, but enjoying higher quality economic growth; an economy that is less factor- and investment-driven, shifting towards a pattern of growth driven by services and consumption; propelled by innovation and with market forces determining the allocation of resources. In the past few years, lower output growth in China has already spilled over into many sub-Saharan African countries (through direct and indirect channels). The aforementioned adjustment will undoubtedly continue to play out – albeit in varying degrees – across Africa.

From an African perspective, simply put, this means that the traditional ways of connecting to China's growth are no longer as effective as they once were because the capital spending cycle that drove the Chinese economic narrative in the past has diminished. It is merely a logical progression that investment – measured as a share of China's gross domestic product (GDP) – will decline in the coming years. That said, urbanisation is critical to Beijing's domestic plans; for instance, another 100 million people will live in cities across China by 2020, equating to additional investment of around 6% to 8% of GDP each year. In addition, in terms of the

One Belt One Road policy, China is generally expected to channel nearly USD 1 trillion into projects across the region, suggesting infrastructure development will continue to spearhead economic development. Therefore, Africa's abundance of resources remains central to China and the region's ability to grow. And perhaps more significantly, over a longer time horizon, Africa's vast agricultural potential too offers tremendous opportunities.

Significantly, the new phase of development means that many Chinese corporates that have been reshaping global trade and investment ties and, in doing so, built up enormous capacity and competitive advantages will need to externalise to a greater extent. The trend is particularly acute – albeit not limited to – those companies connected to the 'old growth model' in the Mainland, such as construction companies, real estate developers, engineering firms, and heavy machinery and vehicle manufacturers.

It is already abundantly clear that Africa's growing markets matter more to China every year. China's total sales to Africa have more than doubled since 2009, from USD 47bn in 2009 to USD 106bn in 2015, and remained above USD 100bn in 2016. Since 2010, China's sales to Africa have increased by an average of around 15% year-on-year (YoY) each year, which is nearly twice the speed of growth recorded by Chinese exporters elsewhere. Clearly, given many years of below trend growth in advanced economies, China has made a concerted effort to recalibrate who it sells to, and Africa's larger markets – like Nigeria and South Africa – have become increasingly important.

Chinese exporters are concentrating their efforts on Africa's largest economies – notably South Africa, Nigeria and Egypt. The three regional heavyweights accounted for 40% of China's exports to Africa last year – up from 37% in 2009. As a proxy for rising consumer demand, Chinese exports of finished clothing and footwear, for instance, have increased by 23% p.a. since the global financial crisis, led by Nigeria and South Africa.

Chinese investment in Africa

It is fair to say that so far, the rapid ground-swell in consumer demand across Africa has been reflected predominantly in the growth of total imports from China. Nevertheless, with each passing month, this is gradually changing. China played an enormous role in reversing Africa's marginalisation in global trade flows, the world's second largest economy now doing this in investment. Central to this, China's state-led projects and product sales have spurred an inflow of Chinese individuals into cities across the African continent. Many thousands of these individuals are pursuing their own enterprises in wholesale and retail trade, restaurants, hotels and manufacturing (Cardenal and Araujo, 2014). What has become increasingly visible from Johannesburg to Lagos is the rapid rise of commerce – led initially by diplomacy – which has invigorated commercial enterprise, embedding a wide range of small- to medium-sized Chinese companies in non-resource sector activities, particularly in services.

Now, more than ever before, the growing share of China's investment in Africa is aimed at locking in markets for manufacturing exports in what could be simplistically characterised as sunset industries. Just like Chinese ventures in other emerging markets, state-led projects have tended to focus on construction (35%) and resource-extraction (25%); while private firms have tended to invest in manufacturing (36%) and services (22%) (Shen, 2013). Chinese private investments in manufacturing typically aim to sell goods to the African markets, where, as noted already, China's exports are expanding at a faster rate than elsewhere. Indeed, according to Fu et al. (2013) the reasons cited by Chinese firms for investing abroad are to seize the local market; increase global market share; use local sales networks; and access preferential trade policies.

Looking ahead, it is a simple logical progression that outbound investment will continue to follow Chinese sales. Indeed, double-digit increases in unit labour costs (exacerbated by 40% appreciation of the renminbi from 2005 to 2014) eroded the cost competiveness of Chinese exporters. Moreover, it is expected that by 2020, the average wage for workers in China will have increased from USD 400 per month to a minimum of USD 1,000 per month (Lin, 2016). Thus, already in preparation for this, labour-intensive enterprises are investing in R&D to propel them up the value chain and/or shifting to capital-intensive areas with higher added value. Nevertheless, many more will have to move to lower wage regions.

Overall, China's FDI stock in Africa has increased from USD 13bn in 2010 to USD 32.3bn in 2015. According to an impressive data set by Johns Hopkins University, led by Deborah Brautigam, China's FDI inflows into Africa have averaged USD 2.8bn each year over the past decade, totalling a cumulative USD 20bn and including nearly 3,000 individual deals (SAIS China-Africa Research Initiative).

Predictably in terms of scale and size, the most significant investments have focused on a few resource-rich countries, led by South Africa (25%), Nigeria (10%), Zambia (9.7%), Sudan (7.9%), Zimbabwe (7.1%) and Democratic Republic of Congo (6.5%). These are the only countries that have attracted a cumulative total of more than USD 1bn in investments from China in the past decade. This reflects the top-heavy investments in natural resources and the related infrastructure – roads, railways and ports – required for the extraction and transportation of those minerals.

That said, given that the average deal size is generally below USD 10m, two-thirds of Africa's countries have hosted at least 30 Chinese deals over the same period. Herein is evidence of the reach of China's engagement in Africa. As a proxy for this wide reach, according to MOFCOM there are an estimated 3,171 Chinese firms and affiliates registered in Africa. Interestingly, one third of these firms have set up in East Africa, led by Tanzania, Ethiopia and Kenya. West Africa makes up another one-third and is dominated by Nigeria – which alone accounts for one-in-ten Chinese firms in all of Africa. Southern, North Africa and Central Africa make up the remaining third.

Even though around one-third of China's total inflows have been in extractive industries, finance (20%), construction (16%) and manufacturing (15%) make up around half of total FDI (Pigato and Tang, 2015). More importantly, in recent years, it is China's investments in non-resource sectors, like commercial services, wholesale and retail trade, and real estate, which are growing most rapidly. For instance, in 2016 according to Mergermarket Group, who focus on mergers and acquisitions (M&A) deals in energy, mining and utilities slumped to half of the 2015 levels, whilst the consumer and financial services sectors have taken up the deal-making slack, expanding rapidly.

In particular, manufacturing investment has increased significantly in recent years. As noted previously, Chinese manufacturing firms have begun relocating to countries with lower wage rates, including several in Africa. In the past, the key motivation for manufacturing firms to invest in Africa was to circumvent US and EU trade restrictions on Chinese products. However, today this is no longer the case.

The top reason for investing in Africa is to gain access to largely untapped local consumer markets and avoid competition in an increasingly saturated Chinese market (Gu, 2009). Importantly for African development (and China's brand in Africa) manufacturing-related investment is proving to be a critical job creator, creating twice as many jobs as extractive projects. In fact, an interesting data set hosted by FDI Markets, which specifically tracks global green field investments, shows that despite ranking ninth by capital investment and seventh in terms of number of projects for the year 2015, China created the most new jobs in Africa (FDI Markets, 2016). Further confirming the shift towards substantial private sector participation, the majority of these jobs were created by private-owned companies, such as Foton, Huawei and ZTE. In fact, according to MOFCOM data, over half the projects – in number and value – are privately owned (Shen, 2013).

A few examples are given below:

- China's largest exporter of refrigerators, Hisense, started manufacturing flat-screen televisions and refrigerators at its electronics factory in South Africa in 2013.
- Chinese footwear manufacturer, the Huajian Group, in collaboration with the China-Africa Development Fund, has earmarked around USD 2bn to build up an export base in Ethiopia. It will eventually employ 200,000 workers. Already, Chinese exports of textiles are being used in the production of clothing, which explains why exports of plain-weave cotton fabric and synthetic yarns and fibres expanded from USD 3.8bn in 2009 to USD 6.5bn in 2013.
- Chinese Telecoms firms are tapping into the world's second-largest market. The number of mobile phones in use is expected to rise from 629m in 2013 to 1.2bn by 2017. China – a producer of about one-and-a-half billion units per annum (global sales were 1.895 billion units last year) – has recognised the opportunity. Of course, China manufactures many international brands, including for Samsung, Apple, LG and Nokia, but it is its home-grown brands that specialise in low-cost entry-level handsets – not just Huawei and ZTE but also Gionee, Infinix, Itel, and Tecno – that have found growing markets in Africa. As a sign of things to come, firms like Tecno have plans to build manufacturing plants in Nigeria.

- Millions of customers (and many more millions of potential customers) to serve means that Chinese telecom companies are rolling out communications towers and base stations across Africa. The three major Chinese players in this field are the equipment manufacturers Huawei Technologies, ZTE (Zhongxing Telecommunications Equipment Corporation) and Alcatel-Lucent Shanghai Bell Ltd Co (ASB). They are active in 50 African countries but have chosen several hubs from which to roll out their telecommunications strategy on the continent. These hubs include Kenya, Nigeria and South Africa.
- Chinese car makers are setting up more production facilities closer to their target markets, including South Africa, which is partially a reason for the relatively weak export volume of cars. For instance, Chinese truck manufacturer Foton has switched from importing pre-built vehicles to setting up assembly plants in Nairobi and Uganda. Furthermore, Kewalram Chanrai Group is partnering the car maker to establish an automobile assembling plant that will produce the Foton range of vehicles in Lagos.
- The multitude of infrastructure projects throughout the continent is giving Chinese heavy equipment manufacturers opportunities for much-needed orders, but increasingly they are looking at setting up production facilities. For Sany, even though opening a manufacturing plant in Africa is 'unrealistic' now, according to the general manager of Sany Southern Africa, Xiao Jiang, an assembly plant is in the planning stages as a first step in the process. According to Shantui Vice President Richard Li, '[I]n the not too distant future we plan to start production and manufacturing within the various regions of Africa, with an understanding as to which companies are able to produce our parts under license, with our priority to focus and establish a strong presence in South Africa first'. LiuGong, XCMG and Zoomlion are also believed to be looking for opportunities for expansion in Africa.

It is important to note that unlike more mature economies, investments in Africa are largely unable to support Chinese firms' efforts to move up the value chain. Chinese companies are globalising via joint ventures, strategic partnerships and/or M&A deals. Importantly, this can help them in moving up the value chain (thereby offsetting rising costs). So far Europe has been the partner of choice, attracting twice as much investment as the US since 2008. At this stage, only a few select African firms offer Chinese firms the skills and technology they seek.

It is worth pausing here to note the following: it is probably also fair to suggest that China's investments in Africa are likely to be greater than the data indicates. Visual evidence would suggest that the headline numbers do not neatly align with the vast numbers of engineers, tailors, traders and entrepreneurs and so on, who are seen across the continent in a wide range of sectors – from textiles, shoes and tanneries, to food products, restaurants, wholesale and retail centres and other service providers (Cardenal and Arauju, 2014). Put plainly, the fact that China accounts for less than 5% of Africa's total FDI stock, but accounts for 15% of Africa's annual trade, does not quite align.

Already back in 2005, Yao and Yin (2005) found that most private firms interviewed did not file applications for their investment projects abroad. Meanwhile, recent developments in the regulatory approvals process may make tracking more difficult. The aim is to simplify the approval procedures, including removing the need for prior reporting to the National Development and Reform Commission (NDRC) of investments below USD 100m. Nonetheless, given that the average deal size in Africa is below the threshold, many outbound investments are not necessarily being reported. Many Chinese firms have been in Africa for some time, growing revenue streams and diversifying to become largely independent entities. Many are expanding without necessarily going through the approval processes outlined above. According to Shen (2013), Nigeria reports that there are nearly three times as many Chinese projects than Chinese data currently indicates. Similarly, other governments report a greater number of Chinese projects than China's official figures state – in Zambia (2.5 times the official figures), Ethiopia (2.6 times), Rwanda (3.6 times), Ghana (5.5 times) and Liberia (7 times). Therefore, it seems reasonable to postulate that official data understates Chinese investments in Africa by at least USD 10–20bn.

Why Africa will continue to matter

Africa's cyclical growth prospects are sound. It is very difficult to argue that the cyclical slowdown in global demand was not the reason for the continent's growth decreasing to below 3.0% YoY from over 5.0% YoY in 2014, as measured by the IMF for sub-Saharan Africa. Indeed, there are a number of important structural trends supporting economic growth prospects.

The first and foremost trend is demographics. Demographics in isolation does not determine the future economic trajectory, but rather serves as the scaffolding for an economy's growth potential. Promisingly on this score, Africa's population is swelling rapidly, providing a compelling array of opportunities and challenges. Since the year 2000, the continent's population has expanded by 200 million to exceed 1 billion. Future growth projections are even more seismic; population growth for the next decade will average 2.2%, compared to 0.9% in Asia. By 2050 Africa's population will number almost 2 billion, implying that one in five of the world's inhabitants will be African. Of course, rapid growth means Africa's population is also exceptionally young. At present, Africa's median age is 19.7 years compared to an average of 32 years in Brazil, Russia, India and China. China's example shows that a youthful and growing population can be an asset and serve as a platform for rapid economic growth. Of course, a few important preconditions are necessary, but should Africa meet those, the long-term outlook for services and manufacturing is positive.

Also, when coupled with robust economic growth, population growth will support the emergence of the continent's consumer base – providing support to local firms, creating economic opportunities and attracting foreign investment. Indications of the manifestation of the above are already evident. Sub-Saharan

Africa's per capita income has increased by 70% since 2000, compared to growth of 15% between 1990 and 2000. Within the next five years Africa's spending power will increase by 25%. Consumer growth is being supported by a rising middle class. Though most African households hug the low-income band, many are increasingly able to dedicate a share of their daily and monthly income to non-staple goods and services. The comparatively rapid per capita economic expansion in these countries will elevate welfare. However, when combined with financial deepening and a broadening of property rights, it is likely to result in a more leveraged emerging market consumer over the next two decades. As a result, a 'shopping' culture is likely to stimulate consumption-based industry and services.

Africa's population is not only rising but rapidly urbanising, providing support to the continent's ongoing economic advance. Around 40% of Africans currently reside in urban areas, but, at current growth rates (the swiftest in the world), more than half of Africa's population will be urbanised by 2030. In fact, within the next four decades another 800 million Africans will either migrate to, or be born in, urban areas. For some countries this shift will be particularly profound. Nigeria will see 140 million new urban entrants in the next 40 years. Also by 2050, 14 African countries – including Angola and South Africa – will be more than 80% urbanised.

Naturally, these trends are leading to the mushrooming of Africa's prominent commercial capitals. Mega-cities such as Kinshasa, Lagos and Cairo are swelling. Since 2000, Luanda has expanded at an annual average rate of 6%; currently around one in four Angolans lives in the capital city. Interestingly, 70% of all urban growth in the next two decades will take place in smaller towns and cities in Africa. The pace of urbanisation in Africa is placing immense strain on existing urban infrastructure systems, exacerbating an already prevalent shortfall in infrastructure investment requirements across the continent.

Poor urban planning is also increasing pressure on commercial hubs, adding to congestion, and hindering the provision of basic services to urban inhabitants. Between 1998 and 2014, spending on African infrastructure rose at a compound annual rate of 14%, outstripping the growth of global infrastructure investment. This growth has been driven largely by increased funding from non-OECD governments – particularly China. The private sector is still the largest single source of funds. Rapid growth has attracted many multinational companies within and outside Africa. While this growth has been substantial, the size of the investment gap is huge.

Across the world, technological enhancements are fundamentally altering the way individuals and firms connect, communicate and transact, providing new avenues of commercial opportunities. Unlike in the past, Africa has not been left stranded. The continent's population has vigorously embraced technology in general, and telecommunications in particular, as a means to enhance socio-economic prosperity. In no area has the terrain altered more seismically than in mobile telephony. Whereas in 2000 there were 15 million mobile subscriptions in Africa, by the end of 2010 there were over 500 million, and this has increased to almost 800 million today.

Over the next five years, east and central Africa will enjoy the highest mobile subscription growth rates in the world. Already, Nigeria is the world's tenth-largest mobile market. Meanwhile, more Africans are connecting to the internet. Currently, there are around 120 million Internet users in Africa. While penetration is relatively low, growth rates have been profound – between 2000 and 2011, Internet usage in Africa grew by 2,527%, compared to a world average of 480%. New fibre-optic cables will raise connectivity. A range of mostly privately funded cables set to land, or having already landed, on Africa's east and west coasts will dramatically alter connectivity. Provided intra-regional backhaul networks are built, this will lower costs for a wide range of African internet users. Evidence of the potential economic gains from greater ICT access is mounting. According to the World Bank, for every 10 percentage point (pps) increase in broadband penetration, economic growth could be lifted by 0.73 pps in typical African economies, and an extra ten phones for every 100 people in a country could boost GDP by as much as 0.8 pps.

Unlike in other, more nascent, areas of economic potential, Africa's natural resource wealth is renowned. Africa has a dominant share in a number of core commodities. Currently, Africa holds 95% of the world's platinum group metals (PGM) reserves, 90% of chromite ore reserves, 85% of phosphate rock reserves and more than half of the world's cobalt. Meanwhile, Africa's potential is equally alluring in a range of commodities for which future production prospects are elevated. For instance, Africa possesses roughly one-third of global bauxite reserves but accounts for only 8% of global bauxite mine production.

Importantly, Malthusian concerns about the Earth's ability to nourish a population of 7 billion people, expected to rise to 9 billion by 2050, are growing. In order to feed the world's population in 2050, food production will have to increase by 50–70%, necessitating a total average annual net investment in developing world agriculture of USD 83bn. Given these concerns, attention is increasingly turning to Africa. It is estimated that over 60% of the world's available and unexploited cropland is in sub-Saharan Africa (SSA). Of Sudan's 105 million ha of cultivable land, only 16% (or 16.6 million ha) had been cultivated by 2009. A similar ratio is evident in the Democratic Republic of Congo (DRC), where less than 10% of the country's 80 million ha of cultivable land has been cultivated. The Congo River Basin alone holds 23% of Africa's irrigation potential, with the Nile River Basin holding a further 19%.

Africa's financial services sector is responding rapidly to the continent's changing economic reality. Rising incomes, technological enhancements and rapid urbanisation are bringing more people within reach of a broader suite of financial services – in so doing providing profound support to economic growth assertions. Developments in the banking sector have been most dramatic. South Africa is dominant in the African financial services space, accounting for over 30% of Africa's banking assets, around 80% of all life insurance premiums, and half of all non-life insurance premiums. Of the total assets held by Africa's top 100 banks, 46% were held by South African institutions. Banking growth has created a host of new corporate champions. Innovative strategies have been pivotal in unlocking new opportunities. Rapid technological changes are reducing transaction costs, bridging geographical strains, expanding markets, and inspiring investment from large financial institutions, in so doing altering Africa's commercial terrain.

Overall, less than one in five African adults has an account at a formal or semiformal financial institution. Future growth projections for Africa's financial services sector are stellar. At current growth rates, Africa's financial services sector could make up around 20% of the continent's collective GDP within the next decade, compared to 10% today. Much of the new growth will come from retail banking. The banking industry in 16 key African countries could boost its financial assets by 248% to USD 1.37tr by 2020. Angola may see bank claims increasing more than ten-fold, from USD 25bn in 2009 to USD 262bn in 2020. Robust financial systems are a critical cog in ensuring more rapid and inclusive growth. Most critically, the expansion of financial services has the ability to create new jobs, establish a formal identity for millions of market participants, and provide greater safety than currently predominant cash-based systems.

Conclusion

Even though African countries are relatively open to Chinese investment, which has been identified by Beijing as an important consideration in assessing total outward investment strategies, the business environment in Africa remains challenging. According to an EIU (2013) survey of attractiveness for outbound investment, each of the seven African nations assessed – Tunisia (48), South Africa (49), Egypt (51), Algeria (61), Kenya (65), Nigeria (66) and Angola (67) – ranked in the bottom third, out of 67 countries. Unsurprisingly, China's outbound investment to the US and Europe rose by 48% YoY and 21% YoY in 2012 respectively. Meanwhile, outbound investment to Africa expanded by 11% YoY.

That said, even though the internal conditions in Africa – from the business environment to government efficiency and infrastructure – may lag mature economies, they compare favourably to China in the 1990s when many of the Chinese MNCs cut their teeth. The forces pushing Chinese firms abroad offer opportunities for Africa.

China is a visible force for development and growth across Africa, led by dazzling growth in bilateral trade and investment. It is upon the crest of state-led investment projects that rising tides of corporates and individuals have (and will continue to) shift their gaze towards Africa. It seems that this trend will continue to grow – especially as industrial restructuring in coastal China forces some labour-intensive firms to relocate to other parts of the developing world, including Africa.

There is no doubt that since the turn of the century, a number of important internal changes, including better macroeconomic management, improved institutional credibility, better quality and economic growth have complimented the emergence of China as an important trading partner and source of capital.

However, it is also probably fair to say that Africa's favourable structural drivers have proven most relevant in attracting the interest of China's corporates. Looking ahead, Chinese FDI in Africa is set to double to USD 50bn and trade could reach USD 300bn over the next five years. However, China's global footprint is incredibly deep and wide and Africa still accounts for a relatively small share of China's external flows. Indeed, for Africa to attract a larger share of Chinese capital and corporate externalisation, the coordination of trade and tax policies is necessary, infrastructure and financial sector development requires further prioritisation, while public governance and accountability constitute a critical prerequisite and require continual attention. Most importantly, the quality of human capital requires constant attention as people (in concert with soft and hard infrastructure) play the most crucial role in differentiating Africa from the emerging market herd.

References

Cardenal, JB & Araujo, H 2014, *China's Silent Army*, Allen Lane an imprint of Penguin Books, United Kingdom.

Economist Intelligence Unit (EIU) 2013, *China Going Global Investment Index*. Available from: www.eiu.com/Handlers/WhitepaperHandler.ashx fi=China_Going_Global_English_version.PDF&mode=wp&campaignid=ChinaGoingGlobal. [10 April 2017].

FDI Markets 2016, African investment report, United Kingdom.

Fu, X, Suyu, L & Teili, L 2013, 'Determinants and impact of outward investment from China', *University of Oxford and Guangdong University of Foreign Studies*. Available from: www.tmd-oxford.org/sites/www.tmd-oxford.org/files/publications/SLPTMD-WP-049.pdf. [10 April 2017].

Gu, J 2009, 'China's private enterprises in Africa and the implications for African development', *European Journal of Development Research*, vol. 21, no. 4, pp. 570–587.

Lin, JY 2016, *Continent Holds Answer to Wage Conundrum in Chinese Enterprises in Africa*, China International Press, Haidian.

Pigato, MA & Tang, W 2015, *China and Africa: Expanding Economic Ties in an Evolving Global Context*, World Bank Washington, DC.

Shen, X 2013, 'Private Chinese investment in Africa', World Bank, Policy Research Working Paper 6311.

UNCTAD 2012, 'World investment report 2012', United Nations Conference on Trade and Development. Available from: http://unctad.org/en/Pages/DIAE/World%20Investment%20Report/WIR2012_WebFlyer.aspx. [10 April 2017].

Yao, Y & Yin, H 2005, 'Chinese outward investing firms: A study for FIAS/IFC/MIGA', China Centre for Economic Research, Peking University.

20

THE RETURN OF BILATERALISM

China, post-Brexit Britain and Trump

Erik Berglof and Vince Cable

Introduction

Until the Brexit vote, economic relations between China and the UK were supposed to be experiencing a 'golden era', and Chancellor Philip Hammond has since declared that the relationship now is 'more important than ever'. Yet, as the two nations are forced to renew their vows, they are doing so in a context of unprecedented uncertainty about life post the EU-UK divorce and the basic rules of the game in international trade.

The case for the UK leaving the European Union was sold as an opportunity to strike new and innovative bilateral deals with the rest of the world, including with China. Free from the shackles of a much loathed EU bureaucracy and the sclerotic economies on the continent, the UK would unleash its true trade and growth potential. The election of President Trump, on the other hand, reflected a scepticism about the benefits of trade more generally and, in particular, to the US itself. Multilateral agreements and the international institutions set up to enforce them are, almost by definition, unfavourable to the US. Bilateral trade deals have to be renegotiated under the broad banner 'America First'. This US 'unilateral bilateralism' threatens to unravel more than half a century of progress on international trade and investment. The British government, therefore, is planning its post-Brexit trade strategy based on an optimistic view of world trade, which its main ally is trying to undermine.

For most of the post-war era, the rules of trade have been constructed on a global, multilateral, basis through the GATT (General Agreement on Tariffs and Trade) and, then, the World Trade Organization. There have been exemptions, within GATT/WTO rules, to permit the formation of regional integration projects like the EU (along with NAFTA, ASEAN and others). And there have been periods, as in the 1980s, when the energy behind regional integration led to growing fears of 'trade blocs' fragmenting the global, multilateral system.[1]

The completion of the Uruguay round of multilateral negotiations in 1998 partially allayed these concerns and took trade negotiations into new areas such as services, intellectual property and foreign investment rules. The admission of China to the WTO in 2001 further strengthened the prospects of a genuinely global, multilateral, system. But in parallel there was a further spate of bilateral agreements – an estimated 250 notified to WTO by 2003 – which led to a growing determination to advance the multilateral agenda through the Doha round. The faltering of the Doha negotiations also triggered a fresh burst of interest in trying to deepen trade (and investment) integration through so-called 'mega deals' like trans-Atlantic (TTIP) and trans-Pacific (TPP) negotiations extending to areas previously virtually untouched such as service sector regulation.

Increasingly, however, bilateral preferential trade agreements (PTAs) have become the principal arm of trade policy. Since 2005 the share of world trade accounted for by PTAs has increased from 40% to more than half.[2] These agreements have become increasingly sophisticated. Many of them now cover trade in services and include provisions for technical barriers to trade, phytosanitary measures and intellectual property rights. Perhaps more importantly, PTAs also have come to extend to areas withdrawn from multilateral negotiations such as investment protection, competition policy and government procurement.

While the bilateral approach involves both trade creation and trade diversion, the evidence suggests that on balance it has resulted in (modest) welfare gains. However, bilateralism has also increasingly come to be driven by foreign policy, environmental and social concerns which create links across bilateral negotiations. Comparisons of welfare impact from trade between bilateral and multilateral arrangements then become second-order.

The year 2016 has produced a potentially dramatic discontinuity. President Trump has been elected on an explicitly protectionist agenda repudiating the authority of the WTO and with a total rejection of trade liberalisation, whether through the WTO or TPP or NAFTA. He sees the future in terms of bilateral agreements with countries which accept trade (and investment) arrangements on terms favoured by the US, comprising a narrow, mercantilist definition of reciprocity and balanced trade. President Trump thus breaks a tradition of what successive US administrations have called 'gold standard' agreements emphasising market access and broad coverage (using NAFTA as the reference point with little room for asymmetry of commitment).

Importantly, this approach has essentially eliminated US tariffs, certainly for manufactured products, but also largely for agriculture. Complex 'rules of origin' modelled on NAFTA has provided some protection for vulnerable sectors like textiles and clothing. What the Trump administration now has in mind, with a border adjustment tax, effectively a tax on imports, certainly runs counter to the long-term trend towards tariff reductions.

The decision of the UK to leave the EU, or 'Brexit', has also led to a revived enthusiasm for bilateral agreements with the UK seeking to negotiate trade agreements with the EU itself (to replace the Single Market and customs union), the US,

Australia (and other, supposedly sympathetic, countries in the Commonwealth), India and China. The motives are unclear and the prospects uncertain, but the aim appears to be the opposite of the Trump administration: that is, to open up trade and investment opportunities albeit through a succession of bilateral agreements.

Any discussion of potential agreements between China and the UK (and the remainder of the EU) has to be set in this somewhat confusing and rapidly evolving context, as well as a rather unhappy history.

The old bilateralism

Until recently, in historical terms bilateralism was the norm. It was the way trade policy was conducted by European states within Europe and in their dealings with emerging powers (the US and Japan), with their colonial possessions and with other countries – like China – which they were seeking to coerce into a dependent relationship.

Trade policy as we currently understand it, between states, did not really exist until the latter part of the eighteenth century (indeed, internal trade within countries was often difficult). There were sea faring cities in northern Europe, Holland and Italy – as well as Switzerland – which always favoured free trade; while elsewhere (Russia, France, Austria – Hungary), trade was of little importance and formidable barriers existed, and protection was the norm (rationalised in France through 'mercantilist' thinking).

In the 'age of enlightenment', a more liberal spirit prevailed and a systematic move to freer trade occurred with the 1786 France-UK trade treaty. The trend was interrupted by the Napoleonic War and by the appetite of emerging state bureaucracies for customs revenue to finance expanding public expenditure.

The UK later moved, unilaterally, towards freer trade through tariff cuts introduced by Peel and, then, the abolition of the Corn Laws as well as the highly protectionist Navigation Act. A decisive step was then taken to open up international trade through the UK-France (Cobden-Chevalier) treaty of 1860, and there followed two decades of bilateral, liberalising treaties notably between France and its neighbours. But after two decades, the demand for government revenue from tariffs and powerful agrarian interests (especially after the Great Depression) led to a protectionist mode and 'customs wars' (between France and Italy, Germany and Russia inter alia).

The First World War pushed the world to higher levels of protection for both industrial and revenue reasons, including the UK, but with the most aggressive moves by the USA. And the infamous Smoot-Hawley Tariff, introduced in the wake of the 1929 financial crash and depression, led to retaliatory measures, notably by Britain with Imperial Preference while bilateral agreements became the norm for Germany (now under the Nazis).

The US under Roosevelt reversed its protectionist tariff measures (the Reciprocal Trade Agreement Act of 1934), and this led to a proliferation of liberalising bilateral trade agreements – with Latin America, the UK, Switzerland and Scandinavia.

By 1945 the US had negotiated 27 such tariff-cutting agreements covering two-thirds of US imports, and this provided the impetus for the attempt to create a worldwide, free trade system post-war under the United Nations which in turn led to GATT and the WTO.

China and global trade

Pre-revolutionary China was peripherally involved in the evolving trade system but in ways which did not help it to look favourably on trade agreements. Western powers, led by Britain, sought in vain to interest the Qing dynasty in opening up its market to imports (to pay for the tea, silks and porcelain much valued in the West). Polite rejection of overtures from the West (the McCartney mission of 1792/93) led to the use of force to expedite trade, increasingly centred on opium.

China experienced bilateralism through a set of unequal treaties forced upon it starting with the Treaty of Nanjing with the UK – followed shortly after by agreements with the USA and France (in 1844). One feature of the UK treaty, which was to have immense importance (inserted through a supplementary treaty in 1883), was a 'most favoured nation clause' under which: 'should the Emperor hereafter, from any cause whatever be pleased to grant additional privileges or immunities to any of the subjects or citizens of such foreign countries, the same privileges or immunities will be extended and enjoyed by British subjects'.[3] The Chinese accepted the clause to limit foreign pressure, but it had the effect of limiting their negotiating flexibility.

The history of bilateral trade treaties is highly complex and reflects the varied and fluctuating political moods in major trading nations as regards trade. For the most part, bilateral agreements have been used to liberalise trade, emerging from periods of time when economic nationalism was rife. But they were also a means of pursuing political objectives and could involve highly unequal, unbalanced relationships.

A system dominated by bilateral agreements creates not merely complexity but also a hierarchy of discriminations in favour of the products of countries with the greatest negotiating power (or skill). In order to minimise the discriminatory element in bilateral agreements, it is necessary to incorporate a 'most favoured nation' (MFN) provision which was the basis of Roosevelt's 1934 trade legislation (and, less happily, the UK-China treaty of 1843). But the logic of MFN is a multilateral system as, indeed, Roosevelt understood and campaigned for. So if the aim of trade negotiations is to strengthen global free trade, as the UK claims, the UK enthusiasm for a new burst of bilateral treaties is very difficult to understand; though President Trump's eagerness is all too easy to comprehend.

The new bilateralism

After successive, successful rounds of multilateral trade negotiations, a new round – the so-called Doha round – was launched in 2002, supposedly to focus on the trade policy agenda of developing economies which were relatively neglected in efforts to secure agreements between the US and the EU (and, to a lesser degree, other developed economies).

But, at the same time, numerous bilateral agreements were being notified to the WTO or were under negotiation. These differ greatly in scale, ambition and motivation, but what they have in common is a rejection (or neglect) of one of the essential principles of the World Trade Organisation: that the lowest tariff applicable to one member must be extended to all members (the most favoured nation status rule).

The most important of these agreements are regional free trade areas (like NAFTA) or common markets, with free movement of labour and capita like the EU. GATT envisaged (in Article 24) that neighbours, or other like-minded countries, might try to form deeper integration agreements and permitted this, providing they did not raise barriers against other GATT members and eliminated barriers on 'substantially all' of their mutual trade.

The EU is in a different league from other regional groups in the volume of internal trade involved and the depth of integration, which goes way beyond the removal of tariffs to involve the harmonisation and mutual recognition of numerous regulations governing trade in goods and many services, restrictions on trade distorting government intervention, and public procurement and free movement of labour and capital. The members of the European Economic Area have most, if not all, of those commitments.

Outside Europe, most regional integration schemes in Africa, Latin America and Asia fall well short of internal free trade and NAFTA, which does not extend to a common tariff.

There are, in addition, preferential arrangements which the EU has negotiated with potential members, however distant the prospect of membership (as with the Turkish customs union); a set of former colonies; and Mediterranean neighbours. The EU has also sought to develop bilateral agreements with other regional groups – ASEAN and Mercosur – and with individual countries: South Korea and Canada (successfully), Japan (in train) and (so far unsuccessfully) the USA and India.

Although this complex network of arrangements, and its hierarchy of preferences, has added great complexity to world trade and is inherently discriminatory, the EU will claim that these agreements are WTO-compliant, indeed WTO-enhancing, in that they do not create additional barriers to third parties and enable progress in liberalisation to be made in areas like agriculture and services and the opening up of flows of direct investment.

The EU's bilateral footprint is massive, but several other countries have also shown a strong interest in bilateralism. Surprisingly, perhaps, two countries which have been most ambitious are the open, free-trading economies of Singapore and Chile. Since they have few trade barriers of their own, there is little to bargain with, but perhaps they are content, for political reasons, to advertise their free trading credentials and to achieve modest, preferential improvements in access to overseas markets (Chilean fruit and wine; some high-tech products and components from Singapore).

Michele Ruta at the World Bank has carried out an analysis of 52 recent examples of bilateral agreements ranging from preferential PTAs to full free trade areas (FTAs), customs unions and common markets.[4] They vary in terms of depth of integration and their enforcement powers. He makes a distinction between WTO+ agreements which incorporate and deepen existing WTO rules relating to issues like procurement, services, intellectual property and anti-dumping, and WTO Extra agreements which raise new issues not covered in the WTO such as data protection, movement of capital, competition policy, labour and environmental regulation, visas and investment protection.

The rise of China and hyper-globalisation

In understanding these trends in the trade architecture, it is impossible to ignore the changing nature of global economic exchange and the emergence of China. Trade agreements have deepened with the rise of multinational corporations and foreign direct investment (FDI). This 'hyper-globalisation' has increasingly become about harmonising regulation, touching on ever more sensitive aspects of domestic societies, and facilitating the transfer of knowledge across borders, with multinational corporations trying to protect this knowledge from spilling over to competitors, locally and globally.[5] Prior to Brexit and, more importantly, the election of President Trump, world trade integration was on the cusp of 'mega-regionalism' with the possibility of both TPP and TTIP aspiring to harmonise domestic institutions within regional trading blocks.

Both TTP and TTIP were to some extent in part a response to China's transforming influence on international production and trade. The country has in many ways been the main beneficiary of the transformation of global trade: it has become what Arvind Subramanian has called a 'mega-trader', the first since Imperial Britain.[6] Over the last two decades the share of the Chinese economy has gone from less than 5% to 20% of global GDP, while that of the G7 has fallen from close to 70% to slightly above 40%. While globalisation was disruptive in many G7 economies triggering political backlash, it was cohesive in China, where the middle class thrived and, more recently, the rapid rise in inequality since market reforms started has been reversed.[7] The threat of disruption to trade integration, emanating primarily from the Trump administration, could threaten these achievements. China has more at stake than any other country from the maintenance of an open global system of trade and investment. In this sense China is likely to see a friend in the UK government.

Apart from the EU, the pace-setter in bilateral agreements has been the USA, which started by securing agreements with Israel, Singapore, Australia, Chile, South Africa and Morocco (the other NAFTA members, Canada and Mexico, lacking a common trade policy with the USA, have separately secured bilateral agreements with some of the above, and other countries). Critics of bilateralism like Jagdish Bhagwati have argued that the US is now using agreements with compliant small countries to 'advance the agenda of domestic lobbies' with 'extraneous issues', such as those covered in WTO Extra agreements, breaking up coalitions of developing countries to secure a stronger hand in multilateral negotiations: '[T]he process of trade liberalisation is becoming a sham, the ultimate objective being the capture, reshaping and distortion of the WTO in the image of American lobbying interests'.[8] Examples are the imposition of provisions on labour and environmental standards on Central American countries and Jordan, and the imposition of a ban on capital controls on Singapore and Chile (with penalty and compensation mechanisms even when agreed by the IMF).

There are somewhat more generous interpretations of US motivation. One is simply that bilateral agreements may be 'the only game in town'. The multilateral liberalisation process through the WTO has ground to a halt in part because of the reluctance of India in particular, and also Brazil and other emerging markets, to embark on further market liberalisation, at least when bound through WTO rules. The motivation of the Obama administration in promoting the TPP and TTIP was as a second-best to global liberalisation with an attempt to reduce regulatory barriers to trade in a similar manner to regulatory harmonisation within the EU Single Market. That was pre-Trump.

Following the election of Trump, the new administration is committed to bilateralism but from an entirely different set of objectives from its predecessor. It is actively opposed to multilateral trade liberalisation. It does not believe in the benefits of international trade. It is committed to 'economic nationalism' and to pursuing aggressive action against countries which run large trade surpluses with the US, notably China, or are otherwise seen as acting 'unfairly' (like Mexico). We do not know where all this will lead, but there is no pretence or expectation that highly unilateral bilateralism by the US has anything to do with trade liberalisation.

Brexit represents a retreat from trade liberalisation of a different kind and confusingly is being carried out by a government which, unlike Trump's, claims to believe in multilateralism and free trade. Yet this is the first occasion, post-war, in which a country is seeking (by leaving the EU Single Market) to raise trade barriers against itself. It apparently wishes to compensate by negotiating liberalising bilateral trade agreements with other countries outside the EU, including China. We shall look now at how these apparently contradictory objectives can be reconciled.

Brexit and bilateralism

Britain is the first country to test the process of leaving the EU. There are no precedents; the legal principles are disputed; and the politics are highly uncertain.

The first bilateral agreement the UK has to negotiate is with the remaining members of the EU. The UK government has decided to leave the Single Market because it gives overriding priority to immigration control, over trade, though some critics believe that a compromise governing freedom of movement could have been negotiated.

However, negotiating a new trade deal with the EU will not be straightforward. The European Union is insisting that the UK should settle outstanding financial liabilities before trade negotiations can begin, while the UK denies that there are outstanding liabilities and insists on talking about trade. Even if this issue is resolved, there will not be time to negotiate a comprehensive new deal before Britain leaves the EU and so there will almost certainly need to be a transitional arrangement. But even such a transitional agreement may not be agreed and ratified in time by the 27 countries and 39 parliamentary chambers of the EU. It is not yet clear if a temporary continuation of the status quo would require such an agreement. Probably not.

The government's response to the risk of being left in legal limbo is to say WTO rules will apply. But Britain has first to re-join the WTO. Over 40 countries have joined the WTO since Britain joined the EU. They (and the residual EU) will be able to challenge the tariff schedules which Britain puts forward on re-joining the WTO and may demand – unreciprocated – concessions as the price of accepting the new UK tariff schedules.

Even if we neglect these technical and legal problems, the mere fact of falling back on WTO rules would present serious problems in itself. Until a new deal is agreed removing, tariffs and trade barriers, the UK could face tariffs on 90% of its EU exports by value and numerous regulatory hurdles. The car industry will face 10% tariffs and there could be customs checks and/or tariffs on components, disrupting supply chains.

To overcome these barriers, the UK could try to negotiate low or zero tariffs with the EU. But under WTO – MFN – rules, they would have to share the concessions with the rest of the world on a non-reciprocal basis, which the EU may be very reluctant to do. The regulatory hurdles would have to be separately negotiated.

What this analysis shows is that falling back on WTO rules is highly problematic and potentially disastrous. If sense is to prevail, the UK will have to concentrate on reaching an early agreement with the EU, if necessary with an interim arrangement. But it relies for this on the goodwill and cooperation of 27 governments, few of whom have any compelling reason to be helpful.

One consideration advanced to reassure business and the public is the offsetting opportunities of 'trade deals' struck with other countries outside the EU. Some of these will be necessary in any event to replace the preferential agreements with many Commonwealth countries and the EU bilateral agreements with countries like Canada and South Korea. But no new agreements can be reached until Britain has actually left the EU and any prospective trade partner will want to know what agreement the EU has reached with the UK.

The sense of breathless urgency communicated by UK ministers about these exciting new deals belies the reality that not very much is likely to happen for some years.

Even those governments which, perhaps for political reasons, wish to advertise goodwill towards the UK are unlikely to be able to deliver substantial agreements soon. The US is the UK's largest trade partner (unless we treat the EU as a whole). The Trump administration has promoted the UK to 'the front of the queue' but may no longer have a congressional majority when the deal is negotiated. Unusually, the UK has a trade surplus (in goods as well as services) with the USA, which chimes badly with the Trump administration's mercantilist interests. And the US has priorities in its trade negotiations – like securing market access for its private health providers, and guarantees that US companies will not be disadvantaged by policy decisions without compensation – which the UK might find it hard to agree to.

It may be much easier to agree (WTO-compliant) tariff cuts with Australia and New Zealand, restoring some of the preferential arrangements which existed 40 years ago, but these countries have long since moved out of the UK's regulatory orbit and have little interest in aligning regulation with the UK to remove non-tariff barriers.

If future trade deals are to be serious rather than driven by sentiment, they will have to encompass the big emerging markets. Russia is for now cut off by sanctions. The premature attempt by Mrs May to enlist India resulted in an embarrassing fiasco. The Indians made it clear that any concessions on, for example, access for UK financial services firms would be conditional upon the UK relaxing visa restrictions on Indian skilled IT workers, students and visitors. Mrs May was unable to contemplate any relaxation of immigration rules and went away empty handed. That leaves China.

UK-Chinese relations and post-Brexit links

Until very recently, UK-China relations were exceptionally warm. Beneath the rhetoric about 'a golden era' was a hard-headed calculation on both sides. For the Chinese, the UK's commercial strengths – sophisticated financial services, branded consumer goods, world class higher education – offered long-term advantages not shared by, for example, Germany whose capital goods were crucial at an earlier stage of development. The UK welcomed Chinese investment much more warmly than the US or other Western economies even in controversial, sensitive areas like telecoms and nuclear power. It appeared untroubled by a large bilateral trade deficit with China (UK imports from China of £37.6bn in 2014 as against exports of £16.7bn with a partially offsetting services trade surplus of £2.7bn).

It was willing to demonstrate independence from the USA on some matters of importance to China (like the establishment of the Asian Infrastructure Bank). Moreover, the UK provided China with an (apparently) reliable ally within the European Union, arguing against anti-Chinese protectionism. And, of course, as a member of the EU Single Market, the UK was a good 'entry point' to the EU for Chinese investors and exporters. Interests in China, particularly around the People's Bank of China, also saw in the UK an important partner in building its own financial sector and opening it up to the rest of the world.

For the UK, the benefits of a close relationship with China lie in the potential for trade in areas where the UK has a comparative advantage (financial and professional services; creative industries, higher education); the importance of the stock of UK investment in China (with around £6bn in 650 businesses); and the continuing strong links with Hong Kong. The prospect of attracting large volumes of Chinese investment into UK infrastructure has also been a powerful draw (given the perceived constraints on government borrowing).

Some of these assumptions have been undermined by the Brexit vote. The UK can no longer act as an entry point for the EU Single Market, and the future of the customs union and its rules of origin as they will apply to the UK are very uncertain. Government ministers in the Coalition and Conservative governments well-disposed to China have disappeared (at least for the moment). Mrs May is an unknown quantity; perhaps more conscious of security considerations (as with cyberattacks); and her hesitation over Hinkley Point and nuclear power sent a negative signal (albeit since removed). On the other hand, she is less likely to embarrass China by giving lectures on human rights and Tibet.

There is little doubt that the Chinese leadership miscalculated the reliability of the UK as a partner and the risks of Brexit (though so did most of the British political class!). But warm words continue to be uttered, and references to future trade deals have not been as dismissive as those from, say, India. Many of the commercial arguments for business with the UK remain. The Chinese will also have noticed that although the UK is close to the USA (and has invested political capital in the Trump administration), there is none of the anti-Chinese, 'trade war', protectionist sentiment prevalent in the USA. The UK by contrast is still animated by the spirit of Davos Man (as, apparently, is the Chinese leadership).

Moreover, the Chinese will have calculated that the British are anxious to achieve (and have to be seen to achieve) trade deals and are not in a strong bargaining position. Moreover, the UK may be helpful to China if it can weaken the resistance in the West to China's demand for 'market economy status' in the WTO. China is still somewhat far removed from being a market economy, but the direction of travel is broadly liberalising. The rather technical legal issues surrounding 'market economy status' can be subsumed under the bigger geo-political question: if there is US-led 'economic nationalism' directed at China, can the UK be an ally or at least soften the impact? And will a bilateral treaty help in this process?

Negotiating parameters for a UK-China post-Brexit deal

In sketching out what a future deal might look like, we need to consider what the constraints and opportunities are. As mentioned, the key areas of China's interests in its economic relations with the UK are likely to be outside trade as such, and more related to the predictability of policies for energy, transport, planning permission and possibly taxation. For the UK, the main focus is on investment protection and the financial sector, which both are largely outside standard preferential trade agreements, even though investment protection has become a more common feature of PTAs in recent years. In short, to have economic meaning, an agreement must go much beyond traditional trade issues.

Moreover, the timing of the negotiations will matter. As Garcia-Herreiro and Xu have already[9] pointed out, there are serious obstacles to concluding an agreement quickly even if there were the will on both sides to do so. First, the UK cannot formally reach a trade agreement with China until it has left the EU and established its own legal capacity to negotiate and forge bilateral trade agreements. Even if informal discussions with the Chinese counterparts could begin earlier, the British government would prefer to wait until it has reached an EU deal. Otherwise, the more preferable were the agreement with China, the more unfavourable would be the terms of a subsequent arrangement with the EU – and the latter is economically much more important to the UK.

Second, there could be no meaningful discussion in any event since the benchmark for negotiating with third parties will be the agreement with the EU and the tariffs (and other measures) notified to and accepted by the WTO. Third, Chinese companies would no longer be able to export to the EU from a base in the UK, since the UK has indicated that it intends to leave the customs union and EU.

So, are there any existing arrangements on which a China-UK agreement could be modelled? A possible prototype is the China-Swiss agreement, although critics have noted that the agreement seemed one-sided with the removal of remaining barriers on Swiss imports from China with little concrete in return. The UK would expect to push for concessions in two main areas and has a potential negotiating asset if it is willing to endorse China's 'market economy status'.

The UK would undoubtedly want stronger investor protection for UK companies operating in China with provision for independent arbitration. However, we need to put this in context. Less than 1% of UK overseas investment is in China. Realistically, China is most unlikely to concede a fundamental derogation of sovereign decision-making, and, even if it did, formal mechanisms are unlikely to change behaviour. China has already conceded a stronger legal framework and courts for intellectual property protection, but abuses continue to occur, allegedly on a significant scale.

The main area in which the UK could seek improved market access is services, especially financial services. At present, the UK has a small surplus of services trade with China (£2.7bn; 0.13% of GDP), and there is a lot of untapped potential in areas such as creative industries and China's domestic insurance market.

For its part, China, like India, might well want to insist on a liberalisation of the visa regime for Chinese visitors, workers and students. And it has long pressed to remove high-tech goods and services from UK export controls, which are currently restricted as dual-use equipment under arms export licensing.

That said, the 'Golden Era' of Anglo-Chinese relations did not require a bilateral agreement. It required a recognition of strong mutual economic interest and political endorsement from the top. That remains the case for the UK, inside and outside the EU. If a 'trade deal' is useful, it is as a signalling device: not much more.

In fact, ultimately the Trump administration may shape the future economic relationship between China and the UK much more than any trade agreement they conclude. In one scenario the anti-globalisation sentiments fuelled by its protectionism and nativism will seep into their bilateral relationship and undermine what the two countries set out to achieve, together and apart. In another, Trump's 'unilateral bilateralism' and attempts to undermine the multilateral trade institutions will move China and the UK (and the EU) much closer together.

Notes

1 Stoeckel, A, Pearce, D & Banks, G, 1990, *Western Trade Blocs: game, set or match for Asia-Pacific and the world economy?*, Canberra: Centre for International Economics.
2 Heydon, K & Woolcock, S 2009, *The Rise of Bilateralism: Comparing American, European, and Asian Approaches to Preferential Trade Agreements*, 1st ed., New York: United Nations University Press.
3 Spence, JD 1991, *The Search for Modern China*, 1st ed., New York: W.W. Norton & Company, 1990.
4 Michele Ruta Deep Integration and UK-EU Trade Relations World Bank 2016.
5 Baldwin, R 2016, *The Great Convergence: Information Technology and the New Globalization*, 1st ed., Cambridge, MA: Harvard University Press.
6 Subramanian, A & Kessler, M 2013, *The Hyperglobalization of Trade and Its Future*, Working Paper 13–6, Washington, DC: Peterson Institute of International Economics.
7 Baldwin, R 2016, *The Great Convergence: Information Technology and the New Globalization*, 1st ed., Cambridge, MA: Harvard University Press.
8 Bhagwati, J & Panagariya, A 2003, 'Bilateral trade treaties are a sham', *Financial Times*, July 13.
9 Garcia-Herreiro, A & Xu, J 2016, *China's Belt and Road Initiative: Can Europe Expect Trade Gains?*, Working Paper 5, Brussels: Bruegel.

PART V
Conclusion

21

SUMMARY AND CONCLUSIONS

Xuedong Ding and Chen Meng

Chinese outward direct investment (ODI) is a rapidly growing and complex phenomenon. This book aims to offer a multi-perspective, full-spectrum analysis of Chinese ODI. Although such an attempt is perhaps too ambitious, our analysis does provide some valuable updates to the observation and understanding of Chinese ODI practice and addresses some interesting and important emerging issues.

Part I reviewed Chinese ODI over the last decade, from both a practical and a theoretical perspective. Accurately measuring Chinese ODI is never an easy task, due to issues of data availability and consistency. Meng et al. conducted a survey based on over 3,000 merger acquisition transactions. Their findings revealed an evolutionary development path of Chinese ODI: a surge of Chinese private enterprises, shift in strategic motives and investment patterns, and further diversification of investment (by sector, region and method). The most notable phenomenon is perhaps the rapid internationalization process of the private sector and Chinese enterprises' increasing appetite in acquiring high-end intangible assets, such as global market access, knowledge, brand and technology. Lau examined China's economic transition and pointed out that reduced reliance on exports, excessive domestic savings (together with declining rates of return) and aging population are fundamental driving forces for Chinese ODI. At the firm level, Chinese companies are incentivized by multiple motives. Progress in bilateral investment treaties and careful design in investment structures (including the means of investment and choice of funding currency) deserve further attention, as these will in turn facilitate Chinese enterprises' internationalization process. Ding and Gong et al. analysed Chinese ODI from the perspective of the global value chain. China is undergoing a transition in moving upward in the global value chain, and the development of ODI is a natural reflection of such a transition. However, this has to be an incremental journey. There are real dangers derived from policy complacency of ignoring such an incremental approach. Challenges lie on the policy front in terms of how to design and implement a transitional policy framework. Special attention needs to be paid to questions of how to balance the use of inward foreign direct investment and ODI, re-allocate economic resources domestically, as well as maintain China's status of 'world factory' and improve the competitiveness of domestic manufacturing. Buckley made a thorough and detailed review of international business theory. Although emerging market multinational enterprises (MNEs), particularly those from China, may pose some challenges to traditional international business theory, there is no need for a 'special' theory. The dynamics of Chinese ODI can and will be explained by the internalization of other markets – in knowledge, technology and information. An interesting element in the internationalization of Chinese multinationals is their focus, at least in the current stage of development, on the rapidly expanding Chinese domestic market, bringing back technology to compete at home. Government policy is also an important variable in explaining the deviation in Chinese ODI behaviours. This also requires a careful review of recent policy developments.

Part II provided a thorough review of Chinese ODI in relation to policy framework and context. Special light has been shed on recent policy shifts and innovations, such as establishment of the AIIB. Hu provided a detailed introduction to the administrative framework of overseas investments and progress in recent policy reforms. The direction of reform is to further relax governmental control and shift the administration of ODI from review and approval to record-filing. Looking forward, the 'One Belt One Road' Initiative and promotion of international production capacity cooperation offer important guidance on future Chinese ODI development. Based on the 'business-centred, market-orientated, rule-based and government-led' principle, the Chinese government will further enhance management of overseas investments, including improving the ODI service and risk control systems. Zhang noted that Chinese ODI is undergoing three development stages simultaneously (characterised by speed of expansion, degree of maturity and transformation). He shed special light on the progress and outlook of China's bilateral and multilateral free trade and investment agreements (FTAs). Running in parallel with the WTO systems, FTAs have become an increasingly important global policy initiative that may to a large extent shape the future landscape of international trade and cross-border capital flows. Shi provided a detailed examination on the motives, establishment and governance of AIIB. It is anticipated that AIIB will promote connectivity within the Asia region, but more importantly, as an innovative financial architecture introduced by the Chinese government, AIIB will have significant influence in global and regional financial governance as well as policy setting. Meanwhile, development of such a multilateral organisation will also act as a platform for cooperation and a facilitator for overseas investment. Ma and Xie investigated the history and outlook of renminbi (RMB) internationalization. They envisaged that internationalization of the RMB will be a continuous process. As a more widely accepted and recognized currency, the RMB will become another catalyst for promoting flows of trade and investment. Chen and Mei, from a policy think-tank perspective, made a comparative study of Japanese ODI. Their analysis offered important policy implications such as the collective and optimal utilization of foreign aid, policy banking and private capital, support for small and medium-sized enterprises, improvement in administration and the insurance protection system, and a good balance between domestic economic development and overseas investment expansion.

Part III provided an in-depth and dynamic analysis of Chinese ODI from a business practitioner's viewpoint. Orr and Cogman concluded that in the past decade, around 60% of Chinese ODI created little or no value. Its performance record does not look impressive at all. This is partially due to the 'resource curse', and, again, debate always centres on the quality and availability of data. However, this is unsurprising given previous studies on M&A performance (King et al., 2004; Jaffe and Manderlkar, 1992). Orr and Cogman further illustrated the challenges faced by Chinese enterprises while integrating their global businesses post-acquisition. Case studies showed that lack of qualified managers, incompatible management systems and differences in corporate culture are the key hurdles to integration. Liu and Liang offered a detailed case study on Lenovo's acquisition of IBM's PC division. It is interesting to see how strategy was formulated and translated into execution. The learning curve is steep and there is no such thing as 'overnight success'. In our view, the internationalization of Lenovo does not present a 'special' case to explain why emerging market multinationals take a 'different' approach to globalization. On the contrary, this case reinforces the importance of firm-specific advantages (FSAs) (see Buckley), such as management skills, knowledge transfer, learning, adaptation and so on (also see Meng [2009]), which dictate the internationalization process. Zhao's case studies further demonstrate the increasingly active role played by domestic private equity funds. They may to some extent overcome the deficiency in Chinese enterprises' FSAs, but this still warrants further examination. Nevertheless, the examples of PizzaExpress and WeWork provide further evidence for the strategic motives of serving the domestic market and competing at home. Wood & Cao and Shenker et al. added further colour to the execution of cross-border transactions. Based on additional case studies, they demonstrated how legal, regulatory review, tax, labour and other factors would come into play. The capability of successfully executing a deal is also an integral element of FSAs. This is no doubt a very complex decision-making process.

Part IV placed Chinese ODI in a global context. Drawing on his many years of experience in the financial sector in the Southeast Asia region, particularly Malaysia and Hong Kong, Sheng discussed the importance of FDI in the financial services sector in the host country. In the context of the OBOR initiative, he believes that a new model of financial intermediation is required, which could be achieved by investing in the financial services sector. Despite the potentially positive contribution of FDI on host country financial sector development and social development, investment into the financial sector alongside the OBOR region is expected to pick up in future due to the logic that financial service multinationals often follow their industry clients globally (Meng, 2009). The question for host country governments is how to respond to and properly manage this type of FDI, in order to achieve a win-win strategy. Based on his extensive experience of working with

Chinese enterprises, Wu provided an interesting review of Chinese companies' globalization. His observations also touch upon an important emerging phenomenon, namely the rapid development of the internet in China and high-tech companies such as Alibaba, Tencent and Huawei. Their internationalization process may have a more profound and long-lasting impact, and thus deserves further investigation. Sassoon and Blackburne examined Chinese investment in the UK and offered interesting insights from a regional development perspective. It can be seen that there is real demand for Chinese capital and an increasing appetite among Chinese investors. However, there are also mismatches in expectations. On the one hand, local policymakers in the UK need to better understand the motives of Chinese enterprises and try to ensure that interests align. On the other hand, many Chinese enterprises investing in the UK are still at the learning stage. Further, the 'China angle' possessed by some Chinese enterprises may in fact pose potential uncertainty or confusion (if not real barriers) in their business expansion in the UK, because local partners may have a different perception or expectation, and such a difference would affect strategies that Chinese investors may adopt. Maree and Stevens made an intriguing connection between China's economic adjustment, namely the 'new normal', with direct investment in Africa. Chinese investment into Africa has picked up quickly in recent years and this trend is likely to continue for many years to come, given Africa's economic complementarity to China's economic growth and transformation. Africa can leverage Chinese capital to achieve better economic and social development. However, in order to attract greater Chinese investment, the policy framework and infrastructure need to be refined significantly. Berglof reviewed the history of international trade, in particular bilateralism, and compared the different approaches of the UK and the US. He further provided some practical suggestions on how the UK and China can negotiate a deal post-Brexit. The debate is not just about Brexit and the policy of the Trump administration, bilateralism and multilateralism, but more fundamentally about globalization versus anti-globalization, which could have a significant impact upon international flows of trade and investment. This is a much broader context that should not be overlooked, and affects virtually every aspect of corporate internationalization.

We now conclude by focusing on several emerging but important issues, which we think deserve further attention.

Development path

It adds little value to argue simply based on official statistics that China is becoming a net capital exporter. First, official figures tend to underestimate capital outflows. For instance, official data does not capture Chinese multinationals' offshore deposits (earnings generated from foreign operations) that are used to fund overseas acquisitions, including investing through third markets. Sometimes, direct investments can also be disguised under the notion of portfolio investment, for example through a fund structure. Furthermore, the data also hardly captures outward direct investment by Chinese individuals. Very often, this kind of investment takes various forms of capital flight and mainly flows into the overseas real estate sector. One example of how to channel individual deposits offshore is through purchasing universal life insurance in Hong Kong.[1]

Second, official statistics can be quite volatile and dependent on domestic policy. For instance, at the beginning of 2017, the Chinese government tightened foreign exchange controls. Individual purchasing of offshore life insurance products is prohibited. Foreign exchange requests made by individuals and companies are under scrutiny. The NDRC also tightened supervision and guidance on Chinese companies' overseas acquisitions. Investments into overseas real estate, hotels, entertainment and sports clubs, and companies investing into non-core businesses via fund structures or by acquiring a foreign entity that is much larger in size are all subject to tighter monitoring. As a result, according to MOFCOM, in the first quarter of 2017, Chinese non-financial ODI stood at USD 20.5 billion, representing a year-on-year drop of nearly 49%.

This leads to the third point: what is the government's real intention? While the fundamental principles of opening up and relaxation on overseas investment may not change, central government does have concerns about capital outflow being too rapid – particularly if this outflow is primarily driven by 'irrational' investment decisions (sometimes simply due to fear of further RMB depreciation) or even illegal capital flight. This may trigger potential domestic financial instability, and it also means that central government places more weight on the quality, rather than the speed, of ODI. In a different respect, it also reflects the fact that the governance and management system needs to be further refined in order to accommodate the rapid expansion of Chinese ODI. It also implies that we need to take an incremental approach towards complete liberalization of the capital account as well as other necessary financial sector reforms.

In this regard, China is likely to undergo a dual development path, remaining the world's factory while also becoming an increasingly important global investor. Thanks to its huge population and domestic market, China has benefited a great deal from the complete range and high sophistication of its industrial system. It would be unwise and a mistake for China to give up its position in the global value chain as the world's factory. Meanwhile, China is also in a position to export its competitive manufacturing capacity to developing countries (and even to developed countries, as in the case of high speed trains) via the medium of direct investment. ODI also supports the upgrading of domestic manufacturing and enhancement in the global value chain, through continued investment in foreign technology, research and development, know-how and talent. In this way, Chinese ODI will continue to expand steadily. With the appropriate policy framework in place and progress in domestic economic and financial reforms, Chinese ODI will develop in a more orderly manner.

Going global in order to compete at home is a natural response to China's vast domestic market. Such a strategic motive will continue to drive many ODI activities. If the 'China angle' is played carefully, foreign partners also stand to benefit from China's next round of economic growth and transformation. In the long run, Chinese multinationals will become true global investors and competitors. Achieving this will to a great extent depend on the ability of Chinese managers and talent. With the accumulation of sufficient FSAs, Chinese multinationals will undoubtedly reshape the global competitive landscape and exert a major influence on the international economy.

Emerging driving forces: new challenges to theory and commercial practice

Figure 21.1 illustrates some mega-forces that drive the growth of the Chinese economy and very likely the global economy as well. The first layer is urbanization. Over the last 30 years, China's urbanization rate grew on average at 1% per annum. This process underpinned China's rapid economic growth and created great opportunities and demand for jobs, as well as the development of a full range of industrial systems. Nowadays, China's urbanization rate stands at just above 50%. Compared with an average of 75% in other developed economies such as the US, Japan and Western Europe, China's urbanization still has a long way to go, so this in turn will continue to be a key driver for economic growth. This means continuous demand for commodities, goods and services, which are to be acquired or produced either domestically or globally.

The second layer is expansion of the middle class. Some estimate that by 2016, China's middle income population exceeded 200 million. With moderately fast economic growth, China's middle class will continue to swell. This will stimulate domestic consumption and push the Chinese economy to transform from investment-led growth to consumption-driven growth.

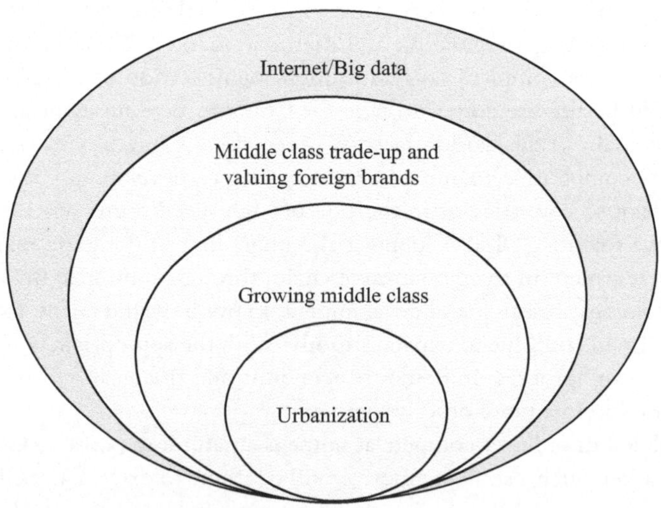

FIGURE 21.1 China's emerging driving forces

The third layer is the upgrading of consumption demand and middle-class living standards. This means that people trade up for better products and services; want cleaner food, water and air; and attach greater value to foreign brands.

These are the more visible forces. The less obvious forces are the internet and big data, and these warrant the most attention. China is promoting an 'internet+' policy. This will further stimulate the application of internet (cloud) solutions and big data algorithms, which lead to technological innovation and disruptive business models. Already, people in China can use their mobile phone to pay for things, shop online or transfer money. They don't need to carry their wallet any more. This is quite a transformation, and, in this regard, China is perhaps even leading the world in some respects. Companies such as Alibaba and Tencent are quickly expanding their commercial empires across national boundaries, building their own ecosystems and competing face to face with other multinationals.

The internet of things (IoT) is penetrating into broader industrial and commercial spaces and is fundamentally redefining and reshaping the boundaries of industry, business models and firms. Behind IoT is cloud computing based on big data algorithms. Rapid learning by computers and machines is advancing the development of artificial intelligence (AI). Such technological development further reduces the cost of information and communications and the way in which knowledge is created, stored, managed and transferred, which is regarded as being at the core of FSAs. Computers will in future replace human beings in some aspects of the managerial decision making process. IT infrastructure has never been such an important driving force for companies. Reductions in transaction costs and greater efficiency gains are the most obvious benefits of IT system improvement. However, access to data and ownership of data often poses challenges, creating barriers to entry.

Let us consider some examples of how the internet and big data can change our world. For instance, they are transforming traditional methods of urban transportation. The application of IoT and big data facilitates the development of driverless cars. They promote the business model of agglomeration in urban commuting, such as Uber in the US and DiDi in China (in fact this agglomeration effect is also evident in the global hotel and tourism business, such as the Airbnb). The online bike leasing business has recently flourished in China. Smart bikes in different colours, equipped with GPS tracker, can be easily found on the streets of more than 100 cities in China, and also in London, Sydney, Singapore and Los Angeles. Customers can easily unlock the bike and pay on their smartphone using an app or through WeChat or Alipay. Several Chinese startups or unicorns, such as Mobike and ofo, now offer more than 10 million bikes, with 100 million registered users.

There are many other examples. For instance, IoT and big data are driving forward industrial digitization. With sensors and software built into equipment, computer systems will automatically monitor and notify the engineers when and where malfunctions might occur. With big data algorithms, companies can significantly enhance the efficiency of their marketing campaigns, with systems automatically matching consumer demand. Some internet companies have started building electric vehicles – looking to make a Chinese version of Tesla. They have set up an R&D centre in Silicon Valley, recruited world-class designers and engineers from Europe, and outsourced car production in Mainland China. In their eyes, a car is no different from other products that people buy online. Their business model is built upon consumer behaviour and earns profits from ongoing services provided post-sale. In this regard, these Chinese enterprises are 'born global'.

IoT and cloud computing are also impacting the financial services industry, namely the development of FinTech. For instance, Goldman Sachs and J. P. Morgan are looking at ways of using computer AI systems to replace humans in some types of financial trading. People also are discussing how the technology behind Bitcoin, known as Blockchain, can be used to change money, business and the world (Tapscott and Tapscott, 2016).

Globalization and policy implications

Much existing literature has demonstrated that globalization contributes to economic growth and improvement in social welfare. Companies with firm-specific advantages tend to grow globally and become multinationals in order to achieve optimal organisation of production activities and allocation of internal resources. We do not believe that the process of globalization can be halted. However, it has suffered some serious setbacks recently and there has been a rise of anti-globalization sentiment. This poses great uncertainty and is a serious threat to the free flow of cross-border trade and capital. Obvious examples are Brexit and the introduction of the 'Putting America First' policy. Local protectionism and political populism are the major causes, but, more fundamentally, this reflects the disparities and challenges in the process of globalization that policymakers need to address and resolve.

In light of this background, as well as the slow progress made in the WTO negotiations and in reform of global economic and financial governance, countries are turning to alternative policy solutions. For instance, bilateral and multilateral free trade and investment treaties are carrying increasing weight in global policy setting. In addition, countries are placing more emphasis on regionalization and view this as a transition to further globalization. This kind of regionalism-based approach can also require wisdom and innovation.

Without any doubt, government policy plays a key role in the pace and process of globalization. The Chinese government recently introduced several initiatives including the OBOR initiative, international production capacity cooperation, the AIIB and BRICs Development Bank. Some of these concepts are being constantly refined based on discussions with various participating countries and parties. While some policy initiatives may be more regionalism-oriented, the open and inclusive nature of these policies mirrors the real efforts made by the Chinese government in promoting further and more sustainable globalization.

It is essential for countries and partners to understand that these policy initiatives need to be progressed based on mutual trust and must be mutually beneficial.

In terms of investment, projects need to be commercially viable and generate long-term economic benefits for both the local partner and the Chinese company. It may be a prime opportunity for countries and regions to 'enjoy the ride' of China's further economic transformation, but, in order to do so, still greater efforts are needed. The Chinese government needs to provide clearer guidance to domestic companies, communicate effectively and efficiently with the international community (in particular with the host country or region), and prioritize project cooperation where it is most commercially viable and visible. Host countries also need to make continuous efforts to improve their domestic infrastructure (both software and hardware) and maintain a transparent, consistent and fair investment policy framework. Chinese companies are also strongly advised to make prudent and rational investment decisions, maintain a good reputation and public relations with local partners and local governments, and invest heavily in the recruitment and training of highly qualified international managers.

Research agenda

Several interesting research agendas have emerged from our analysis. First, we are in a new era of rapid technological improvement and innovation. The development of information technology may, to an unexpected magnitude, affect the way firms do business and reshape the boundaries and the outlook of their organisational structure. The Internet of things and development of artificial intelligence are poised to redefine the creation and transfer of knowledge. A new set of managerial skills and capabilities will be required to address these emerging challenges, and this is of clear interest to the future development of international business and management theory.

Second, government policy warrants further analysis. The impact of new policy initiatives on Chinese ODI is still unknown. The systems of global power and policy are also undergoing profound change, and this will impact significantly on the future development of Chinese ODI patterns and behaviour.

Lastly, as Chinese ODI activities reach a more rational and mature stage of development, the examination of ODI performance becomes increasingly important and urgent. While the availability of large data samples may still be a constraint, more in-depth case studies and longitudinal studies should be carried out. Greater attention should also be paid to investigating the different modes adopted by Chinese manufacturing, technology and Internet companies.

Note

1 For example, person A purchases a USD 10 million universal life insurance product in Hong Kong using a debit card, then pledges the insurance at the bank and receives a loan from the bank. Due to the ultra-low interest rate, the cash dividend received from the insurance product can be even higher than the debt service cost; thus person A not only cashes out his or her local currency into foreign currency offshore but also enjoys risk-free interest rate arbitrage.

References

Jaffe, A & Manderlkar, GN 1992, 'The post-merger performance of acquiring firms: A re-examination of an anomaly', *Journal of Finance*, vol. 47, pp. 1605–1621.

King, DR, Dan, RD, Daily, CM & Covin, JG 2004, 'Meta-analyses of post-acquisition performance', *Strategic Management Journal*, vol. 25, pp. 187–200.

Meng, C 2009, *Multinational Banking in China: Theory and Practice*, New Horizons of International Business Series, Edward Elgar Publishing, Cheltenham.

Tapscott, D & Tapscott, A 2016, *Blockchain Revolution: How the Technology behind Bitcoin is Changing Money, Business, and the World*, Penguin, UK.

INDEX

Note: Page numbers in **bold** indicate tables and page numbers in *italics* indicate figures.

ABP 227
Affymetrix 182
Africa 232–242; banking growth in 240–241; Chinese investment in 234–238; demographics and economic growth in 238–239; economic growth in, trends supporting 238–241; introduction to 232–233; natural resource wealth and economic growth in 240; 'New Normal' and 233–234; technology and economic growth in 239–240; urbanisation and economic growth in 239
Aixtron 169
Alcatel-Lucent Shanghai Bell Ltd Co (ASB) 237
Alibaba **18**, 199, 211–212
Alipay 263
Ali-Yrkkö, J. 48
Aluminum Corp. 38
American Enterprise Institute 216
American Industrials Partners 131
Anbang Insurance Group **18**
Apple 213
Asian Development Bank (ADB) 30, 87
Asian Infrastructure Investment Bank (AIIB) 2, 9, 30, 87–93, 258; Articles of Agreement of 89–90; establishment of 87; global economic recovery and 88; infrastructure funding gap and 87–88; international economic governance and 88–89; as milestone and international development innovation 90–91; as open/inclusive multilateral institution 89–90; as professional, efficient and clean financing platform 92–93; UK investment and 219
Asia-Pacific Economic Cooperation (APEC) 213
Aston Martin 217

Baidu 211, 212
Bain Capital 134
Baker McKenzie 218
Beatrice Offshore Windfarm Ltd (BOWL) 226
Beidahuang Group **18**
Beijing Construction Engineering Group (BCEG) 224
Bhagwati, J. 248–249
bilateral investment treaties (BIT) 42–43
bilateralism 243–254; Brexit and 249–251; China, global trade and 246; critics of 248–249; hyper-globalisation and 248–249; introduction to 243–245; new 246–248; old 245–246; preferential trade agreements 244; Trump and 244–245; UK-China post-Brexit deal and 252–254; UK-China relations and 251–252; United States and 243
Birmingham insights on Chinese investment 222–223
Boston Consulting Group (BCG) 163
BPL 217

Brautigam, D. 235
Brexit: bilateralism and 249–251; Chinese investors views on 228–229; UK-China post 252–254
BRICS Development Bank 2, 30
Bright Food's 180
Brookstone Holding 135
Buckley, P. J. 64

Cameron, D. 218–219
Campeau 141
Cao Dewang 53
capital flight 62
Carillion 224
C.banner 227
CDH Investments **18**
Changan Automobile 223
Changan UK R&D Centre Ltd (CAUK) 223
Changyou 211
ChemChina (China National Chemical Corp.) 8, 17, **18**, **19**, 38, 44, 183, 210, 218
ChemChina-Syngenta outbound deal 128
Chevron 180
China: consumption demand, economic growth and *262*, 263; economic growth, emerging driving forces of *262*, 262–264; exports/imports of goods and services as percentage of GDP *34*; as global investor 2–3; global trade and 246, 259–260; global value chain and (*see* global value chain (GVC)); inbound/outbound direct investments of 35–36, *36*; Internet/big data, economic growth and *262*, 263–264; middle class growth, economic growth and 262, *262*; multilateral financial institutions initiated by 30; national saving rate 34–35, *35*; as net capital exporter 7, 260–261; net ODI stock by sector *55*; new concepts introduced, government 2; ODI and IDI share in developing economies *49*; technology, economic growth and *262*, 263; UK and (*see* United Kingdom (UK), Chinese investment in); urbanization rate, economic growth and 262, *262*; as World Factory 1, 23
China-Africa Development Fund 236
China-Africa Production Capacity Cooperation Fund 75
China angle 227, 230
China Banking Association 219
China-Britain Business Council, China Outbound Conference 226–227
China Construction Bank 221
China Development Bank **18**, 75
China Equity Group 217, 227, 228–229
China-Europe Mutual Fund 75
China Export and Credit Insurance Corporation 75
China Fiberglass 159
China Foreign Exchange Trade System 219
China General Nuclear Power Corporation 183, 219
China Interbank Bond Market (CIBM) 107–108
China International Capital Corporation (CICC) 227, 229
China International Payment System (CIPS) 201
China Investment Corporation 219
China-Japan-ROK Free Trade Area 82
China Jushi 158–159
China-Latin America Production Capacity Cooperation Fund 75
Chinalco **18**
China Life 219
China Mining Association 209
China Minsheng Investment Group 16, **18**
China National Automated Payment System (CNAPS) 201
China National Chemical Corp. (ChemChina) 8, 17, **18**, **19**, 38, 44, 183, 210, 218
China National Petroleum Corporation (CNPC) 17, **18**
China Ocean Shipping (Group) Company (COSCO) **18**
China Petrochemical Corporation (Sinopec) 17, **18**, **19**, 208
China (Shanghai) Pilot Free Trade Zone 9
China South Railway Corporation (CSR) 132
China Three Gorges Corporation **18**, 226
China-US Bilateral Investment Treaty 42–43
China Venture 9
Chinese enterprises: Going Out strategy of 1, 2; most active, by industry **18**; new concepts introduced for 2; outward direct investment by 2–3 (*see also* outward direct investment (ODI)); overseas investments 2–3; private equity industry 15–16; variables of 3
Chinese global M&A 205–214; evolvement strategy for 212; to expand digital offerings 210–212; future for 213–214; history of 206; overview of 205–206;

phase 1, acquisitions to gain market entry 206–207; phase 2, natural resources/tangible assets focus *208*, 208–209; phase 3, evolution of 209–213; proprietary intellectual property and 209–210; talent/intangible assets, accessing through phased investment 212–213
Chinese investors: views on Brexit 228–229; views on UK investment 226–228
Chinese National Offshore Oil Corporation (CNOOC) 17, **18**, **19**, 21, 38, 180, 182, 208
Chinese Telecoms 236
Churchill, W. 57
Cifa 134
CIO magazine 139
CIPS *see* Cross-border Interbank Payment System (CIPS)
CIT Group 8
CITIC Construction 17, **18**, 227
CITIC Pacific 184, 209
CITIC Private Equity 22
Closer Economic Partnership Arrangement (CEPA) 82
CNOOC *see* Chinese National Offshore Oil Corporation (CNOOC)
Cocoon Networks 227
COFCO Corporation **18**
COFCO-Nidera outbound deal 129
COFDI *see* outward foreign direct investment (OFDI)
co-investors, ODI acquisitions and 134–135
Committee on Foreign Investment in the United States (CFIUS) 40, 181
competitive bidding environments 180
ConocoPhillips 208
conquering army syndrome 142
Consumer Business Group (CBG) 213
corporate culture 148–150
corporate governance, FDI projects and 193
country-specific advantages (CSAs) 63
Creat Group 217
credit guarantee commissions (CGCs) 114
Cross-border Interbank Payment System (CIPS) 105
cross-border mergers and acquisitions (M&A) 9–11, *11*, **18**
cross-border transaction opportunities, capitalizing on 177–186; competitive bidding environments and 180; European Commission competition review and 183–184; fiduciary duties and 178–179; introduction to 177; managing issues with 177–178; post-closing integration/operations and 184–185; regulatory approval process and 180–184; United States national security review and 181–183
cross-cultural communication 165
Cross Strait Economic Cooperation Framework Agreement (ECFA) 82
Ctrip 217
Ctrip-Skyscanner outbound deal 128
cultural clash, mergers/acquisitions and 141–142
cultural difference theory 142

deal management, timing and 164
Dealogic 9
Dedrick, J. 48
Dell 205
Deng Xiaoping 35
developed multinational companies (DMNC) 137; factors enabling ENMC mergers with 151–154
DiDi 263
diversification, economic transition and 39
DMNC *see* developed multinational companies (DMNC)
domestically produced consumer goods, ODI and upgrading quality of 38
dual track processes 172–174
Dynex 132

eBay 139, 141
economic transition, ODI and China's 33–45; bilateral investment treaties and 42–43; diversification and 39; domestically produced consumer goods, quality of 38; inbound/outbound direct investments 35–36, *36*; introduction to 33–37; irrational investments and 39–40; local currency financing and 43–45; lower costs and 37; market share/power and, increasing 37–38; national saving rate and 34–35, *35*; natural resources/raw materials, acquisition of 38; as 'New Normal' 33–34; reasoning for ODI 37–40; technology, acquisition of 38; trade follows investment and 39; whole or controlling ownership and 40–42
Economist Intelligence Unit (EIU) 241
economy-based multinational companies (EMNC) 137
EDF/CGN/NNB Group of Companies 183
EDP Renovaveis 226
ElectraNet 128

emerging-market MNEs (EMNEs) 61; factors enabling DMNC mergers with 151–154; organisational form and ownership of **62**
EMNC *see* economy-based multinational companies (EMNC)
European Commission competition review 183–184
European Investment Monitor 220
Everbright 217
Export-Import Bank of China 75
Export-Import Bank of Japan (JEXIM) 113

Fairchild Semiconductor 182
FDI *see* foreign direct investment (FDI)
Federated Department Stores 141
fiduciary duties of directors, international transactions and 178–179
financial diversification, ODI acquisitions and 124–125, *125*
financial sector development, policy implications of FDI on 191–203; impact of FDI 196, **197–198**, 198; introduction to 191; Malaysia case study 193–196, *195*; OBOR Initiative and 198–202; strategic considerations of 191–193
firm-specific advantages (FSAs) 63
Ford 223
foreign direct investment (FDI) 7–8; country-specific advantages and 63; financial sector development and (*see* financial sector development, policy implications of FDI on); financial structure impact of 196, **197–198**, 198; firm-specific advantages and 63; RMB for 101; strategic policy issues in 191–193
foreign investment policy options for China 117–120; capital for foreign aid, method reform for 117; creative solutions needed 119–120; financing difficulties, improving domestic/international capital channels 117–118; go global companies, streamlining approval for 118; risk management system, improvement of 118–119; RMB, internationalization of 119
Fosun Group 17, **18**, 227–228
Foton 236, 237
free trade agreement (FTA) 258; future considerations for 84; going abroad of Chinese enterprises and 82–84; OFDI supported by 82–84; signed by China 82
Fu, X. 235
full-on integration model 128, 129–130
Fuyao Glass Industry Group 53

Gabriel, S. 169
Garcia-Herreiro, A. 253
GE Appliances 214
Geely 38, 133, 185
General Agreement on Tariffs and Trade (GATT) 243, 247
General Atlantic 22, 134, 144
General Electric 38, 152
General Mills 180
General Motors 53
Giant 211
Gionee 236
globalization process 156–162, 264–265; China Jushi 158–159; for Chinese businesses 157–159; inbound investments and 159–161; introduction to 156–157; Jinjiang Hotels 157–158; PizzaExpress 159–160; private equity funds and 161–162; WeWork 160–161
global production sharing, importance of 46, 48
global value chain (GVC) 23–31; background of 23–24; China's current position in 24–26; comparative advantage theory and 24, 25–26, *26*; future development for China's 26–28, *28*; roadmap for China's 28–29; studies of 24; suggestions for 29–31; value added in trade concept 24–25, *24–25*
global value chain, ODI development and 46–58; challenges in China's 55–57; changing trends in production activity *47*; driving forces of China's 50–55; global production sharing, importance of 46–48, *47*; from IDI to, in China 48–50; intermediate inputs, share of 46, *47*; policy suggestions for China's 57–58
Going Out policy 71
Goldman Sachs 134
Goldwind 54
Go Scale Capital 169
Goss International 130
Greater Manchester Pension Fund 224
Gree 169
Greenland Holding Group **18**
Guangming Diaries **18**

Haier Group 17, **18**, 38, 214
Hainan Airline Group 8, 224
Hamleys 227

Hammond, P. 243
Hands, G. 219
hands-off integration model 127–129
Heritage Foundation 9, 216
Hewlett Packard Enterprise (HPE) 205
Hisense 236
HiSoft **18**
HNA 17, **18**, **19**
Hony Capital 134, 158, 217
House of Fraser 217, 227
Huajian Group 236
Huawei Technologies 134, 181–182, 212–213, 221, 225, 236, 237
Hummels, D. 48
hyper-globalisation 248–249

IBM PC 22, 123, 130, 134, 185, 205; *see also* merger and acquisition (M&A) execution strategy
IMF 30
Industrial and Commercial Bank of China (ICBC) 17, **18**
Infinix 236
integration models for ODI acquisitions 127–128
intellectual property, access to 209–210
inward foreign direct investment (FDI): outward direct investment and 7–8; top-three FDI inflow economies and **48**
Ion 132
irrational investments, economic transition and 39–40
Itel 236

Japan, foreign investment experience of 109–120; China's foreign investment policy options and 117–120 (*see also* foreign investment policy options for China); comparison to China 109–110, *110*, *111*; financing barriers, removing through policy finance 113, *114*; lessons from 115–116, *116*; Official Development Assistance role 110–112, *112*; Overseas Investment Insurance System and 115; SMEs and 113–115
Japan Bank for International Cooperation (JBIC) 113, 114
Japan-China Investment Promotion Organization 115
Japan Finance Corporation for Small and Medium Enterprise (JASME) 114
JETRO 115
Jinjiang Hotels 157–158
Jin Jiang International **18**
JMC 223
Johns Hopkins University 235
joint ownership, foreign direct investment and 42
J. P. Morgan Chase & Co. 44
Jushi Group 158–159

Kewalram Chanrai Group 237
Krugman, P. 55
Kuka AG 38, 168–169, 210

Leica 213
Lenovo 17, **18**, 22, 123, 129–130, 134, 185, 205; *see also* merger and acquisition (M&A) execution strategy
Lenovo-IBM PC acquisition strategy 143–151, 259; background and update of 137–138, *138*; compromises and 150–151; corporate culture and 148–150; corporate governance/ownership structure and 145–146; diversity and 147–148; learning approach taken 144–145; overview of 143; planning team 143–144; top team globalization 146–147
Lenovo Way four P's 149
Li, R. 237
Li Keqiang 87
Liu Chuanzhi 143, 144, 149
LiuGong 237
local currency financing, ODI and 43–45
London insights on Chinese investment 220–222
London & Partners 220–222, 228
long-term supply contracts, foreign direct investment and 41–42
Louvre Hotel Group 158
lower costs, ODI and 37

M&A *see* mergers and acquisitions (M&A)
Machnig, M. 170
Made in China 2025 initiative 23, 30–31, 170
Magic Leap 212
Mahindra & Mahindra 129
Ma Kai 219
Malaysia case study, financial sector development 193–196, *195*
Malmström, C. 170
management of ODI acquisitions 123–136; CSR-Dynex example 132; decade review of 123–124; financial diversification and 124–125, *125*; full integration, approach 129–130; future for 135–136;

integration challenges 127; integration models 127–128; minimalist post-deal 128–129; overview of 123; partnerships and 134–135; Petrochina-Ion example 132; progressive integration approach 133–134; relationship-building and 124–125, *125*; resource acquisitions and 124, *124*; selective integration approach 132–133; success rates in 125–127, *126*; turnarounds and 130–132
Manchester Airports Group 224
Manchester insights on Chinese investment 224–225
Manchester's Inward Investment Agency (MIDAS) 224, 225, 228
Mandarin Capital Partners 134
Manganese Bronze 217
market share/power, ODI and increasing 37–38
'Matches made in hell' (O'Neill) 139
Mazda 223
Medion 185
Memorandum of Understanding on Establishing the Asian Infrastructure Investment Bank (MOU) 89
merger and acquisition (M&A) execution strategy 137–154; cultural clash and 141–142; factors enabling ENMC-DMNC mergers 151–154; global challenges of 139–143; introduction to 137; Lenovo-IBM PC 137–138, 142–143 (*see also* Lenovo-IBM PC acquisition strategy); match failures 139, **140**; over-paying and 141; strategic fit, misjudging 139, 141; success in Lenovo-IBM PC 143–151
Mergermarket Group 236
mergers and acquisitions (M&A): cross-border 2; expanding ODI with, 23–24; failed, analysis on 20–22; financing to support 13, 15–16, *16*; outward foreign direct investment and 60; overseas, ten largest **19**; *see also* Chinese global M&A
Merkel, A. 170
MG Rover 222
Midea Group 38, 168, 210
Midea-Kuka outbound deal 129, 168–169
minimalist post-deal ODI management 128–129
Ministry of Commerce (MOFCOM) 2, 73, 235; Administrative Measures regarding Overseas Investment of 73–74; Outbound Investment and Cooperation Guidelines by Countries (Regions) 85–86
MinMetals **19**
Minsheng Bank 21
MNEs *see* multinational enterprises (MNEs)
Mobike 263
Most Favoured Nation (MFN) treatment 83, 246
Motorola 181
Motorola Mobility 214
multinational enterprises (MNEs) 23, 61–62
Murdoch, R. 142
Myspace 139

Nanjing Xin Bai 227
National Development and Reform Commission (NDRC) 73, 180, 238
natural resources/raw materials, ODI and acquisition of 38
net capital exporter, China as 7, 260–261
net international investment position (NIIP) 191
Neul 213, 221
New Bridge Capital 22
New Economic Geography 55
'New Normal': Chinese economic growth as 33–34; investment in Africa and 233–234
News Corp 139, 142
The New Silk Road 60
Nexen Inc. 38, 182, 208
Ng, A. 212
NLFC 114
non-control *vs.* control investments *126*

OBOR *see* One Belt One Road (OBOR) Initiative
OBOR Initiative impact on Chinese ODI 198–202; currency arrangements and 200–202; opportunities, mapping of 202
Odeon 217
ODI *see* outward direct investment (ODI)
Oettinger, G. 169
OFDI *see* outward foreign direct investment (OFDI)
Offshore Investment Management Approach 118
ofo 263
One Belt One Road (OBOR) Initiative 2, 76–78, 108; Africa and 234; currency arrangements and 200–202; FDI areas connected by 199; international cooperation and 28; ODI and 9, 55; OFDI and 60; using RMB as currency, obstacles to 201
ON Semiconductor 182

Organization for Economic Co-operation and Development (OECD) 87
Osborne, G. 89
Osram 169–170
outbound investment challenges 163–174; Aixtron takeover 169; Chinese 163–168, 170–171; cross-cultural communication 165; deal management and timing 164; dual track processes 172–174; execution certainty 166; introduction to 163; Kuka AG controversy 168–169; labour challenges 168; Osram and 169–170; post-acquisition integration 167; protectionism in Europe and 170; tax issues 166–167, 171–172; well thought-out international acquisition strategy, lacking 163–164
outbound investments: business alliances, establishment of 76; defined 71; enterprises to invest abroad, policy improvements for 75–76; financing channels supporting 75; fiscal and taxation support for 75–76; growth of 72; national guidance on, enhancing 76–77; OBOR Initiative and 76–78; outcomes of 73; overseas investment administration 73–75, **74**; overview of 71–73; ramp-up period of 72; risk control system, improving 78; start-up phase of 71–72
outward direct investment (ODI) 7–22, 257–258, 259; 2006–2016 **8**; active management of (*see* management of ODI acquisitions); challenges facing 20–22; cross-border M&A and 9–11, *11*, *12*, **18**, **19**; economic transition and (*see* economic transition, ODI and China's); enterprises/transactions, dynamics of 17; expanding, with M&A 23–24; factors driving 8–9; growth of, 2005–2016 *11*; introduction to 2–3, 7; investment flow distributions 12–13, *13*, *14*; investment preferences, analysis of 17–20, **19**; inward foreign direct investment and 7–8; motives, dynamics of 13, *16*; new era of 7–9; provinces most active in 16, **17**; reasoning for 37–40; rising costs and 50–53; RMB for 101; SOEs and 10, *11*, *12*; survey findings/implications 22; target industries 13, *15*; transaction database/analysis of 9, **10**; trends/characteristics of 9–17; *see also* global value chain, ODI development and
outward foreign direct investment (OFDI) 60–66; actors involved in 62; background 60; challenge to theory of 60–62; development stages of Chinese enterprises' 79–82; flows from selected economies *80*; home country characteristics and **65**, 65–66; meeting challenge of 63–64; new challenges facing 64–66; as opportunity for theory development 62–63; sectoral make-up of 62; stock by industry of China *81*; stock of major countries *80*; suggestions for Chinese enterprises on 85–86; supported by free trade agreement framework 82–84; Uppsala approach to 63
Overseas Economic Cooperation Fund (OECF) 113
overseas investment administration 73–75, **74**; management of 77; risk control system, improving 78; service system, improving 77
Overseas Investment Insurance System 115
Overseas Investment Profit Insurance 115
Overseas Mineral Resource Investment Insurance System 115

partnerships, management of ODI acquisitions and 134–135
Pearl River Piano 54
Peixe Urbano 212
People's Bank of China 40; RMB Public Announcement No.19 98
Petrochina 132
phalanx effect 62
Pinsent Masons 218
Pirelli 44, 218
PizzaExpress 159–160, 217, 259
Plateno 158
Plaza Accord 115–116
pollution/environmental degradation, FDI projects and 193
PopIn 212
Porsche Design 213
PPP Investment Fund 114
preferential trade agreements (PTAs) 244
price discovery, inward FDI and 192
private equity (PE) industry 15–16
Proctor & Gamble 152
progressive integration model 128, 133–134
proprietary intellectual property, access to 209–210
PSA 223
Putzmeister 22, 128, 210

Qiao, G. 148

Ralls 182
Red Rock Power Limited 226
Regional Comprehensive Economic Partnership (RCEP) 82
regulatory approval process 180–184
relationship-building, ODI acquisitions and 124–125, *125*
renminbi (RMB) internationalization 94–108, 258; assets held onshore by non-residents *97*; CIPS 105; clearing network **105**, 106; cross-border, financing 102–103; cross-border trade transactions and 101–102; for current account transactions *99*, 99–101, **100–101**; direct investment cross-border trade transactions and 102; for foreign direct investment 101; inclusion in SDR currency basket 98–99; as international payments currency *95*; as invoice currency 95, **96**, 98; market infrastructure for 104–105; outlook for 105, 107–108; for outward direct investment 101; overview of 94; policies promoting 101–104; portfolio investment and 103–104; as reserve/investment currency 95; role of 94–99; swap agreements 105; trade and direct investment use of 99–101; for trade settlement/financing 94
Repsol 226
resource acquisitions, success rate of 124, *124*
resource allocation, inward FDI and 192
Reuter News 142
Revealed Comparative Advantage (RCA) index 25–26, *26*
reverse break-fee 182
Riot Games 211
Rio Tinto 38
rising costs, China's ODI development and 50–53, *51–52*
risk management, FDI projects and 192–193
RMB *see* renminbi (RMB) internationalization
Royal Dutch Shell 42
Ruta, M. 248

Sailing Capital 135
Samsung 53
San'an Optoelectronics 169
Sanpower Group 135, 217, 227
Sany Heavy Industry 22, 128, 210
Sany Southern Africa 237
Sarovar 158
Scotland insights on Chinese investment 225–226
Scottish Development International (SDI) 225–226
SEC 130
selective integration model 128, 132–133
Shanda 211
Shangdi Guanqun Investment Corporation **18**
Shanghai Automotive Industry Corporation (SAIC) 21, 129, 139, 184, 222
Shanghai Clearing House 219
Shantui 237
Shen, X. 238
Shoko Chukin Bank 114
Shuanghui Group **18**, **19**, 131
Sino-Australia Free Trade and Investment Agreements 9
Sinochem Group 17, **18**
Sino Iron Project 184
Sino-Korea Free Trade and Investment Agreements 9
Sinopec (China Petrochemical Corporation) 17, **18**, **19**, 208
Skype 139, 141
Skyscanner 217
SME Diagnosis Organization 115
SME Revitalization Organization 115
smiley-faced value curve 54
Smithfield 131
SMRJ 115
social inequality, FDI projects and 193
SOEe *see* state-owned enterprises (SOEs)
Special Drawing Right (SDR), RMB inclusion in 98–99
SsangYong Motor Company 21, 129, 139, 184–185
State Administration of Foreign Exchange (SAFE) 2, 43, 44, 73, 74, 217
State Council's Guiding Opinions on Boosting International Production Capacity and Equipment Manufacturing Cooperation 72
State Development & Investment Corporation (SDIC) 226
State Grid **18**, **19**, 128
state-owned enterprises (SOEs) 10, *11*; *vs.* non SOEs **19**; outward foreign direct investment and 60
State Power Investment Corporation **18**
strategic fit: assessment of 139, 141; defined 139
Subramanian, A. 248
Sunseeker Yachts 217

Supercell 211
Suzuki 223
Syncrude 208
Syngenta AG 8, 38, 183, 210

TCL 207
technology, ODI and acquisition of 38
Tecno 236
Tencent 17, **18**, **19**, 199, 211
Terex Corp. 38
Tesla 264
Thomson Multimedia 207
3Com 134, 181
3Leaf Systems 182
TPG 22, 134
trade blocs 243
trade follows investment, economic transition and 39
Transatlantic Trade and Investment Partnership (TTIP) 23
Trans-Pacific Partnership Agreement (TPP) 23
Trump, D. 37, 39, 51, 84, 166, 243
Tsinghua Holdings **18**
turnaround integration model 128, 130–132
2Wire 181
two-step loans 113, 114

Uber 263
UK-China Economic and Financial Dialogue (EFD) 219
UK-China Infrastructure Alliance 219
UK-China Joint Economic and Trade Commission 219
UK-China post-Brexit deals 252–254
UK-China relations, bilateralism and 251–252
Unico 21
Unilever 42
United Commercial Bank 21
United Kingdom (UK), Chinese investment in 216–230; Birmingham insights on 222–223; Brexit and, Chinese investor views on 228–229; Chinese investors insights on 226–228; context for 218–219; current state of 216–218, **218**; introduction to 216; London insights on 220–222; Manchester insights on 224–225; policy implications/recommendations 229–230; Scotland insights on 225–226; by sector, 2005–2016 **217**
United States: bilateralism and 243; national security review 181–183
unit labour costs, international comparison of *28*
Unocal 180

value added in trade (VAiT) 24–25, *24–25*
Vensys 54
Vienna Hotels 158
Volkswagen AG 42, 53
Volvo 38, 133, 185

Wall Street Journal 169
Wanda Group **18**, 54, 217
Wang, Z. 46, 51
Wang Huishen 226
Wang Jiahua 209
Ward, S. 148
WeChat 263
Weetabix 217
WeWork 160–161, 259
Wolverhampton Wanderers Football Club 227–228
World Bank 30, 240
World Trade Organization (WTO) 206, 243, 244, 247

XCMG 237
Xiao Jiang 237
Xi Jinping 87, 89, 198, 213, 218–219, 224, 233
xPerception 212
Xu, J. 253

Yang Yuanqing 143, 144, 145, 147, 148
Yao, Y. 238
Yin, H. 238
Yoplait 180
Yu Chengdong 213

zero VAT rate and tax exemptions 75–76
Zhejiang Geely Holding Group 217
Zhong Shan 40
Zhou Xiaochuan 40
Zhuhai Yinlong New Energy Co. 169
Zijin Mining Group **18**
Zoomlion Heavy Industry Science & Technology Co. 38, 134, 237
ZTE (Zhongxing Telecommunications Equipment Corporation) 184, 236, 237